D0072622

Feminization of the Clergy in America

Feminization of the Clergy in America

Occupational and Organizational Perspectives

TABOR COLLEGE LIBRARY
Hillsboro, Kansas 67063

PAULA D. NESBITT

New York   Oxford

Oxford University Press

1997

Oxford University Press

Oxford   New York

Athens   Auckland   Bangkok   Bogota   Bombay   Buenos Aires
Calcutta   Cape Town   Dar es Salaam   Delhi   Florence   Hong Kong
Istanbul   Karachi   Kuala Lumpur   Madras   Madrid   Melbourne
Mexico City   Nairobi   Paris   Singapore   Taipei   Tokyo   Toronto

and associated Companies in
Berlin   Ibadan

Copyright © 1997 by Oxford University Press, Inc.

Published by Oxford University Press, Inc.
198 Madison Avenue, New York, New York 10016

Oxford is a registered trademark of Oxford University Press

All rights reserved. No part of this publication may be reproduced,
stored in a retrieval system, or transmitted, in any form or by any means,
electronic, mechanical, photocopying, recording, or otherwise,
without the prior permission of Oxford University Press.

Library of Congress Cataloging-in-Publication Data
Nesbitt, Paula D., 1948–
Feminization of the clergy in America : occupational and
organizational perspectives / Paula D. Nesbitt.
p. cm.
Includes bibliographical references and index.
ISBN 0-19-510686-5
1. Women—Clergy. 2. Ordination of women. 3. Episcopal Church—
Clergy. 4. Unitarian Universalist Association—Clergy. I. Title.
BV676.N47   1997
262'.14'082—dc20   96-22281

1 3 5 7 9 8 6 4 2

Printed in the United States of America
on acid-free paper

Preface

Louisa Woosley had hoped that her husband would become a Cumberland Presbyterian Preacher, but when he showed little interest she embarked on her own occupational journey into the ministry. She was ordained by her congregation in 1889, but her ordination was denied by the denomination's governing synod, endorsing her instead as a lay evangelist. Forty-nine years later she would be elected moderator, leader of the same synod.[1] Had her husband gone into the ministry, Woosley may have put her energies into supporting his career, living it instead of her own.

Capitola Sumner Law was not as fortunate. The daughter of a Christian (Disciples) minister, she convinced her young husband that he should enter seminary, and then attended seminary along with him. Although she chose not to be ordained, perhaps wisely given her husband's temperament, she became an active lay co-pastor with him. According to her daughter, Capitola and the congregation would seek opportunities to send her husband traveling on church business so that she could remain at home to preach and pastor the church. Many thought she was the better of the two at both preaching and pastoring. Unfortunately Capitola, my great grandmother, died in an accident while only in her thirties, and I can only imagine where her passion for the ministry might have led her as she gained self-confidence and congregational support, and what marital conflicts might have ensued.

Many Protestant women have responded to their own desire for ordained ministry by marrying clergy, seminarians, or prospective candidates for ordination. Under the "shadow occupation" of minister's wife, they effectively have gained opportunities to co-pastor while not having to confront ambivalence or outright hostility within their congregations or denominations, much less their own personal hesitancies, or friction from their husbands. In short, their social location provided them with opportunities they otherwise might not have had. Susanna

Wesley, wife of a Church of England cleric, was paradigmatic in this respect. Covertly preaching and pastoring under the auspices of Sunday evening meetings in the rectory, her gatherings drew consternation from Wesley's associate pastor when her husband was away on Church business, because more people attended her services than his.[2] Although admittedly many other ministers' wives have had no such aspirations and some have had little interest in ordained ministry altogether, the role of minister's wife nonetheless traditionally has represented a safer choice for women who have felt called to a religious vocation. Woosley, not having such a safe option, had to break her own fresh ground. Although she was the first woman ordained in her denomination, she suffered severe retaliation as a consequence, before her triumph nearly a half-century later.

I didn't hear my great grandmother's story until after I had entered my own ordination process in the Episcopal Church, but it subsequently lent support to my interest in studying women and ministry, including women's struggle for legitimation and the sometimes highly creative ways they have pursued their vocational passion in social circumstances where acceptable roles for women have been sharply restricted. According to the story, Capitola's theology and my great grandfather's theology differed sharply, as did their ministerial styles. Explanations for such gender differences have variously been attributed to biological essentialism, with dissimilarities based on innate differences between men and women, or to socialization and other social constructionist arguments. Whatever their hypothesized genesis, all such explanations irreducibly point to gender as a key contributor to how people differentially experience the world, the various interests and commitments they develop, the opportunities they obtain, the constraints placed upon them, the theodicies they consequently form, and the moral reasoning they use to support them. Such differences raise intriguing speculation as to what religious organizations themselves might be like today, as well as how their scriptures, doctrines, or traditions might differ if women had shared equal authority and influence over their formation and development. The potential for widespread change in both the ideology and social behavior of organized religion as an outcome of realigning the gender balance among those with substantive power or influence, then, is at the heart of my current interest in this study on the structural effects of women's influx into the ordained ministry and the prospect of occupational feminization.

One of the more remarkable aspects of this research has been to encounter the extent of internal divisiveness that the subject of women clergy has triggered within religious organizations, not to mention the increased conflict between denominations that do and don't ordain women. Much of the divisiveness appears rooted in an earnest commitment to the religious basis of traditional gender arrangements, where women's place has been justified on perceived human inferiority to men, on divinely mandated subordination, or on separate but ostensibly equal status, all of which have been interpreted and promulgated by men.

At the time the original wave of this research began (1987) as my Ph.D. dissertation, I noticed an ambivalence over digging too deeply into issues related to women clergy in the various religious organizations I contacted for data. How concerned really are denominational leaders that women clergy have opportunities similar to those of men, that women and men are compensated equally for equivalent work, or that women have equal access for advancing into positions of denominational authority, should they desire that career path? Over the years I've met men and women strongly committed to gender equality in their religious organizations, but too often others' resistance has worked against their progressive efforts, which ultimately produced ambivalent results. Now, as a full-time academician in a United Methodist seminary and a nonstipendiary parish priest, I continue to pursue such questions through the lens of a detached insider. Or perhaps, more realistically, I utilize a methodology of *intense ambivalence* to balance an objective research agenda with my own personal interest, a method which was taught as well as modeled by a former teacher and mentor, William Sims Bainbridge.

Perhaps it's no coincidence that this manuscript should be completed in Denver—the site of the Episcopal Church rupture following the 1976 General Convention's decision to ordain women to the priesthood. As I was interviewing the Very Rev. Sandra Wilson, rector of St. Thomas Episcopal Church in Denver and a member of the women clergy sample of this analysis, Bishop James Mote, rector of St. Mary's, the first parish to break away from the Episcopal Church over women's ordination, coincidentally was present at the interview site. Rev. Wilson voluntarily introduced herself to him, not knowing who he was. The contrast of these two clergy speaking briefly to one another, an elderly traditionalist European-American male and a young progressive African-American female, symbolize the diversity and the conflict over both the ministry and the direction of the church. Other denominations portray similar diversities and conflicts.

Over the years, many women and men from various religious traditions have continued to offer important suggestions and insights for this study. Clergy, seminarians, and laity from various denominations—United Methodist, Evangelical Lutheran (E.L.C.A.), United Church of Christ, American Baptist, Episcopal, Roman Catholic, Unitarian Universalist, Reform and Conservative Jewish traditions—have shared their comparative perspectives. Foremost have been students and alumni of Harvard Divinity School and The Iliff School of Theology, who have discussed their career aspirations and the challenges they subsequently encountered. These have included struggles by progressive women seeking to enter their denomination's ordination process or, once ordained, to work within a traditional theological and organizational framework. Some women have chosen to reject denominationalism altogether, and instead have developed post-Christian communities or spiritual direction practices. But for women who embrace ordination, difficulties in getting through the process continue: sex-biased concerns over required psychological tests or professional assessments; denominational committees preoccupied with a husband's ambivalence about a wife's vocation while wifely ambivalence over a male candidate's vocation is overlooked; and widespread use of "gatekeepers"—clergy and lay leaders who hold the power to help, hinder, or halt a woman's prospects for ordination and a subsequent career. Once ordained, women then face the challenge of obtaining employment, especially if they are seeking a paid full-time position. In this respect, the United Methodist itineracy system has been the most helpful of all denominations in facilitating placements for women where the conference bishop and cabinet are committed to affirmative action. However, as several United Methodist clergywomen have pointed out, much work yet remains to be done, especially in appointing capable women as senior ministers of larger, wealthier congregations.

I'm grateful for the support and critique of many colleagues in the development of this study. Among those who have been especially helpful are Dr. Mary Sudman Donovan, Dr. Joanna Gillespie, the late Dr. Catherine M. Prelinger, Rev. Sandra Hughes Boyd, Rev. Dr. Suzanne Hiatt (whose methodological challenges originally helped me to refine the accuracy of data collection), Revs. Nan and Jim Hobart, Rev. Lynn Scott, Dr. William Silverman, and the Episcopal Dioceses of Colorado, Massachusetts, and Oregon; all have helped me gain important access to materials and contacts. I've also appreciated the support of Dr. Annemette Sørensen, Dr. David Riesman, and Dr. Roderick Harrison, who oversaw the original wave of this research during the late 1980s; the Harvard Department of Sociology for a grant during the original data collection, and the joint Ph.D. Program in Religion and Theological Studies between Iliff and the University of Denver for a grant to update and expand the data. Finally I would like to acknowledge the excellent assistance of statistical consultants Dr. Karen Butler, University of Denver; Cheri Minton and Nancy Williamson, Harvard University; of faculty computing specialists Carol Taylor and Jennifer Moore-Evans, University of Denver; of my secretary Shirley Kaaz, Iliff; of graduate research assistants Rev. Lucretia Fehrmann, Claire Nord, Rev. Susan Pierce, and Rev. Delbert Watkins for their work on the six-year update and verification process; and of graduate research assistants Elizabeth Azevedo, Lea Harding, Susan Crow, Jo Winn, Bob Miller, and Rev. Linda McMillen for other contributions.

Denver, Colorado   P. D. N.
March 1996

Contents

Introduction   3

ONE

Tradition or Transformation: Women's Struggle over Religious Authority
and Leadership   9

*Organizational Development and Opportunities for Women's
Leadership*   14

Women's Leadership in American Religion   15

Women's Entry into the Clergy   21

The Effects of Occupational Feminization on the Ministry: A Study   26

TWO

Clergy in Two Religious Organizations   29

Life Chances: A Comparative Study 1920–1994   32

Ordination in Two Religious Traditions   36

The Data: Two Decades of Women's Influx   38

THREE

Ordination and Entry Jobs: Critical Criteria   41

Job Placements   41

Gender   44

Ordination Status   46

Education   47

Age   49

Prior Occupational Experience   50
Marital and Family Status   52
Demographic Effects on Entry Placements   54

FOUR

The Second Job: Key to the Career Path   57
Separating the Women from the Men   58
Gender and Ordination Status   62
Gender and Job Mobility   63
Beyond the Second Placement   67
A Career Perspective   70

FIVE

Clergy Careers over Time: A 60-Year Portrait   73
Job Mobility and Career Attainment   73
Women's Place in Clergy Couples   79
Men's Careers and the Appearance of Occupational Stability   80
Clergywomen's Opportunities for Leadership   86

SIX

Decline and Fall of the Young Male Cleric   90
The Graying of the Clergy   91
Second Career: Asset or Liability?   94
Lamentations: Where Have All the Young Men Gone?   100

SEVEN

Feminization and Backlash   107
Proliferation of New Ordination Tracks   115
Gender, Backlash, and Educational Inflation   123
The Deconstruction of Full-Time Work   124
Gender Segregation in the Clergy   126
The Mixed Blessings of Tokenism   130

EIGHT

Structural Change in the Ministry   135
Shortage or Surplus: The Supply and Demand of Clergy Labor   140
Alternative Clergy Labor Supplies   143
Clergy versus Laity: The Emergence of Clericalism   145

Professionalism and Deprofessionalization   149

A Future of Nonstipendiary Clergy   154

Occupational Feminization and Male Exodus   158

Occupational Change and Organizational Response   159

NINE

Clergy Feminization: Controlled Labor or Liberationist Change?   161

   The Future of Women Clergy   162

   Women and the Future of the Clergy   165

   Women Clergy and the Future of Liberationist Change   165

   *A Concluding Unscientific Postscript on Gender and Organized
      Religion*   173

Appendix A   Clergy Job Titles Aggregated by Job Level   178

Appendix B   Demographic Variables   186

Appendix C   Mean (average) Career Trajectory   190

Notes   191

Bibliography   245

Index   269

Feminization
of the Clergy
in America

Introduction

A nglican clergyman John Wesley, in the midst of developing his Methodist movement, urged one of his associates to halt women's preaching in his circuit. "If it were suffered, it would grow, and we know not where it would end."[1] Implicit in Wesley's words may have been an apprehension over power that women in influential positions might exert. Indeed, if women's influence were to grow, where might it have ended? Whereas Wesley was quite concerned with women not holding authority over men, citing scriptural rationale (1 Tim. 2:12),[2] perhaps Wesley and his men were also concerned with the possibility of losing control of their burgeoning religious movement, or the prospect of its lessened appeal to men should it be significantly associated with female leadership.

Women in the ordained ministry have been the focus of considerable public interest and controversy, perhaps more so than any other professional occupation. Like Wesley two centuries ago, male religious leaders in a number of denominations have been preoccupied with how the increase in women interested in preaching and ordained ministry might affect their denomination, including whether their cumulative presence would inhibit membership, contributions, or the prospect of attracting more young men into the clergy, or whether women might collectively take over the organization and, attendant with it, radically change denominational doctrine, theology, liturgical language, and direction. Differences in the types of positions that men and women clergy have obtained are given substantially less attention. Yet studies over the past two decades consistently have shown that women clergy, like their sisters in secular occupations, face a "glass ceiling" regardless of whether a denomination has ordained women for a decade or a century. Occasional cracks have allowed a few women to move into leadership positions, offering hope to scores of other women clergy. But female leadership in mainline denominations remains at token levels.

Although Wesley subsequently modified his position toward women, allowing

3

them a preaching presence that was tightly controlled, opposition to women grew as a backlash movement after his death.[3] Women's ordination within British Methodism wasn't approved until 1973. Strides toward women's participation in ordained ministry on the same basis as men predictably have been followed by waves of backlash, whether the issue at hand has been women's lay preaching, ordination, or pressure for equality at all levels of religious leadership. Such a backlash has been sweeping many U.S. religious organizations over the last several years, putting pressure on whatever occupational gains women clergy have made in recent decades. Concurrently, the proliferation of women clergy has over the last twenty years been blamed for an array of organizational ills, including decreased organizational vitality and decline.[4] How religious organizations respond to backlash accusations may be but symptomatic of the extent of their myopia, or perhaps lack of sincere interest, in attacking the particular roots of organizational malaise.

Over the years, women have brought diverse agendas to ordination, resulting in differing ramifications for both the clergy as an occupation and their religious organizations. It can be argued that some women have been ordained with the professionalized understanding that they are continuing the mores of submissiveness and forbearance that have engendered the development of an infrastructure of female support upon which male occupational opportunities traditionally have depended. As such, women's entry into the ordained ministry may represent a continuous trend of female commitment within organized religion that historically has been expressed through volunteer and charitable work and through youth education. Relying on Douglas's hypothesis of the dual privatization of the religious and the domestic spheres among nineteenth-century Victorian upper- and middle-class European Americans,[5] one could argue that the large-scale movement from professional homemaker to church professional was a logical one. But such a perspective doesn't explain the sudden, exponential increase in women seeking ordination since 1970, nor the increased widespread activism for gender-related issues such as inclusive language within religious organizations.[6]

Women also have sought ordination with concurrent commitments to ideological change and consequent social transformation of both their religious organizations and wider society. Rev. Alison Cheek, director of the feminist liberation theology program at Episcopal Divinity School and one of eleven women to be irregularly ordained to the Episcopal priesthood in 1974, today advises women to seek ordination only if they want to change the church. Says Cheek, "When women come to consult me about going into the ordained ministry, I'm apt to tell them that I believe that women should only do that if they intend to work to change the system. Otherwise they are undermining women's protest against unjust structures by helping cement them into place."[7] While women with transformative agendas are still being ordained, the results of this study show that structural changes allowing newer ordination tracks with local study programs that disproportionately attract women actually facilitate the inclusion of more traditionalist perspectives among female ordinands. This development also is having negative effects on the employment prospects and, to a lesser degree, the networking ability of seminary-trained women clergy.

Beginning Easter 1988, the World Council of Churches announced an ecumenical decade for churches in solidarity with women, with the aim of empowering women to challenge organizational structures, as well as to respond to pressing social issues in their various cultures.[8] Nearly through this decade, we need to seriously reexamine what "solidarity with women" actually has meant within religious organizations that conceptually affirm women's full participation, but have been passive in helping them to obtain viable opportunities to exercise that participation. Because the First Amendment of the U.S. Constitution guarantees the separation of church and state, religious organizations in this country have not been externally pressured to make substantive changes or eliminate gender discrimination. Although some denominations have responded with internal equal opportunity and affirmative action guidelines, these have succeeded primarily in assisting women into entry-level positions. Some women clergy interviewed for this research expressed doubt about their denomination's commitment to help women attain mid-level and higher placements—concerns supported in the quantitative data of this analysis.

Over the last twenty years, several important studies have been conducted on how well women are being assimilated and accepted as clergy, including attitude change by congregations, other clergy, and denominational leaders, and the occupational challenges that women clergy yet face. The most ambitious of these was Carroll, Hargrove, and Lummis's *Women of the Cloth* (1983), which evaluated the prospects of women clergy across nine U.S. mainline denominations. A comparative study designed to update this research has just been completed. Other multidenominational studies have compared and evaluated gender differences in clergy leadership and pastoral styles.[9] Recent single-denominational studies include those on women clergy in the American Baptist Conference,[10] Southern Baptist Convention,[11] Church of God,[12] Episcopal Church,[13] United Methodist Church,[14] United Presbyterian Church U.S.A.,[15] and Reform and Conservative Judaism.[16] Studies on similar trends related to women clergy have been conducted in Canada,[17] Australia,[18] and Europe.[19] In the Roman Catholic Church, studies have focused on interest in women's ordination[20] and the emergence of female lay pastors as an alternative organizational response to the dilemma of a diminishing clergy supply and denominational refusal to ordain women.[21] Taken together, they provide important cross-sectional and comparative benchmarks for the history of women's entry into the ordained ministry and their subsequent careers.

Much of the advocacy literature arguing for women's ordination is of sociological interest from the standpoint of studying feminist religious arguments and understanding the agendas that women have sought to bring to their clergy commitments. This literature, theologically based and justified, typically debates prevailing religious doctrine used against women's ordination or to limit the role that women clergy may hold. Some of this literature has exposed beliefs and practices considered sexist or demeaning to women; some has challenged both the social and the moral legitimacy of the structure of organized religion itself, including ordination rites and the very definition of "church," or it has advocated women's exodus from organized religion, claiming that it is irredeemably misogynist. The thrust of this material expectedly has appeared during ongoing denominational struggles prior to women's ordination.[22] Combined with the sociohistorical literature on women and religion, these writings have been crucial for challenging the gender subordination supported by organizational doctrine, worship, language, and ordained leadership. Religious organizations also have responded with advocacy literature of their own, including tracts portraying exemplary case histories of women clergy who "made it" in terms of holding responsible, although not always authoritative, positions in their congregations; booklets on biblical women; women's leadership materials; and policies on affirmative action for women clergy.[23] Advocacy has taken a slightly different kind of confrontation in evangelical Protestantism, focusing on exegetical analyses of biblical texts as a means for justifying the authority that women can hold either as ordained clergy or as religious leaders, typically through development of androgynous understandings of deity or attempts to reconcile supernatural phenomena with natural causation.[24]

Because religious organizations can slip into theological arguments at the expense of sociological realities, a sociological approach is particularly helpful when examining the dynamics of those who become marginalized when opportunities are relatively distributed. Yet the danger of such an approach is reductionism: sociological arguments can homogenize the clergy with other professions while ignoring a crucial difference between religious and secular vocations—namely, the eschatological element—that can influence occupational decision making in terms of how job opportunities are defined and selected, and how occupational success is measured. Some clergy interviewed for this study, who had stayed in particular jobs that ceased to be occupationally or personally satisfying, stayed there passively, attributing their situation to divine intention (e.g., "this must be where God wants me"). Others described the acceptance of a new job at a lower level than their previous one as a way of being of service, or of ministering ("God urged me to take this position"). But there also is evidence that male clergy traditionally have tended to think in ways similar to those in secular careers: in successive moves to positions of greater budgets and other socioeconomic resources, and to organizational authority and leadership.[25] Although this may be a valid generalization for European-American men beginning their careers as young adults, it cannot be assumed to apply equally to women, people of color, or second-career men or women, nor necessarily to any other individuals deeply influenced by religious concerns. Sociological reductionism, as well as theological idealism, can result in a distorted sense of the real gender tensions within religious organizations today.

Chafetz has argued that research exploring the increase of women in the labor force too often focuses on changes in women's attributes—what she equates as "supply-side logic"—without also examining the "demand side," the opportunities that women actually may have.[26] The supply of opportunities not only is relative to organizational need and resources but their distribution also can be relative—opportunities presented on the basis of gender, age, race, or sexual orientation. The differential attainment that results consequently becomes a function of the quality of opportunities.

The approach used in this analysis departs slightly from traditional sociological literature, which assumes a utilitarian, rational-choice model as the normative mode of occupational reasoning, whereby people automatically will move to higher level jobs should the opportunities arise, independent of other considerations. Two qualifying distinctions are made in the treatment of clergy occupational data. First, clergy upward job mobility and attainment of higher level positions are not to be valued so much as *better* or *more desirable* than as measures of opportunity for greater autonomy and authority that may enhance one's chances to contribute insights or talents to influence denominational doctrine, direction, and practices. In this manner, many higher level positions do offer distinct benefits for those with a transformative agenda. Second, job mobility and attainment are treated as independent concepts. In the occupational literature based on the career experience of European-American men, job mobility and attainment have been perceived as interchangeable concepts, reflecting rational-choice assumptions stemming from male career-development patterns. As such, mobility analysis has ignored the implications of women and minorities who are more likely to experience forced, lateral, and downward job mobility—the result of different opportunities and attainment outcomes. Differences between occupational mobility and attainment proved to be crucial in this analysis, given the sharply divergent career paths for men and women clergy.

Differing from most other research on women clergy, this study takes a longitudinal approach to occupational feminization, examining the careers of both female and male clergy across more than six decades. It also compares the careers of male clergy over time, before and after the large influx of women during the 1970s and 1980s. In this manner, both the longitudinal and the comparative aspects of this study offer a comprehensive picture of the dynamics involved in occupational feminization, including the extent to which the entry of women is responsible for occupational or organizational change.

The selection of the two religious organizations for this study was initially based on public availability of clergy data—a limitation which proved to be fortuitous. The two denominations studied are of markedly different size, with divergent histories of women's ordination, denominational polity, and occupational structure. One maintains linkages with classic conservative Christian tradition, where clergy are ordained on the belief of Apostolic succession—the laying on of hands across generations of clergy from the Apostolic era. The other claims no direct contemporary relationship to Christianity, although it is deeply rooted in liberal Protestant Christian tradition.

Both denominations—the Episcopal Church and the Unitarian Universalist Association—have a large European-American constituency that has limited the possibility for cross-racial analysis, particularly as it may interact with gender. There is evidence that racism compounds gender discrimination for many women clergy of color, not only in predominately European-American denominations but also in integrated and intraracial environments. For instance, it has been observed that in several African-American denominations and in those that are multiracial—typically in Methodist and Baptist traditions—men have dominated religious leadership and have justified their control and subordination of women, partly in response to the racism that men experience in the surrounding society.[27] Based on anecdotal discussion with Asian-American women, this type of interaction appears within other racial groups as well. Therefore, the sexism occurring within constituencies subject to racism expectedly should be evident as well.

The data on clergy careers from these two denominations involve additional limitations. Those who don't survive their denominational screening processes prior to ordination unfortunately do not appear. The subjectivity of who gets admitted, particularly related to women applicants, has been a recurrent theme in both interviews and anecdotal discussions.[28] Additionally, the analysis cannot reliably generalize about gender dynamics involving clergy in smaller Protestant groups where little or no data are publicly available, nor can it attempt to speak for female lay leaders in denominations that don't ordain women, such as the Roman Catholic and Orthodox churches, nor in denominations that don't ordain clergy at all. American Reform and Conservative Judaism have much in common with mainline Protestantism, not only in many shared cultural values shaping American religiosity[29] but also in the pattern of women's entry into the rabbinate, the controversies over their presence, and their access to substantive occupational opportunities. While any generalizations to the Jewish rabbinate should be made cautiously, it is hoped that this analysis may pose questions for reflection on the career prospects of the increased numbers of women being ordained to the rabbinate.

This research makes a critical assumption that a set of factors distinctive to American culture exists that have had harmonizing effects on shaping the norms for religious organizations and their clergy across various traditions.[30] Supporting this assumption, the results of this study did find several strong similarities in clergy careers across two very different religious organizations—similarities which included increased educational resources of more recently ordained clergy; a steady movement toward occupational feminization in terms of the female gender ratio; a proliferation of multiple ordination tracks; tendencies toward job segregation with women concentrated in lower level positions; and an increase in second-career men and women clergy. These trends not only share similarities with secular occupations, especially those which have experienced increased concentrations of women,[31] but also hint at structural changes within the ordained ministry itself, with profound ramifications for reshaping the organization and polity of these denominations.

Clergy in leadership positions hold authority to interpret religious doctrine or ideology within the framework of their tradition, and to develop policy for ensuring a tradition's survival. Male concern over the possibility of losing authority or control over a religious movement such as Wesley's, or an entire religious tradition, may be linked to the underlying structure of how male gender identity is constructed in our culture. If so, it would help to explain why heated debates over issues related to women clergy or sexual orientation occur in proximity with one another. But to more fully explore this thesis will take another book. This volume begins the task by exploring some of the surface issues related to gender and religion—those involving the growing movement toward occupational feminization of the clergy, the resulting implications for both ordained men's and women's careers, and the substantive changes that are occurring within their constituent religious organizations.

Tradition or Transformation

Women's Struggle over Religious
Authority and Leadership

A lexis de Tocqueville, observing America during the period of the Second
Great Awakening, noted an intimate link between religious ideology and the
political quest for liberty.[1] Not unique to the United States, the interaction of
religious belief and social formation has provided a powerful source of regulation
in both economic and political realms, as well as reinforcement of the social
arrangements that have given stability to our institutions. Religion also has provided the moral substance for confrontation, with traditionalism cast as antithesis
to transformation. Over the past three decades, one need only look at the role
of religious ideology in empowering people to seek secular change, nowhere
more evident than the role of the Rev. Dr. Martin Luther King, Jr., and the
black church during the civil rights movement. Other recent movements have
been stirred by Latin American and feminist liberation theologies. Religious ideology also has supported the political efforts of groups seeking a different type
of change—one that represents the reinstitution of tighter social regulation and
control. Such a resurgent linkage between religious ideology and political activity utilized to define, delimit, and control human social relations is poignantly evident to women who have struggled against the strictures of scripture,
doctrine, and tradition of their religious organizations—strictures that too often
have circumscribed their participation in religious communities and in wider
society.

A religion's ability to control behavior depends in part on an ideology that
defines, articulates, rationalizes and maintains hegemony on theological or moral
grounds.[2] Moral justification for a particular social order, grounded in the religious authority of a believing community, can demonize various groups seeking
social change by attributing negative cosmic consequences to their attempts.
Where religions have become institutionalized over time, religious tasks typically
have been differentiated by gender, with such actions justified through scriptural

explanations, typically fortified by reference to divine manifestation, divine will, or religious attributions of natural law.[3]

Noting a tie between religious pronouncements of what was divinely willed and human arguments that one's accomplishments in this world would add to God's glory on earth, Weber believed that such a linkage had provided unusual opportunity for achievement in American society, supported through social mores of self-sacrifice and forbearance—the very mores that reinforced women's acceptance of gender role divisions and circumscription to provide domestic support for the economic activity of husbands, fathers, and other men.[4] Women's supporting roles often have been theologically sanctified as contributions having divine value or blessedness, and reasoned as morally necessary for the good of society. Those making such distinctions and providing rationalizations have been men, who have assumed responsibility for visible leadership activities while allocating to women the subordinate tasks, traditionally those related to family, home, and domestic activity. While this dichotomy has cut somewhat differently along racial lines in the United States, the basic pattern nonetheless is consistent.[5]

Such gender dichotomies in religious roles and responsibilities, have appeared in virtually all forms of religious societies, from tribal organization to western institution. As Weber points out, despite attributions of gender equality at various times in world religious traditions, men have virtually monopolized priestly responsibilities, the setting forth and administration of religious doctrine, public participation, and professional religious training.[6] For instance, traditional Judaism limited direct participation in the divine covenant to men through the rite of circumcision, including opportunities and responsibilities to study the Torah, to interpret and teach religious tenets, and to form *minyans* for community prayer and ritual. Women took part through virtue of marriage and family, and some rituals centered in the home. Only over the last several decades have American Jewish women more commonly participated in the religious community rituals and leadership activities traditionally ascribed to men,[7] including ordination to the rabbinate, now open to women in all but the Orthodox branch.

Christian denominations historically have segregated gender roles on the basis of various New Testament scriptural exhortations emphasizing the rightful dominance of men over women.[8] Men have utilized both the authority of scripture and the weight of accumulated tradition to circumscribe women's religious roles, particularly in those denominations where women have sought to hold the same sacramental responsibilities and authority as men. While most Protestant denominations now ordain both men and women, the struggle to justify women's ordination by countering both scriptural and traditionalist arguments has been both lengthy and intense, and continues in the Roman Catholic and Orthodox traditions. Struggles over women's ordination and women's rightful religious realm have been revived in some denominations that previously had affirmed it, such as the Southern Baptist Convention and the Reformed Church, as support for women clergy has sharply eroded in recent years.

In Islamic tradition, the *Shari'ah*, or Divine Law, instructs gender segregation according to tasks and duties based on the differing natures and constitutions of men and women. Religious responsibilities within the family and the community have been the exclusive domain of men.[9] Muslim women seeking to justify more equitable gender arrangements by showing the corruption of the Q'uran's intent over time have been viewed by traditionalists as rebelling against Islam. Furthermore, women's rebellion is attributed to be the result of men's irresponsibility. Argues Nasr, to the extent that women no longer feel the authority of the religious tradition upon themselves, men should assume the blame for having "ceased to fulfil their religious function and [for having] lost their virile and patriarchal character."[10] This argument has appeared within conservative Protestant Christianity as well, particularly in relation to male responsibility for inhibiting the female independence that is manifested by feminism.[11]

Where religious ideology and practices have been utilized to justify dominance and superior social status by those with the greatest access to power, any challenges for an equal share of authority inevitably collide with those religious precepts and accumulated traditions that have maintained the status inequality. Central to the underlying conflict over gender roles in worship and religious life is the issue of authority and whether divine authority—and consequently human authority—should rest disproportionately on one constituency, such as men. With authority as the ground for legitimating social as well as religious power, dominant constituencies have used legitimating rationale such as their divinely pronounced superiority or divinely delegated rulership over others as justification for racist and classist, as well as sexist, social arrangements. In short, the characteristics of a dominant group typically become justified on religious grounds so as to maintain legitimation of its authority and, consequently, its privilege. Where this occurs, spiritual authority becomes conflated with social authority, affecting how justice is defined, interpreted, and administered in the name of social morality.

Mainline religious organizations, traditionally holding substantial cultural authority in the United States,[12] also have provided linkages for ruling class or status groups to solidify their social authority. For instance, the Victorian ideal for European-American middle-class and upper-class women that privatized them to the domestic sphere as moral exemplars[13] predictably resulted in working-class aspirations of being able to afford a homemaker spouse as a symbol of a man's— and his family's—upward social mobility and consequent social virility. To the extent that mainline religious organizations have supported and perpetuated this ideal, they have facilitated both class and racial cleavages, as well as the stereotypical thinking, that has fortified men's leadership and limited women's participation in both organized religion and wider economic society.

How conflict over authority is dealt with depends to some extent on the normative mode of social reasoning within the dominant group. For instance, religious communities strongly influenced by Enlightenment philosophy may be preoccupied with rational consistency between religious ideology and gender roles. Conversely, groups with greater tolerance for the mystical or nonrational element may be open to women as sacred spiritual leaders[14] while paradoxically justifying on religious grounds their subordination to men in the profane world of daily life. Some conservative, spirit-centered Protestant groups have justified such a dichotomy on the basis that even a cock's crow was used for God's prophecy (Lk. 22:34, 60). Women have been allowed to proselytize and preach based on their perceived divine use as spiritual vessels for religious authority, while at the same time they have been required to adhere to subordinating interpretations of biblical gender arrangements in daily social relations.[15] But to the extent that women in such religious groups also participate in a secular society with more egalitarian gender mores, some evidence has accumulated that they feel heightened tension in maintaining distinct boundaries between leadership in the sacred and subordination in the profane realms.[16] The double consciousness that such participation engenders—of their own legitimated role circumscriptions in contrast to those of others with whom they may develop secular relations of respect and trust—increases the potential for such women to make transformative linkages between the lives of others and their own. Consequently, how women manifest their religious leadership, the opportunities offered by their religious community, and the transformative agendas they bring may differ not only in relation to their racial and socioeconomic social location but in how knowledge is constructed and legitimated within their religious tradition, as well as the extent of their public participation in a heterogeneous, wider society.

Women have been stereotyped as having a single transformative agenda at the expense of ignoring varying cultural experiences and interests, particularly those which cross racial and social class lines. Marital status also can differentiate women's interests or agendas. To the extent that women are heavily dependent on their husbands for social status and are isolated from substantive interaction beyond the religious community, they expectedly would uphold the privilege granted their social location through their husband's standing and oppose efforts to undermine male privilege. For instance, Nason-Clark's multidenominational study tends to illustrate this point in her finding that female clergy hold more liberal biblical and theological perspectives than do clergy wives.[17] Indeed, women's differing race, social class, and marital privilege have generated internal conflicts that have diluted the cohesion of women's movements for social change. Internal controversies and conflicts, while profoundly important in developing more equitable understandings of justice, consequently have inhibited the efficacy of new agendas seeking to confront or replace established regimes, and have served to benefit those who continue to dominate the religious organizational leadership.[18] Yet only when transformative agendas are generated out of widespread internal support across diverse constituencies can they be less likely to enact the same repressiveness as those they seek to replace.

The consequence of transformative gender relations can be significant. Gender-related changes in scriptural, doctrinal, and ethical interpretation across various religious traditions have important secondary effects on the wider community in which members of religious groups interact—namely, in extended family relationships, the workplace, and politics. Feminist theological arguments in both conservative and liberal religious traditions have taken seriously this possibility, pointing to the potential utility of religion for the political empowerment of women. Change in theological understanding of the structure of divine and, consequently, human authority, as well as the language with which it is communicated, has been expected to manifest new structures of opportunities and enhanced prestige as women, and other previously marginalized constituencies, gain fresh access to authority. Schaller's observation that men are drawn to theologically conservative congregations while women constitute two-thirds of the membership in theologically liberal congregations underscores the empowering importance of such religious ideology.[19]

Furthermore, with evidence that female seminarians tend to be more liberal theologically than males and more inclined to perceive the function of the church in terms of social reform,[20] one can hypothesize that, should the percentage of women in positions of significant religious authority reach a threshold level, widespread change can be expected in religious ideologies and behaviors related to gender and sexuality—those which traditionally have delimited women's roles, responsibilities, and opportunities in their religious communities and shaped expected behavioral norms for social interaction.[21] Likewise, to the extent that religious ideology promulgated by female religious leadership supports beliefs and practices that advance female empowerment and equality in the sacred realm, particularly in those traditions which de-emphasize discontinuity between the sacred and daily life, there should be increased pressure for egalitarian gender relations in both religious and secular spheres. Women's continued movement into positions of religious leadership in numerous denominations during the political and economic turbulence at the close of the twentieth century optimistically could herald both a religious and a social transformation, forming new linkages across not only gender but also racial/ethnic and sexual orientation lines, if the evidence of their more egalitarian and congregationally empowering leadership style are any indicator.[22]

But given the close alignment of socioeconomic stability and reinforcing religious ideology that Weber and Durkheim each observed but valued in different ways, conservative forces among a dominant group, as well as those who perceive their own interests to be aligned with that faction, should be expected to vigorously work against any changes in ideology that could undermine the religious authority that has sanctioned their social privilege. Therefore, any significant change in gender relations likely will not go unchallenged. Put simply, how far will male dominance of religious authority and organizational control be eroded before women become subverted from increasing their share beyond marginal levels of influence? Overt backlash movements reasserting religious tradition with strongly circumscribed gender relations as a means of reinforcing social stability have developed in certain religious sectors since the early 1980s, supporting the likelihood that women's influx into religious leadership and the ensuing pressure for gender-related changes have reached a critical level. Direct attacks against religious feminism by Mormon and conservative evangelical church leaders, as well as Pope John Paul II's equation of feminism with heretical goddess worship,[23] illustrate their concern with the implications of women gaining greater religious and social power. Yet, for women who have tasted greater autonomy, opportunity, and self-esteem as a result of empowering religious ideology, will—or can—they return other than by force to a traditionalist environment? The gendered struggle over religious authority expectedly will continue.

Organizational Development and Opportunities
for Women's Leadership

Weber observed that when a religious community is faced with surviving beyond its founding generation, it typically develops institutional means by which the emergent tradition can be preserved. [24] As religious groups bureaucratize, the organizational structure often develops a conserving bias in its religious worldview and worship practices as it seeks consistency with what it believes are the understandings of early members. The process of codifying beliefs and tradition, such as done through canonizing scripture, risks reductionism as it loses relation to both the cultural context out of which beliefs and tradition emerged and the diversity of argument and counterargument surrounding them. Silence in scripture or tradition, particularly on issues relating to gender and sexuality, has been assumed as prohibition, especially by denominational theologies strongly dependent on Enlightenment rationalism and positivism for the development and maintenance of their authoritative basis. For instance, Christian denominational arguments against women's ordination have utilized declarations based on biblical positivism that women weren't named among the disciples or sanctioned for ordination under the emergent church structure. [25] Reliance on reductionistic positivism, as well as natural law justifications for doctrinal efficacy, produces a retardation of organizational change, facilitating the maintenance of authoritative control by the constituency that dominates the tradition's leadership.

Weber also made two important observations about women's opportunities to participate in religious leadership. First, religious sects composed primarily of the disprivileged classes more frequently tended to grant equality to women. Such groups were found within early Buddhism and Christianity, religions rooted in socioeconomic and ideological conflict with prevailing religious traditions whose practices privileged some while marginalizing others. [26] The Buddha, who sought to rectify the caste determinism of Hinduism, admitted women to the Sangha (Order of Monks), although he was concerned that they would negatively affect the purity and consequently the life span of religion. [27] Women's leadership activities in early Christianity are most notably evident in the initial Pauline communities. Women as well as men served as deacons, as leaders of "house church" communities, and occasionally as apostles. [28] Weber believed that Christianity's egalitarian appeal to women had been critical to its spread and eventual success over competing rival religions that excluded women, especially Mithraism. [29] Islam, during Muhammad's lifetime and immediately afterward, not only offered women greater freedom and social esteem than the mores of surrounding cultures, but women prayed in mosques and were counted among the earliest Islamic scholars. [30] Other emergent Buddhist-Taoist sects and, later, European and American spiritualist and pacifist sects attracted women, notably the Quakers, offering them egalitarian status and benefiting from their leadership and missionary efforts. [31]

Weber further observed that as new religious groups organize or "routinize," formalizing their leadership structure, codifying and canonizing scripture as an ideological reinforcement for their organizational development, women typically become marginalized from positions of religious responsibility. [32] By the emergence of the Buddhist canonical literature, about two centuries following the death of the Buddha, not only had women become excluded from the Sangha but female gender was viewed as both an obstruction to religious perfection and a sexual distraction to the (male) clergy. Likewise, following Muhammad's death, women's status steadily declined over ensuing centuries.[33] Women's opportunities for leadership in early Christian communities also were short-lived. Radical in its notion of gender parity in matters of the spirit, early Christianity represented a subversive social force to more stratified gender relations in the surrounding cultures. Furthermore, Parvey argues that when the early church lost its millennialist belief in the immanence of the return of Christ and transformation into the Kingdom, it also lost the theological rationale for egalitarian social life—and consequently egalitarian gender relations.[34] Women's participation also may have threatened to dominate the early church prior to development of a formalized structure, with the marginalization of women from leadership occurring out of a twofold male concern for the church's survival and fear that men would abandon the Christian movement. Its survival involved the need to minimize high extant sociopolitical tension with Rome, as well as with the surrounding cultures, and to some extent incur political legitimacy without changing key tenets of Christian beliefs. The epistles of Timothy, setting forth the emergent leadership structure of the newly forming tradition (1 Tim. 2–6), specifically note maleness as a requirement for ordained leadership; by then, women were proscribed even from teaching roles. In some gnostic sects of that era, women still could be priests,[35] but both their leadership and the sects themselves, along with androgynous religious imagery, became forcibly eliminated as a heretical threat to the more dominant strains of Christianity. Although Christian women subsequently did retain some opportunities for religious leadership through gender-segregated religious orders,[36] they remained subordinate to male clergy. Thus, the acceptability and consequent legitimation of women's authority in religious circles have involved fluctuations in socioeconomic and political conditions, gender-related norms and taboos in the surrounding culture, and internal concerns, such as change in organizational structure and membership, accompanied by change in legitimating authority and doctrine.

The mechanism for women's subordination, then, seems to have been a combination of ideology justified by selected elements of tradition interacting with political and economic exigencies of the day, which historically were echoed in denominational exhortations of women's higher calling to self-sacrifice, moral purity, and segregated yet theoretically equal vocations, particularly in times when the group's male hegemony was under threat.[37] Nowhere has this been more explicit than in Pope John Paul II's 1994 apostolic letter *Ordinatio Sacerdotalis*, which reaffirms the priesthood as open to men only, despite profound shortages of male ordinands.[38]

Women's Leadership in American Religion

Relying on Weber, Carroll et al. have characterized the history of American women's religious leadership as a three-stage cycle: (1) *charismatic groups*, where women are evident as founders and important leaders; (2) *consolidating and orga-nizing groups*, where women become restricted from leadership and channeled into gender-segregated roles, usually following the death of the founding genera-tion; and (3) *maturing and institutionalizing groups*, where women's leadership becomes publicly visible, but typically in ways that are marginal to organizational authority.[39] As a model, it relies on Weber's concept of routinization: as religious movements gain political and social legitimacy, they become more bureaucratic, institutionalized, and identified with both socially and politically dominant groups and their mores.

Charisma in the Weberian sense connotes an extraordinary power and conse-quent authority that is attributed to a leader on the basis of particular personal traits rather than formal credentials.[40] As charismatic leaders, women have a strong tradition of founding and leading new Pentecostal, Holiness, and Spiritualist movements. Such groups place substantial authority on the spirit whether in a mystical or pietistic sense, with relatively low concern for organizational structure and occupational credentials, such as ordination. During revivalist worship, gen-der, racial, and social class differences become submerged; women and others normally marginalized can be respected as vessels of divine communication. Women who have assumed religious leadership of such groups typically have been subjected to suspicion, scorn, ostracism, or death when their throngs conflict with traditionalist or rationalist sects or denominations in the surrounding society. For instance, New England Puritan Anne Hutchinson, the educated daughter of an Anglican clergyman who taught that inner truth was available to all and threatened the hegemony of the local Puritan clergy, was tried, convicted, and ostracized by the local clergy and their constituencies, and died shortly thereafter.[41]

Evangelical and Pentecostal women preachers were integral to the transforma-tive revivalism of the early nineteenth-century Second Great Awakening.[42] For instance, Barbara Heinemann led the Amana (Society of True Inspiration) com-munity;[43] Phoebe Palmer was central to the Holiness movement; Aimee Semple McPherson founded the International Church of the Foursquare Gospel; Alma White built the Pillar of Fire Church; and Jemima Wilkinson, who combined Quaker spiritualism with revivalist preaching, founded the Universal Friends com-munity.[44] Women have been particularly prominent in founding black spiritualist churches, such as Mother Leafy Anderson, founder of the Eternal Life Christian Spiritualist Church; Sister Moore, the Redeeming Christian Spiritualist Church; and Sister Wilma Stewart, the St. Joseph's Spiritual Church.[45] Outside of preach-ing and worship, however, women typically were scripturally bound to subordina-tion under men in their daily life. This paradox, based on sharp sacred-profane distinctions in matters of spiritual empowerment, offered women temporary respite from subordinate status in contrast to the more rationally dependent, Enlight-enment-influenced religious traditions emphasizing the routinization of charisma and the rationalized consistency between the holy and daily life.

Women leaders of groups that remained small or loosely organized, as well as those consisting predominately of women, the destitute, or other socially mar-ginalized constituencies, have tended to attract little concern provided that gender or sexual mores of the surrounding society aren't violated. African-American slave women were the locus of cultural and religious transmission, instilling elements of cultural survival and religious values into young children before they were sold or moved away.[46] Careful to provoke little interest among European-American religious communities, they played a crucial role in keeping alive resistance to domination. By contrast, both Shaker and Oneida communities, simply advocating gender equality achieved through sexual mores considered deviant to their surrounding society, attracted substantial public consternation.

While some religious groups have waned with the death of the founding female leader, others have been able to bridge the transition by developing an organizational structure, but one that typically has ended up marginalizing or eliminating women from leadership. For instance, Barbara Heck had been responsible for building the first Methodist church in America,[47] but nearly two centuries would pass before the first Methodist woman would be ordained to full clergy status. The Seventh-Day Adventist Church, inspired by Ellen White, the Christian Science Church founded by Mary Baker Eddy, and Aimee Semple McPherson's International Church of the Foursquare Gospel would become established within American Protestantism, but the leadership subsequently was taken over by men.[48] A notable exception was the American Shaker movement, which preserved dual-gender leadership beyond the founding generation, although the movement had waned markedly by the close of the nineteenth century.[49]

Once religious movements become institutionalized, women have few opportunities to assert influence over the formation of their tenets and tradition. This has particularly been the case for Pentecostal and Evangelical groups that were far more egalitarian prior to institutionalization.[50] Economically and politically dominant religious organizations have offered women some visible leadership opportunities, but the extent of their authority has been tightly controlled, either through gender-segregated religious orders, boards, commissions, or assemblies, or by co-opting them into male dominant groups. For instance, Roman Catholic and Episcopal religious orders, as well as Protestant deaconess movements, provided important opportunities for women to found or lead various communities and head organizations, although they effectively were segregated from direct influence on doctrinal or traditional church authority.

Among mainline Protestant denominations, women's leadership opportunities have been primarily of two kinds: presiding over gender-segregated congregational committees, guilds, Sunday School, and special fund-raising events; or working outside the congregation in institutional, deaconess, or missionary work.[51] Missionary appointments, appealing particularly to graduates of Protestant-influenced women's colleges, offered a milieu geographically separate from the sponsoring religious organizational structure, often with conditions not unlike the autonomy and authority that women leaders have held at the charismatic stage. Women gained experience in lay missionary work with other women, in ministering to soldiers during the Civil War, or in assignments to other countries primarily as teachers, nurses, or as social service and administrative staff. Smith writes that "the mission field was, in fact, the first area of American life where women achieved a more or less equal professional status with men."[52] Smith adds that missionary work attracted women deeply committed to women's rights. Such women found substantial opportunities for lay, and eventually ordained, leadership, in both foreign and domestic missions—the latter responsible for Christian conversion on what was considered the American frontier. Women's missionary organizations, although in their early years segregated from other denominational bodies, eventually challenged the male-dominant organizational structures with their initiative, influence, and fund-raising acumen.

Across denominations, women's organizations were efficiently run and financially solvent, often more so than those run by men.[53] Some women's missionary organizations resultingly were merged into the denominational structure—for example, in the Episcopal Church (1920) as in several other religious organizations, where men took over the leadership including management of the sizable budget, allotting to women only marginal roles.[54] As women's missionary boards and auxiliaries were involuntarily incorporated into the male-dominant organizational structure, or voluntarily but naively so, women subsequently became keenly aware of their marginalization, not only by losing control over their financial assets but also in the more progressive positions on social issues they had been able to take prior to merger.[55]

The male co-optation of successful female-led groups—whether religious communities or missionary societies—exemplifies the process of *organizational masculinization*. Not only does it illustrate the fluid nature of gender roles as related to occupations and organizations, but it points to the critical element of competition with women over the desirability of the resources they control—whether economic, occupational, or organizational. As such, then, women themselves cannot be said to be decreasing occupational or organizational desirability where there are significant resources at stake. The relationship between institutionalization of a religious group and marginalization of women from leadership[56] also occurs when the resources are political rather than economic. This has been evident in the political rise of fundamentalist and conservative evangelical movements into the cultural mainstream of the late 1970s and 1980s, and in the black church during the civil rights era, where important political gains could be made in partnership with widespread European-American moderate and liberal support. In both instances, men shared the prospect of upward social mobility and esteem within the politically dominant culture; they also had the fear of downward social mobility should their somewhat precarious gains be lost.

Lynd and Lynd observed in *Middletown* that religious beliefs and practices may be the most slowly changing of all human social activity, but the well-established mainline denominations have exhibited an increasingly liberalizing trend over time.[57] Women's leadership, where allowed to flourish within mainline organizations, has tended toward the liberal side not only in ideology but also in ecumenism. Women-led groups such as the Women's Christian Temperance Union or those involving human rights—abolitionism, suffrage, literacy, education, and peace—frequently crossed denominational boundaries. While divisions have existed among Protestants, Catholics, and Jews, and along racial lines, women's groups have tended to be demographically more fluid than male-dominant groups.[58]

Women-led groups also have tended to integrate religion with political concerns. Said Frances Willard, leader of the Women's Christian Temperance Union, which arose as an offshoot of religious revivalism in an attempt to improve women's relationship to men, "We speak about the germ of a new church in which, as Christ declared, there shall be neither male nor female. . . . We speak, too, about the germ of a new political party. . . ."[59] Liberal transformation arising out of concern for the oppressive edges of tradition has provided a powerful foundation for fortifying feminist movements, whether grounded in the frustration of generations of women seeking roles in religious leadership closed to them, in the development of feminist biblical scholarship and theology, or in the more radical solution of post-Christian feminist forms of religious community, belief, and practice. Yet liberal social concerns, including deliberate empowerment of marginalized groups where the newly empowered represent no socioeconomic or political threat to the privileged, can serve many purposes, as the results of this study will show.

A Cultural Context for Women's Ordination

A sociohistorical sketch of women's religious leadership can provide important cultural insights into both the gendered division of religious labor and women's ensuing struggles for power. Nowhere are these dynamics more evident than in the myriad gender-related issues that emerged prior to granting women's ordination in U.S. mainline religious organizations[60] and the actual leadership struggles that surrounded the process of legitimating women's ordination.[61] To the extent that the United States traditionally has been regarded as a *promised land* by European Americans and more recently by other immigrant groups, the resulting intensified religious fervor has heightened the perceived stakes involved in the gendered struggle for power, manifested in the issue of women's ordination. Ironically, it also may have facilitated this effort in several distinct ways.

First, with the European-American migration into the frontier,[62] the prestige of family heritage and social standing often became leveled with those from non-privileged backgrounds,[63] facilitating development of congregations that were democratically organized and maintained. As such, more egalitarian emphasis was placed on what one could do or contribute than on maintaining one's traditional place or role. Second, high geographic mobility enhanced by the frontier mitigated Protestant denominational rivalries and facilitated greater tolerance for religious pluralism. New communities emerged virtually overnight, with European-American settlers coming from diverse backgrounds. As they moved west, they were more often than not replaced by migrants with even more diverse pasts and perspectives. A sense of freedom to move on if a community didn't suit the liking of migrants suggests that entrenched, competing religious organizations were less likely to develop. Third, the diversity of religious groups and the proliferation of new congregations created a demand for both lay and clergy leadership, which translated into opportunities for women as well as men willing to accept such a challenge. The more visible socioeconomic roles that pioneer women were able to assume, combined with the high demand for religious leaders despite many congregations' inability to pay a substantive salary or, in their terms, *not able to afford a man*, led to a cultural receptivity conducive to women missionaries, preachers, and other religious leaders in congregationally oriented denominations.[64]

Fourth, Evangelical and Pentecostal religious groups, as well as pietistic and separatist movements, gave women greater opportunity to preach, teach, and otherwise take substantive religious leadership roles that were reserved for men in more socioeconomically elite denominations. This in turn offered them wider public visibility. Where women could gain experience in religious leadership, their ensuing social visibility challenged eighteenth- and nineteenth-century European-American stereotypes of a "woman's place," especially within the strongly Enlightenment-influenced intellectual and religious circles of the middle and upper classes. If women were effective preachers among revivalist groups, for instance, why couldn't they likewise be so in the larger, mainline congregations?

Fifth, Douglas argues that by prohibiting state religion through the First Amendment to the U.S. Constitution, religious organizations and their leadership became economically dependent on local congregations, which offset the authoritative power that clergy had held in the colonial era.[65] Disenfranchisement created a combination of social pressure and economic leverage that could be exerted by lay membership should a minister unsettle powerful interests in the congregation. Douglas claims that this loss of direct authority was a major contributor to the decline in clergy prestige, and points to European-American clergy and women's roles concurrently being privatized to religious and domestic spheres respectively, with both held to similar moral ideals and standards of behavior and benefitting mutually from successful collaboration on various reform movements.[66]

Sixth, the effects of nineteenth-century U.S. industrialization, which moved the locus of economic production—and male labor—out of the home and established norms that privatized middle- and upper-class women away from the public sphere, gave impetus to women's participation in religious organizations as a culturally accepted social, educational, and vocational outlet where they could utilize their skills and education in a variety of ways. The bifurcation of the ministry into discrete specialties of theologian and pastor resulted in the latter's coming to emphasize experience, piety, and nurture over intellect, and becoming equated with parish ministry, according to Douglas. As such, the pastoral realm was more conducive to the education and deployment of women as missionaries, lay pastors, counselors, and social workers, and as teachers to women, children, and the socioeconomically disenfranchised. Douglas contends that the very conflation of the religious and domestic spheres, and the effeminate qualities expected of the European-American minister and matron, engendered a hostility among ministers over women's attempts to enter their professional domain.[67] Ironically, the proximity of these two spheres, and the social acceptance of women's involvement in each, provided the very opportunities for women to assert their interests in political, social, economic, and ultimately religious organizational reform—the last by challenging the gender limitation on ordained ministry. At the 1848 Seneca Falls convention on women's rights, hosted by the Wesleyan Methodists, women's ordination was formally stated as one of the movement's goals.[68]

As women gained organizational and public experience in a range of ministerial activities, the male clergy leadership continued to refuse recognition of women's endeavors as professional ministry. Of the Episcopal Church, Donovan writes, "In the period between 1850 and 1919, women developed a wide range of ministries. . . . Symbolically, the women were viewed as handmaidens, as those who prepared the way for the priests, the Church's authentic ministers."[69] Furthermore, women's ensuing marginalization as their boards, missionary societies, and other groups were co-opted into the formal denominational structure subsequently radicalized them, as they saw expected gender equality in leadership disintegrate. Many turned toward supporting women's movements for ordination.[70]

Another factor involves the introduction of critical biblical scholarship that effectively relativized the absolute power of scripture and the clergy as interpreters of divine intention. Critical scholarship, opening the way for the use of cultural context to theologically question, demythologize, or utilize an array of alternative reinterpretations of the authority of scripture, also laid the foundation for feminist analysis, with Schüssler Fiorenza's axial hermeneutic of suspicion[71] that has empowered emergent theologies to confront male-biased scripture, doctrine, language, and ritual. Feminist religious scholarship had begun to emerge in the 1880s, as women explored and questioned female status in scripture, leading to the 1895 publication of Elizabeth Cady Stanton's *The Woman's Bible*, the year in which the interreligious World Conference of Women held special liturgies, sang hymns, and proclaimed women's equality as a divinely ordained struggle.[72] After several decades of latency promulgated by a backlash against women's equality movements, two world wars, and the Great Depression, contemporary feminist religious movements gathered significant momentum in the 1960s, heralded by Valerie Saiving's essay "The Human Situation: A Feminine View" (1960) and Mary Daly's *The Church and the Second Sex* (1968)—works which became pivotal in catalyzing arguments over women's ordination during the subsequent decade.[73]

Thus the historical pattern of geographic mobility, the disenfranchisement of church and state, the ensuing shifts toward congregational authority and autonomy, women's opportunities and experience as grassroots religious leaders and role models, the co-optation of many lay women's religious organizations and women's resultant radicalization, changes in clergy roles, and the relativization of religious scholarship all have contributed not only to movements committed to reformulate religious ideologies and rationally justify women's ordination but also to the reformation of religious tradition in ways that seek to empower rather than subordinate women. But to what extent have women traded handmaiden status for authentic recognition as ministers on the same basis as men? Predictably, tensions and resistances to change in traditional gender arrangements have emerged, particularly in access to ordained leadership positions.

Women's Entry into the Clergy

While some evidence does exist that women were occasionally ordained in Christian communities until the eleventh century,[74] ordination was not to the same offices with responsibilities and tasks identical to those of men. Although women have had greater access to ordination in religious bodies where the rite represents a congregational acknowledgment of spiritual gifts rather than a simultaneous acknowledgment of both spiritual and organizational authority, such ordinations haven't typically granted access to leadership authority over men.[75] Women's entry into the same ordination process as men began for U.S. mainline denominations only in the mid-nineteenth century.

The process of opening ordination to women, including opportunities for leadership, hasn't occurred without strife. While denominational leadership and laity consistently have been more supportive of movements to ordain women, it has been the male clergy—those most affected occupationally—who have put up the most resistance.[76] Male clergy have expressed a variety of concerns about granting women's ordination, which have included fears of an exodus among clergy colleagues; anxieties that women would *take over the church*, especially since women already constitute a majority of lay membership in most denominations; hesitancies over women's ability to minister in dangerous neighborhoods; questions of whether women could be competent administrators, could be respected as authorities, or could competently counsel men on sex or hear their confessions; fears that women would sexually tempt male clergy, that they would cause male impotency, and that they would lower male morale; apprehensions that men would lose legitimate access to sacred vestments and activities otherwise associated with women in daily life, or that menstruating women would contaminate the purity of sacraments or sacred ritual; and beliefs that women's exclusion should be just compensation for men's inability to bear children.[77] Some concerns have been more theological, relying on scriptural positivism to delimit women from ordination, particularly in denominations emphasizing rational consistency between the sacred and profane spheres. In Roman Catholic argument, since the priest sacramentally represents the person of Jesus Christ, priests therefore must be male.[78]

Other apprehensions have been more ethical, such as men shirking their religious responsibilities by delegating them instead to women.[79] Consternation over possible ramifications for changing traditional gender roles is evident in the words of the Rt. Rev. Kenneth E. Kirk, late Anglican Bishop of Oxford:

> The wife and mother would be severely tempted to arrogate to herself a sexual equality with, if not superiority to, her husband analogous to the position of her ordained unmarried sister; dangerous strains would be introduced into domestic life; and the integrity of the Christian doctrine of the married relationship would be gravely challenged.[80]

Where women feel empowered to reject traditionally subordinate, self-sacrificial roles reinforced by religious doctrine and tradition, then negative ramifications for men could ensue in declining domestic and economic support services, in increased competition for jobs and organizational leadership, and for control of doctrinal and religious authority. As such, the ordination of women and the prospect of occupational feminization raise intriguing questions as to what realistically will be the impact of women clergy over time on their religious organizations and the membership, and on empowering more assertive female participation in other sectors of society. Certainly the patriarchal equation for social cohesion would be radically altered.

Many of the earliest ordained women sought to transform not only their religious organizations but also the structure of society, to make it more egalitarian for women. Antoinette Brown was the first woman ordained in the United States, as a Congregational minister in 1853, following a protracted struggle for admission to Oberlin seminary and subsequent refusal by her denomination to license her upon her graduation in 1850. Brown, as women who would be ordained over the next two decades, was an experienced social worker, lecturer, and laborer for the abolitionist and women's rights movements, which proved to be valuable insurance when only a few years later she was forced to give up her ministry position owing to internal strife.[81] Taking her husband's name, Blackwell, she subsequently joined the Unitarian Church, deeply involving herself in preaching, working on the suffrage movement, and writing on the interrelationship of Darwinism, religion, and feminism.[82] Olympia Brown, the first woman minister to have national denominational recognition, was ordained as a Universalist minister in 1863. She likewise was a strong advocate of women's suffrage.[83] In the decades that followed, women were ordained in more than a dozen congregationally oriented denominations. Many took ground-breaking leadership on an array of social and women's issues. Women ordained near the turn of the century began to seek ordination less for ideological than for pragmatic reasons, such as to further their missionary work to assist or copastor within their husbands, or simply eligibility for a clergy discount when traveling with their clergy spouses.

By the turn of the century, at least 3,400 women had been ordained. Women represented 3.3 percent of all employed European-American clergy, but constituted proportionally fewer (1.1%) of African-American clergy.[84] Backlash against women's ordination had begun to reverberate through the denominations, spurred as much by preoccupation with the decline in both quality and quantity of male ministerial candidates as by the presence of women. Women were discouraged from seminary and ordination.[85] If ordained, they found it difficult to get congregational appointments. Where denominational officials once had supported women clergy, they now grew resistant to helping women find congregations. Some denominations, such as the Methodist Protestant Church, revoked women's ordination altogether.[86] In other denominations where women's status was more tenuous, women's role were sharply delimited. The Methodist Episcopal Church, South, for instance, in 1906 sharply restricted women's roles and no longer recognized women as preachers or church officers.[87]

By 1910, the number of women clergy had dropped nearly 80 percent, to less than 700. Yet by 1920 the number of women clergy had more than doubled,[88] with much of this increase accounted for by strides that women had made in Holiness and Pentecostal groups. The Assemblies of God, the largest predominately European-American Pentecostal denomination, had formally recognized women's ordination in 1914, although women weren't given the right to vote within the denomination until 1920.[89] Although struggles for women's ordination persisted in other Christian denominations and in Reform Judaism, they were largely without success. At the 1920 worldwide Anglican Lambeth Conference, the consecration of deaconesses had been declared to be an act of ordination,[90] but this resolution was revoked at the next meeting in 1930. The decade of the 1920s, according to Bendroth, was one in which unrest over women's roles peaked.[91] This also was an era of increased resistance against women ministers.[92] Although Presbyterian and Methodist women were granted ordination as local deacons during this period, few women pursued it. Methodist women, for instance, wouldn't be assured job placements, which ironically was a necessary precondition for their ordination.[93]

During the Depression, women clergy had even greater difficulty finding and keeping placements, owing in part to the desire to give men paying jobs if congregations could afford to do so, which fed a growing prejudice against women clergy. Women were encouraged to train for parish assistants or religious educators rather than as ministers.[94] Although the Assemblies of God did fully open their ordained pastorate to women in 1935, Blumhofer writes that attitudes about what was considered appropriate religious roles for women had become so internalized that the resolution had little effect.[95]

Wartime and repressive regimes have facilitated women's ordination, although once peace returns the denominational authority initially tends to deny the permanence—or legitimacy—of women's status, much like what has occurred in secular occupations. One of the most poignant examples involves Florence Li Tim Oi, who was ordained an Anglican deacon, and subsequently the first Anglican woman priest, during the World War II Japanese occupation of China. Immediately after the war, the ordaining bishop was censured and Oi ordered not to exercise her priesthood. Women's ordination wasn't granted in her church nor her ordination formally recognized until 1970. During the religious revival following the collapse of the Chinese Cultural Revolution, Oi served a congregation of about 1,000 members in Guangzhou.[96] Also during the communist regime in Czechoslovakia, at least three women were secretly ordained to the Roman Catholic priesthood as a means of continuing the religious tradition under political repression. Following the dissolution of the communist government, the Vatican has refused to recognize the validity of their ordinations.[97]

World War II did generate subsequent change in several religious organizations' policies toward women's ordination. Socioeconomic exigencies involving the postwar boom in population, and the rapid expansion of both church membership and congregations, created a high demand for new clergy. The African Methodist Episcopal Church began ordaining women in 1948, followed in 1956 by the United Methodist and United Presbyterian (U.S.A.) Churches, which opened full ordination privileges to women. The Presbyterian (U.S.) Church and Southern Baptist Convention granted women's ordination in 1964.[98] A similar movement was occurring in Europe and elsewhere during these years. By 1958, forty-eight members of the World Council of Churches ordained women on the same basis as men.[99] The Roman Catholic Church remained steadfast against women's ordination, but at Vatican II (1963) a crucial sentence acknowledged that it would be "very important that [women] participate more widely also in the various fields of the Church's apostolate,"[100] which opened up new lay roles for women in worship and teaching, including admission to ministerial preparation in Roman Catholic theological schools.

The most recent wave of U.S. denominations granting women's ordination crested in the early 1970s, when the Lutheran Church in America and the American Lutheran Church granted full ordination to women (1970), the Mennonite Church in North America ordained its first woman (1973), the first female rabbis were ordained in Reform (1972) and Reconstructionist (1974) Judaism, the Episcopal Church voted to ordain women to the diaconate (1970) and to the priesthood (1976), and the Evangelical Covenant Church approved women's ordination (1976). Conservative Judaism opened its rabbinate to women in 1983.

In 1970, women had accounted for less than 3 percent of clergy overall, representing an actual decline from 4.1 percent in 1950.[101] But the rate of women seeking ordination increased markedly in the mid-1970s and early 1980s across denominations, regardless of whether they had only just opened ordination to women or had ordained women for a century. For example, in the United Church of Christ (U.C.C.)—the denomination which had ordained Antoinette Brown— less than 3 percent of the clergy had been female in 1970, similar to the ratio of women overall. But by the early 1980s, U.C.C. seminary enrollment was over 50 percent female.[102] Harvard Divinity School, which began admitting women only during the 1950s, graduated a class in 1972 that was 11 percent female; less than fifteen years later, women would represent over 50 percent of the student body.[103] Overall, by 1990 the gender ratio of U.S. and Canadian A.T.S. (Association of Theological School) seminaries was 30 percent female, with female ratios in evangelical seminaries somewhat lower and those in mainline liberal seminaries substantially higher.[104] Jewish traditions that ordain women have experienced similar increases in female seminarians.[105] Overall in 1990, women represented about 9 percent of all U.S. clergy.[106] By 1995, the number of women clergy had risen to 50,000.[107]

Internationally, movements for women's ordination in mainline religious organizations have increased sharply. For instance, women were granted ordination to the Lutheran pastorate in Japan (1970), Malaysia (1986), Indonesia (1987), Latvia (1989), Hong Kong (1990), India (1991), Tanzania (1991), Singapore (1994), and Romania (1995). Likewise, in the Anglican communion, women were admitted to the priesthood in Hong Kong, Macao, and Kenya (1971); Canada (1976); New Zealand (1977); Uganda (1983); Ireland (1990); The Philippines (1991); Australia and South Africa (1992); and England and Scotland (1994). The German synod of the Old Catholic Church, a denomination in communion with the Roman Catholic Church, agreed to women's ordination in 1994. And in 1995, the first female Conservative rabbi in Latin America was ordained.[108] Women clergy in the Scandinavian state churches have become commonplace; for instance, nearly a quarter of the Church of Sweden clergy are female.[109] To date, none of the Orthodox traditions—Christian or Jewish—ordain women. Nor do the Roman Catholic Church, some Anglican, and some conservative Protestant denominations.[110] Ecumenically, women's ordination has been used by both the Vatican and internal Anglican factions as an overwhelming obstacle to meaningful discussions of intercommunion. But other changes are on the horizon for clergy in most mainline denominations, which may seriously affect for better or worse women's occupational prospects, as Chapter 8 will show.

The Effects of Occupational Feminization on the Ministry: A Study

"Nothing worse could happen to the church than feminization," wrote a Presbyterian layman at the outset of the Depression.[111] Although feminization itself may be regarded simply as an objective process of increasing the ratio of women relative to men to the extent that the church—and its clergy—become predominately female, such change typically has been associated with devalued prestige. Feminization, in secular occupations, also has been connected with diminished authority and socioeconomic rewards, either through external restructuring and benefiting other occupations, or through the internal reconfiguring, partitioning, and de-skilling of various constituent jobs. Additional effects of occupational feminization typically have included changed job opportunity and mobility structures, depressed compensation, strong competitive pressure by men for senior positions, a depletion of young men making the clergy their career choice, especially those considered to be "the best and the brightest," gender segregation, and a backlash against women's occupational presence.[112]

Feminization, as a result, has come to imply a set of symptomatic socioeconomic changes, mostly adverse, for the bulk of women and men in an occupation, related to their jobs and their career trajectories. Often the implicit assumption has been that women are the cause, or problem, of diminishing job opportunities and rewards—an assumption which too often has gone untested. Outside of feminist circles, the increased presence of women has never been heralded enthusiastically nor claims made that more women will add prestige to an occupation, nor that they will help to *raise* salaries for men. In the marketplace, women still have less socioeconomic and political currency despite affirmative action programs that have sought to raise their visibility and value. Even where signs of occupational malaise might be widely evident prior to the influx of women, it is important to ask why the blame for declines in compensation, prestige, and power nonetheless is placed upon women. As a corollary, it also is critical to explore why so many men have been hesitant to associate with women as equals. Although such questions extend beyond a sociological study of the effects of women's influx into the ordained ministry over the past twenty-five years, they do suggest foundational issues that will discussed in the concluding chapter.

Assuming a diversity of agendas that women have brought to their ordination, what ramifications or outcomes can be predicted for occupational or organizational change as the overall ratio of women clergy continues to increase? To what extent is women's ordination a professionalized continuation of the mores of submissiveness and forbearance that effectively have generated women's domestic support for men's opportunities in secular work? Or, to what extent are women seeking ordination with a concurrent commitment to religious and social transformation, particularly related to gender? And what ramifications may ensue when women clergy become sharply divided between these two hypothetical extremes? If women's entry into the ordained ministry is continuous with women's extensive history of lay volunteer and paid work within their religious organizations,[113] such continuity doesn't explain the exponential increase in women seeking ordination nor women's widespread activism for gender-inclusive religious language since 1970.[114]

Occupational feminization also raises the issue of potential structural change in the ordained ministry. For instance, if a shift in the gender composition of an occupation is the result of wider socioeconomic changes, such as an altered demand for clergy services, shifts in the supply of prospective male entrants, varying socioeconomic conditions affecting organizational revenues, a proliferation of new jobs, diminishment of well-paying positions, increased job skill requirements, higher or lower compensation, or altered rewards in terms of prestige or upward social mobility relative to other occupations,[115] then an increased ratio of women being ordained would suggest that structural occupational changes have already begun.

Other studies have shown that female clergy, once ordained, have not had equivalent opportunities, job placements, or treatment to that of men, even when their education, age, and prior experience may be similar.[116] Whether denominations have ordained women for a century or barely two decades, women clergy seem to be disproportionately absent from those placements traditionally coveted by men—namely, as leaders of large, affluent congregations or as denominational bishops or executives. Is such a gap the result of women's free choice or forced circumstance? If women's opportunities in maturing and institutionalizing religious organizations are marginal to those of men, to what extent might these organizations be actively co-opting their labor into subordinate or sex-segregated positions? From such questions, three points of investigation emerge: (1) how the clergy as an occupation might be changing overall, either in a way that has facilitated women's entry or in response to their presence; (2) how occupational change in the clergy might similarly or differentially affect the opportunities, rewards, and constraints for newly ordained women and men; and (3) how women's ordination might interact with various structural changes occurring in religious organizations themselves.

The following analysis investigates the first point—how the clergy as an occupation is changing—from an empirical perspective. The embedded research questions are: To what extent might a greater amount of occupational change have occurred prior rather than subsequent to the large influx of women? What might an analysis of career trajectories between recently ordained male clergy and those of several decades ago say about possible long-range changes in the occupation's opportunity structure? And, how might women's integration into the ministry accelerate such change? Finally, to what extent does the gender ratio seem to be changing significantly and permanently?

Exploration of the second point—how occupational change affects newly ordained clergy—will assess empirically whether opportunities for women clergy resemble those of men. Are there signs that the occupation is becoming well integrated or remaining sex segregated by type and level of job? Over several job changes, are there significantly different occupational outcomes attributable to gender? For instance, do women clergy have the same amount of denominational authority and resultant prestige as men ordained at the same time? To what extent do clergy careers reflect modifications in other occupations where a comparable gender shift has occurred? Furthermore, to what extent are men still interested in the clergy? And if so, are they similar demographically to men who would have sought ordination in earlier generations?

Both structural change in the clergy and a shift in gender composition suggest major adjustments in religious organizations themselves, which is the third point of this analysis. If patterns of gender segregation should continue to accompany women's influx, where women are concentrated in subordinate jobs regardless of their qualifications, then it is possible that women's labor may be directed in response to changed internal socioeconomic or structural needs. If substantial occupational change has occurred prior to the large influx of women, then it suggests that organizational needs in response to external socioeconomic, political, or cultural factors may have affected the clergy independent of gender-related issues.

Emerging from the three points above, the following hypotheses frame the following study of clergy occupational feminization.

1. Similarities will be evident when comparing male and female clergy careers across different types of religious organizations.
2. Gender will be a significant variable in differences between female and male clergy careers.
3. Evidence of occupational change will have preceded the sharp influx of women clergy during the 1970s.
4. Male clergy careers will have been more affected by changes preceding rather than following the sharp influx of women.
5. Female clergy careers should be more adversely sensitive to the increasing influx of women than should men's careers.
6. Trends toward occupational feminization in the clergy should be consistent with feminization trends in secular occupations.

The objective of this research, to set forth a detailed analysis of the dynamics surrounding women's influx into the ordained ministry, seeks to respond to the question of what responsibility gender, in contrast to various socioeconomic or political forces, may have had in creating those structural symptoms so often associated with occupational feminization, such as declining occupational power and prestige, job differentiation, and segregation. Yet the implications of clergy feminization undeniably hold important consequences for the struggle between maintenance and change in religious traditions and their host organizations, with reverberations for other social institutions—the family, the workplace, the government—in which religious peoples participate.

Two

Clergy in Two Religious Organizations

All major religious traditions that ordain clergy have specified at some point in their development that ordination is a rite belonging exclusively to males.[1] Ordained leadership historically has served as an occupational anchor to tradition, responsible for writing, interpretation, and maintenance of scripture, doctrine, sacred ritual, or custom; for inspiring members to apply religious tenets to daily life; for encouraging members to commit themselves and their resources; for exhorting them to conform with the religious community; and for conserving and perpetuating religious heritage.[2] Such responsibilities have helped men to organize and shape emergent religious movements into religious institutions.

Ordination, etymologically meaning "to set into order" (L. *ordināre*), signifies an authorization or designated appointment.[3] It sets apart those with professional authority and responsibilities to speak for a religious organization and to oversee its viability over time. Ordination in contemporary mainline denominations normally follows a formalized acknowledgment of having mastered specialized knowledge culminating in an advanced degree, one or more internships in a local congregation, and often an oral or written examination. Religious groups with strong congregational authority, and either a literalistic interpretation of scripture or strong authoritative emphasis on personal inspiration, have tended to shun ordination rites, relying instead on lay leadership. The Society of Friends, for instance, believes that God ordains and the church "records"; likewise, the Salvation Army "commissions" rather than ordains its officers.[4] Islamic tradition, while not ordaining clergy, does have functionaries such as the *imam* who leads a mosque's religious prayers and is considered to be titular head of the local religious community, or who is a highly respected religious scholar.[5] These examples are similar to ordination in that they delegate greater religious responsibility, if not authority, to certain individuals. Taken together, they overwhelmingly have tended to be dominated by men.

Congregational groups affiliating with a denomination but maintaining final authority typically have ordained clergy in a single rite, dependent on recognizing and affirming a candidate's perceived "call"[6] to ministry. Usually there are additional denominational stipulations if one's ordination is to be recognized beyond the local congregation. Denominations with centralized hierarchies have more complicated processes, often ordaining clergy twice: the first is usually regarded as a probationary or preparatory status, prior to a second ordination granting full preaching, pastoral, or sacramental privileges, including opportunities to hold senior leadership positions within the denomination. Christian denominations rooted in the Orthodox, Roman Catholic, Lutheran, Anglican, and Methodist traditions normally ordain clergy first as transitional deacons and second as elders, pastors, presbyters, or priests.[7] Those subsequently selected as bishops are consecrated to their office. Some denominations also either license lay leaders or ordain clergy to minister in a local congregation or, a certain geographic region.

Historically new clergy—ministers, priests, rabbis—learned their profession through apprenticeship to senior clergy, as well as through continued study. Professionalization of the clergy, through formal seminary training and specific denominational requirements, became normative in many religious organizations during the ninteenth century, similar to professionalization movements in medicine and law. The contemporary usage of *profession* normally refers to a specialized type of occupation with distinct attributes, such as (1) a theoretically grounded body of knowledge acquired through long, intensive training; (2) the authority to assess what is in the best interests of clients and to prescribe a course of action; (3) the autonomy to make decisions about the occupation without external controls, such as in selecting and training candidates or peer evaluation, (4) community support for the profession's authority to set its own standards and to self-govern; and (5) a subculture with particular symbols, language, and internal peer networks.[8] Clergy subculture involves special vestments, meetings, associations, networks, and other activities distinct from those of lay members. Clergy also have substantial autonomy in determining their own norms, including self-censure, although the recent widespread rise of litigation over clergy sexual abuse has tightened controls on internal autonomy and has affected public perception of clergy professional accountability.

The clergy as an occupation usually has been understood to be a single, paid career beginning in young adulthood, reflecting the norm for the European-American male labor market. In many socioeconomically poorer congregations, clergy tasks and responsibilities often have had to be handled on a part-time or nonstipendiary basis. Nonetheless, most clergy have aspired to full-time pastorates, where they could concentrate their religious commitments. Full-time positions are considered to be an internal labor market[9] bound within a religious organization. Although some denominational crossover may occur, with clergy ordained in one denomination but employed in another, such situations represent special circumstances. For instance, Donovan describes a female Episcopal priest holding her first clergy position in a United Methodist congregation and subsequently being ordained to the priesthood there, primarily because of the lack of job vacancies in Episcopal churches nearby, although an inference suggests that the tight job market likely was related to her gender.[10] A few instances of denominational crossover in job placements occur in data for this analysis, as well.

Following ordination, common entry placements for most clergy either have been in associate positions within large congregations or as sole clergy (e.g., vicar, extension minister, solo pastor) responsible for small congregations. For men, subsequent moves ideally have tended toward successively larger congregations in terms of members and budgets, and occasionally supervision of a clergy staff, with a few eventually moving into denominational leadership positions. In congregationally oriented organizations, denominational executive positions may be seen as a lateral move, carrying more prestige within the denomination but lacking the external, community prestige and internal socioeconomic leverage that oversight of a large congregation brings.

Clergy status, according to Parsons, is related to the prestige of a congregation's membership.[11] Although most clergy are located in congregations, a variant career pattern involves those clergy who, instead of a parish track, pursue their careers in denominational schools and seminaries, hospitals, or agencies under denominational sponsorship. Organizationally, specialized ministries not financially supported by a congregation have had less prestige and political leverage within the denomination.

Both clergy and secular occupations involve hiring and deployment processes with positions linked in job ladders, and individual jobs linked within career trajectories. The denominational job ladder for clergy, whether formally defined or informally communicated, tends to reflect traditional career aspirations. In the past, many clergy passively "waited for calls" from other congregations rather than actively managing their careers in a manner more characteristic of secular occupations. Mainline denominations historically have corresponded to dominant American cultural strains,[12] and there is substantial evidence that male clergy have indeed tended to make career decisions in ways similar to secular workers, through aspiring to positions of greater budgetary and socioeconomic resources, and to increased denominational authority.[13] Within religious organizations the hierarchical level of authority held, the number of clergy supervised, the amount of membership growth and financial resources overseen, or the extent of one's own compensation package traditionally have been used as informal measures of occupational success.[14] Ironically, women ministers historically have been very good at building up small congregations, but seldom have been rewarded by being allowed to remain there or to move to larger congregations, as have male clergy.[15]

Over the past two decades, there has been some discussion over whether women and men value the same criteria for defining occupational success. Gender differences have been identified in occupational interests and expectations among both seminarians and clergy, with women more focused on mastery and enjoyment of tasks in particular jobs than on treating those jobs as steps to higher level positions within a context of upward mobility across the career life course.[16] Whether perceived gender disparities are due to mentoring differences, socialization, personal conflicts, or to assessments based on their divergent positions and realistic prospects for attainment, this has yet to be fully determined. Lehman found few significant differences across four denominations between male and female ministers in time spent on various tasks, the importance they placed upon them, or, controlling for denomination, desire for formal authority,[17] which would suggest that gender differences at lower occupational levels may be socially and situationally influenced rather than intrinsic. Secular research also suggests that there are strong similarities in terms of how men and women value income, prestige, or the "goodness" of a job.[18] Consequently, female as well as male clergy should be expected to value opportunities for full-time employment, higher income, autonomy, and sufficient authority to influence their congregation or denomination.

Life Chances: A Comparative Study 1920–1994

Occupationally, life chances have been described as the sum of opportunities and rewards, offset by constraints, that affect job choices.[19] *Opportunities* are represented by available job placements offering either intrinsic or extrinsic rewards such as autonomy, creativity, increased responsibility, authority, prestige, potential for occupational advancement, and salary. For this analysis, the most critical determinant of whether a position represents an opportunity is the amount of organizational authority that it offers. The reason lies in the centrality of the clergy for interpreting, influencing, and maintaining the continuity of their religious tradition, including their greater likelihood than laity to be regarded as representatives or spokespeople for their denomination. Access to authority for women clergy is particularly crucial should their occupational agenda include change or transformation in gender relations within the religious organization, its beliefs, and practices. Access to opportunities depends upon *personal resources* such as ordination, seminary, college or prep school affiliation, academic degrees, applicable skills, and, to some extent, demographic factors such as gender, race or ethnicity, age, a clergy parent with accumulated years of denominational networks, recommendations by clergy in positions of denominational esteem, and marital status, which for men traditionally has included the free support services of a spouse—the traditional "minister's wife"—to help build his career. *Organizational resources* for determining opportunities include job vacancies—either new positions or those created through vacancy chains[20]—and both formal and informal employment processes ranging from denomination-wide computerized job and candidate matching networks to local deployment officials who communicate or broker job openings.

Much of the concern over occupational feminization involves the effect of increased women's ordination on the occupational life chances of male clergy. Less concern typically has been expressed on the effect of the increasing ratio of women on the life chances of female clergy. To study the comparative effect, including the effect of various personal and organizational resources for access to opportunities, male and female clergy occupational biographies have been analyzed over a period extending from 1920—a point when, according to U.S. Census figures, there were fewer than 1,800 women clergy—to 1993, when women numbered more than 33,000, or 11.6 percent of American clergy overall.[21]

Despite sizable differences between the two denominations selected for this analysis, the Episcopal Church and the Unitarian Universalist Association (U.U.A), both share a common history with U.S. Protestantism: Episcopalianism, resulting from its break with the Church of England following the American Revolution, American Unitarianism as the liberal descendent of New England Puritanism, and Universalism likewise having descended from Congregationalist tradition.[22] Many have entered the U.U.A. from predominantly Protestant and, to a lesser extent, Roman Catholic and Jewish backgrounds. Neither the Episcopal Church nor the U.U.A. are among the largest denominations, nor are they the most typical of American mainline religious organizations. Both tend to attract an educated, upper-middle-class membership.[23] Both denominations also have strong historical ties to the Northeast,[24] although the Episcopal Church has widened its geographic representation, particularly in the South. In denominational organization and utilization of clergy, Unitarian Universalism is similar to Protestant congregational polity where local congregations have nearly complete autonomy, with the denominational organization primarily providing structure and support for affiliated congregations. Organizationally, the Episcopal Church's hierarchal structure is based on the nearly 2,000-year tradition of Apostolic succession, yet in practice it combines episcopal and congregational styles of polity, with self-supporting parishes hiring their own clergy subject to formal approval by diocesan (i.e., regional) bishops.

The highly different organizational structures and deployment practices of the Episcopal Church and the U.U.A. provide an excellent challenge for identifying occupational trends that can be generalized beyond denominational particularities. Also, having very different histories of women's ordination and experiences of women clergy, they present a potentially distinctive contrast for women's careers. The U.U.A., with no official doctrine, creed, or authoritative body of scripture or practices,[25] has not had to justify women clergy on religious grounds. Furthermore, given its social justice orientation and more than a century of experience with Unitarian and Universalist women clergy, the U.U.A. should be expected to offer the most equitable opportunities for women clergy of any denomination. The Episcopal Church, in marked contrast, has only a recent history of women's ordination, which was justified against objections of scripture, religious authority, and tradition.[26] Balancing the Episcopal Church's liberal constituency has been a strong traditionalist sector constituted by a conservative elite with an Anglo Catholic or *high church* religiosity and a conservative middle class with a Protestant evangelical *low church* orientation. Both of these groups, having opposed women's ordination during the 1970s, create a coalition that represents a conservative strain on matters of gender and sexuality.[27]

The two samples consist of 399 female and 974 male Episcopal, and 77 female and 119 male U.U.A. clergy occupational biographies. Clergy were selected in ordination cohorts at ten-year intervals ranging from 1920 to 1950, and in five-year intervals ranging from 1970 to 1990 (Tables 2.1 and 2.2). Selection was based on the year of the first, or only, ordination. All Episcopal clergy are originally ordained to the diaconate, although those subsequently ordained to the priesthood have additional occupational opportunities open to them. Consequently,

Table 2.1. Episcopal Sample of Clergy, Compared to All Ordained to the Diaconate for Selected Years, 1920–1990.

Cohort	Sample			All Ordained (Diaconate)	
	Female	Male	Total	Total	Percentage Female
1990	150	150	300	435	43.4
1985	126	150	276	499	31.9
1980	75	154	229	360	21.7
1975	38	165	203	311	12.2
1971	7	0	7	a	a
1970	3	170	173	413	0.7
1950		130	130	274	0.0
1940		25	25	166	0.0
1930		25	25	169	0.0
1920		5	5	115	0.0
Total	399	974	1,373	2,742	

a Clergy total for 1971 was not included since the only clergy ordained that year relevant to the sample were women who had completed seminary by June 1970 and, had they been male, would have been ordained then.

Sources: *Journal of the General Convention 1922–1991; Episcopal Clerical Directory, 1975–1993; Episcopal Clergy Directory 1972; The Clerical Directory 1956–1968; Stowe's Clerical Directory, 1920–1953.* The 1950 and later sample years include clergy who subsequently left the ministry. Total clergy ordained must be considered an approximation, because of conflicting dates across various denominational documents.

Table 2.2. Unitarian Universalist Sample of Clergy, Compared to All Ordained for Selected Years, 1930–1990.

Cohort	Sample			All Ordained	
	Female	Male	Total	Total	Percentage Female
1990	19	17	36	36	52.8
1985	23	18	41	41	56.1
1980	25	13	38	38	65.8
1975	6	22	28	28	21.4
1970	2	19	21	21	9.5
1950	1	17	18	18	5.6
1940	0	8	8	29	0.0
1930	1	5	6	54	14.8
Total	77	119	196	265	

Sources: *Unitarian Universalist Association Directory, 1961-1993; Unitarian Year Book, 1921-1959,* Universalist Church of America, *The Universalist Directory, 1948-1953; Universalist Register, 1920;* Universalist General Convention, *Universalist Biennial Reports and Directory, 1940–1941; The Universalist Directory 1922-1958.* The 1950 and later sample years include clergy who subsequently left the ministry. The 1950 and earlier cohorts are a combined total of Unitarian and Universalist clergy. Total clergy ordained must be considered an approximation, because of conflicting dates, omissions, and incomplete data across various annual directories. Occupational biographies were constructed where information was sufficient to do so.

priesthood status is treated as a separate variable. Only Unitarian Universalist clergy holding fellowship status with the U.U.A. are included.[28] In both samples, the women represent the denominational population of female clergy ordained in the years selected, except for Episcopal women ordained in 1990. Episcopal men and women clergy in the 1990 cohort and men ordained in 1920, 1930, and 1940 were selected from clergy ordained those years through use of random numbers, while Episcopal men ordained in 1950 and at five-year intervals between 1970 and 1985 were selected from all those ordained through a stratified systematic formula.[29] Clergy received from other denominations but not actually ordained are excluded from the study. Also excluded are biographies with insufficient data to be verified. Since the 1970 Episcopal General Convention authorized women's ordination to the diaconate to begin in 1971, women who had completed seminary as of June 1970 but were ordained in 1971 are included in the 1970 cohort, since had they been male they would have been ordained that year. Three women were identified with an ordination year of 1970: two had been consecrated as deaconesses who were then regularized as deacons, and one was ordained as a deacon in December. The group of women ordained in 1970/71 represents *the original cohort of women clergy in the Episcopal Church.* Biographies were subsequently verified and updated to 1993 by cross-reference with other denominational documents, yielding at least a 95 percent verification rate for both samples.[30] Finally, a small sample of interviews (N = 30) was developed consisting of female and male clergy whose occupational data were selected for this analysis, with clergy ordained in other years, with Episcopal and U.U.A. denominational officials, and with clergy of other denominations, primarily for assistance in reflecting on the statistical results and clarification of deployment processes.

The career biography approach not only provides a means for longitudinal analysis but also presents several other methodological benefits. A representative sample of clergy from the entire denomination can be selected, assuring geographic diversity. This approach also tracks clergy migration, job changes, and, to some extent, nondenominational employment. The sample is independent of clergy cooperation or accurate recall of job histories that affect survey or interview research. Additionally, those ordained and subsequently leaving the ministry altogether are included. In a few cases, "leavers" were found to return many years later.

Minority racial status has been shown to affect careers in ways similar to gender. For instance, a 1989 Presbyterian (U.S.A.) panel study reported that preference for racial/ethnic minority clergy ranged from 4 to 10 percent among various groups sampled, compared to 28 to 81 percent for white clergy; preference for female clergy ranged from 0 to 2 percent, compared to 48 to 86 percent for male clergy.[31] Consequently, an interaction effect between race and gender should be expected.[32] Although race wasn't listed in denominational directory data, a racial variable was constructed based on partial information available.[33] Overall, only a small number of minority-race clergy were identified—about 6 percent of each sample. In both samples, the largest minority racial group is African American. All U.U.A. minority-race clergy in the sample are male. Of minority-race Episcopal clergy, 18 percent are female. Because of the variable's heuristic construction, the statistical results should be considered definitive for European Americans but not necessarily for other clergy.

The statistical methods depended on the objective of the particular test, sample size, and specific variables used. Descriptive results examining associations between variables primarily utilized cross-tabulation with significance evaluated by chi-square tests and analysis of variance. Multivariate regression was used primarily to analyze gender and other independent effects on job level. Event history analysis, utilizing maximum likelihood estimates based on Cox proportional hazard-rate modeling, evaluated time-dependent prospects for upward job mobility. The 1950 and earlier cohorts often were collapsed to serve as a control for testing the stability of occupational trends, as well as for identifying subsequent trends.

Should career trajectories of male clergy in both denominations be similar over time, including the period when Episcopal men only were ordained, then occupational changes evident for men prior to the large influx of women should be attributable to causes other than feminization. Also, should the career trajectories of women clergy be substantially similar in both denominations, then arguments such as denominational beliefs and practices, polity, occupational structure, or lack of experience with women clergy[34] cannot be responsible for differing occupational outcomes between men and women clergy.

Ordination in Two Religious Traditions

Unitarian Universalist Association

Each denomination has more than one ordination status. The U.U.A. has three types of ordination: the traditional *minister*, who normally specializes in parish ministry; the *minister of religious education*, an ordination status developed in 1981 that replaced the certification process for parish religious educators; and the *community minister*, instituted in 1992 for those specializing in nonparish ministries. U.U.A. clergy may hold more than one type of ordination. Officially, Unitarian Universalist candidates must be *called*, or hired, by a parish before they can be ordained. Consequently, clergy supply is linked with selective demand. Local congregations can ordain candidates without denominational approval, but if a minister wishes to hold denominational fellowship—which offers both national recognition and opportunities for jobs in other congregations—the process of seeking fellowship resembles steps toward ordination in other denominations. Acceptance into *preliminary U.U.A. fellowship* entails a probationary period and may occur while prospective ministers are completing seminary. Following graduation, and after three years of preliminary fellowship, ministers are eligible for *final fellowship*. U.U.A. clergy also are in *associate fellowship* during their probationary period or if they are neither working full time nor active in ministry. Those subsequently in *full fellowship* normally hold or actively seek full-time parish placements.[35]

Prior to women's ordination, Universalist and Unitarian women have had a long history of religious involvement as preachers. Judith Sargent Murray, an advocate of Universalism and women's rights, held a local Universalist preacher's license as early as the 1790s; other Universalist women joined her in the opening decades of the 1800s.[36] The first Universalist woman ordained with full denominational authority, Olympia Brown (1863), and the first woman ordained in the Unitarian Church, Celia Burleigh (1869), led the way for nearly seventy other Unitarian and Universalist women who were ordained by 1890. After the turn of the century, women clergy, as well as prospective candidates, tended to be discouraged by the male leadership of the two denominations, a primary concern being that the presence of women ministers would hurt a "manly" image that the leadership desired for their denomination.[37] This was a trend shared by other religious organizations of that era. Evident from the early Universalist and Unitarian directories, the number of ordained women declined sharply, particularly after 1930, and remained at virtually token levels until the mid-1970s (cf. Table 2.2).

The Episcopal Church

Episcopal ordinations reflect a very different process. Candidates initially are ordained to the diaconate either as *permanent deacons*, who consider the diaconate to be their vocation, or as *transitional deacons*, who have taken the denominationally required General Ordination Examination and who usually are ordained to the priesthood at some point during their first diaconal year. The permanent diaconate theoretically is considered a separate and equal ministry,[38] although considerable overlap exists between deacons and priests in certain placements and job tasks. Additionally, deacons and priests can be ordained to serve in a local congregation only, with subsequent movement requiring the diocesan bishop's approval. Many dioceses accept aspirants to the ordination process based on projected job openings at the time an applicant normally would be ready for ordination, but additional candidates may be admitted, particularly if they are planning nonstipendiary ministries.

Women's ordination first became a major issue in the U.S. Episcopal Church during the 1960s, when the ordination status of deaconesses was brought forth for debate. This may have had echoes in earlier discussion over deaconess status, which culminated in the 1920 Anglican Lambeth declaration of deaconess consecration to be an ordained status, although church leaders quickly backed away from this position. Following the 1964 Episcopal General Convention decision that deaconesses indeed were a ministerial order, Bishop Pike of California formally recognized a deaconess on the same basis as ordained male deacons, which set off considerable furor within the denomination. The 1968 worldwide Anglican Lambeth Conference summarily agreed that deaconesses who had received the "laying on of hands with appropriate prayers" were within the ordained diaconate,[39] which opened the way to women's ordination. At the 1970 Episcopal General Convention, women's ordination to the diaconate on the same basis as men was approved, with ordination to the priesthood failing only in the clergy vote. At the next triennial General Convention (1973), women's ordination was resoundingly defeated by conservative coalitions. Devastated and frustrated, eleven female deacons presented themselves to be ordained by three retired bishops on

July 29, 1974. These irregular ordinations set off further turmoil within the church, including substantial hostility directed at the new female priests. Four more women were ordained to the priesthood by a retired bishop on September 7, 1975. During this period, several male deacons chose to delay their ordination to the priesthood until their female colleagues also could be ordained. The 1976 General Convention approved the ordination of women to the priesthood, by declaring that gender was not a limiting factor on ordination or ability to hold the offices of bishop, priest, or deacon.[40] By the end of 1977, about 100 women had been ordained as priests.[41]

But in 1976 a *conscience clause* was also passed as a way to minimize schism by those opposing women priests, which stated that, "no bishop, priest, or lay person should be coerced or penalized in any manner" for acting according to their convictions on the matter of women's ordination.[42] The effect in the Episcopal Church enabled some dioceses to refuse to ordain female deacons or priests. In some cases a diocese might support women's ordination, but a bishop could refuse to ordain women or to admit them if they had been ordained elsewhere. In other cases, bishops would allow another bishop to enter the diocese to ordain women, thus upholding church policy while not violating personal conscience. Through the early-mid 1990s, only one diocese—Fond du Lac (WI)—continued to prohibit any ordained women. Four more dioceses have ordained women to the diaconate but not the priesthood—Eau Claire (WI), Fort Worth (TX), Quincy (IL), and San Joaquin (CA).[43] When it became evident that a female bishop would soon be elected, a structural change occurred within the Episcopal Church at the 1988 General Convention. Congregations were allowed a conscience clause enabling them to substitute an *Episcopal visitor* for necessary rites, such as confirmations and ordinations, if their current bishop were unacceptable to them. Following the 1988 election of the first female bishop, Barbara Clementine Harris, congregations opposed to women's ordination formed a national synod in defiance of the denomination's organizational structure.

As many as 20,000 clergy and laity may have broken away from the Episcopal Church following the 1976 decision to ordain women to the priesthood, but Sumner points out that subsequent internal schisms within the breakaway groups and legal conflicts over property only decreased the efficacy and viability of such movements.[44] Some clergy sought standing in the Roman Catholic Church. In 1993 another faction, which had been associated with the defiant synod, broke away from the Episcopal Church, the trigger issue being denominational support for the continuing consecration of women to the episcopate.[45] Overt resistance to women clergy within the Episcopal Church has been allowed to continue as a way to avoid further divisive organizational conflict, although at the expense of women clergy.

The Data: Two Decades of Women's Influx

An interesting correspondence arises between the years of the greatest increase in U.U.A. women clergy and the period when Episcopal women's ordination to the priesthood was granted, lending evidence to clergy feminization as an occupation-wide trend affected by external socioeconomic and cultural influences characteristic of the late 1970s. The trend toward occupational feminization is particularly visible when comparing the increasing ratio of women's ordinations over the last twenty years in these two denominations (Figure 2.1, cf. Tables 2.1 and 2.2). The growth of U.U.A. women ministers appears to have peaked with the 1980 cohort, where nearly two-thirds of candidates ordained that year were female. Subsequently the gender ratio has settled to slightly more than 50 percent female annually.[46] Since the first Episcopal woman was ordained in 1970, the annual ratio of Episcopal women being ordained has risen steadily, to more than 40 percent female by 1990.

Since the U.U.A. recruiting process theoretically is *closed*, to the extent that to be ordained a candidate must be *called* to a parish, the change in gender composition implies that either women are entering with superior qualifications and have a competitive edge over men in obtaining calls, or that fewer men are actually seeking ordination. If female clergy have succeeded by outcompeting male candidates for ordination, then women should show evidence of greater personal resources, such as superior education. Yet the data reveal just the opposite: U.U.A. men are being ordained with a significantly higher level of education than women ($p < .001$). More likely, the changing gender ratio reflects not only a growing female interest in ministry as a career choice but also a marked decline in male interest.

Although the number of Episcopal men ordained increased markedly in 1985, which was the largest male cohort in the data since 1970, male ordinations in 1990 were at their lowest level of any cohort examined since 1940 (cf. Table 2.1). At the

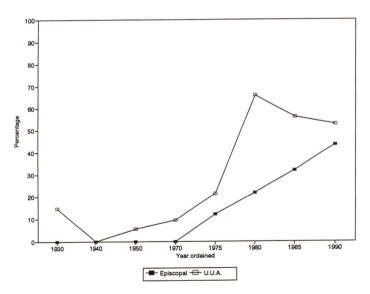

Figure 2.1 Episcopal and U.U.A. women clergy as a percentage of all ordained, 1930–1990.

same time, the large 1985 and 1990 cohorts of new Episcopal clergy, in contrast with the 3.1 percent decline in Episcopal congregations and the 13.5 percent decline in church communicants between 1980 and 1990,[47] suggest that occupational crowding is likely, which should be manifested in an intense competition for entry placements. If crowding effects from secular occupations[48] are valid for the ordained ministry, then women should be expected to fare adversely relative to men in entry positions. Furthermore, based on secular occupations that have feminized,[49] gender-related differences should expectedly increase in occupational opportunities and attainment as the ratio of women increases—differences that benefit the proportionately fewer men, rather than the women, entering the ministry. The next three chapters will explore these prospects in more detail.

⌣· Three ·⌣

Ordination and Entry Jobs

Critical Criteria

Earlier research on women clergy identified a relationship between the length of time that women have been ordained and increased support among male clergy for feminism.[1] But to what extent does such liberalized attitudinal support become translated into actual employment opportunities?

Entry placements, which often serve as training positions, represent a foundational foothold in the clergy occupational structure. Yet several criteria may affect the type of entry position that clergy obtain, such as gender, age, and amount of education at the time of ordination, type of ordination one holds, other occupational experience, and marital or family status. To the extent that these criteria positively or negatively influence job placements, they become resources or liabilities. Particular resources when combined may interact with one another in quite different ways. For instance, a youthful age at the time of ordination may be an important asset when combined with male gender, but may be neutral when linked with females. Several potential resources, and how they interact with gender are explored separately in this chapter. But first, a methodological note is necessary on the range and comparison of clergy jobs in the Episcopal Church and the Unitarian Universalist Association.

Job Placements

Most clergy job placements are situated in local congregations, either as the sole ordained functionary or as part of a multiple clergy staff. Since congregations vary in size and socioeconomic status, jobs with the same title can differ widely in the amount of socioeconomic resources available. Such resources include the size of the congregational budget, amount of opportunity to develop substantive internal and outreach programs, size of the clergy compensation package, amount that the congregation contributes to the denomination, and prestige of the congregation, both within the denomination and in the local community. Small congregations with few members and a tight budget may barely support one paid, full-time clergy. Or, they may receive denominational financial support for part of the clergy stipend. Or, further, they may either hire a clergyperson part-time or share clergy with one or more other congregations. Small, financially poorer congregations tend to be in inner cities, neighborhoods in socioeconomic transition, and rural areas. The most financially stable congregations, which typically offer the greatest socioeconomic resources, are those with endowments often established long ago or with rental income from other property; they tend to be in prosperous downtown sectors and in socioeconomically elite neighborhoods. While many clergy may actively seek job opportunities in congregations that are financially disadvantaged, there is ample evidence that they also tend to be attracted to locations offering full-time employment, a staff, and ample budget for internal and outreach programming.[2]

Clergy placements outside the congregation may involve denominational administration, teaching in denominational schools and seminaries, counseling in private agencies, chaplaincy work on college campuses, or chaplaincies in hospitals and urban agencies. In recent years, more clergy tend to have professional training or experience in areas such as law, finance, social work, or counseling—a trend supported by the data in this analysis. Such experience can be utilized either as a specialized skill in a traditional job placement inside the denomination or in an ecumenical or secular agency. In the latter situation, clergy additionally may hold a part-time or nonstipendiary denominational appointment.

Placements are obtained through both formal and informal networks. In purely congregational systems, clergy must find their own placements, usually with some informal help by regional or denominational officials who may consult with them as well as the congregations. Episcopal systems such as the Roman Catholic and United Methodist churches appoint clergy to congregations and can move them at will. In the Episcopal Church, some positions may be filled by the diocesan bishop—normally those which are financially dependent on the diocese—while others are filled by the sponsoring congregation, school, or institution. Newly ordained Episcopal clergy are the most likely to be appointed, usually for a short-term or temporary position; thereafter, they are responsible for finding their own positions within the denomination, as in congregational organizations. The Episcopal Church and several other denominations also have developed national employment agencies utilizing computerized matching between position descriptions and clergy profiles. Computer searches have been useful for affirmative action purposes in identifying potential female and racial minority candidates. Informally, employment decisions may be strongly influenced by denominational deployment officers who choose to give or withhold a recommendation. Denominational officials interviewed for this research also noted that if their recommendation is negative, the congregation's interest in a candidate usually is terminated.

Other ways in which clergy are contacted about placements include recommendations from influential lay members, other clergy, denominational officials, and seminary deans or presidents. The subjectivity involved in relying on personal recommendations of key insiders has resulted in accusations of special privileged access to an "old boy network" that particularly functions to exclude women. For example, an Episcopal priest interviewed for this research admitted that a college fraternity connection was the critical factor in obtaining one of his rectorships. Another priest acknowledged that a persuasive boarding school classmate was pivotal in his being hired as rector. No women interviewed for this analysis attributed placement opportunities to any similar kind of network.

Since the types of positions that clergy hold tend to be more similar than different across denominations, most job titles can be analyzed, equated, and positioned in a job ladder based on the amount of organizational authority and autonomy that each position represents. The typical clergy career pattern has been to move from smaller to larger congregations, from supervised to solo or supervisory positions, and from local to regional or denomination-wide responsibilities, with higher status granted to the latter jobs.[3] While critiques have been made of the job ladder as being of questionable interest to women clergy,[4] the interview data tend to support women's general interest in full-time denominational employment rather than part-time positions supplemented by full-time secular work. Similarly, where women attain positions of authority or influence, they have greater opportunity to work for change in organizational ideology or practice in ways that are more affirming of women. As Lehman found in his multidenominational study, women clergy did not desire formal authority less often than men.[5]

For this analysis, a job ladder with nine hierarchical levels has been developed for the 41 Unitarian Universalist and 153 Episcopal job titles identified in the samples. Only positions associated with the denomination, a denominational school, hospital, or agency are included. Other unaffiliated jobs are coded separately according to the type of secular work. Each denominational job ladder ranges from entry placements to the highest leadership positions in the denomination. Three ordering criteria are used: (1) the amount of authority that a position commands; (2) the extent of autonomy a position affords for exercising leadership, including opportunities to change customary practices in the congregation or work site; and (3) whether a position normally is held prior or subsequent to other positions with similar levels of authority and autonomy. Where titles differ markedly across religious organizations, such as Episcopal *bishop* and Unitarian Universalist *denominational executive*, the proportional authority each title holds within its denomination has been the major criterion for structuring comparisons.[6] Appendix A lists the aggregated job titles for each denominational sample within the nine hierarchical levels. Job levels 1 to 3 are considered entry and lower-level positions, such as an assistant or associate minister/rector, representing some authority and autonomy but also usually supervision at the work site. Levels 4 to 6 represent mid-level positions, such as interim or temporary "in charge" placements (level 4), and have considerable autonomy at the work site. Episcopal vicars and U.U.A. extension ministers (level 5) have substantial autonomy and authority, although are dependent on denominational financial support and supervision. Episcopal rector or U.U.A. minister of a self-supporting parish with fewer than 500 members is the most common position at level 6. Levels 7 to 9 represent senior or executive positions, including leaders of the largest parishes, cathedral and seminary deans, bishops, and denominational executive officers.[7]

Whether or not jobs are full-time presents another challenge. Although some positions were listed as part-time in the directories, others were not specified. Where either the size or the financial condition of a congregation was disproportionately low to the ratio of clergy on staff, all but the senior-ranking clergy were coded as part-time positions. If only one clergy appears at a congregation, the position was coded as full-time regardless of size or budget, with the assumption that a denominational salary supplement might be available.[8] The bias toward coding positions as full-time provides a conservative estimate of part-time or nonstipendiary employment, which can serve to accentuate the significance of any gender differences in employment status that appear in the data.

The first two years after ordination typically are considered to be a training period for clergy in both denominations. For U.U.A. clergy ordained in 1970 and later, men had on the average a two-month waiting time compared to slightly more than six months for women—a gender difference that was statistically significant ($p < .05$).[9] Overall, Episcopal female and male clergy had no difference in waiting time for a job. The denominational difference may be partly the result of the larger number of part-time and nonstipendiary placements available in Episcopal parishes and, according to the data of this analysis, the greater tendency for Episcopal women clergy to hold part-time and nonstipendiary appointments. Although women ordained to the diaconate in 1975 lagged about two years behind men in ordination to the priesthood, owing to their ordination not officially beginning until 1977, for those ordained in 1980 this lag averaged less than two months and disappeared altogether for those ordained in 1985 and 1990.[10] Gender, then, affects the outset of clergy careers differently by denomination. But to what extent does the U.U.A. gender difference disappear once ministers are in their entry placement? And, to what extent are Episcopal clergy able to maintain gender parity in the type of entry placements they get?

Gender

Gender appears to make a significant difference in the early stages of career development, whether in waiting time for an entry placement among U.U.A. clergy or in different types of positions obtained among Episcopal clergy. The most common first job title among both men and women is *minister* for U.U.A. clergy and *assistant* among Episcopal transitional deacons.[11] Despite men and women most commonly having the same (modal) job title, when all titles were assigned one of the nine job levels, men on the average held higher level placements. This was the case for U.U.A. ministers ($p < .05$) and Episcopal deacons subsequently ordained as priests ($p < .01$); the pattern appeared across the 1970 to 1990 cohorts before controls were added for age or education.

Table 3.1 shows the consistent gender differences in the average level of entry placement. The *index of dissimilarity* provides a slightly different perspective on gender inequalities among entry placements by showing the percentage of women who would need to hold higher level positions in order to eliminate gender differences.

It is important to note that in both denominations, the trend toward gender

Table 3.1. Average Entry Job Level and Index of Dissimilarity for Episcopal Priests and U.U.A. Ministers, 1920–1993.

Cohort	Episcopal			Unitarian Universalist		
	Men	Women	Index of dissimilarity (%)	Men	Women	Index of dissimilarity (%)
1990	3.1	2.8	15	5.0	4.8	16
1985	3.3	2.7	18	5.3	4.9	24
1980	3.2	3.1	9	6.0	4.7	37
1975	3.2	3.0	24	5.3	5.2	13
1970	3.5	2.6	35	5.5	4.0	50
1950	4.1			5.2	a	
1940	4.0			6.0		
1930	4.1			5.0	6.0	33
1920	3.8					
Total	3.5	2.8		5.4	4.8	
(N)	(830)	(291)		(98)	(54)	

a Missing job title information for this cohort.

Episcopal priests are grouped by the year ordained to the transitional diaconate. Job levels range from 1 to 9. Index of dissimilarity represents the percentage of men or women who would have to change job level for gender differences to be eliminated.

parity in entry placements for each denomination peaked *shortly before* the ratio of women reached 30 percent or more per cohort (cf. Tables 3.1, 2.1 and 2.2). This often is considered to be a threshold level after which, in secular occupations, signs of gender-related job segregation begin to appear.[12] The appearance of this pattern in the data suggests a definite relationship between occupational feminization and the tendency to segregate women into lower level ministerial placements from the start of their careers.

Men in both denominations also were more likely than women to hold entry placements considered traditionally normative to the clergy, such as *assistant* or *associate, minister* or *rector, minister* or *priest in charge, vicar,* or *extension minister* ($p < .01$, for each sample). Normative jobs historically have had more visible linkages to upward mobility on an occupational job ladder, especially for Episcopal clergy aspiring to rectorships. The data show women more often clustered in entry jobs without proven linkages to opportunities for upward mobility, such as *chaplain, intern, minister* or *priest in residence,* or in positions on denominational staffs. Their significantly lower tendency for parish placements ($p < .01$, for each sample) suggests that women may not be getting the same exposure as men to the types of jobs more likely to be associated with upward mobility and denominational leadership.

In a related trend, male priests were significantly more likely to have full-time entry jobs than female priests, for every clergy cohort examined since 1975 ($p < .05$). Such differences didn't occur among U.U.A. ministers, which could be a reflection of the proportionately fewer part-time positions in this denomination. For female priests, however, neither marital status nor whether they had children made any difference in their likelihood to have a part-time or full-time placement. While no salary information was available for the data, this trend suggests some strong gender differences in income from job placements, since part-time positions seldom carry fringe benefits such as health insurance.

Overall, gender differences in entry placements in the 1990s appear to virtually mirror those of the early 1970s, despite far more women now being ordained. This trend suggests that structural factors may be at work, such as occupational differentiation and job segregation by gender, rather than situational factors particular to denominational doctrine or polity, its history of women clergy, or marital and family constraints. The next step is to look at how gender interacts with other demographic criteria.

Ordination Status

Ordination status affects the job level that clergy normally hold. Episcopal priests and U.U.A. ministers may hold placements at any level. Similarly, U.U.A. ministers of religious education and community ministers officially are not restricted to certain positions, although clergy interested in a range of positions usually seek dual ordination. Episcopal permanent deacons are eligible for the same types of entry placements as transitional deacons, but since deacons cannot perform all of the sacramental tasks they are restricted from becoming rectors and consequently from most positions at level 6 and above. Most diaconate positions are part-time or nonstipendiary.

Sizable gender differences appear in these newer ordination tracks—Episcopal permanent deacons and U.U.A. ministers of religious education. *All* of the ministers of religious education ordained in the years selected for this analysis were female. While the ratio of permanent deacons to priests has increased overall during the last twenty years ($p < .005$), and particularly so since 1980, the permanent diaconate also has been feminizing. In the 1970s, only about 20 percent of all permanent deacons in the sample were female. The female ratio more than doubled in 1980, then peaked at 59 percent female in 1985. While the 1990 ratio had returned to the 1980 level of 46 percent female, other data show that the 1994 ratio of candidates preparing for ordination to the permanent diaconate was again 59 percent female,[13] suggesting that ordinations to the permanent diaconate have been near or above 50 percent female annually since 1980. The impact of both the proliferation and the feminization of these newer ordination tracks will be discussed in chapter 7.

Although transitional deacons in the data were significantly more likely to hold higher level entry placements than permanent deacons, the number of priests holding the title of *deacon* in their entry placement has more than tripled since 1980, with twice as many female (18%) as male (9%) priests having jobs with this title. This trend indicates not only a shift over time in the direction of entry placements for priesthood training, but it also may point to female priests being tracked differently than males, particularly in a way that may put them into the same entry job pool with permanent deacons.

Overall, differences in placements between transitional and permanent deacons has widened over time, especially for men (Figure 3.1). For instance, the

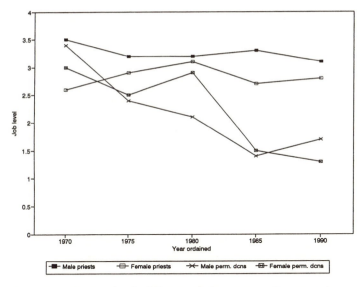

Figure 3.1 Average level of Episcopal clergy entry placements by gender and ordination status, 1970–1990.

average entry job level for male permanent deacons ordained in 1970 was 3.4, but only 1.7 for those ordained in 1990. During the same time, the average entry job level of male transitional deacons declined only 0.4 between 1970 and 1990. The disparity between female transitional and permanent deacons was much smaller. Taken together, these changes suggest that the role of the permanent diaconate in relation to priesthood may be undergoing substantial redefinition, a possibility that will be discussed in chapters 7 and 8. Yet any occupational conflation between these ordination tracks that disproportionately affects women at the outset of their careers may shape both the experience they gain and their subsequent qualifications for future jobs.

A similar conflation in entry placement occurs between U.U.A. women ordained as parish ministers and ministers of religious education. Women ministers in every cohort year examined from 1970 onward have held positions that overlap with the job pool of ministers of religious education, while *no* men in this analysis were found to have held such placements. The stability of this pattern suggests that some amount of structural gender segregation in U.U.A. placements may exist in a way that could disadvantage female parish ministers seeking to gain experience and consequently opportunities similar to those of men.

Education

Education has been shown to be an important resource for occupational opportunities and resulting attainment, as well as for upward job mobility within secular occupations.[14] The amount of education that candidates hold at the time of ordination, then, should be expected to positively affect their entry job placements. Episcopalians and Unitarian Universalists are considered to be among the most highly educated of all denominations,[15] with resultant emphasis on educational preparation for their clergy. Clergy ordained as U.U.A. ministers or Episcopal priests typically hold a Master of Divinity degree at the time of ordination.[16] Even so, the average educational level of priests and ministers in the data shows a sizable increase over time, dramatically rising since 1950 (Table 3.2), which supports an overall trend of increasing educational attainment across most of this century.[17]

Comparatively, clergy in the two denominations differ in education. U.U.A. ministers in the sample on the average hold higher educational credentials than Episcopal priests. Male ministers were the most highly educated of all, having significantly more education than female ministers ($p < .001$) or priests, and averaging one or more advanced degrees in addition to their Master of Divinity degree. As a trend this supports Almquist's research that the higher a group's educational attainment, the more men's educational level exceeds that of women.[18] Furthermore, men's higher educational credentials suggest that their lower recent cohort ratios are more likely due to a paucity of male candidates than women outcompeting men for opportunities to be ordained.

Education should act as a resource for clergy in finding entry placements. Ministers with more education at ordination did begin their first job sooner ($p < .001$). Among Episcopal priests, few gender differences appeared except that women were more likely than men to hold one or more advanced degrees in addition to their Master of Divinity degree ($p < .005$). Consequently, women should be at least as well positioned as men to attract similar entry job opportunities. Overall, education was a significant predictor of a higher level placement

Table 3.2. Average Level of Education at Time of Ordination for Episcopal and U.U.A. Clergy, 1920–1990.

| | Episcopal | | | | Unitarian Universalist | | | |
| | Transitional Deacons | | Permanent Deacons | | Parish Ministers | | Ministers of Religious Education | |
Cohort	Men	Women	Men	Women	Men	Women	Men	Women
1990	6.1	5.8	3.5	4.0	6.9	5.8		5.0
1985	6.0	6.0	2.4	2.7	6.6	6.1		3.5
1980	5.7	5.6	2.4	4.3	7.0	6.4		2.5
1975	5.2	5.2	2.7	4.0	6.8	5.6		1.0
1970	5.2	5.3	3.5	3.0	6.8	5.5		
1950	4.8		1.0		4.1	6.0		
1940	4.1				5.4			
1930	3.0				3.2	2.0		
1920	2.7							
(N)	(645)	(296)	(124)	(96)	(114)	(66)	(0)	(6)

Educational levels are represented as (1) associate degree, or continuing education certificate; (2) bachelor's degree; (3) bachelor's degree plus certificate; (4) master's degree in field other than religion; (5) master's degree in religious field, other than B.D. or M.Div; (6) Master of Divinity degree (includes B.D. prior to 1975), three-year professional degree normative for ordination; (7) two or more master's degrees; (8) doctoral degree prior to a religious degree; (9) Doctor of Ministry degree; (10) other doctoral degree earned following a religious degree; (11) More than one doctoral degree. Cases with dates of degrees not listed are excluded.

among both U.U.A. ministers and Episcopal transitional deacons, even when controlling for gender ($p < .05$, for each sample).[19]

Sharp educational differences also appeared by ordination status. Ironically, U.U.A. ministers of religious education had significantly lower educational credentials than women ordained as parish ministers ($p < .0001$). Those ordained exclusively as ministers of religious education typically held certificates from denominational extension programs rather than seminary degrees.[20] Similarly, in the Episcopal data, permanent deacons had much less education than transitional deacons ($p < .0001$). Permanent deacons also were much less likely to have attended seminary, with most educational preparation taking place at the congregational or diocesan level. The significance of this type of education will be discussed in chapters 7 and 8.

Age

How age affects decisions to enter ordained ministry and influences subsequent career opportunities has become an important issue in an era of frequent occupational change in the United States, accelerated by waves of corporate restructuring and downsizing that have characterized American business and government since the early 1980s. The effect of these dislocations in creating a large, older labor pool seeking work has been compounded by the increased economic need for two incomes to maintain a standard of living for many middle- and working-class families, and the growing number of predominately female, single-parent families. Ordained ministry has been perceived as a viable second-career choice for many men and women over the last fifteen years.

Age was available in the Episcopal data, based on year of birth, but it had to be estimated for U.U.A. clergy, based on the year in which ministers completed their first college degree or certificate. Such an estimate assumes that ministers do have college degrees and that they were earned directly following secondary school graduation—assumptions which can introduce bias into the data since women, if they marry, tend to complete college degrees later than men.[21] To explore this methodological concern, the actual age of Episcopal clergy was compared with an age variable constructed from year of first college degree or certificate. The average difference between actual and constructed ages—about one year—was not statistically significant for Episcopal women or men. Table 3.3 illustrates the similarity between these two age variables and compares constructed ages in the two samples. The chief disparity between the samples in the 1970 women's cohort is likely the result of Episcopal women having been seminary trained well before becoming eligible for ordination in 1970/71. Otherwise, the general similarities between constructed age in the two samples suggest that constructed age for the U.U.A. sample can be used with some reliability to indicate major age effects or trends.

Women were significantly older at ordination than men in both denominations ($p < .0001$ each sample). This trend also was evident among both Episcopal transitional deacons and permanent deacons, and across cohort years. A second trend in the data involves the steadily increasing age at ordination over the last seventy years in both denominations. This increase has been particularly apparent

Table 3.3. Median Actual and Constructed Ages of Episcopal Priests and U.U.A. Ministers at Time of Ordination, 1920–1990.

	Episcopal				Unitarian Universalist	
	Actual Age		Constructed Age		Constructed Age	
Cohort	Men	Women	Men	Women	Men	Women
1970–1990	31	39	29	38	28	36
1990	37	44	36	42	37	37
1985	36	40	34	38	37	38
1980	30	36	29	38	28	35
1975	30	32	28	30	26	33
1970	28	41	26	41	27	27
1950	29		25		25	27
1940	27		26		27	
1930	25		25		25	23
1920	26		26			
(N)	(843)	(299)	(783)	(291)	(111)	(65)

Constructed age was based on year that first higher education degree was completed. Most first degrees were bachelor's degrees; the few exceptions involved about an equal number of associate degrees and master's degrees. Cases were eliminated where no degree dates were given.

since 1970. For Episcopal and U.U.A. male clergy, the trend was highly significant ($p < .0001$, each sample), and was also significant for Episcopal women ($p < .0001$), regardless of ordination status. The aging trend across cohorts was not significant for U.U.A. women, which likely is a consequence of their consistently greater age diversity in relation to the sample size.

Age, however, had no effect on waiting time between ordination and beginning an entry placement. Once ordained, older women and men were just as likely as younger clergy to be assimilated quickly into the occupational structure. However, other differences did appear. While age made no difference in the level of entry placement for Episcopal transitional deacons, older men and women were more likely to remain in their job significantly longer than younger clergy ($p < .0001$).

Conversely, while age made no difference in the length of time that U.U.A. clergy held their first placement, older clergy were less likely to hold higher level placements ($p < .05$) even when controlling for gender, year ordained, and education. When age was added to education and ordination year in multivariate regression models, education was a strong predictor of higher level entry placement ($p < .001$) for women ministers only, which suggests that education for women may help to offset the negative effects associated with age. Furthermore, older women ministers tended to have somewhat more education than younger women at the time of ordination ($p < .10$), a tangible asset for their employment prospects.

Prior Occupational Experience

Some men and women clergy listed work experience prior to ordination in their occupational biographies. Table 3.4 shows the different types of prior occupational

Table 3.4. Prior Occupational Experience of Episcopal Priests and U.U.A. Ministers.

	Episcopal		Unitarian Universalist	
	Men	Women	Men	Women
No experience listed	80%	75%	90%	82%
Of clergy listing experience:				
Religion-related	32%	38%	75%	100%
Professional/educational	26	24	25	
Semiprofessional	13	13		
Managerial	14	8		
Administrative	5	13		
Labor, misc.	6%	3%		
(N)	(659)	(299)	(119)	(77)

U.U.A. women include ministers of religious education, some of whom hold dual degrees as ministers.

experience in the two samples. Since this information is optional, the following analysis should be regarded as exploratory rather than definitive.

Although younger U.U.A. ministers may obtain higher level entry placements, is it their youth which is critical, where parishes perhaps may be investing in the potential for a longer career, or is the crucial aspect their lack of secular occupational experience, which could affect their occupational expectations and facilitate their socialization as clergy? Male ministers who had listed any occupational experience prior to their ordination (10% did so) ranged up to age 40 at the time of ordination. Interestingly, no men ordained over age 40 listed any prior occupational experience, which suggests that there may be a possible concern over calling attention to second-career status. Most of the experience listed was in religion-related fields (70%); none in religious education. The remaining 30 percent was in secular education. U.U.A. women listing prior occupational information (18% did so) had worked primarily in religious education.

As a general trend, the data concur with a Presbyterian study noting the most frequent prior experience for second-career clergy to be religion-related work, followed by education.[22] Presumably, then, prior religion-related experience might act as an occupational resource for higher level entry placements. Yet for U.U.A. ministers, it had a negative effect on the level of their placement, similar to age at ordination. However, when age and experience were included in the same regression equation,[23] the negative effects of occupational experience remained significant ($p < .05$) while those of age did not, which suggests that the more critical criterion may be lack of prior occupational socialization which could interfere with ministerial formation.

Prior occupational experience had a very different effect on the level of entry placement for Episcopal transitional deacons subsequently ordained to the priesthood. Overall, 20 percent of male and 25 percent of female transitional deacons had listed some prior occupational experience. The type of experience was diverse, although the most frequent type was religion-related (37%), followed by professional and education-related (26%), semiprofessional (13%), managerial (12%), administrative (8%), and manual labor (5%).[24] Regression analyses show positive effects of religion-related ($p < .005$) and semiprofessional ($p < .005$) experience for the prospect of obtaining higher level entry placements despite controls for ordination year, gender, ordination status, age, and education, which concurs with earlier research that had identified easier acceptance for second-career entrants.[25] Prior occupational experience also remained positively associated with higher level entry placements when regression equations were run separately for men and women. However, when taking prior occupational experience into account, younger clergy were more likely to have higher level entry placements, which suggests that younger second-career clergy may be particularly well positioned for desirable entry-level placements. Not only is there a subtle but important difference between simply older age versus increased age combined with skills gained in other occupations,[26] but the asset value of secular skills appears to decline as age increases.

The difference between how the two denominations value prior occupational experience may be a result of their varying size and occupational structures. The much smaller U.U.A. is a more *closed* occupational system,[27] where ministers are more closely aligned with the traditional norm as key criteria for higher level placements: ordained young and with substantial education rather than work experience. Closed systems provide more control over occupational socialization. In contrast, the Episcopal Church represents a more *open* system with a larger, diverse occupational structure. As a result, priests who deviate from the traditional norm typically have more opportunities available to them, although these may vary sharply in quality and pay.

Marital and Family Status

Marriage and family have been assumed to have negative effects on women's careers owing to their disproportionate responsibility for domestic work and child care. At the same time, the notion of a solid marriage and family traditionally has been viewed as an important asset for occupational success in secular occupations and in the Protestant clergy, both which have assumed male incumbency.[28] Despite the theological rationale from Luther's time onward that has supported marriage for clergy, the sociological reality also has meant the availability of a minister's wife who, since the time of Katharine von Bora (Luther's wife), traditionally has donated substantial time to church activities and, in many ways, has functioned as a lay co-pastor among women's groups in the congregation.[29] This additional labor source represents an important asset to congregations having only one paid clergy position. While there is some evidence that married women clergy have higher prestige than women who are single,[30] suggesting that marriage serves as an occupational resource, few minister's husbands have the time or interest to intensely involve themselves on a volunteer basis as ministers' wives traditionally have done, nor have congregations expected them to do so. Consequently, women clergy—single or married—not only may be missing a traditional occupational asset available to men but added constraints that married women face, including greater geographical limitations and consequently fewer opportunities for full-time and higher level placements, greater domestic responsibilities, and family and child-care obligations, may disproportionately suppress their careers.[31]

Although marital status wasn't available in the U.U.A. data, Episcopal male priests were significantly more likely to be married than females ($p < $ .00001) (Table 3.5).[32] While secular professions also tend to have a greater concentration of single women than men,[33] this trend in the clergy data could suggest as well that male priests have a greater occupational incentive and consequent benefit from marriage than females. Of those who were single at ordination but who subsequently married, marriage for both men and women took place on the average within three years after ordination. Of those clergy ordained in 1970 and later who had children, the average was 2.5 children for both men and women. When the effects of marriage and children on entry-level positions were analyzed, several trends appeared. First, neither marital status nor children were found to have any effect on women's entry placements. Married men, however, were significantly more likely to have a full-time placement ($p < $ .05) and to hold a higher level position ($p < $ .05) than single men. When parenthood was substituted for marital status, fathers similarly were more likely to have higher level, full-time placements. In separate regression models for men and women, where controls were added for year ordained, age, and education, marriage continued to be directly related to higher level placements for men ($p < $ .01) but not for women. Children, controlling for marital status, had no effect for men on entry placement, which suggests that the presence of a wife is the more important influence.[34]

Table 3.5. Marital and Parental Status of Episcopal Priests.

Cohort	Never Married	Married	Divorced/Widowed	Remarried	Children
	Marital Status				*Parental Status*
1990					
Men	13%	82%	1%	4%	65%
Women	24	66	1	9	63
1985					
Men	10	90	0	0	78
Women	21	77	1	1	70
1980					
Men	13	85	0	2	79
Women	25	65	8	2	69
1975					
Men	15	78	1	6	76
Women	43	40	10	7	47
1970					
Men	13	76	3	8	82
Women	63	38	0	0	38
1950 and earlier					
Men	13	81	4	3	79
1970–1990					
Men	13	82	1	4	77
Women	26%	66%	3%	5%	62%

Demographic Effects on Entry Placements

Taken together, the preceding variables—gender, ordination status, education, age, prior occupational experience, and marital status—have differing effects on entry placements. Table 3.6 compares how these influence the level of entry placement in two different models for each denomination: one for all clergy in the two samples, and the other for only those ordained either as transitional deacons and subsequently as priests, or as (parish) ministers.

For U.U.A. clergy, the models show little significant influence on entry placement other than ordination status. This likely is due to the effect of large variance in the data given the small sample size. However, when prior occupational experience that hadn't been religion-related was included in the models,[35] it did have a negative effect on entry placement ($p < .01$), which supports the likelihood that skills gained in secular employment are not an asset for second-career ministers.

Predictably, given the shorter history of women's ordination in the Episcopal Church, the occupational picture is less optimistic for women priests, despite the apparently more open occupational structure and greater diversity of positions. Put

Table 3.6. Criteria Predicting Level of Entry Placement for Episcopal and U.U.A. Clergy Based on Multivariate Regression Analysis.

Model: Variable	*Episcopal*		*Unitarian Universalist*	
	All B	Transitional Deacons B	All B	Parish Ministers B
Age at ordination	−.008*	−.003	−.011	−.009
Male gender	.271***	.333***	.368	.356
Year ordained:				
1990	−.470***	−.313*	−.170	−.189
1985	−.404***	−.253+	−.027	−.060
1980	−.200+	−.170	.545	.536
1975	−.210+	−.191	−.074	−.088
1970		regression line		
1950 and earlier	.568****	.623****	−.003	.027
Ordained:				
Priest	.984****			
Parish minister			2.411****	
Marriage	.213**	.251**		
Education	.046**	.015	−.008	.003
Prior occup.				
experience	.246***	.230**	−.492	−.519
Constant	2.065	2.888	3.041	5.325
Adj. R Sq.	.266****	.112****	.251****	.009
(N)	(1,310)	(1,099)	(159)	(148)

**** $p < .0001$ *** $p < .005$ ** $p < .01$ * $p < .05$ + $p < .10$

The regression line represents the ordination year 1970, against which other years are compared. For example, Episcopal clergy ordained in 1950 and earlier had significantly higher-level entry placements than clergy in later years, despite controls for the other variables listed.

simply, men are placed in higher level entry positions than women, despite whatever resources women may have. The advantage of male gender cannot be explained away by year of ordination, age, education, prior secular work, marital status, or ordination status. Although marital status was shown to affect men only, it is included in the combined models primarily as another control to challenge the strength of the gender effect on entry placements. Since the Episcopal Church has ordained women priests for only a generation (20 years) or less, the data illustrate the reality that strong occupational resistance to women still exists in the 1990s. Furthermore, these results suggest that little permanent headway has been made in occupational equity among equally qualified women and men at the outset of their careers. Treiman and Hartmann define discrimination as referring to occupational outcomes regardless of intentions.[36] Episcopal women clergy, then, continue to experience gender discrimination despite greater opportunities to enter and survive the ordination process.

Yet there are other important influences on Episcopal entry jobs. First, while permanent and transitional deacons may be eligible for the same entry placements, the significant effect of ordination status suggests that they may be tracked into different types of placements, which is substantiated in the data by the overwhelming tendency of permanent deacons to hold positions that are nonstipendiary or part-time. The strong gender differences in entry placements, including women's greater likelihood to hold part-time positions regardless of marital or family status, suggests that female transitional deacons are much more likely than males to share a job pool with permanent deacons. Second, both education and age at ordination affect entry placements in the model that includes all deacons (Table 3.6), suggesting that these variables may be important to the occupational prospects of permanent deacons. Third, clergy ordained in 1985 and 1990 were more likely to hold significantly lower level entry placements than those ordained in 1970. The importance of cohort year in the model that includes all deacons suggests that there has been a marked change over time in how the permanent diaconate is being utilized in the church. Fourth, because prior occupational experience has a positive effect despite taking into account the other variables, the ordained ministry in the Episcopal Church appears to be a viable option for second-career clergy interested in translating some secular experience into their new vocation. Fifth, the importance of marriage for higher level placements cannot be overlooked for men. It can be said, then, that younger, married men with substantial education and some previous occupational experience are the best positioned of all to attract high-level entry placements that not only will pay a full-time salary but more likely will launch them into an upwardly mobile career pattern.

In sum the U.U.A., a denomination with a longer history of women's ordination and with a congregational polity, seems to be somewhat more egalitarian for women ministers in obtaining entry placements. But as U.U.A. women move into their next position, where they might have greater opportunities for autonomy in using the skills they have developed, access to larger budgets, more authority to supervise others, or to have influence on their congregations and the denomination, how will they fare in relation to men? And will Episcopal women clergy fare any better relative to men, or will the sharp gender difference evident from their first placement become more accentuated as they journey through their careers? The next chapter analyzes gender and other differences in second and subsequent placements.

⌣· Four ·⌣

The Second Job

Key to the Career Path

Since entry placements are considered to be a training experience, the second placement becomes a more useful predictor of the direction that clergy careers will take. Despite whether a placement is chosen from a range of opportunities or represents the only option when a job change becomes necessary, taken together the first two placements often set forth a pattern of job tracking that shapes much of the clergy career life course.

The length of time that clergy hold their first placement varies by denomination. Among Episcopal clergy, the first placement averages about three years, a duration that was remarkably constant from 1920 for men and from 1970 for women until 1985, when the average duration shortened to under three years for both men and women. While older clergy tended to remain longer in their entry placements ($p < .0001$), gender made no difference in duration. U.U.A. ministers had held their first placements about five years on the average until 1980; thereafter, the average duration shortened to less than four years. Placement duration was similar for both men and women.

Denominational differences may be explained by a greater range of part-time and nonstipendiary placements available to Episcopal clergy, which increases job mobility for those interested in seeking full-time placements. On a smaller scale, evidence from the data suggests that there also has been an increase in part-time placements within the U.U.A. in recent years, which may partly account for the increased job mobility. Another possible explanation may be the development of vacancy chains[1] as a result of increased retirements by predominantly male clergy ordained in the post-World War II growth era for American mainline denominations. In a small denomination, with clergy supply more closely matching demand than in the Episcopal Church, clergy retirements would create proportionally more opportunities for job mobility.

Both men and women have opportunities for changing positions, measured by movement from first to second placement, in about the same length of time according to the data. But the range of opportunities that men versus women have, as well as their desirability, may be another matter. Gender differences in the level of second placements become sharply apparent in both denominations. For the following analysis, clergy ordained exclusively as permanent deacons or as ministers of religious education have been excluded unless otherwise stated, in order to compare opportunities and attainment among men and women clergy with somewhat more similar career objectives and qualifications.

Separating the Women from the Men

With the increasing ratio of women clergy over recent years, gender differences have widened in both the type and level of positions that clergy hold in these two denominations. Among Episcopal priests, the title of the second placement illustrates the strong disparity between men and women as their career trajectories begin to take shape. For women, regardless of when they were ordained, the most frequent (modal) second job title is *assistant* or *associate*, the same as their entry placement, represented at job level 3 in the data. The modal second job title of men consistently is *rector*, a position at level 6, indicating that they move upward rather than laterally from their first to second placement. Although the modal second job title among both U.U.A. female and male clergy ordained between 1970 and 1985[2] has been *minister*, a position at level 6, two-thirds of the male ministers hold this title but less than half of the female ministers do so, which suggests that there is a wider variation in the type of jobs that women hold. More than three times as many female as male ministers move into support staff or administrative positions in their second placement. This difference may reflect committed career choices differentiated by gender, but it also may be indicating limitations on opportunities for women to obtain placements similar to those of men.

Comparably, male priests were much more likely than females to hold jobs considered traditionally normative to the priesthood in *both* their first and second placements ($p < .01$) regardless of the year they were ordained, which suggests that the structure of men's opportunities may be consistent with positions that historically have been linked to upward career mobility and the possibility of denominational leadership. Among clergy with jobs that were *not* normative, male priests tended to hold denominational administrative positions while females held jobs such as educational or hospital chaplaincies. Thus, even in the less typical positions, men worked in job placements more centrally located within the religious organization—placements which more likely would position them for opportunities of greater influence and authority over time. This result supports a similar trend in other denominations where women have been disproportionately concentrated in specialized ministries, in some cases because they were blocked from parish placements traditionally held by men.[3]

Both men and women priests were more likely to hold full-time second placements than in their entry position (Table 4.1). But among those holding part-time placements, women were disproportionately represented ($p < .0001$). The main

Table 4.1. Percentage of Episcopal Priests and U.U.A. Ministers with Full-Time First and Second Placements, 1920–1990.

	Episcopal				Unitarian Universalist			
	First Job		Second Job		First Job		Second Job	
Cohort	Men	Women	Men	Women	Men	Women	Men	Women
1990	87	73	94	76	69	87	100	100
1985	82	59	86	77	77	71	70	91
1980	76	50	89	70	91	80	100	89
1975	73	60	85	78	65	60	77	33
1970	83	50	91	80	72	0	88	100
1950	95		98		39	0	62	0
1940	88		91		43	—	100	—
1930	92		100		100	100	100	100
1920	100		100					
(N)	(824)	(284)	(727)	(211)	(99)	(61)	(68)	(37)

Part-time placements where not stated in job title are estimated based on the ratio of clergy to parish membership (Episcopal) or parish total expenditures (U.U.A.); this construction tends to assume more placements are full-time than actually may be the case. Only clergy holding denominational placements are included. Erratic percentages in the Unitarian Universalist data are the result of low female cohort numbers (1970 N = 2; 1930, 1950 N = 1), and greater difficulty in estimating placements from earlier Unitarian and Universalist directories.

career contingencies for women—marriage and children—made no difference in their employment status. Similar to entry placements, men who were married or had children were significantly more likely than other men to hold full-time employment ($p < .05$). Those men who did have part-time placements typically held two or more denominational jobs concurrently ($p < .05$), while women were more likely to hold an additional secular job—a trend which has persisted from the early 1970s. It also illustrates women's interest in full-time careers as well as their commitment to ordained ministry despite their lower likelihood of earning a living from it. This continuing trend further points to a discordant combination of denominational and secular work for women especially when attempting to accumulate denominational employment benefits, work continuity, exposure to other denominational job opportunities, and the same internal labor market experience as their male counterparts. All U.U.A. ministers were much more likely than Episcopal priests to hold full-time placements, and no gender differences appeared among those who did hold part-time settlements.

Despite similarities among men and women ministers in their entry placements, strong differences did appear in the job level of their second placements. For example, the second placement of all male ministers ordained in 1980 (a year when the gender ratio was 66% female) was at level 5 or higher, but little more than half of female ministers ordained that year held second placements above level 4. The gender difference for the 1980 Episcopal cohort is also striking. While entry placements for men and women ordained that year had been nearly identical (see Table 3.1), men moved into significantly higher level second placements ($p < .0001$). Table 4.2 illustrates the similarity among women priests over the years in

Table 4.2. Average Second Job Level and Index of Dissimilarity for Episcopal Priests and U.U.A. Ministers, 1920–1993.

	Episcopal			Unitarian Universalist		
	Average job level		Index of dissimilarity	Average job level		Index of dissimilarity
Cohort	Men	Women		Men	Women	
1990[a]	4.5	3.3	41%	2.0	3.0	100%
1985	4.4	3.8	17	5.1	4.7	16
1980	4.5	3.9	21	5.9	4.5	36
1975	4.6	3.8	26	5.2	4.3	59
1970	4.4	3.7	45%	6.1	3.5	94
1950	4.9			5.4	[b]	
1940	5.1			6.4		
1930	5.5			6.0	3.0	92%
1920	5.2					
(N)	(734)	(212)		(71)	(36)	

[a] The 1990 Episcopal and U.U.A. cohorts do not represent complete data on second placement, since the average duration of entry placement is three years for Episcopal priests and five years for U.U.A. ministers.
[b] Job title data are missing for this cohort.

Episcopal priests are grouped by year ordained to the transitional diaconate. Job levels range from 1 to 9. Index of dissimilarity represents the percentage of men or women who would have to change job level for gender differences to be eliminated.

the level of second placement, despite the year they were first ordained, and the persistent difference when compared to male priests. Such a pattern also is evident among U.U.A. ministers.

To explore possible underlying causes for the persistent gender differences in the second placement, a range of variables were tested in multivariate regression equations for each sample (Table 4.3). Unlike the entry placement, prior occupational experience had no effect on the job level of the second placement in either denomination, and so was dropped from further analysis. Overall, the importance of male gender for holding a higher level placement in both the Episcopal ($p <$ .0001) and U.U.A. ($p < .05$) denominations, which could not be explained away by ordination year, age at ordination, education, taking time out between placements, or level of entry placement that one had held, emphasizes the importance and persistence of the gender disparity. Additionally, among U.U.A. ministers, younger age at ordination ($p < .01$) and continuous employment between first and second placements ($p < .05$) positively affected the level of position they held, as well.

When equations were run separately for men and women (not shown), the effects of age, education, and other variables differed somewhat by gender. For a higher level placement, U.U.A. women ministers significantly benefited from higher educational credentials ($p < .05$), younger age at ordination ($p < .005$), and having been ordained before 1980 ($p < .05$). These variables were not significant for men, which implies that these may be effects of occupational feminization for women. Ordination prior to 1980 suggests a *tokenism* effect, where women who are proportionally few in number have relatively better opportunities for higher

Table 4.3. Criteria Predicting Level of Second Placement for Episcopal Priests and U.U.A. Ministers Based on Multivariate Regression Analysis.

Variable	Episcopal Coefficient (B)	Unitarian Universalist Coefficient (B)
Male gender	.648****	.841*
Age at ordination	.006	−.041**
Education	.030	.121
Year ordained:		
1990ª	−.015	−2.038*
1985	.072	.487
1980	.142	.125
1975	.085	−.454
1970	regression line	
1950 and earlier	.450***	.160
Entry job level	.242****	.186*
Duration of entry job	.032	.074+
Time out between jobs	−.003	−1.759*
Constant	2.492	3.847
Adj. R Sq.	.120****	.355****
(N)	(934)	(96)

ª The 1990 Episcopal and U.U.A. cohorts do not represent complete data on second placement.

**** $p < .0001$ *** $p < .005$ ** $p < .01$ * $p < .05$ + $p < .10$
The regression line represents the ordination year 1970, against which other years are compared. For example, Episcopal clergy ordained in 1950 and earlier had significantly higher level second placements than clergy in later years, despite controls for the other variables listed.

level placements—prospects which fade as the female ratio increases within an occupation.

Gender difference in the less occupationally feminized Episcopal data suggest different organizational effects on clergy careers. Men ordained in 1950 and earlier were significantly more likely to hold higher level placements than men ordained in 1970 or later ($p < .005$). There were no significant differences over time for women. This pattern suggests either that there may be a surplus of clergy competing for relatively fewer higher level placements, or that there has been a proliferation of new, lower level placements since the 1950s. There is evidence to suggest that both alternatives have occurred, which will be discussed further in chapters 5 and 6.

Additional demographic variables that were available for Episcopal but not for U.U.A. clergy were tested in separate equations for female and male priests: whether they were married, had children, had received academic or other types of honors, had published, or their fathers had been clergy. Also included in these equations were ordination year, education, and whether the entry placement had been part-time or full-time. Both marriage ($p < .001$) and having held a full-time entry placement ($p < .001$) were important predictors of second placement level for male priests, even when controlling for all of the other variables. For female priests, having had a full-time entry placement also was significant ($p < .05$), but marital status had no effect. Instead, having public honor or recognition positively affected women's second job level ($p < .05$), despite controls for the other variables. These findings run counter to the traditional occupational myths that suggest that marriage and family responsibilities explain why women do not have—or pursue—high-level job opportunities.[4] The results also support other research that has shown that women must continually rely upon external standards such as education, honors, or other credentials for their career placements.[5] Furthermore, although the importance of marriage and children in predicting the level of men's job placements may suggest a positive bias in opportunities for men who represent the traditional clergy norm (i.e., married, with children), it also may reflect high male motivation as well as female domestic support for their career aspirations. Most important for both men and women, however, was the priority of full-time entry placements in predicting higher level second jobs. Since women—married or single—were significantly more likely to be found in part-time entry placements, their disadvantage becomes yet more apparent.

Gender and Ordination Status

When jobs held by men and women in the alternative ordination tracks were analyzed, gender differences among Episcopal permanent deacons persisted into the second placement. Male deacons held higher level positions than females. This disparity becomes particularly important when comparing their second placements to those of priests. The slight decline since 1980 in the average job level of second placements among women priests while those of men have increased somewhat (Table 4.1) suggests that the second placement levels of permanent deacons and female priests may be converging while that of male priests is diverging from all others (Figure 4.1). By the 1980 cohort, male priests have come to

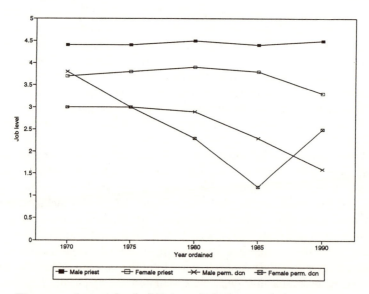

Figure 4.1 Average level of Episcopal clergy second placements by gender and ordination status, 1970–1990.

average more than a full job level above all others. This shift toward occupational conflation between permanent deacons and women priests, combined with female priests' lower likelihood of holding full-time placements and their greater tendency to have supplemental employment outside the denomination, suggests that they may be sharing a job pool that, for the most part, is distinct from the pool of opportunities for male priests. The implications of this trend will be discussed in chapters 7 and 8.

While women U.U.A. ministers held significantly lower level placements than men ($p < .05$), there was no evidence of conflation with ministers of religious education at this point in their careers.

Gender and Job Mobility

Job mobility, defined as the rate of occupational change across various jobs, is the mechanism that connects or sequences various placements within a career trajectory, and measures to some extent the job opportunities presented to men and women over the course of their career.[6] Although the data show that opportunities for job mobility are readily available to both women and men, the pattern of women's lower job level attainment in both samples suggests that the *quality* of opportunities differs by gender. This probability has been borne out by other research showing salary inequalities between men and women. For instance, Episcopal Church Deployment Office data show that male rectors and vicars, ordained about the same time as the 1980 cohort of this analysis, have averaged a 20 percent higher stipend than women in similar positions ordained the same years.[7] Research on other U.S. mainline denominations has shown similar disparities.[8]

Critical to mobility analysis is whether a move is made by choice or is forced. *Choice* mobility, based on opportunities such as additional autonomy, authority, compensation, prestige, socioeconomic resources for one's job, developing new skills, positioning oneself for a future move, realigning occupational, and personal priorities, or believing that God is calling one toward a particular placement, entails a desired personal, occupational or ecclesial benefit that distinguishes it from *forced* mobility. The latter is based on time boundaries of a particular position, such as in interim placements, or forced departure owing to family constraints, relocation of one's spouse, or other stipulated conditions, such as required resignations by Episcopal assistants and associates when a parish changes rectors. Forced mobility in secular occupations also has been enacted as a means of reducing labor costs and preventing workers—particularly women—from accruing seniority.[9]

Since entry placements for both Episcopal men and women clergy are primarily parish assistant or associate positions, whose occupants normally must offer their resignation if the rector retires or leaves, then forced mobility itself should affect men and women equally. Yet it is evident that male priests moving into higher level second placements are able to capitalize on the higher level opportunities available when the entry placement ends, even though marriage or children have not been shown to constrain *women's* employment and thus to force them into less advantageous placements. Women, then, become more subject to the vicissitudes of forced mobility for a longer span of their careers.

A similar result is evident in the U.U.A. data. Although male ministers are slightly more likely than females to have held entry positions as an *interim minister*, they therefore are exposed to more forced job mobility. Yet all but one of the men in the data holding interim placements moved into a traditional parish minister position for the second job, indicating that forced mobility is not a liability for men in this denomination either. However, women ministers were four times more likely than men to move into interim positions in their second placement, with only 25 percent subsequently moving into a traditional parish minister placement, suggesting that gender may make a crucial difference in being able to capitalize on the opportunities available when one needs to change jobs. Additionally, women in their second placement were more likely than men to move to a *lower* job level than their entry placement, suggesting that for women there is substantially more risk of *downward* mobility when changing placements.

While differences between first and second placements have suggested that men are advancing into higher level positions, more precise ways of analyzing mobility from one job to another can give a better picture of what differences actually may exist between men and women clergy and how these have changed over time. Just as holding a higher level entry placement predicts that one will hold a higher level second placement (Table 4.2), holding a lower level entry placement is associated with a greater probability that the second placement will represent an upward move in job level. This illustrates an important relationship between occupational attainment and mobility, and why it is imperative to analyze both of these dynamics. If one has high attainment early in the career, which tends to be the pattern for U.U.A. clergy, there is relatively less opportunity for upward mobility in subsequent placements. Additionally, while those who hold lower level placements early in their careers may have substantially more opportunities for upward mobility, their overall attainment still may end up at a modest level. Other factors, such as differences in a denomination's organizational structure, also can affect clergy prospects for upward mobility and attainment. For instance, the U.U.A. has proportionally fewer hierarchically differentiated positions than larger, more centralized structures such as the Episcopal Church. As a result, U.U.A. ministers have more opportunities to be sole minister of a congregation early in their careers, but they also have fewer subsequent opportunities to move into positions overseeing large congregations with multiple staff, or into denominational executive positions. Translated into a job ladder, typical U.U.A. entry placements at level 6 leave little room for upward mobility. The mobility analysis expectedly showed that the U.U.A. upward mobility curve was much flatter than that for Episcopal priests who had access to a wider range of hierarchically stratified positions.

Gender differences in the percentage of clergy who moved up one or more job levels between entry and second placement were not significant in either denominational sample. The disparity, however, resided in the *size* of the increment. Being male predicted a significantly larger increase in job level for both Episcopal ($p < .0001$) and U.U.A. ($p < .05$) clergy among those who had already changed positions, based on regression analysis, even when controlling for ordination year, education, age at ordination, level of entry placement, length of time in entry placement, and whether more than a year had lapsed between placements. Besides gender, education was positively associated with the size of the job-level increase for Episcopal priests ($p < .005$), although education had no effect on upward mobility for U.U.A. ministers.[10] When equations were run separately for men and women, significant differences appeared only in the Episcopal data. Larger job-level increases were evident for men ordained before 1970 than subsequently ($p < .0005$), suggesting that the magnitude of higher level opportunities has declined since the 1950s. While differences over time weren't evident for female priests, those who remained longer in their entry placement ($p < .05$) were more likely to have a greater increment in job level, which intimates how devastating the effect of forced mobility may be on women's careers.

Although ordinary least squares (O.L.S.) regression models were used to examine possible explanatory variables such as gender, education, or year ordained in order to determine their influence on the size of increment in job level between one placement and another, the disadvantage of such models is that they can include only those clergy who already have moved to the next placement. Those clergy who haven't yet changed positions (i.e., *censored observations*) are excluded, which results in limiting the number of cases that can be analyzed. This problem introduces the possibility of bias into the results, particularly for smaller samples such as the U.U.A. data and the Episcopal female cohorts.[11] For this reason, further mobility analyses have used Cox proportional hazard-rate modeling, an event history analysis method that allows cases to be included regardless of whether mobility actually has occurred.[12] In utilizing Cox modeling, the censoring—or *job change*—variable has been constructed in two different ways. The first construction considers upward mobility only where there has been a year or less between placements.[13] The second construction captures upward job mobility regardless of the amount of time between placements. Duration of entry placement is the exposure time. For U.U.A. clergy, upward job mobility was directly related to remaining in continuous employment. Furthermore, all ministers taking time out between placements had been ordained prior to 1980. However, for Episcopal priests, whether they remained in continuous employment or took time out between placements made no difference in their upward mobility prospects.

For both Episcopal priests and U.U.A. ministers, the most significant influence on the likelihood for upward mobility into their second placement was having held a lower level entry position (Table 4.4). Male gender was a significant predictor for Episcopal priests ($p < .01$), as well as for the U.U.A. model, when ministers of religious education were included in the equation and their ordination status controlled (not shown).[14] No other variables were significant for U.U.A. clergy in any of the Cox models tested. The larger Episcopal sample additionally showed a significant tendency for younger age to predict upward mobility ($p < .005$), suggesting that a combination of youth and male gender sharply increases the prospects for priests to move to a higher job level quickly. This was confirmed when separate models were run for men. For women, however, education rather than age was the critical resource for upward mobility ($p < .01$), which supports

Table 4.4. Maximum-Likelihood Estimates of Upward Mobility from Entry to Second Placement for Episcopal Priests and U.U.A. Ministers, 1920–1993.

Variable	Episcopal Coefficient (B)	Unitarian Universalist Coefficient (B)
Male gender	.306**	.901
Age at ordination	−.015***	−.031
Education	.032	.141
Year ordained:		
1990[a]	−.418*	−16.331
1985	.043	1.064
1980	.110	−.560
1975	.041	−.355
1970	regression line	
1950 and earlier	.435***	.729
Entry job level	−.501****	−.819****
−2 log likelihood	6534.719	155.718
X^2	176.681****	42.29****
(N)	(1,099)	(153)
Censored observations	52%	84%

[a] The 1990 Episcopal and U.U.A. cohorts do not represent complete data for second placement.

**** $p < .0001$ *** $p < .005$ ** $p < .01$ * $p < .05$ + $p < .10$

Maximum likelihood estimates utilize Cox proportional hazard-rate modeling. The censoring variable is movement to a higher level second job, with the duration of entry job as the exposure time.

previous research in secular occupations linking women's education as an objective measure of their qualifications with upward job mobility.[15] Additionally, male priests ordained in 1950 and earlier were significantly more likely than men ordained in 1970 or afterward to experience early upward job mobility ($p < .005$), a trend that will be discussed in chapter 5.

Both gender and age generally have been regarded as the two most critical criteria for defining and assessing appropriate role behavior for occupations as well as for human social organization. Predictably, both gender and age at the time of ordination have been found in this analysis to influence job mobility. Although a lack of significant age effect on mobility for U.U.A. clergy does suggest that youth, by itself, doesn't necessarily result in being tracked quickly into higher level positions, other tests show that younger clergy—especially younger men—held higher level second placements and that the size of job-level increase between entry and second placement was negatively affected by older age ($p < .05$). This suggests that age may have a greater impact on job attainment than on mobility. Among Episcopal priests the trend appears to be reversed: younger age was significantly associated with early upward job mobility ($p < .005$), but not with level of the second placement or with the size of job-level increment, indicating that perhaps younger clergy may be "tracked" into increasingly higher level positions early in their career but not necessarily at the expense of opportunities for older clergy. That the effects of age on upward mobility and attainment are mixed, in both denominations, suggests that this may be an occupation into which both men and women may enter as a second career and experience at least some advantageous occupational opportunities.

Beyond the Second Placement

"I think if you'd track a seminary class over the years, you'd find that by the time men and women reach, say, their third assignment, men are significantly ahead, both in size of church and salary," sociologist Jackson Carroll has pointed out.[16] In *Women of the Cloth*, Carroll et al. observed that gender differences in placements grew across the career. By the third and subsequent placements, 92 percent of the men but only 60 percent of the women participating in their study were sole or senior pastors.[17] Overall, this two-tier disparity between men's and women's placements has been well observed across a variety of mainline denominations over the past twenty years. The results of this analysis show similarities to these earlier studies. In positions considered either solo or senior pastorates, whether interim or permanent (i.e., job level 4 and higher), 76 percent of the male priests held such positions in their third placement, compared to 52 percent of the female priests. The outlook was more egalitarian for U.U.A. ministers, with 89 percent of men and 81 percent of the women ministers holding placements at level 4 or higher, although this likely is influenced by the relatively few lower level positions in this denomination.

Another gender disparity occurs in the *frequency* of job mobility. U.U.A. women ministers remained in their second placements a significantly shorter time than men ($p < .005$), averaging 3.8 years compared to men's 6.3 years. Similarly, women priests remained in their second placements for a shorter time than men ($p < .005$), averaging 3.6 years compared to 4.3 years for men. The pattern was similar for subsequent placements as well, which may be an indicator of the lower level—and perhaps less desirable—jobs they hold and the greater likelihood that their mobility may be forced rather than by choice. Secular research has documented women's more frequent job mobility, particularly in temporary, seasonal, and lower level placements,[18] which suggests both that women may be utilized more frequently as a source of auxiliary labor and that their job mobility more likely may be forced.

Gender disparities in upward mobility between second and third placement also persisted for Episcopal priests in the Cox models utilizing the variables shown in Table 4.4. The significant predictors for upward mobility into the third placement were ordination at a young age ($p < .0001$), male gender ($p < .05$), and holding a lower level second placement ($p < .0001$), despite controlling for year of ordination. When the models were run separately for men and women, young age was important for men only ($p < .05$), which suggests that the combination of being young and male is especially effective for career tracking into higher level placements in this denomination.

While in secular occupations it has been argued that women are more likely to take time out during their career for raising children, which may affect the jobs they choose,[19] male clergy in both samples took significantly more time out than female clergy over the course of their careers, despite controls for cohort year ($p < $

.05). The data, then, suggest that women clergy are no less committed than men to their careers. Furthermore, taking time out between placements had no effect on upward mobility from second placement for women or men in either sample. It did, however, affect attainment in the third placement, which suggests that a two-tier job stratification system may exist, with those ministers and priests more likely to take time out clustering primarily in lower level placements, and those seeking high-level positions remaining in continuous denominational employment. Among priests, however, time out between placements had a negative effect on attainment only for men ($p < .01$), which may be an effect of women's overall likelihood to be in lower level placements where occupational penalties for time away aren't severe. It also may indicate significant job penalties for men interested in nontraditional career patterns.

An interesting difference between the two denominations emerged in those who held positions that were less than full-time. While no gender differences were evident among U.U.A. ministers in full-time employment, men holding part-time placements were somewhat more likely to have concurrent *secular* employment rather than another position elsewhere in the denomination ($p < .10$). This trend is reversed for Episcopal priests working part-time, where men more likely hold an additional denominational placement and women additional secular work. The consistency of this pattern over the first three placements suggests that U.U.A. male ministers may be choosing secular employment because of greater socio-economic or other opportunities that it affords despite evidence that men overall have the greater opportunities *inside* their denomination as well. The secular work of women priests likely occurs for very different reasons: women are turning to secular work probably as the result of an inability to obtain full-time positions or to obtain jobs that may be more professionally commensurate with their interests and skills. As in earlier placements, male priests held full-time third placements more frequently than females ($p < .0001$) and, again, marital status made no difference for women.

Overall, gender differences among U.U.A. ministers seem to have become embedded in different career paths by the third placement. The high correlation between male gender and a higher level previous (.49) and current (.20) position suggests that men are strongly associated with higher level placements.[20] Additionally, the percentage of women ministers holding third placements at level 3 or lower was more than twice that of men. Other gender differences emerged in O.L.S. regression models: men moved to parishes with larger budgets than did women ($p < .05$), and men took charge of larger congregations than did women ($p < .10$). This was the case regardless of the year they had been ordained. Thus, even where ministers may move laterally, male ministers were advantaged in terms of inheriting slightly larger congregations with somewhat greater financial resources.

In the larger, more stratified Episcopal sample, gender differences were even more visible despite the year of ordination. For example, the average third placement level was 3.9 for female and 4.9 for male priests ($p < .0001$), a disparity substantiated in regression models which indicated that male gender, despite controls for ordination year and a range of other variables tested, consistently predicted higher level attainment ($p < .0001$). Another important influence on the level of third placement was younger age ($p < .005$). Other tests showed that the age effect became more evident in ten-year increments, but was especially negative for men ordained over age 50.[21] Another variable that emerged with a surprising significance for the third and subsequent placements was the effect of having a clergy parent ($p < .05$), which suggests some evidence of inheritance as a resource for higher level attainment among Episcopal priests.

Subsequent upward mobility from third to fourth placement was similar to previous patterns. Among U.U.A. ministers, male gender was significant for upward mobility ($p < .05$) utilizing Cox models similar to those for earlier placements. Among Episcopal priests, gender itself was not significant. But when the models were run separately for men and women, younger age was significant for men ($p < .05$) but not women, which suggests that opportunities for upward mobility continue to be substantially greater for young male priests. Further tests using O.L.S. regression models, however, revealed that higher level Episcopal attainment for the fourth placement was directly related to male gender ($p < .05$), as well as not taking time out between placements ($p < .05$), with year of ordination held constant. In short, men across the years and over several job placements, especially when able to maintain continuous denominational employment, consistently have greater attainment prospects than women.

The number of clergy holding five or more placements over their career diminishes sharply. For U.U.A. ministers, the sample was so small that only basic trends could be discerned: those ordained younger ($p < .10$) and those ordained in 1950 or earlier ($p < .10$) tended to hold higher level placements. Whatever gender differences may exist have become embedded in these and other variables. The gender disparity did persist for Episcopal priests, with men linked to higher level fifth placements ($p < .05$) despite controlling for ordination year. Besides male gender, other important predictors in the same model were higher educational credentials ($p < .005$), not having taken time out between placements ($p < .05$), and having held a higher level fourth placement ($p < .0001$).

Another way to examine job data is by comparing gender differences in the *most recent* placement held. Such an analysis gives a snapshot of what occupational conditions currently are like among clergy who are still active in each respective denomination. Table 4.5 illustrates the significant differences in the average level of latest clergy placements.

In other tests, Episcopal regression models revealed that male priests currently hold higher level placements than females ($p < .00001$) despite controls for ordination year. Higher education credentials ($p < .0001$) and younger age at ordination ($p < .001$) also are important predictors of current Episcopal placement level, controlling for ordination year and gender. When the models were run separately by gender, age was critical for men but made no difference for women, which may be a reflection of women's concentration in lower level placements. While the basic trends were similar in the U.U.A. regression models, none were statistically significant, which may be a result of both the smaller sample size and wider variance in the U.U.A. sample.

Table 4.5. Average Level of Most Recent Placement for Episcopal Priests and U.U.A. Ministers.

Cohort	Episcopal			Unitarian Universalist		
	Men	Women	Index of dissimilarity	Men	Women	Index of dissimilarity
1990	4.0	3.3	24%	4.9	4.6	21%
1985	4.9	3.9	27	5.6	5.3	15
1980	5.0	4.3	25	6.1	5.2	19
1975	5.1	4.6	24	5.8	5.0	40
1970	5.0	5.1	48%	5.8	4.0	92
1950 and earlier	4.3			5.3	5.1	67%
(N)	(705)	(286)		(82)	(60)	

Job levels range from 1 to 9. Index of dissimilarity represents the percentage of men or women clergy who would have to change job level for gender differences to be eliminated. The gender difference in average job level is significant in both Episcopal ($p < .0001$) and U.U.A. ($p < .05$) samples. Clergy who left the ministry are excluded.

A Career Perspective

As an illustration of how the career paths of women clergy can differ from those of men, Episcopal priests present a particularly vivid case. Clergy in this denomination traditionally have held an average of five placements over their career spanning more than thirty years, based on men ordained in 1950 and earlier.[22] Because those ordained since 1970 are holding placements for shorter periods of time, a comparative profile for men and women priests can be sketched for these five placements (Table 4.6). Although both men and women overall share the modal job title of *rector* in their third placement, only women in the original, 1970/71 women's cohort and the more recent 1985 women's cohort most often held rectorships at this point in their career. That female clergy ordained in 1985 are currently being hired as rectors in their third placement suggests that more parishes are open to female candidates than a decade ago. Even though this is an encouraging sign

Table 4.6. Composite Career Path over First Five Jobs for Episcopal Men and Women Priests, Ordained as Deacons 1970–1990.

	Men		Women	
	Modal Title	Average Job Level	Modal Title	Average Job Level
Job 1	associate	3.5	assistant	2.8
Job 2	rector	4.6	assistant	3.7
Job 3	rector	4.9	rector[a]	3.9
Job 4	rector	4.9	interim	4.3
Job 5	rector	5.1	interim	4.0

[a] Although *rector* was the modal third title for women priests overall, this actually was the case only for those ordained as transitional deacons in 1970–71 and 1985. For women ordained in 1975, the modal title was *assistant*, and among women ordained in 1980, it was *interim*.

Modal title is the most common title held. The modal titles were compared across ordination years, and generally were consistent for all cohorts.

for women, the data show that men still have much greater prospects for obtaining such placements.

Table 4.6 shows that most of the upward mobility for male priests occurs between the first and second placement, with continued small increases in average job level across other placements. While other results point to men tending to reach the highest level attainment of their career by the third placement, Table 4.6 suggests that some upward mobility continues across their career life course. Women also peak in their modal attainment with the third placement, but on the average they continue to experience some upward mobility, although unlike men they are more prone to downward mobility toward the end of their career.

The statistical evidence of sharp gender disparities across the careers of U.U.A. ministers and Episcopal priests aligns with other research on clergy in mainline religious organizations that consistently has found that women hold lower level positions beyond entry placements, more often work less than full-time, and are paid less than men.[23] Despite ordination year, male priests in the data held higher level placements and had more upward mobility than females. Ordination at a young age and not taking time out between placements affected men's careers in various ways such that, taken together, they suggest an implicit tracking for young male priests over the first several jobs.

While gender differences may be somewhat less explicit for U.U.A. ministers, they nonetheless persist, particularly when assessing who tends to become minister of parishes with larger budgets or more membership. These gender disparities are strongly reminiscent of the historical pattern for women clergy over the past century: the marginalization of women to low-income or rural parishes that, as Gibson summarized, "cannot support men with families" and consequently where there are more vacancies.[24] It also is similar to Cowan's results for women in the Reform rabbinate, where women not only become concentrated in smaller congregations but earn less then men in similar positions.[25]

In summary, from the second placement onward, male and female clergy careers unfold in very different ways. Gender is a powerful corollary and predictor of career differences. Where gender isn't explicitly independent of the influences of other variables, it was apparent that gender becomes embedded in them. Furthermore, the lack of effect that marriage and children have had on the careers of Episcopal women priests, combined with women's tendency to hold secular jobs in addition to part-time or nonstipendiary denominational work, suggests that they are committed to full-time careers and that their lower attainment is the probable result of fewer substantive opportunities for women within that denomination. Whether their secular work is the result of preference or perhaps a realistic assessment of more limited career opportunities within the church cannot be teased out of the statistical data. The women clergy interviewed for this analysis overwhelmingly indicated that they preferred full-time placements on a par with those of their male colleagues. They also ideally wanted to change how they as clergy might function in such placements when compared to how they have seen them enacted in the church.

The results, then, lend support to the first and second hypotheses: (1) *similarities were evident between U.U.A. and Episcopal women clergy when compared*

with their male colleagues in holding comparatively lower level positions; and (2)
gender differences consistently appeared, either as independent or as embedded
effects, across the first five placements of clergy careers in these two denominations.
Overall trends in upward mobility and attainment, as well as how the careers of
male clergy have been affected by the large influx of women over the past two
decades, will be investigated in the next chapter.

·· *Five* ··

Clergy Careers over Time

A 60-Year Portrait

Given the longer history of women's ordination as Unitarian and Universalist ministers, as well as the less stratified occupational structure of the current U.U.A., one would expect to find fewer gender differences among U.U.A. ministers than among Episcopal priests. Although the statistical data show that this is the case, the persistence of gender disparities within the U.U.A. suggests that women clergy aren't fully integrating into the occupation much beyond lower to mid-level placements.

While an ideal of complete gender equality might not accurately reflect personal choices or constraints, women nonetheless tend to hold disproportionately assistant, associate, or interim appointments; to work in smaller congregations with more limited budgets; to hold specialized positions less likely to lead to promotions; and, for Episcopal priests, to work part time regardless of marital or parental status. All of these conditions suggest both lower salaries and a narrower range of opportunities than those of their male colleagues. The implications of such findings will be explored in the discussion that follows.

Job Mobility and Career Attainment

While occupational literature traditionally has assumed that job mobility means movement in a steadily upward trajectory, such assumptions have been based overwhelmingly on the secular careers of European-American middle-class men. Job mobility also occurs laterally or downward, as the data of this analysis have shown. Job mobility becomes complicated by theological reflection, manifested in the notion of a *call*, especially if clergy forgo more attractive job opportunities[1] because of a belief that remaining in a current placement, or perhaps moving to a lower level position, represents God's will calling them to do so. Yet one denominational executive noted how many clergy had applied to fill the rectorship of a wealthy urban parish, stating that they felt called to this placement, while at the same time he was unable to find any clergy called to serve a vacant remote, rural congregation. In this manner, the notion of call may show some consistencies with the more utilitarian assumptions of secular career choices. Furthermore, despite theological intention, the actual importance of a sense of call in clergy job selection appears to be problematic. For instance, a 1989 Presbyterian study found that only 11 percent of pastors felt called to their present position; the more popular reasons for accepting their placements were location (22%), good characteristics (20%), congregation's potential (12%), and program (12%).[2]

Job attainment similarly affects both the quantity and quality of opportunities as these interact with personal interests, assets, and constraints. Clergy, for example, whose preferences are sufficiently strong for rural ministry positions in the mountains to affect the placements they accept consequently are unlikely to attain high-level positions within their denomination, owing to limitations on the range of job openings they will consider. This would be an illustration of what Kerckhoff calls a *socialization model of attainment*, which is shaped both by one's choices among various opportunities and how well one performs.[3] This has been the dominant model for career analysis based upon European-American men. Kerckhoff also describes an *allocation model of attainment*, where the selectivity of opportunities resides not with the person but with the organization. In this case, different opportunities are made available to disparate groups based on their race, gender, or other characteristics. The results of the mobility analysis in chapter 4 suggests that although the *quantity* of opportunities for women to change placements was at least equal to that for men, the *quality* of those opportunities appeared to differ markedly, implying that gender differences in clergy occupational attainment must be considered within the framework of the allocation model. Consequently, the findings of women clergy consistently averaging lower attainment than men, whether measured by job level or parish resources such as budget or membership size, must be interpreted not in relation to women's choices or lower ability as the socialization model would suggest, but with respect to distinct limitations placed on the opportunities that are allocated to them, in contrast to those of their male colleagues. That women's lower attainment tends to increase as the annual ratio of women ordained reaches 30 percent or more suggests that the distribution of opportunities may fluctuate with the relative concentration of a subordinate group. Opportunities, then, become a mechanism of social control over occupational feminization.

Since women clergy average lower levels of attainment than men over their careers, opportunities for job mobility—especially *upward* mobility—become particularly important for women seeking to advance their careers toward increased denominational influence and authority. As Table 4.6 illustrates, prospects for upward mobility typically differ at various points in one's career. Therefore, knowing when the timing is most auspicious for upward movement can be important in assessing whether to take advantage of a particular opportunity, should it present itself.

Table 5.1 shows the pattern of upward mobility at five-year intervals over the first twenty years of Episcopal and U.U.A. clergy careers. From these patterns,

Table 5.1. Percentage of Episcopal Priests and U.U.A. Ministers with Upward Job Mobility at Five-Year Intervals.

Cohort	Sex	Episcopal Years				Unitarian Universalist Years			
		1–5	5–10	10–15	15–20	1–5	5–10	10–15	15–20
1985	F	55	—	—	—	18	—	—	—
	M	63	—	—	—	36	—	—	—
1980	F	60	28	—	—	19	5	—	—
	M	58	39	—	—	0[a]	11	—	—
1975	F	41	39	34	—	0	0	0	—
	M	58	36	30	—	21	0	0	—
1970	F	33	80[b]	33	17	0	0	—	0
	M	51	28	8	8	23	0	11	13
1950 & earlier	F	—	—	—	—	0	0	0	100[c]
	M	64	32	22	14	22	0	0	0

[a] All men ordained in 1980 entered at job level 6, the highest of any cohort year in the data.

[b] Upward mobility is unusually high in years 5–10, as women's ordination to the priesthood was granted in 1977.

[c] The 1950 and earlier Unitarian Universalist female cohort had only one case with sufficient job information for this analysis.

Percentages were calculated by comparing job levels at the beginning and end of each five-year interval.

three trends are evident: (1) the first five years are highly important for the likelihood of upward mobility in one's career; (2) the probability of further upward mobility decreases over time; and (3) women clergy—ministers and priests—ordained prior to 1980 experience comparatively low upward mobility, except for the original cohort (1970) of Episcopal women whose upward mobility between years five and ten increased substantially—likely the result of the Episcopal Church's 1976 decision to ordain women to the priesthood. It's also important to recall the increase in lower entry-level placements since 1980, discussed in chapter 3, which may suggest that the higher upward mobility in recent cohorts is an artifact of a lower starting point.

The first five years, then, are critical to the pattern of upward mobility likely to develop within clergy careers.[4] In the maximum likelihood estimates of upward mobility between first and second placement for Episcopal priests (Table 4.4), the importance of male gender suggests that men's advantage in inducing early upward mobility increases the prospect for higher attainment over their careers. The more evenly distributed upward mobility pattern of women priests suggests not only that opportunities for upward movement do exist but that more frequent job changes beyond the first two placements do result in overall job-level gains (cf. Table 4.6). That women experienced upward mobility in smaller increments also suggests that they must expend much more energy in the mobility process for whatever they attain. Conversely, if clergy—female or male—remain in lower level placements for more than a short time early in their career, they risk fewer job changes during the period when opportunities for upward mobility are likely to occur, and consequently may have lower career attainment than those who move more frequently. Such clergy may risk becoming locked into flat career trajectories.

The greater tendency for women clergy to experience *downward* mobility compared to men (Table 5.2) cannot be ignored. Neither can the relationship between the higher female ratios of the 1980 and later cohorts and women's greater tendency to have more downward job mobility than men ordained these same years. Although clergy in higher level placements have fewer opportunities for further upward mobility, with more chance of lateral or downward mobility, women's tendency to have *both* lower level placements and more downward mobility than men suggests that other mechanisms—such as sharply constricted opportunities—may be operant. Where opportunities for women constrict in relation to increased female cohort ratios, such patterns further suggest that the supply of opportunities may be controlled in relation to concerns about the prospect of occupational feminization.

The net effect of job mobility, when combined with the level of positions that one attains, constitutes a *career trajectory*. The norm for clergy career trajectories has included at least one placement as a rector or minister overseeing a self-supporting parish. The trajectories of men and women who have attained at least this level of placement are compared in Figures 5.1 to 5.4. Those who left the occupation before their twentieth year after ordination have been excluded from this portion of the analysis.

Figures 5.1 and 5.2 show a gender gap in attainment ranging from 13 percent for those ordained in 1990[5] to 34 percent for those ordained only a decade earlier in the Episcopal Church. Interestingly, the original cohort of women clergy, ordained in 1970/71, had higher attainment relative to men than any subsequent cohort except 1990, despite the obvious limitation on their attainment until 1977. Moreover, this original cohort had a higher percentage attainment in the first decade after their ordination to the diaconate than any subsequent cohort of women priests in the data. Admittedly, this may be a tokenism effect of the novelty

Table 5.2. Percentage of Episcopal Priests and U.U.A. Ministers with Downward Job Mobility at Five-Year Intervals.

Cohort	Sex	Episcopal				Unitarian Universalist			
		Years				Years			
		1–5	5–10	10–15	15–20	1–5	5–10	10–15	15–20
1985	F	7	—	—	—	24	—	—	—
	M	5	—	—	—	9	—	—	—
1980	F	6	26	—	—	14	15	—	—
	M	6	12	—	—	11	0	—	—
1975	F	11	13	10	—	0	0	0	—
	M	6	14	17	—	0	0	0	—
1970	F	0	0	0	17	0	0	—	100[a]
	M	9	15	15	15	0	9	0	13
1950 & earlier	F	—	—	—	—	0	0	0	0
	M	8	17	15	14	0	15	0	21

[a] The 1970 Unitarian Universalist female cohort contained only one case.

Percentages were calculated by comparing job levels at the beginning and end of each five-year interval.

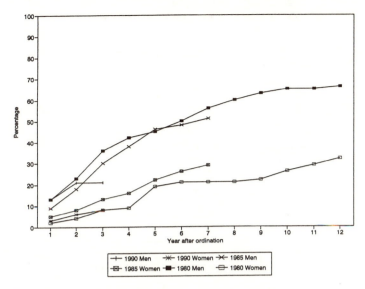

Figure 5.1 Percentage of female and male Episcopal priests attaining level 6 positions who were ordained to the diaconate, 1980–1990.

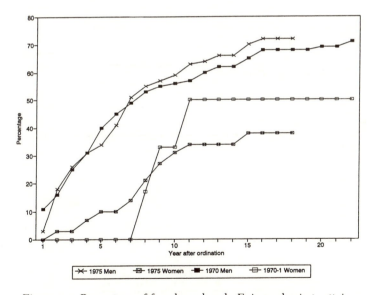

Figure 5.2 Percentage of female and male Episcopal priests attaining level 6 positions who were ordained to the diaconate, 1970–1975.

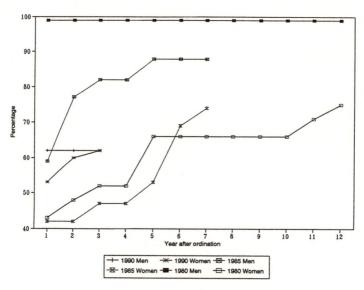

Figure 5.3 Percentage of female and male U.U.A. ministers attaining level 6 positions who were ordained 1980–1990.

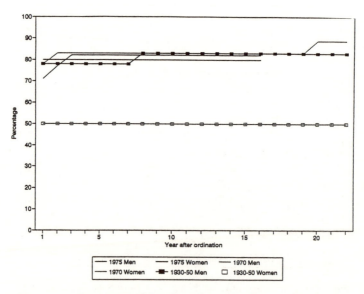

Figure 5.4. Percentage of female and male U.U.A. ministers attaining level 6 positions who were ordained 1930–1975.

of women priests during the late 1970s and the small cohort size ($N = 8$ priests), such that even a few parishes interested in women rectors would likely result in placements for this group. But the demand for women clergy in high-profile positions obviously has not kept up with the emerging supply in subsequent cohorts. Overall, twice the percentage of male (58%) to female (27%) priests ordained to the diaconate in 1970 or later have held level 6 or higher placements, which concurs with the Episcopal Church Deployment Office findings that women priests are only half as likely as men *ever* to become vicars or rectors (job level 5 or 6).[6] However, the data do show some optimism: the raw number of women attaining level 6 placements or higher between 1987 and 1993 had tripled when compared to earlier years.[7]

A gender gap, although smaller, emerged for U.U.A. ministers (Figures 5.3 and 5.4), even though most placements in this denomination traditionally have been at level 6. The gender disparity becomes evident from 1980 onward, coinciding with those years when the cohort ratios have been over 50 percent female.[8] Where the female gender ratio is high, men surpass women in attainment from the very start of their careers. As with the original cohort of Episcopal women clergy, U.U.A. women ordained in years where the ratio of women to men was very low benefited occupationally from a tokenism effect.

The attainment curves reinforce the importance of those patterns that showed the greatest amount of upward mobility occurring during the first five years of men's careers, and point to the value of the smaller yet steady increments that women make over the ensuing ten years. With few exceptions, the consistency of the attainment curves over time is striking, for both men and women. The persistent gender difference in attainment, when combined with the greater tendency for downward mobility among women ordained in 1980 and later, lends evidence to a decline in women's opportunities relative to men. The likelihood that such a decline either may be part of an overt backlash to the increase in women clergy or a result of various structural changes within religious organizations that have disproportionately affected women clergy will be discussed at length in the next three chapters.

Women's Place in Clergy Couples

Sociologist Talcott Parsons believed that marriage between professionals would be both personally and professionally destructive.[9] Additional stresses occur with the compounded "fishbowl" pressure of clergy life in the church.[10] Clergy couples have noted the potential for stress where one spouse may be asked to leave a good placement for the sake of the other's career, as well as the role overload that typically has accompanied the clergy occupation.[11] Furthermore, while there traditionally have been additional role expectations for female spouses of male clergy to participate in congregational life, whether they are lay or ordained, such expectations have been minimal for male spouses of female clergy. Where a woman minister or priest holds a shared position with her spouse, the pressure of increased subordinate-role expectations from the congregation, in addition to any disproportionate domestic or child-care responsibilities, can result in the woman's ending up with the supportive role. As one clergy respondent in a Presbyterian study wrote, "Many of our people still see me in the roles of 'super-equipped pastor's wife.' At this stage in my life, that's not a problem." Another clergywoman in the study was less positive about her husband's congregation, who wanted her to be a volunteer "pastor's wife."[12] Female co-pastors also have noticed more subtle inequalities, such as being addressed by their first name while their husbands are called by their clergy title.[13]

Rallings and Pratto, studying two-clergy couples in ten Protestant denominations, observed that wives were more likely than husbands to have subordinate placements and to face issues such as balancing multiple roles, conflating work, and family life, and to have greater responsibility for household tasks, similar to dual-career couples sharing the same secular occupation.[14] They also observed gender-related inequalities in both status and salary for the female partner.[15]

The ability to find available placements in the same geographic location for both clergy spouses is a primary concern for two-clergy couples.[16] While some couples may opt to share a single position (e.g., co-minister, co-rector), Sawtell observed that for United Church of Christ (U.C.C.) couples this tends to be primarily a choice for the newly ordained. Because clergy must split a single salary, not only does this result in a lower income but there are complications for pension contributions and disability insurance. Women in U.C.C. clergy couples also disproportionately worked part time, although Sawtell found that some men worked part time in order to provide child care. Both Sawtell and respondent comments from a Presbyterian study suggest that women who do take time out from their career to care for children full time may be doing so at least partly because of an inability to find placements.[17]

A few clergy in the data were identified as being part of two-clergy couples: 5 percent of the Episcopal priests and 4 percent of the U.U.A. ministers.[18] This is comparable to Sawtell's 1988 estimate that 6 percent of all U.C.C. ministers are part of clergy couples.[19] All Episcopal members of two-clergy couples in the data were ordained in 1970 or later, with the largest concentration of couples in the 1980 and 1985 cohorts. U.U.A. male members of clergy couples ranged from the 1950 cohort. While more female than male members of Episcopal two-clergy couples held nonparish positions and lower level placements, their career pattern was not significantly different from that of women clergy overall. Nor were there differences among U.U.A. women ministers who were or weren't part of two-clergy couples. Thus, any occupational disadvantage seems to be characteristic more of gender differences than of women's marital status.

Men's Careers and the Appearance of Occupational Stability

While concerns have been raised over the impact of occupational feminization on the careers of men, little attention has been given to studying longitudinally what has happened to male clergy careers over the last several decades. In the remainder of this chapter and in the next chapter, I will argue that various forces have coalesced to maintain the opportunity structure of male U.U.A. ministers over time, in contrast to pronounced declines in opportunities for male Episcopal

priests. It also should become evident how the influx of women clergy has inter-
acted with these trends.

Table 5.3 compares changes over time in the average job level of the first four
placements held by men who either were ordained in 1950 and earlier or in 1980
and subsequently. Data from chapter 4 showed that the first four placements
roughly represent the first decade of ministry for male Episcopal priests and the first
two decades for male U.U.A. ministers. These two periods also compare an era
well prior to the large influx of U.U.A. women ministers and priests with the more
recent, feminized cohorts. The data of these two denominations show an important disparity: *more recently ordained male priests hold lower level positions than
their counterparts three decades earlier, a pattern not evident among male ministers
despite the large influx of women since 1980.* Since the attainment of male ministers does not seem to be adversely affected in more recent years, when the annual
ratio of women ordained has consistently exceeded that of men, the occupational
decline experienced by male priests can be attributed to factors other than the
presence of female priests. Furthermore, since chapter 4 did show that gender
differences exist among both U.U.A. and Episcopal clergy—differences that favored men—the U.U.A. male opportunity structure likely is being maintained
through gender-related dynamics, such as differential opportunity arrangements
that facilitate job segregation, with women disproportionately clustered either in
slightly lower level positions or as ministers of smaller membership, lower budget
parishes.

Occupational changes are not unrelated to organizational shifts. This linkage
is particularly critical for clergy, since they represent the dominant occupation in
religious organizations. Perhaps the most visible illustration of this relationship
involves the decline in membership that both the U.U.A. and the Episcopal
Church have experienced since 1970 without corresponding decreases in the number of clergy being ordained, trends which will be discussed further in chapter 8.
The consequences, however, differ by denomination. Among U.U.A. ministers,

Table 5.3. Average Level of Entry to Fourth Placements for Male Episcopal Priests and
Unitarian Universalist Ministers, 1920–1993.

Placement	Episcopal			Unitarian Universalist		
	Ordained 1950 or earlier	Ordained 1980 or later	Index of dissimilarity	Ordained 1950 or earlier	Ordained 1980 or later	Index of dissimilarity
Job 1	4.1	3.2	33%	5.4	5.4	13%
Job 2	5.0	4.5	17	5.8	5.2	15
Job 3	5.2	4.9	12	5.3	6.0	35
Job 4	5.2	4.8	17%	5.5	7.0	93%[a]
(N)	(184)	(358)		(25)	(41)	

[a] Only one minister ordained in 1980 or later had moved to a fourth placement.

Job levels range from 1 to 9. Index of dissimilarity represents the percentage of clergy who would need to change job
levels for the two groups to be equal. The number of clergy in each grouping is an overall total of those who have held
at least one denominational position. Not all clergy have held four placements. Data for second to fourth placements
are incomplete for clergy ordained 1985–1990.

men ordained in the 1970s were found to hold their placements somewhat longer than men ordained in 1950 and earlier, which may reflect elevated competition for desirable positions throughout the 1970s. Concurrently, a decline in the number of men ordained in 1975 and 1980 indicates a possible alleviation of occupational crowding and resultant tight job competition among men. Since the data show that women ministers on average haven't been significantly competitive with men beyond the entry placement, a decreased occupational crowding *among men* may be responsible for men's ability to maintain levels of attainment similar to that of clergy ordained in 1970 and earlier.

Conversely, male priests ordained in 1970 and later seem to have adjusted to occupational crowding by shortening the average tenure of their placements, which could reflect extremely tight job competition as they seek to *find* desirable placements. For instance, among male priests ordained prior to 1950, the average length of second and subsequent placements had ranged up to nineteen years. From 1950 onward, the average duration of these placements was reduced to seven years or less. The shortened job duration for those ordained in 1950 may have been the result of increased opportunities from sharp growth in both church membership and number of congregations. Since data from this analysis showed that Episcopal men ordained in 1950 and earlier had significantly higher level entry and second placements, and much greater upward job mobility over the first two decades of their careers than men ordained in 1970 or later, the shortened job durations from 1970 onward, combined with lower level placements on the average, suggest that fewer high- or mid-level opportunities were available by the early 1970s, with proportionately more placements at mid to lower levels and at less than full-time employment. Similar to the U.U.A., there was a decline in the number of Episcopal men ordained during 1975 and 1980, and markedly so in 1990. However, unlike the U.U.A., the disjunction in Episcopal clergy supply and demand, estimated in 1995 to be about 7,200 stipendiary positions for more than 14,000 Episcopal priests,[20] is so great that the effects of occupational crowding among male priests are still prevalent.

Because of noticeable occupational change over time in the level of placements held by male Episcopal priests, it's important to discern whether this has any direct relationship to women's ordination and occupational feminization. Figure 5.5 compares the percentage of male priests who have held entry placements at job level 5 (e.g., vicar) or above, and then moved into second placements at job level 6 (e.g., rector) or higher. Only two-thirds as many male priests ordained to the diaconate in 1970 started their careers at level 5 or higher as did men ordained in 1950; by 1990 this percentage had dropped another third. Since the data show that entry placements typically have averaged about four years until recent cohorts, the first sharp decline in the ratio of men moving to rectorships or other positions at level 6 and higher in their second placement appears to have occurred in the mid-1940s, with another marked decline around 1974—a period still prior to the church's formally allowing women's ordination to the priesthood and women's eligibility to compete with men for these positions.[21] Furthermore, while the percentage of men in mid-level entry placements has declined since 1950, even more dramatic may be a trend in the 1990 cohort that reverses a decline in men

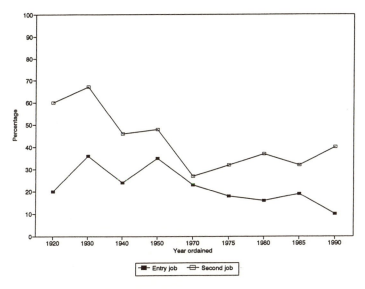

Figure 5.5 Percentage of male Episcopal priests with at least level 5 entry or level 6 second placements, 1920–1993. Data for second placement are incomplete for clergy ordained in 1990.

ordained between 1970 and 1985 who attained rectorships in their second placement. Thus, *whatever declines have occurred in opportunities for male priests to become vicars or rectors relatively early in their career has not been due to the ordination and influx of women.* Instead, the influx of women appears to be associated with a *reversal* of the decline in the ratio of men moving into rectorships for their second placement, particularly for men ordained in 1990, a cohort year when the number of male priests is estimated to be the lowest of any year examined in this analysis since 1920 (est. $N = 143$; cf. Table 2.1), and the female ratio is the highest (est. 52%). This suggests that opportunities for male clergy in this denomination may be sensitive to occupational crowding and competition *from other men* rather than from the presence of women. If so, alleviating the crowding from other men has helped to maintain men's attainment structure in both the Episcopal Church and the U.U.A., despite the very different organizational arrangements of these denominations.

Yet another way of illustrating patterns in male clergy career attainment over time is by comparing men who have held level 6 or higher positions at some point in the first decade of their careers. Declines in attainment become highly visible, particularly when comparing Episcopal men ordained in 1940 and earlier with those ordained in 1950 and in 1970. Despite church growth during the 1950s, Figure 5.6 shows that a lower percentage of men ordained in 1950 held level 6 or higher placements during the 1950s than did their predecessors a decade earlier. Furthermore, the average trajectory of men ordained in 1950 forms a line highlighting the sharp disparity between the 1950s and 1970s in attainment among Episcopal male priests. This suggests that the 1960s were particularly crucial for

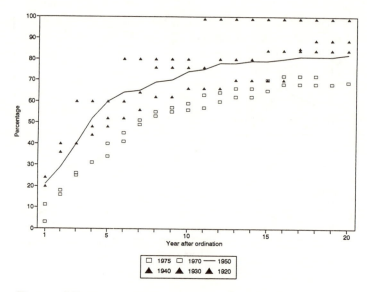

Figure 5.6 Percentage of male Episcopal priests attaining level 6 positions or higher during the first two decades of their careers, by ordination year. Those who left the priesthood prior to their twentieth year have been excluded.

the development of a declining male opportunity structure—the decade immediately *preceding* women's ordination. Furthermore, that men ordained in 1975 and subsequently have experienced proportionally higher attainment as the ratio of women priests has increased, while women's attainment hasn't similarly increased (cf. Figures 5.1 and 5.2), reinforces the likelihood that neither women priests nor occupational feminization have hindered men's opportunities for mid- to high-level attainment.

The attainment pattern of male U.U.A. ministers hasn't discernably changed over time, clearly illustrating that the influx of women hasn't affected their opportunities for obtaining traditional ministerial placements at level 6 or higher. The constancy of their attainment likely is the result of a narrower occupational structure with proportionally more mid-level positions, relatively fewer new and part-time jobs, a closer relationship between clergy supply and parish demand, and, most important, decreased occupational crowding among male ministers in recent years.

An important mechanism helping to disproportionately position male clergy to maximize attainment opportunities is the growing tendency to hold job titles considered to be traditionally normative for clergy in their respective denominations. The most common normative titles are *bishop, rector, vicar, associate,* and *assistant* among Episcopal priests, and *parish minister* and *extension minister* among U.U.A. ministers. The ratio of male priests holding traditional job titles overall has increased substantially, especially when compared to priests ordained in

1950 and earlier ($p < .005$). While this trend was not significant in the U.U.A. data, both male ministers and male priests were significantly more likely than females to hold traditional job titles ($p < .01$), which was the case in every ordination cohort. This tendency appears to be a segregating means that enables men to maximize opportunities for positions traditionally linked in a job ladder toward denominational leadership.

The difference between male priests ordained earlier and more recently becomes yet more dramatic when examining career trajectories leading to senior leadership. Constricted leadership opportunities that evidently occurred during the 1960s (cf. Figure 5.6) are particularly visible when plotting a twenty-year career trajectory for male priests ordained since 1920 (Figure 5.7) who have held senior-level positions at level 7 or higher. Among priests ordained prior to 1950, 45 percent had held such placements within the first two decades of their careers, compared to only 13 percent of those ordained in 1970. As with mid-level attainment, the ratio of Unitarian Universalist ministers holding senior-level placements has not changed substantially over time, indicating that men have similar senior leadership opportunities today as in earlier years.

Since no U.U.A. women and only seven Episcopal women were found in the data to have held senior-level placements, females present little competitive challenge for male attainment prospects. The locus of competition, then, seems to be

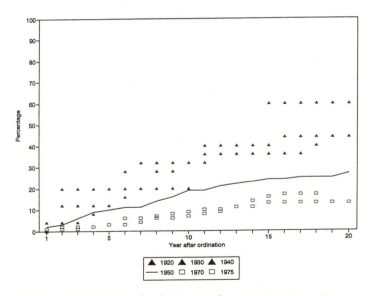

Figure 5.7 Percentage of male Episcopal priests attaining senior-level positions during the first two decades of their careers, by ordination year. Senior-level positions are those at job levels 7 to 9. Those who left the priesthood prior to their twentieth year have been excluded.

among men. Furthermore, that diminishing high-level leadership opportunities for male priests are evident *prior* to women's ordination suggests that structural changes in religious organizations, including male clergy oversupply and declines in the number and financial resources of congregations, may be critical to any explanation of the fewer mid- to high-level job opportunities evident. The closer linkages between clergy supply and demand in the U.U.A. similarly may partly explain the lack of change in male clergy attainment over time. While clergy retirements may open up some potential for upward mobility, any imbalance in either a denomination's membership or parish financial resources relative to the supply of male clergy will result in a relative decline in the proportion of men likely to attain high-level positions.

Although race as a variable is used only in an exploratory manner because of only partial information available, the ratio of minority-race U.U.A. male clergy attaining a senior-level placement was similar to the ratio of minority-race men in the sample. In the Episcopal sample, European-American men were overrepresented in senior-level positions while the opposite trend was evident among women attaining these positions. Women of color were disproportionately overrepresented among all women who attained one or more senior-level placements. Furthermore, the women of color were all African American, although this racial group constituted only about half of the women identified as probable minority-race in the sample. The combination of overrepresented European-American men and minority-race women in relation to the proportionally few senior-level positions held by women overall suggests that women's attainment may be a function of tokenism, whereby women are selected for visibility in addition to their qualifications to fill an allocated supply of higher level positions.

Overall, occupational differences among male clergy over time were fewer than those between men and women clergy in their respective denominations, which suggests that occupational stability for men has resulted in the continued marginalization of women. If this is correct, then the likelihood is high that occupational gender segregation is accounting at least partly for whatever stability and constancy have remained in the career trajectories of male clergy in relation to structural changes within religious organizations that have created pressure leading to occupational decline. Such changes will be discussed in chapter 8.

Clergywomen's Opportunities for Leadership

Women's opportunities for leadership in various religious organizations have waxed and waned in historical cycles. Tucker writes of Zwingilian Reformer Katherine Zell who, although not allowed to be ordained, was so passionately committed to ministry that she was accused of "disturbing the peace" and, following her husband's death, of "seeking to take over the pulpit."[22] Nevertheless, Zell persisted.

Women's perseverance also is evident in the data of this analysis. Despite Unitarian and Universalist histories of women in ministry for more than a century, the first woman called to be a senior minister—of a parish with more than 500 members—occurred in 1987 (she wasn't in the U.U.A. sample). Episcopal women have had a slightly higher attainment record. Although 9 percent of the male priests ordained between 1970 and 1990 in the data attained senior-level placements compared to 2 percent of the women priests ordained during these years, an inequality that was statistically significant ($p < .001$), nonetheless the number of women in such positions has tripled since 1987. Only women ordained in 1980 or earlier have attained such placements, however, while men ordained through 1985 did so. One especially noteworthy example is Mary Adelia McLeod, a member of the 1980 cohort who, in 1993, was elected the Episcopal Church's first female diocesan (Vermont) bishop.

The Episcopal Church's hierarchical occupational structure appears to have facilitated the concentration of women in lower level positions, while the U.U.A.'s less differentiated occupational structure has encouraged greater parity for women to attain mid-level positions at some point in their career. However, the U.U.A. advantage fades when considering either the qualitative differences between men and women clergy in their parish budgets or membership sizes, or the dearth of women ministers in senior-level positions.

The disproportionate absence of women ministers and priests from positions of authority over large congregations and in denominational leadership, based on the data, is consistent with the results of other studies on women clergy in mainline Protestantism and Reform Judaism.[23] The gender disparity is particularly visible in large congregations with multiple clergy, where the senior minister, pastor, rector, or rabbi overwhelmingly is male. Consistently, even local congregations that publicly support women clergy have tended to prefer men for senior positions. At the outset of the 1980s, Carroll et al. had discovered in their nine-denomination study that congregations having had a positive experience with women clergy were subsequently no more likely to choose a woman than a man.[24] There also is evidence that laity still tend to defer to a male minister if one is present.[25] Lehman had found in his Presbyterian data that congregations perceiving their viability at stake tend to view women clergy as less competent than men.[26] Similarly, a 1989 Presbyterian survey found that 84 percent of the pastoral and 55 percent of the lay member respondents admitted that they preferred a male pastor to head their congregation. None preferred a female.[27] It seems, then, that the most women can hope for is a *lack* of gender preference. Consequently, women's deployment in interim positions, particularly evident in the Episcopal data (cf. Table 4.6), may not necessarily be the "breaking-ground" strategy it has long been perceived to be, as an informal means of affirmative action to familiarize congregations with women clergy as possible candidates for their permanent minister or rector.

The United Methodist Church has successfully placed more women in senior leadership positions than any other denomination, which seems to be largely the result of all ordained ministerial appointments made by the conference (i.e., regional) bishop, with support from the cabinet of officials responsible for administration and deployment matters. Since ministers can be moved at will, and usually are rotated within ten years, there is a steady turnover of senior-level placements. Where the bishop and cabinet have been supportive of women clergy, they have been given substantive opportunities, although one minister interviewed for this analysis critiqued appointments as being made "from the good ol' boy system," and often with a racial as well as gender bias. The results of Schmidt's study affirmed this minister's analysis that equitable deployment can be problematic.[28] Neverthe-less, the United Methodist deployment system has yielded positive results for women clergy: Royle found that female United Methodist ministers were more likely to have full-time placements and at higher salaries than women in the Lutheran, Presbyterian, or Disciples of Christ traditions,[29] the latter group which, like the Episcopal Church and the U.U.A., may offer deployment assistance but does not centrally control or distribute ministerial placements.

Overall the leadership structure of both denominations, headed and domi-nated by men, has accommodated women's ordination and entry into the occupa-tion with opportunities for employment, but all too typically at lower level place-ments from which upward mobility has resulted in neither women achieving parity nor women threatening the organizational control and consequently the religious influence that men traditionally have held. Rather, the results suggest that women clergy are not less committed to their careers, but are developing them through a separate, subordinate set of occupational opportunities, manifesting a *glass ceiling* through which only a few women clergy are able to ascend. Furthermore, the results demonstrate that men are continuing to attain those positions most likely to lead to high-profile careers. If anything, they are doing so at women's expense. That this trend persists in two diverse religious organizations underscores the systemic nature of gender segregation in placements.

In sum, the mobility and attainment analysis lends further support to the first and second hypotheses: (1) *similarities in female and male clergy careers were evident across two different types of religious organizations*; and (2) *gender differ-ences were sharply evident in clergy career trajectories, particularly in attaining mid-level and senior-level positions*. Additionally, the analysis supported the third and fourth hypotheses: (3) *there was evidence of negative change in occupational opportunities for male priests that preceded women's ordination*; and (4) *the careers of male clergy were not at all adversely affected by the presence of female clergy*. If anything, occupational feminization has enhanced men's careers by decreasing the pool of candidates considered to be seriously competitive for mid- to high-level positions—a pool which includes few women.

Reskin and Roos observed that various secular occupations have feminized as a result of men's declining opportunities for upward job mobility, compensation, and autonomy.[30] Declines in men's opportunities for upward mobility and attain-ment are most evident in the Episcopal data. Although the U.U.A. has maintained its opportunity structure for male clergy over time, it has done so through a limited supply of men and a near exclusion of female clergy in senior leadership. Thus, there is evidence to support the sixth hypothesis: *trends toward occupational femi-nization of the clergy tend to be consistent with feminization tendencies in secular occupations*.

While certain cultural conditions may precipitate or enhance opportunities for women to found religious movements, which traditionally have been the chief means for women to hold leadership positions in religious groups, other cultural conditions, such as denominational support for women's ordination and equality of ministerial opportunities on the same basis as men, are yet more vulnerable to shifts over time—whether as an active response to concerns over occupational feminization, as an active backlash movement in attitudes toward gender equality, or as a passive change as women disproportionately become caught by shifts in the occupational structure precipitated by economic concerns affecting religious organizations. The most visible shift affecting both occupational feminization and the support for women clergy has been the decline of the young male cleric that traditionally had been normative to the occupation, a trend whose magnitude will be discussed in the next chapter.

Six

Decline and Fall of the Young Male Cleric

R eskin argues that the feminization of secular occupations is preceded by changes that make them less attractive to men, such as reduced opportunities for mobility or autonomy and declines in prestige and earnings.[1] Related to opportunities for upward mobility, the data of this analysis have pointed to a decline in attainment among Episcopal priests, and to U.U.A. ministers apparently maintaining their attainment through a decreased number of men ordained after 1975, combined with a near exclusion of women from high-level placements.

While the clergy as a profession traditionally has had relatively low earnings, given the amount of educational preparation typically invested in a career, historically it could expect a level of prestige well above secular occupations with comparable earnings. There is some evidence that clergy occupational prestige had remained relatively stable into the 1950s,[2] but increased widespread accessibility to higher education for middle- and working-class Americans and the proliferation of professional specialties served to challenge the ordained ministry with secular alternatives. Growing concern over role ambiguity and conflict from within the occupation further eroded its professional stature.

In this manner, clergy prestige has appeared to fluctuate in relation to the amount of formal education or professional knowledge represented within a religious community's membership, including available secular alternatives. Where few members have had substantial education, clergy have enjoyed high prestige. In the past, selection for monastic or ordained orders also often served as a means of upward social mobility, particularly for men otherwise not having access to the prospect of a formal education. Similarly, some religious orders have offered women opportunities to pursue higher education and scholarship that they wouldn't otherwise have had.

The widespread European cultural influence of the Protestant Reformation, which placed a high value on literacy for both men and women so as to be able to read and reflect upon scripture, led to greater access to education among the middle and lower classes, paralleling earlier emphases on literacy developed within Rabbinic Judaism and Islam. Yet rising literacy and education also have had a secularizing relationship with religion, first by facilitating the development of other professional specializations that subsequently have encroached upon many of the traditional clergy roles and functions, and second by emphasizing individual access to the sacred through theologies of immanence or personal relationship with the deity, such as those developed in Quakerism, born-again Evangelicalism, and Pentecostalism. The result has been greater emphasis on egalitarianism among worshippers, serving to decrease dependence on clergy as divine-human mediators.

Various other causes have been attributed to declines in clergy prestige. Douglas argues that the disenfranchisement of religion from state support created a dependency of clergy—and their religious organization—on local congregations for socioeconomic survival, a relationship which tended to suppress not only the authority but the persuasive sway that clergy traditionally had held on matters of public interest.[3] Instead, Douglas argues, clergy were socially and morally privatized away from the public realm, with those who contradicted the political and economic interests of influential members of their congregations risking loss of their jobs. This theory offers an intriguing partial explanation. Yet Hutchison writes, "Laments concerning 'ministerial decline,' laid end to end would form a wide and solid line from 1630 to 1930 and, if valid, would document the ending of all ministerial influence in America sometime before the Revolution."[4] Nor does a disenfranchisement theory account for the powerfully influential public activism of African-American churches and the high prestige with which they have held their clergy leadership, nor does it explain the declines in clergy prestige in English and European state churches.[5] The relative position of clergy to their membership in terms of education and socioeconomic status appears to be the more comprehensive predictor.

Yet two symptoms explicitly associated with the loss of prestige in secular occupations have been occupational feminization and a concurrent sharp decline in capable young men seeking to enter the occupation, resulting in both a feminizing and a graying of these occupations. Both trends, linking a decline in prestige and opportunities for upward mobility, attainment, and compensation with the vanishing supply of young men, are evident in the data of this analysis.

The Graying of the Clergy

Sixty years ago, men typically went to seminary straight from college and were ordained shortly after graduation, if not beforehand. Over the past two decades, the increasing age of male as well as female seminarians in most U.S. denominations has been well documented. Larsen, in his comprehensive study of A.T.S. (Association of Theological Schools) seminaries, noted that the average age of seminarians enrolled in Master of Divinity degree programs had risen from 25 years in 1962 to 34 years by 1991, with only 38 percent of all seminarians under age 30.[6] This trend has been attributed to be a reflection of an overall aging of the U.S.

population. While the rise in average seminarian age has been conspicuous over the last two decades, as an overall trend it is not that recent. Gustafson had noted it among seminarians in the early 1960s, particularly among Episcopalians.[7] Wilson had identified a similar trend as early as the 1950s among newly ordained clergy in the Church of England.[8]

Even among conservative Protestant seminaries that attract a disproportionate concentration of young men, McKenna has identified a "two-humped curve"— seminarians under age 25 and those in their mid-thirties.[9] The aging trend hasn't been quite as marked in Jewish seminaries.[10] But although the age increase in most denominations has leveled off since 1988, it is unlikely to reverse in the near future.

That aging among male seminarians had been identified in the Episcopal Church by the 1960s, prior to granting women's ordination, or for other denominations prior to the sharp influx of women, underscores the importance of this trend *preceding* occupational feminization. Furthermore, since the ages of women clergy in this analysis have increased across the years at a rate generally similar to those of men (cf. Table 3.3), the trend of rising ages may be attributable to structural factors related to the occupation itself, perhaps the differing nature of opportunities and rewards relative to other occupations, or to external factors outside the occupation altogether.

Men traditionally have had a wider variety of occupations, organizations, and positions on a career ladder open to them than women have had. Given the ratio of men over age 35 who are drawn to seminary, the ordained ministry must offer particularly attractive attributes as a second-career choice for men—for instance, the opportunity to mentor others.[11] Among those who apply to various graduate schools for vocational retraining, Sarason found a desire for "meaning" as an important focus in those decisions.[12] Since religion deals with eschatological meaning as well as spiritual mentorship, ordained ministry may represent a logically attractive vocational choice.

Older seminarians have been regarded by one seminary dean as a "restless young professional group," with their decision to enter seminary part of a continuous service-oriented vocational theme after having tried another field such as law, business, or human services, and either finding the norms of secular work too confining or desiring additional training in religion.[13] Larsen and Shopshire associated the trend toward older seminarians with the generation of Vietnam-era youth, although they did not find evidence that the decision to enter seminary was influenced by moral idealism acquired during the sixties. The three motivations for entering ministry identified in their 1986 A.T.S. study and in Larsen's 1991 update—*experiencing a call, church influence,* and *wanting to address the wrongs of the world*—were generally consistent across age groups.[14] Others have regarded the influx of older seminarians with more skepticism, suspecting those identified with the "me" generation as perhaps more interested in serving their own needs through ministry than those of others.[15] Since Larsen and Shopshire found less concern among older seminarians about making occupational moves for the sake of climbing a career ladder, and a similar willingness to start at the bottom of the occupation, those needs they might be seeking are more likely psychic, existential, and religious than socioeconomic and pragmatic.

Since 1980, the median age at ordination for men and women in both the Episcopal and U.U.A. samples has been above age 35, which suggests that the majority of those ordained in the last decade are second-career clergy. No generational skew was evident, even though both denominations have been characterized by strong internal social movements reflecting liberal idealism. Just as likely, decisions to enter seminary have been influenced by factors independent of age or generation, such as a long-term interest or a pragmatic need to make a career change.[16]

The structural shifts in human resource utilization by U.S. business, including waves of plant closures, organizational restructuring, and downsizing, led to the elimination of 3.5 million jobs during the 1980s alone.[17] As a result, career change has come to represent a substantial forced choice, particularly among older workers less likely to be hired elsewhere at similar occupational levels and salaries. This likely has contributed to the aging trend since 1980 (cf. Table 3.3), as well as explaining in part the relatively even distribution of ordinand ages across generational lines. The impact on the clergy, however, has been a sharp influx of new ordinands who are both older and have a greater diversity of skills and occupational experience than what has traditionally characterized the occupation.

Age diversity conflicts with the traditional concept of career trajectory, historically formed from the work experience of European-American males. Malony and Hunt have adapted a career-development model to the clergy that consists of five stages:[18]

preparation: college and seminary, traditionally occurring during a candidate's early twenties

entry level: up to the fifth year following ordination, associated with one's late twenties to early thirties

advancement: typical movement from smaller to larger congregations during one's thirties and forties

maintenance: career plateau following the last advancement, typically occurring during one's late forties to early sixties

decline: reduced responsibilities in preparation for retirement, normally occurring between one's late fifties and seventies

Based on secular occupations, clergy with ages above the normative boundaries of each stage should be expected to experience negative effects on their careers. For example, clergy ordained in their thirties and early forties might expect to advance quickly through their age association with the *advancement* stage, but would be less likely to advance as far as younger clergy with more years available in that stage.[19] Clergy ordained at an older age would more quickly be age-identified with the *maintenance* stage. As such, men and women clergy ordained over age 50 would be expected to have little identification with the *entry* and *advancement* stages, and consequently have less opportunity for upward job mobility. How, then, does older age at ordination affect opportunities to develop a career in the clergy, and what gender differences may interact with age?

Second Career: Asset or Liability?

Age traditionally has been regarded as a liability for those who change careers in secular occupations, particularly in middle age. Despite the 1967 U.S. Age Discrimination in Employment Act, those who made changes in their forties or later within secular occupations have reported greater difficulty, with length of unemployment in the transition period directly related to age.[20]

Based on age, the career-stage model not only has served as a normative guide within religious organizations but to some extent has been prescriptive both for clergy expectations and for evaluating their career progress. Major age deviations from where one is expected to be could become a career liability if others perceive one as "too old" for a position. Carroll et al. found age to be viewed by Lutheran officials as more crucial than gender in whether clergy received calls (i.e., job placements).[21] Similarly, an E.L.C.A. (Evangelical Lutheran Church in America) pastor interviewed for this analysis recounted advice by a denominational official that he needed to make any major career moves by age 50. Second-career Episcopal clergy similarly have been considered too old for the traditional path of occupational development in that denomination.[22]

One distinct advantage that second-career clergy bring to their new vocation is a high level of education, based on the data of this analysis. Although younger clergy averaged more education overall at time of ordination ($p < .0001$), older clergy were more likely to hold at least one advanced educational degree *besides* the Master of Divinity degree. For example, 71 percent of the male U.U.A. ministers ordained at age 40 or later held a master's or doctoral degree *in addition to* the Master of Divinity, compared to about 35 percent of men ordained prior to age 40 ($p < .05$). About 38 percent of female ministers ordained after age 40 held an additional advanced degree, compared to 18 percent of those ordained younger. Similarly, about 35 percent of female and 41 percent of male Episcopal priests ordained over age 40 held advanced degrees besides the Master of Divinity, compared to 13 percent of female and 20 percent of male priests ordained prior to age 40.

Roos has called age a "crude proxy for experience."[23] However, the kind of experience that age represents may affect its efficacy. Larsen identified the largest percentage (45%) of second-career seminarians, those entering seminary over age 30, as having come from professional occupations such as law, medicine, and education.[24] The data presented in chapter 3 show that two types of such prior occupational experience—religion related and semiprofessional—positively affected prospects for higher level entry placements among Episcopal clergy, while prior occupational experience had a negative effect on U.U.A. clergy entry placements despite controls for ordination year, gender, and education. However, both the asset and liability value of prior occupational experience had disappeared after the entry placement while the effects of age did not, which suggests that the proxy value resides in the duration rather than the content of prior experience. In short, younger second-career clergy were found to be better positioned for higher attainment than their older counterparts.

Because age and gender both are considered to be key aspects of occupational segregation and discrimination, the interaction of gender with age can disproportionately penalize older women.[25] Age, then, expectedly would exacerbate whatever negative gender effects might occur. However, because of the significantly negative impact that gender has been found to have on clergy careers, older age may *appear* to have little impact on women, owing to the age effects becoming embedded in the suppressing effect of gender on attainment. Consequently older as well as younger women would be expected to have plateaued career trajectories more closely resembling the *maintenance* stage for most of their careers.[26]

The data support the traditional career-stage paradigm as a model of clergy mobility and attainment (Figure 6.1), although with some modifications. Older age negatively affected attainment in the second placement of U.U.A. ministers, but instead it negatively affected upward mobility of Episcopal priests (cf. Tables 4.3, and 4.4). Since the U.U.A. has less job stratification, age effects on attainment rather than mobility logically would be expected. In contrast, prospects for upward mobility in the more stratified Episcopal denomination become as important as attainment. That age constrains careers according to the key contingencies in each denomination suggests that its effects do influence occupational prospects for second-career men and women. However, the age breakpoint appears to differ by denomination and gender. For male ministers, ordination over age 50 severely

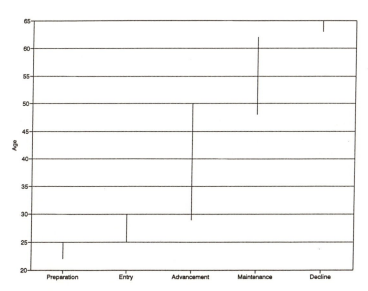

Figure 6.1 Career stages by normative age range. Based on
H. Newton Malony and Richard A. Hunt, *The Psychology of
Clergy* (Harrisburg, Pa.: Morehouse, 1991), 122–123; cf. Donald
E. Super, *The Psychology of Careers* (New York: Harper &
Brothers, 1957).

inhibited the likelihood of holding level 6 placements; for women ministers, the breakpoint was age 40. Male priests ordained through age 60 were able to obtain level 6 placements (e.g., rectorships), although few did so. Similarly, female priests ordained up to age 60 had substantive opportunities relative to their younger colleagues, although only one woman ordained over age 50 in the data held a placement higher than level 5.

For second-career clergy interested in holding a high-level denominational position, the prospects are less auspicious. Senior-level placements were strongly age as well as gender sensitive. In both the U.U.A. and the Episcopal Church, the median age at ordination was 27 for those who had held level 7 and higher placements. Of the male ministers who had such positions, all had been ordained before age 35; 73 percent had been ordained prior to age 30. Possibilities were more optimistic for Episcopal priests, since those having held senior-level placements ranged up to age 45 at ordination for men and age 43 for women. While second-career Episcopal clergy have a wider range of positions open to them including opportunities for denominational leadership than in the smaller, less stratified U.U.A., clergy ordained in their thirties in both denominations appear to have more substantive opportunities for attainment up the occupational job ladder.

While the careers of Episcopal and U.U.A. clergy tend to conform to the career trajectory pattern, they also challenge it. First, the data suggest that men interested in senior-level, denominational leadership positions constitute the only group for which the model's age boundaries are crucial. Second, Malony and Hunt designate the *maintenance* stage as beginning in the late forties, although the data suggest that it more likely may begin in the early fifties. Third, the traditional career pattern appears to be inadequate for predicting upward mobility and attainment among women clergy. Their lower level mobility and attainment regardless of age short-circuit the *advancement* stage. Irrespective of age, women's careers tend to resemble the *maintenance* stage shortly after their first placement. The greater likelihood of women being ordained at an older age than men in this analysis and in other multidenominational studies[27] supports the prospect of sharp gender segregation between female and male career paths. Additionally, where denominational officials use age norms for recommending clergy for placements, women become doubly disadvantaged.

The interacting gender and age bias of career-stage assessment raises a concern about why it persists in organizations officially open to female as well as male clergy. For instance, expectations that major career advancement should be completed shortly after age 40 directly conflict with women's primary child-bearing years and the consequent multiple commitments for child care that women disproportionately face.[28] Furthermore, since a woman bears the greater flexibility in marriage for geographic relocation based on her husband's career, for part-time or volunteer work so as to mesh with family responsibilities or the husband's attitude toward women working, and for assuming auxiliary roles for the sake of a spouse's occupation, nowhere more demanding than the classic minister's wife,[29] such commitments additionally constrain a woman's own career opportunities if not aspirations, especially during the *advancement* stage.

Where prior occupational experience may serve as a resource at career entry (cf. Table 3.6), first-career clergy having limited resources other than youth may perceive themselves at a disadvantage. This may be a valid assessment for Episcopal priests as well as U.U.A. ministers seeking higher level placements early in their careers, illustrated by an Episcopal deployment officer's comment that most congregations in his diocese were seeking a priest who could "walk on water," with skills well beyond the norm for clergy. He also emphasized the importance of maturity in recommending clergy for placements—a maturity he found more prevalent in second-career clergy. "Generally first career people haven't 'been around'; [but] the pews are full of people who *have* 'been around,'" he observed. But lack of maturity was equated by this officer with unemployment at any time other than at career entry—a perception which could work against older clergy who were out of the workforce prior to ordination and against women priests at any age who, in this research, were more likely to hold lower level positions subject to forced mobility, with the consequence of higher risk for at least short-term unemployment.

Despite the growing number of second-career clergy and the evidence from this analysis that they bring particular assets, such as substantial education and, for some denominations, prior occupational experience, interviews with deployment officials pointed out that several occupational stereotypes or *myths* about second-career clergy continue to govern thought and decision making. Several clergy regularly consulted on deployment decisions spoke negatively of "second and third career men" entering because they "just couldn't cut it" in business or their previous occupation, who were idealistic and had "become disappointed with the realities of life," or who were "sixties generation, still trying to find themselves." Older women were described as housewives "whose children are gone," "divorcees," or women who've been working around the church so long "they think they might as well run it."[30] Wilkes's interviewees recounted similar concerns, such as older seminarians who may be carrying "psychological baggage" from previous career frustrations and would not be "self-starters."[31] Similarly, Steinfels has reported denominational concerns that seminaries may be drawing applicants "unable to achieve success in secular careers."[32]

A second myth involving occupational viability was that second-career clergy would have second-rate careers. This too has been unsubstantiated in the data, with the exception of those ordained well beyond age 50 and the suppressing effect that gender has for women. That age produced mixed effects on career dynamics suggests that the deeper issue may be one of a difference between *normative* and *elite* careers. Normative careers, represented through mid-level positions (e.g., parish minister or rector), cannot be considered "second-class" nor do the data show an absence of opportunity for such positions among second-career clergy ordained by age 50. Additionally, Carroll et al. found age to be an asset for both female and male clergy in being able to work well with middle-aged laity and those in business occupations—the two demographic groups typically most influential within congregations.[33] The evidence does point to women—of any age—being significantly less likely to have a normative career, however. Similarly, elite careers were even more exclusive on the basis of gender than age.

A third myth involves concerns that second-career clergy will bring secular expectations in terms of higher salaries and benefits than congregations can afford. Secular organizations have hesitated to hire older employees, concerned that they would be harder to socialize and educate, would expect higher compensation, would make larger claims on employee benefits, particularly health and disability insurance, and likely would extract pension benefits sooner than workers anticipating a thirty or forty year career. As a result, younger workers have been perceived as a better investment.[34] Yet two deployment officials interviewed had remarked that in their experience the opposite was true. Older clergy were more willing to accept positions on traditional terms, including long hours, sometimes very difficult working conditions, and the likelihood of working for low compensation. Since second-career clergy are more likely to have some accumulated financial resources and retirement assets, they may be less dependent on the traditionally low wages of the occupation. Although it might be argued that employers feel a greater pressure to pay them more than younger males, or females of any age, it is possible that such pressure is self-imposed as a vestige of age-associating such clergy with the *advancement* or *maintenance* stages despite the recency of their ordination. Younger clergy more often challenged the occupation with salary and benefits expectations similar to those for secular professions, according to the deployment officials interviewed. "Generally younger clergy expect top pay when they come out of seminary," one official noted, then added that he had a folder of such clergy who still didn't have jobs.

One of the main issues underlying the persistence of occupational mythology may involve the lower potential of second-career clergy for exclusive socialization and investment in the traditional clergy norms within mainline denominations— norms set, dominated, and maintained by European-American men ordained overwhelmingly in their twenties. Additionally, female as well as older male seminarians are more likely, according to Larsen's study, to attend seminaries with moderate to liberal theological stances and, for those over age 40, to identify themselves as liberals.[35] Although Stone's research suggests that second-career men can be the most conservative of all seminarians,[36] their exposure to moderate and liberal scholarship on contemporary social issues may result in a substantial disparity between second-career men and their first-career colleagues more likely trained in conservative seminaries. Age, then, as well as gender and race, may induce a heterogeneity of experience and expectations by integrating insights and expertise from other careers and perspectives. Whether leaving behind expectations of a single-career norm that may have included warnings that their decision to change careers was not wise, of racial-role expectations particularly where one is a minority in a predominately European-American denomination, or of gender-role expectations that may have included explicit biases against their choice of a clergy career, clergy who have broken past socialization patterns present a dilemma for resocialization in tight conformity with traditional clergy norms and their supporting ideology.

Second-career socialization responses typically take one of two forms: either an individual tends to overconform as a means of becoming accepted, or one flexibly integrates denominational expectations with perspectives gained from personal experience resulting in strategic or negotiated conformity. Since occupational socialization among the latter is less easy to regulate, the persistence of occupational mythology among denominational officials may serve as a metaphor for the lower controllability and consequent decreased desirability of such clergy. Not unexpectedly, concerns for maintaining organizational tradition have been linked with early socialization into it.[37]

Perhaps, then, it is the socialization process when begun early in a career rather than chronological age itself that leads to the development of vested interests in tradition maintenance.[38] Schrank and Waring, avoiding the determinism implied in this argument, contend that the combination of older chronological age and substantial power, prestige, and knowledge of an organization also can lead to innovation and change,[39] illustrated by the progressive stance that some denominational leaders have taken on controversial issues such as women's ordination and human sexuality.[40] Nonetheless, the potential for ideological conflict between second-career clergy and those preoccupied with tradition maintenance is likely to be exacerbated as the concentration of men and particularly women ordained at an older age continues to increase, augmented by the ongoing retirements of clergy who were ordained primarily in their twenties.

The pluralism that second-career men, women and people from racially diverse backgrounds represent implicitly threatens a clergy class solidarity. Given the experience of second-career clergy as adult laity, it is realistically possible that they may identify more strongly with laity than would clergy ordained at an early age. In denominations where professional boundaries depend on strong clergy-laity distinctions, second-career clergy more likely would be expected to seek changes in an egalitarian direction, eroding clerical elitism and consequently exacerbating internal occupational strife.

One trend that may serve as a partial response to professional socialization concerns is the redeployment of retired clergy despite a strong supply of active clergy, such as in the Episcopal Church. That retired clergy, mostly ordained in their twenties, might share the same job pool for interim and part-time positions as active women clergy who, studies have shown, tend to be the most theologically liberal of all[41] suggests that the deployment of retirees might have a controlling effect on occupational conflict and change. Further implications of utilizing retired clergy as an alternative labor supply will be explored in chapter 8.

The ordained ministry is atypical among professions in that it presents some significant opportunities, even at moderate levels, for second-career entrants. As the U.S. labor market continues to eliminate more white-collar jobs than it creates[42] with the multiple-career trend predicted to continue, the relative attractiveness of the clergy as a second-career alternative should result in a persistent stream of candidates older than the traditional norm. The implications for religious organizations are profound when considering not only the traditional recruitment emphasis on young first-career men and a denominational leadership historically composed of such clergy but also the internal conflicts that are likely to ensue. Unfortunately the occupational prospects are not as optimistic for second-career female clergy, as gender presents an even greater occupational barrier than age. Yet as the supply of young men continues to dwindle, women are coming to represent an important if not commensurately valued source of clergy. Occupational tensions related to the continuing ordination of second-career men and women are likely to persist in the years ahead.

Lamentations: Where Have All the Young Men Gone?

Embedded in the rising age of new clergy over the last two decades is a sharp decline in the ratio of young men choosing the ordained ministry as their career.[43] Table 6.1 illustrates the dwindling percentages over the last sixty years of clergy ordained by age 30 in the two denominational samples. Since 1930, the ratio of Unitarian Universalist male ministers ordained by age 30 has declined nearly 60 percent while the ratio of young male priests has dropped about 80 percent. Table 6.2 depicts the decrease in Episcopal young single men seeking ordination, illustrating a shortage that rivals the deficits that the Roman Catholic Church has faced.[44] While some decrease in young men would have been expected after ending the military draft and the Vietnam conflict by 1975, the sharpest dip occurs between 1980 and 1990, well after these two events. Furthermore, Tables 6.1 and 6.2 suggest that the trend of fewer young men had appeared at least by 1970 among U.U.A. ministers and as early as 1940 among Episcopal priests. Since the Episcopal trend actually precedes the decline in mid- to senior-level attainment that first became apparent among men ordained in 1950 (cf. Figure 5.5), factors other than a decreased opportunity structure or increased access to higher education, much less women's ordination, must be involved. Because this aging trend of male ordinands doesn't appear in the Unitarian Universalist data prior to 1970, the reasons likely are particular to the Episcopal Church's larger denominational structure, where perhaps substantively greater need to recruit more clergy for vacancies in rural and socioeconomically less desirable locations and for missionary work has created both opportunities and occupational receptivity for older men. Additionally, that young men should be the fewest in the 1990 cohort, a year when young men's opportunities for attainment in the Episcopal data appear to be greater than in the previous two decades, and in the U.U.A. data are at least

Table 6.1. Percentage of Episcopal Priests and Unitarian Universalist Ministers Ordained by Age 30 for Selected Years, 1920–1990.

Cohort	Episcopal		Unitarian Universalist	
	Men	Women	Men	Women
1990	18	12	31	33
1980	51	29	62	44
1970	65	13	68	100
1950	67		86	100
1940	72		88	—
1930	96		75	100
1920	100			
(N)	(582)	(177)	(71)	(40)

Ages for the U.U.A. sample were constructed (see Table 3.3).
The U.U.A. women's cohorts were small for 1970 (N = 2), 1950 (N = 1), and 1930 (N = 1).

Table 6.2. Percentage of All Episcopal Male Priests who were Ordained by Age 30, According to Marital Status for Selected Years, 1920–1990.

Cohort	(N)	Single at ordination	Never married	Married after ordination	Married at ordination
1990	(99)	2	2	0	16
1980	(140)	19	7	12	31
1970	(159)	19	8	11	45
1950	(129)	30	14	16	36
1940	(25)	52	4	48	20
1930	(25)	76	4	72	20
1920	(5)	80	0	80	20
(N)	(582)				

The percentages in columns 3 and 6 total the percentage of column 2 in Table 6.1, except where rounding off has resulted in slight discrepancies.

comparable with previous years, suggests that decreases in occupational opportunities likely are not responsible for the dwindling supply of young men. Just as easily, the recent decline could be the result of the drop in church membership during the 1970s; with fewer youth exposed to sustained denominational influence, the ordained ministry less likely would be considered as a career option in early adulthood.[45]

The declining supply of young men also raises a question about the extent to which the clergy as an occupation remains attractive or viable. Compared to other professions, such as medicine or law, which also expect a three-year advanced degree, one or more years of internship, a written or oral examination, a credentialing process that includes an oath or vow, and an orientation toward human caring or justice, clergy traditionally have been very poorly paid. Additionally, clergy compensation has continued to decline relative to these other professions.[46] The twofold relative decline in compensation and clergy prestige, which historically served to offset low wages, raises a serious concern about occupational viability for young people who are less likely than second-career clergy to have other financial assets. For instance, the average student loan debt of graduating seminarians nationwide was $19,000 in 1993.[47] Furthermore, once ordained, most denominations do not assure full-time placements.

Attempts to standardize clergy compensation have met with resistance by congregations, which often have negotiated compensation based upon what they were able to pay and what the market would bear. Part of the impetus for standardization has been to make congregations aware of the gap in their perception that clergy are well paid, despite evidence that clergy earnings are usually lower than that of their membership.[48] For instance, in 1990 the average U.U.A. ministerial salary and housing package was $32,479 while nearly one-third of the membership earned more than $40,000 per year.[49] Whereas men have traditionally tended to equate occupational success with income,[50] perceived downward socioeconomic mobility in relation to laity expectedly would have a twofold negative effect on clergy prestige and male morale. Standardization furthermore would benefit those at the low end of the pay scale—often disproportionately female and minority-race clergy[51]—while depressing compensation for those at the high end. Understandably, then, movements toward salary standardization would contribute to a decreased economic attractiveness for those clergy most likely to cluster in well-paying positions: men ordained at an early age.

The perception remains that the decline in young male candidates has been precipitated by the influx of women, generating a mood of "clergy crisis" among some denominational leadership. Not only can the large influx of women clergy not be a causal variable in the decline, but it also has not significantly affected men's competition for mid- to higher level placements, according to the data of this analysis. Buchanan discusses a linkage between masculinity and institutional vitality in the mind of Episcopal Church leaders that is not unreminiscent of the masculine revitalization movement among Unitarian clergy at the turn of the century.[52] With the traditional measures of institutional vitality being membership growth and increased budgets, the decline in mainline denominational membership since 1970 and budgets that have become increasingly strained not only neatly parallel recent declines in young male clergy and the increasing ratios of women, but have become linked as a perceived causal relationship by many denominational leaders. Furthermore, where institutional masculinity has been dependent on the notion of male virility, as well as an absence of occupational feminization, the twofold preoccupation with institutional and occupational decline evident in most mainline denominations in recent years becomes more understandable. The emphasis since 1980 on evangelism and revitalization movements, frequently called *renewal*, underscores this linkage, particularly where these factors have tended toward reaffirmation of male-dominant gender roles.

Accompanying the most recent wave of revitalization movements has been the chorus of lamentations over *declines in leadership* and the *loss of the best and the brightest* candidates for ministry. Illustrating the linkage between these two trends, Nester points out that concerns for renewal have led to an attitude, in the United Methodist Church, that "things would be going well if only our pastors had 'leadership' abilities."[53] Embedded in such laments is a twofold assumption that "leadership" and "the best and the brightest" are associated with being male and ordained at an early age. The preoccupation with a perceived declining quality, as well as quantity of ministerial candidates, also commonly has been expressed with phrases such as the "norm [having] slipped" and "top intellectuals" not enrolling in seminaries. Such normative slippages seem to constitute (1) a declining number of young male clergy, (2) a recent decline in entry and second placement levels from those of clergy ordained in 1950 and earlier, and (3) somewhat lower prospects for career attainment among men, especially in opportunities to hold senior leadership positions. Yet religious leaders have admitted that their perceptions tend to be based as much on intuition as on any statistical evidence, and that what is meant by "quality" has yet to be defined.[54] Evidence from this analysis shows an *increase* rather than a decline in the level of education brought to the clergy, when excluding those in the newer, alternative ordination tracks. Additionally, with clergy ordained over age 40 bringing additional advanced degrees and expertise, as the data have shown, one legitimately may question which sector of "the best and the brightest" has been lost.

Tests to identify a decline in "the best and the brightest" in this analysis were made in two ways: first, by comparing clergy who hold undergraduate degrees from elite colleges and universities; and second, by comparing those clergy who either graduated with honors or were elected to an academic honor society.[55] Overall, the ratio of men and women with degrees from elite schools has not significantly changed since 1970, in either sample. While young male Episcopal priests ordained between 1950 and 1975 were more likely than second-career men ordained the same years to have graduated from elite schools, these were the only cohorts to show any relationship between age and elite education for either men or women. Among U.U.A. clergy, age made no difference in elite educational background for any male or female cohort.

The ratio of male priests who either hold degrees with honors or belong to an academic honor society (Phi Beta Kappa was the most common) shows no decline over time (Table 6.3). This information was not available for the U.U.A. sample. Furthermore, with the highest concentrations of *young* men with such credentials occurring in the 1980 and 1990 cohorts, the data suggest that while the volume of young men has declined significantly, their academic talent—which can be an indicator of "the best and the brightest" status—has if anything risen over time.[56] While the elite credentials are similar between men and women priests ordained in 1980 and later, the exceptionally high concentration of women with such credentials ordained during the 1970s suggests that the first decade of women priests represented a disproportionate concentration of "the best and the brightest."

The influx of women and second-career men also has bridged the gap between a smaller pool of young male seminarians and the available educational resources of many North American seminaries. The importance of these newer demographic sources of seminarians is readily apparent to theological educators and, on the whole, to their sponsoring religious organizations. The disparity between the demographic tradition for denominational ministerial committees (i.e., young and male) and the demographic reality of those attending seminary today has created substantial tension between denominations and their seminaries, particularly where the latter have disproportionately high concentrations of women and

Table 6.3. Percentage of Episcopal Priests Holding a Degree with Honors or Membership in an Academic Honor Society, 1920–1990.

Cohort	Men Ordained by Age 30	All Men	All Women
1990	17	4	4
1985	3	5	5
1980	13	8	6
1975	4	5	10
1970	6	5	13
1950	4	2	
1940	11	12	
1930	8	8	
1920	0	0	
(N)	(432)	(843)	(299)

second-career men. Denominations have criticized seminary standards for admission, and put pressure on seminaries to raise them without concurrently offering additional financial support to bridge the deficit that otherwise would result.[57] Underlying this tension between denominations and seminaries is the conflict between denominational committees seeking to control the candidate and seminary selection process, and seminarians who become ordained via the *back door*. It is not uncommon for seminarians, particularly women, to enter in a nonordination track degree program and then decide to seek ordination prior to graduation. Additionally, many women who have encountered gender prejudice in their own region or diocese have attended seminaries in more liberal judicatories, entering the ordination process there. While denominations may deny ordination to any applicant, they are more hard-pressed to do so if applicants have done well academically and have succeeded in their seminary field placements. Furthermore, with evidence that women and second-career men are more likely to attend theologically moderate and liberal seminaries,[58] this constituency would represent both a demographic and an ideological challenge to denominational ministerial committees concerned with tradition maintenance, institutional vitality, and increasing the proportion of young male clergy.

Trends most likely to facilitate an increase in the ratio of young men would be a sharp growth spurt in denominational membership, offering substantial opportunities for autonomy and influence early in clergy careers; either increased compensation for the clergy or a relative decline in earnings among other professions; increased use of technology within religious organizations and the clergy; and renewed public leadership visibility that rejuvenates the prestige value of the clergy.[59] For instance, the recent masculinization of nursing has had much to do with increased potential earnings relative to occupations requiring similar amounts of training, with expanded opportunities that encroach on fields traditionally reserved for physicians, with the development of a new body of knowledge and expertise no longer entirely dependent on that taught in medical schools, and a consequent fresh articulation of the occupation's self-definition as a profession. Precipitating this change, during the early 1980s many women had left or avoided nursing altogether for more lucrative occupations, resulting in an ensuing shortage relative to the growing demand for health care, which elevated salaries. According to Kilborn, wages for registered nurses by 1988 were as high as $50,000 annually in large metropolitan areas.[60] Additionally, the reskilling and reprofessionalization of nursing have included a renewed emphasis on high levels of education and training that augment a hierarchicalization likely to provide sufficient status, as well as authority and prestige differentials, for those at the top. Men's growing entry into nursing predictably has resulted in a disproportionate concentration of men in high-level positions.[61] From this example, movements to remasculinize the clergy likely would benefit men more than women.

Conservative Protestant denominations have been less affected by a declining supply of young men. The invigorated political stance of many such organizations since the late 1970s, as well as a receptivity to applying technological advances in electronic media and music in a way that appeals to the sensibilities of a youth culture, has resulted in a resurgence of opportunities for young male leadership in thriving churches with expansive budgets and attractive salaries. In such organizations, the role of women also has been more explicitly delimited, with tight controls if not exclusion of female clergy and lay leaders seeking ministries other than to women and children. Additionally, in a secular job market that holds little promise for male or female college graduates, to step into fast-track positions offering substantial opportunities for organizational and political influence offered by some conservative Protestant religious organizations, young men with religious inclinations have a highly desirable alternative to secular work.

It is less likely that the church will hold a strong attraction for large numbers of young men in mainline denominations. Overall projected increases in clergy jobs and earnings are expected to be *average* between 1990 and 2005, with a 9 percent growth rate projected over this period.[62] Furthermore, full-time placements and opportunities for upward mobility are expected to become increasingly more competitive in coming years, as rising costs and inadequate finances limit both clergy compensation and opportunities for advancement.[63] Since studies on secular occupations have identified the percentage of women to be negatively tied to earnings,[64] the increased ratios of women being ordained and willing to accept depressed compensation likely will continue. Furthermore, as Reskin and Roos have observed for secular occupations that have feminized, declining opportunities for upward mobility, increased training costs without compensatory increases in salary, and feminist challenges to the type of practices that have fast-tracked men into leadership tend to diminish occupational attractiveness for men.[65] Yet simply attempting to weed out the women and second-career clergy will not increase the supply of young men, and can risk further depleting religious organizations of talented and productive clergy.

While the exodus of young men from the ordained ministry and priesthood has been strongly lamented over the last decade, nowhere has the arrival of second-career or women clergy been celebrated. The structural biases of religious organizations and their constituencies become conspicuous. The crux of the issue may be fear of the loss of power over organizational maintenance, oftentimes conflated with the concept of tradition and the privilege that such power has bestowed on men. That laments over the loss of those who historically have been counted upon for tracking and grooming into leadership placements—in what Peterson and Schoenherr have termed a "crown prince" system[66]—tend to come from the very constituencies who themselves have benefited most from that tradition cannot be ignored. Neither can the potential for change that clergy with other socialization experiences, perceptions, interests, and theological exposures—namely, women and second-career men—bring with them to the profession. The responses have ranged from resistance through outright exclusion, organizational co-optation, job segregation, and restructuring of the religious organization itself in order to utilize women's labor while preserving male control over interpretations and formulations that traditionally have served to legitimate the social order of its constituency. These issues will be discussed further in the next two chapters.

In sum, the third and fourth hypotheses were supported in this section of the analysis. *Not only was there further evidence that occupational change preceded the sharp influx of women clergy during the 1970s and that male clergy careers were* more affected by changes stemming from causes preceding rather than following the sharp influx of women, but the decline in young male clergy has little to do with occupational feminization. Additionally, in accord with the sixth hypothesis, trends toward occupational feminization in the clergy appear to be consistent with feminization trends in secular occupations, including implications for women in occupational remasculinization efforts.

~· Seven ·~

Feminization and Backlash

Of the challenges facing women clergy, one of the most frustrating has been the growing backlash against their presence in many religious organizations, as much through passive occupational restructuring as through overt resistance. Not uncommonly, occupational authority and socioeconomic rewards are restructured, either *externally* to other occupations or influential status groups or *internally* through occupational reconfiguration, job partitioning, or de-skilling of various jobs.[1] Consequently, feminization has come to imply a set of symptomatic changes, mostly of an adverse socioeconomic or political nature, not only for men but particularly for women who either remain in the occupation or subsequently enter it.

Gender backlash in ministry has arisen in waves across time and historical circumstance. Both liberal and conservative denominations experienced its force against the strides that women had made during the nineteenth century, particularly in missionary work and in breaking into ordained ministry. Of explicit concern to denominational leadership at the close of the century had been a perceived decline in male participation, causally interpreted as a diminishment in organized religion's masculine vitality. According to Douglas, the nineteenth century had witnessed a decline of the male-dominant theological tradition in liberal Protestantism without the concurrent rise of a sustained and comprehensive feminism that could provide an embracing ideological alternative. Out of that void came the most vocal laments from clergy over the loss of "religion in the old virile sense," in the words of Henry James, Sr.[2] Such commiseration brought a resurgence in masculine idealization and a reassertion of male authority.[3] Observes Tucker, "The Unitarian leadership, thinking that it could recover its lost institutional vigor by building a 'manlier' ministry, strengthened its central office in Boston and did its best to dislodge female clergy while blocking others from joining them."[4] As chapter 1 pointed out, some denominations also discouraged women from ministerial careers or revoked their opportunities for ordination altogether.

Another wave of backlash, gathering strength in the wake of the 1920 passage of the Nineteenth Amendment to the U.S. Constitution, which granted the vote to women, took a toll on women clergy. According to Tucker, many women left the ministry as a result of discrimination by their denomination and indifference in the parish.[5] Backlash to women clergy was even more virulent and sustained in conservative Evangelical and Pentecostal Protestantism. Barfoot and Sheppard attribute a shift in the symbolic function of Pentecostal religious leadership during the 1920s from *prophet* to *priest* as the catalyst for a rapid decline of women in leadership positions,[6] exemplifying how bureaucratization can be utilized as a structural backlash response. Such reactions may be triggered in part by a need to strengthen and solidify male control of the religious organization, either to manage increased growth and prosperity or to minimize potential erosion of its religious market share, combined with apprehension that females could not be as effective in such organizationally vital roles.[7] In 1931, the Assemblies of God restricted women's ordination altogether to evangelistic ministry, reserving the administrative and ritual ordinances exclusively for men.[8]

The backlash against women clergy was sustained by the Depression, with women finding increased difficulty in obtaining salaried placements or holding onto them if a male were available. Women's ministry during these years took on a characteristic pattern of assuming nearly defunct congregations, rebuilding them, and subsequently losing their leadership to male ministers once the congregations were financially viable.[9] Women interested in pursuing a religious vocation were encouraged to pursue fields such as music or religious education, or to train as lay parish assistants. During the 1930s, according to Bendroth, fundamentalist religious organizations marginalized women to auxiliaries which were substantially narrower in social concerns than had been their nineteenth-century counterparts.[10] Even in the most liberal denominations this trend was evident. Of the eight Unitarian and Universalist women originally identified in this analysis as ordained or licensed in 1930, seven soon dropped out. A decade later, in 1940, no women were ordained and fellowshipped in either denomination.

Ratios of women ministers also declined among groups originally founded by women, such as Aimee Semple McPherson's International Church of the Foursquare Gospel. Two-thirds of the ordained ministers had been female when she died in 1944, but by 1978 the female ratio had declined to 42 percent.[11] Similarly in other denominations where women had played strongly inspirational roles in their founding, the ratio of women leaders declined. Despite Phoebe Palmer's early importance to the leadership of Church of the Nazarene, women pastors had declined from about 20 percent in 1908 to 6 percent by 1973.[12]

With the post–World War II growth in denominational membership and consequent demand for clergy, opportunities opened up for ordained women during the 1950s and 1960s. But as denominational growth plateaued and mainline membership levels began a precipitous decline from their 1960s peak, some religious organizations, including the Episcopal Church, which in 1970 had opened the ordained diaconate to women, faced clergy oversupply. Additionally, feminist concerns for equal rights were being pushed within mainline denominations as elsewhere, catalyzing an influx of women into seminaries and into the ordination process. During the late 1970s and early 1980s, the rapid rise in the ratio of women being ordained in U.S. mainline denominations, as well as sustained pressure for inclusive language and equal opportunity, had incited another wave of backlash.

The current backlash may be reaching full force, as the overall ratio of female clergy continues to rise with ongoing male clergy retirements. Some religious organizations, such as the U.S. Southern Baptist Convention, the Presbyterian Church of Australia, the Evangelical Lutheran Church of Latvia, and the Christian Reformed Church in America, either have reversed or failed to ratify earlier policies supporting women's ordination as a result of ultraconservative factions gaining support and eventual dominance of denominational agendas.[13] Other denominations, such as the Lutheran Church of Australia and the U.S. Episcopal Church, have experienced renegade synods and schisms over denominational support for women clergy and, more recently, women bishops.[14] At its 1994 General Convention, the Episcopal Church passed a resolution weakening the church canon (III.8.1) that had guaranteed access to ordination without regard to gender by formally acknowledging for the first time as a recognized church position the theological legitimacy of those who either explicitly oppose or support women's ordination.[15]

Nielsen claims that women's power is more likely to be challenged while it is still growing, prior to consolidation.[16] Essentially a defensive posture, backlash represents a complex movement manifested in different ways among various constituencies. Chafetz and Dworkin argue that backlash emerges when a movement has grown sufficiently large or successful that it is seen as a threat to both material and status interests of those in either organizational or cultural positions of power and privilege.[17] This may explain why gender concerns persist long after women have been formally acknowledged as fully competent to gain and maintain access to positions of responsibility and authority. For women clergy, the *good news* that backlash movements offer is that women have made sufficient cultural and organizational strides in challenging the prevailing norms that they are perceived as a significant force to fend off. In short, their inroads have dealt a serious blow to the dominance and control of those heavily invested in maintaining the ideological assumptions and vocational norms that have undergirded access to religious leadership. But the *bad news* of such movements means that for women clergy not to lose occupational or ideological ground, they must work as concertedly as they had done to gain original access to ordination, including sizable collaboration with supportive constituencies. According to Cockburn, successful equal opportunity policy has meant that women must "confront head-on men's sense of owning the organization."[18]

Four common types of backlash appear in the contemporary struggles that women clergy face. The first comes from those nostalgic for what they believe the clergy—and the religious organization—once represented, usually a perceived universe in which they either were dominant or, if in a subordinate position, knew how to obtain passive access to power. A second type of backlash appears from previous supporters who passively begin to undermine the backing that they had given women when they were few in number and more politically vulnerable. A third type involves those deeply concerned about potential loss of dominance where women venture beyond what they have determined is their *place,* while a fourth comes from those unsupportive all along but now perceive growing support for their adversarial position.

The first backlash, from nostalgic constituencies, can be comparatively benign, often more concentrated in negative comments than in direct action. Either those within the clergy who preceded the large influx of women or others who nostalgically wish for a return to the "good old days," when clergymen and their denominations held mythic portions of public authority and prestige, may tend to blame the women's influx into the clergy for an array of occupational ills that, according to the previous two chapters, displayed pathological symptoms well prior to women's sizable presence. Such comments are grist for other forms of backlash, including perceived support and increased momentum for overt action against women.

A second, more efficacious form of backlash comes from well-meaning supporters who gain the trust of women through having helped them achieve access but who subsequently seek to limit or stifle their achievement.[19] Such individuals are considered to be structural underminers. Like the nostalgic constituencies, such men seldom choose direct confrontation with women, preferring instead tactics that undermine their efforts while appearing to be supportive colleagues. In a situation affecting one of the women priests in this analysis, an Episcopal rector seeking only female candidates for a part-time assistant position in his parish rejected this woman, considered by her female colleagues as only a lukewarm feminist, on the basis that she seemed "too angry." This phrase turned out repeatedly to be a metaphor used by older, moderate-to-liberal men for women who admit to feminist views or, not smiling enough, appear not sufficiently deferential. Cockburn documents negative attributions by men in secular occupations against women who become "more sparing with the smiles."[20] "If you are too strident they hang you in the wind and leave you to dry," commented one female priest in the 1990 cohort who was interviewed for this analysis. She then added, "On the other hand, if you have half a brain, it's hard not to be strident."

Cowan's study of female rabbis shows that they have faced similar difficulties in being labeled "troublemakers" if they are assertive, while men are rewarded for similar behavior.[21] Women consequently become caught in the bind of being unable to have legitimate access to the same behavior as their male colleagues for dealing with situations involving bigotry, discrimination, tokenism, and absence of mentors and role models, as well as a lack of socialization that has produced for men a sense of social entitlement. This bind can be far more politically complex and potentially devastating than those situations that European-American men typically encounter. Men would call such a context emasculating, terminology that descriptively fits the male bias affecting women, racial minorities, or other nondominant groups. At the same time, women perceived as passive tend not to be given serious consideration for sole pastorates or mid- to senior-level placements.

Another version of structural undermining involves those who appear personally concerned when women experience occupational advancement. For instance, women interviewed by the Episcopal Committee on the Status of Women claimed that, while many men believed they were supportive of women, they became resistant when women sought to move away from subordinate positions,[22] a theme echoed in interviews with women clergy for this analysis. Mentorship of women clergy clearly seems not to include grooming for leadership positions, unlike many mentorship arrangements for men.

An abusive variant is that group considered to be personal underminers—men who prey on women one-by-one in situations where women are dependent on them, and who pretend to be women's ally all the while undercutting their opportunities. A woman priest interviewed for this analysis, part of the 1990 cohort, recounted how her diocesan deployment officer, who had been hired partly because of his open-mindedness about women's ordination, subsequently told her as she was seeking work that he wouldn't forward her paperwork to a parish looking for a rector because they weren't ready for a woman. From an informal network she heard a very different story from a member of the parish's search committee, who encouraged her to apply.

Yet another form of backlash comes from a male constituency less overtly supportive of women with a strong desire to maintain control of privileged access and attainment that their male gender attribution has given them. This is the arena where open conflicts are most likely to emerge, and where *the rules are changed* as women seek to enter positions considered desirable by men. Connell has argued that heterosexual men articulate their sexual politics in institutionalized forms, such as bureaucratic procedures or the manipulation of labor market structures and processes.[23] An explicit example of how such politics highlight the struggle to maintain gender dominance is the *conscience clause* instituted in the Episcopal Church when women's ordination to the priesthood was approved, as a means to minimize possible schism by opponents.[24] Stendahl has argued that the conscience clause over women's ordination adopted by the (Lutheran) Church of Sweden in 1958 had facilitated an overt resistance against women clergy that continued until 1982, when it was dropped.[25] The Episcopal Church's 1988 passage of an *episcopal visitor* provision to allow parishes to utilize the services of an alternative bishop rather than their own, occurring immediately prior to the election and consecration of the denomination's first female bishop, provides another example. Effectively, the move eroded the bishop's ecclesial authority, and it was repealed in 1991. The formation of a maverick synod (Episcopal Synod of America) of disaffected parishes and dioceses wishing to be free from possible oversight by a female bishop was also allowed. More organizational change occurred in 1994, when the General Convention, with one woman diocesan and two women suffragan bishops, amended the Episcopal Church constitution to limit the number of suffragan bishops that a diocese could elect.[26] Similarly, following the 1992 United Methodist Church General Conference, when three more women were elected to the episcopate, denominational discussion erupted over the need to reassess and perhaps change the way in which bishops were elected.[27] Each organizational change technically hasn't denied women access, but it effectively has abraded their opportunities and acceptance.

Other instances have involved clergy hiring practices. A female interim rector interviewed for this analysis recently was called by the parish to become its permanent rector, in a situation similar to that which had occurred with one of her male colleagues less than a year earlier. In her case, however, a furor within the male leadership of the diocese ensued, pressuring the parish to recant its call. The parish refused to do so and hired her anyway. Shortly afterward, a diocesan policy was issued against any further hiring of interim clergy as permanent rectors. Subsequently, a male associate was appointed "in-charge" rather than "interim," so that he could then be called as rector. A similar "no succession to senior minister" rule in the Presbyterian Book of Order has been argued to work against women moving above associate or interim positions.[28] Since women have had to demonstrate their skills in situations where congregations had no prior role models, and since Carroll et al. found that recognition of women's ministerial competency remains individualized rather than generalized into a more enthusiastic attitude toward subsequently hiring women,[29] the interim-to-rectorship can be a far more critical means of access for women than men. Additionally, since interim placements are one of the primary modes of access for women seeking to move beyond a staff-level position, according to the data for this analysis, a restructuring of the rules by which interim clergy are deployed effectively cuts off another means of women's access to higher level placements.

Backlash also comes from a male constituency that has been directly unsupportive of female clergy from the outset, and that has formally maintained as much distance as possible from them. Unlike the more passive aggressive tactics of the "underminers" and the "rule changers," this constituency willingly takes the offensive in developing and sustaining confrontation verbally aimed at re-excluding women clergy. While their arousal can come as a sudden outburst in an emotionally charged situation, typically a conflict is strategically chosen where passive support from the other backlash constituencies can be counted upon. Such a constituency is reminiscent of the resistant minority against women clergy that Lehman found in his Presbyterian study to have a disproportionately powerful voice in church affairs.[30] Tactics have been applied especially vigorously in religious organizations where the legitimacy of women's ordination has been reopened to question. This male constituency less likely consists of those men considered to be the "best and the brightest," but rather whose primary credential for occupational attainment over women has been their male gender attribution and who may be the most at risk not only in occupational competition with women but also in being supervised by women. Where the ability to exercise power over others interacts with gender subordination in the construction of male identity, men perceiving themselves as having little power in relation to other men likely would be even more concerned about a lack of power over women.[31] As Lehman and others have documented, the greatest resistance to female clergy has come from male clergy, particularly those closer to a peer level.[32]

Undergirding the political divisiveness and the ensuing backlash against women within many religious organizations today appears to be a desire for preserving authority and entitlement among a ruling group. Lehman's research on women clergy identifies a "maintenance dynamic," where organizations rationalize their actions in terms of maintaining the present structure at the cost of competing interests that potentially could change it.[33] This also has been a basis for charges of heresy. Since those in positions of dominance are more likely to resist change that poses a direct threat, an appeal to the authority of scripture sets up an objective intransigence that allows proponents of resistance to refrain from taking personal responsibility for their views.[34] Rather, such proponents may become *defenders of the faith*. Where religious tenets have been utilized to maintain and enforce traditional justifications of male dominance, then it is not unlikely that various arenas of change, such as inclusive language, process and feminist theologies, and progressive stances on social issues involving gender and human sexuality, as well as the increasing presence of women in roles of at least limited denominational authority, suggest multiple targets for a backlash oriented toward tradition maintenance. As the proliferation of women signifies change in numbers if not in organizational dominance, substantial socialization pressure may be put upon men to support tradition maintenance as a condition of hiring or promotion, as Stendahl found occurring in the Church of Sweden.[35] Furthermore, where tradition maintenance can be handled effectively at senior leadership levels, typically through means such as undermining or rule changing, the detonation tactics of the more overtly hostile group are less likely to flourish. But when the challenge to tradition maintenance becomes sufficiently pervasive, and the overtly hostile constituency perceives support from other constituencies, open conflict is more likely to emerge.[36]

Complicating the struggle over authority and dominance is the necessity for a subordinate constituency, not only to define by contrast those who are dominant but to serve their needs and to undertake the labor that they would prefer not to do. As Cockburn points out, "Men subordinate women but are dependent upon this subject woman they have created."[37] Other interpretations of men's dependency on women have alluded to a male fear of a latent power that women are attributed to have. For instance, Bendroth cites fundamentalist comments such as men being made to commit sin, or become weak, because of women—phrases which echo similar pronouncements against women in Christianity's early centuries.[38]

Women form yet another constituency involved in backlash movements. Ammerman points to the clash between traditionalist and moderate Southern Baptist women over support for female pastors.[39] Such women may hold traditionalist perspectives about male supremacy and resent the encroachment of female clergy into placements where women, rather than men, have either direct authority or leadership responsibility over them. As Chafetz and Dworkin observe, female incursion into male positions represents a status threat to antifeminist women.[40] This was apparently the case following the election of the first Episcopal female diocesan bishop, Mary Adelia McLeod, part of the 1980 cohort of this analysis. At her consecration ceremony, Jane Shipman, representing the ultra-traditionalist Episcopal Synod of America, read a protest statement that asserted that, "the present ungodly rage of feminism has swept aside the biblical, historical and theological issues of headship and obedience for the language of equal rights,

self-fulfillment, empowerment, the jargon of the secular world. . . . If you ordain this woman, you will have to answer before the throne of God."[41] Episcopal
Presiding Bishop Edmund Browning proceeded with consecrating McLeod.
Where women wield substantial influence but defer to men as authority figureheads, women's access to power depends on a clear subordinate role where
there is no risk of competition with men or potential for backlash. The presence of
women clergy upset such a balance. Furthermore, given the subordinate status of
women in the church, the work of lay women risks losing prestige when done in
the same environment as that of women clergy. Yet while Carroll et al. had found
that lay women rather than men tended to give women clergy the most overt
resistance, they also observed that this was the constituency most likely to experience positive attitude change toward women's ordination following the departure
of the female minister.[42] As a result, women unlike men involved in backlash
movements represent a more volatile constituency—one over which men must
maintain constant vigilance and control to ensure conformity.

Backlash battles and end-run skirmishes may utilize intimidation, patroniza-
tion, and trivialization among other tactics, but what has made the "underminers"
and "rule changers" so dangerous to women's opportunities has been the co-
optation of women to accomplish their ends—from gaining control of lay women's
missionary societies early in this century[43] to contemporary decisions about ordaining and deploying women clergy. Additionally, indifference over how structural changes in religious organizations may negatively affect women, as well as
men of color, can produce the same effects as overt backlash campaigns.

Structural backlash, catalyzed by tight economic conditions within religious
organizations interacting with wider economic trends, can result in a requisite
sacrifice of one or more constituencies over others. Chafetz points out that sustained political conflict typically results in shifts toward traditional values and
gender roles that hold gender equality and inclusiveness movements responsible
for the current socioeconomic conditions.[44] Lehman's research suggests a trend
toward opposition to women clergy typically surfacing at those points where congregational or organizational viability is perceived to be at stake.[45] Where men
truly fear losing control of religious leadership or their religious organization
altogether, despite whether their reason is a strategic concern over matters of male
privilege, altruistic doubt that religion would maintain its socioeconomic "staying
power" under female leadership, or theological conviction that the organization's
socioeconomic malaise is the result of divine repercussions against women in
positions of leadership, requisite sacrifices can be deemed both necessary and for
the good of the organization. The sacrificial group either may be targeted or,
because of its more vulnerable social location, merely be caught in a riptide of
various changes necessitated by socioeconomic stringency. The dynamics of reor-
ganizing clergy work into new horizontal and vertical forms whereby women
become disproportionately concentrated into lower level and marginal sectors is a
form of structural backlash. It also holds important implications for how male
dominance is structurally maintained through the gendered redivision of labor,
which will be explored in the remaining sections of the chapter.

Proliferation of New Ordination Tracks

Job differentiation as part of occupational restructuring lends itself to being utilized as part of a process of backlash. Wrote Weber, "priesthoods have always, in an interesting shift of roles and also in the interests of traditionalism, protected patriarchalism against impersonal relationships of dependence."[46] The process of occupational differentiation and hierarchicalization has benefited those in positions of privilege by allowing them to focus or specialize in certain tasks, while delegating those tasks that are less important, prestigious, or desirable.[47] Such a process has resulted in the proliferation of new positions, evident in both the Episcopal and U.U.A. data of this analysis. For instance, of all Unitarian Universalist job titles held by ministers ordained in 1970 and later, 54 percent were not found among any ministers ordained in 1950 and earlier. Similarly, 46 percent of all job titles held by Episcopal priests ordained in 1970 and afterward were not found in the 1950 and earlier cohorts. While Episcopal men ordained in 1940 and earlier had averaged seven or fewer different entry job titles, and those ordained in 1950 and 1970 averaged fourteen titles, among clergy ordained in 1990 there were twenty-four distinct entry job titles in the data.

Differentiation also facilitates the development of specialized labor supplies—which become skewed not only demographically but also organizationally in terms of who fills which positions. Coinciding with the diminished supply of young men, new labor supplies—namely, women and older men—have filled auxiliary positions while those placements most likely to lead to high-level attainment disproportionately continue to be occupied by men ordained at an early age.

Occupational differentiation also is manifested in the proliferation of multiple ordination tracks in both denominations of this analysis. The trend toward female gender segregation in the new ordination tracks has been particularly sensitive to the increasing ratio of women clergy overall, which was shown in chapter 3. Furthermore, sharp educational discrepancies were found to appear between the newer and traditional tracks, with clergy ordained in the traditional tracks—U.U.A. minister and Episcopal priest—holding significantly higher levels of education. Despite denominational descriptions of the newer tracks as distinct and equivalent ministries, this analysis shows them to be serving distinct but subordinate occupational functions to those of the traditional track.

Unitarian Universalist Association

The development of additional ordination tracks in the U.U.A. chronologically coincides with the increase in ordained women. Two specialized ordained ministries have been developed: the *minister of religious education*, instituted in 1981, and the *community minister*, in 1992. The latter was developed for clergy wanting nonstipendiary ministries recognized within the church. Such clergy might work in organizations involving advocacy or social services; hospital, school, or military chaplaincies; or pastoral or therapeutic counseling. The U.U.A. had experimented with such ministries in the late 1960s and early 1970s, but they were discontinued because of the difficulty in developing standard criteria for evaluating them. Although over 50 percent of the community ministers listed in the 1993 *U.U.A. Directory* (N = 14) were female, the two clergy in the data ordained as community ministers were male.[48] There has been some concern that community ministers would be held in lower esteem by parish ministers, thus differentially affecting their ordination status.[49] In the data, their education and initial placements didn't differ substantively from other ministers. However, it is still too early to discern whatever direction this ordination track may be taking, or its potential effect on clergy career opportunities.

MINISTER OF RELIGIOUS EDUCATION   Beginning in 1981, the minister of religious education became an ordained status eligible for U.U.A. fellowship. This step, coinciding with the point where the majority of all new ordinands with U.U.A. fellowship had been female for the previous three years, formally represented yet another stride in the professionalization of religious education by replacing the director of religious education certification program that had been created in 1967 to formally recognize "qualified religious educators."[50] The field of religious education, once a male stronghold, had feminized during the Depression. While the loss of jobs, decline in salaries, and conflation of religious education with secretarial, administrative, and other congregational tasks occurring at the advent of the Depression had disproportionately discouraged young men in the field, Furnish points out that other professional issues that had been building throughout the 1920s came to a head with the economic collapse at the end of the decade. Those involved intensified competition over authority between a congregation's pastor and religious education director, congregational feelings that the professional religious educator was out of touch with their needs, and an emergent neo-orthodox theology that scorned the earlier generation's philosophical perspective of education and science being the core of sociomoral and religious salvation. By 1938, women constituted over 75 percent of religious educators.[51]

The development of the minister of religious education as an ordination track has served multiple purposes, including a bolstered prestige for religious education, the utilization of ordination as a means by which to attract and hold good religious educators in a competitive job market, the ability for parish ministers to specialize in civic outreach or pastoral counseling by delegating educational activity, and an increased emphasis on hierarchical differentiation as a buttress to a perceived overall decline in clergy occupational prestige. Although it was conceived as a distinct professional status, supervising all educational activity while the parish minister handled the preaching, pastoral, and administrative duties, hierarchically the parish minister has been more likely to supervise all activity in the congregation including religious education.

Based upon interviews for this analysis and from denominational salary data, the minister of religious education effectively is subordinate to the parish minister, in both pay and prestige.[52] Those ordained exclusively as ministers of religious education in the data were entirely female; they tended not to be seminary trained; and their job titles conflated with those of female but not male parish ministers, as pointed out in chapter 3. In comparison, of all ministers of religious education listed in the 1993 *U.U.A. Directory* (N = 64), more than 80 percent were female. Additionally, 73 percent of the men but only 29 percent of the women held dual ordination as parish ministers. Discussions with female ministers of religious education who returned to seminary as a means to also qualify for ordination as a parish minister, and with women having held lay religious education positions but seeking ordination instead as a parish minister, have emphasized both the subordinate status and limited career options of this alternative ordination track as it has evolved. That the few male ministers of religious education also overwhelmingly held dual ordination as parish ministers suggests that this may be a strategy to increase flexibility in obtaining job opportunities. However, the data did not show this strategy to be particularly effective for women.

Part of the reason that dual ordination seems not to offer as many opportunities for women has to do with the occupational overlap between ministers of religious education and female parish ministers. In the U.U.A. data, 45 percent of clergy ever serving as religious education director and 29 percent of those ever holding a minister of religious education position were women ordained exclusively as ministers. No men in the data had held either title. Furthermore, that female parish ministers were more likely to have held positions as associate minister or on the denominational staff—positions closer in job level to those of ministers of religious education than to those normally held by male ministers— illustrates how the occupational prospects of women in these two ordination tracks seem to be much more closely aligned. The conflation also suggests a disproportionate concentration and consequent pressure to crowd women into lower level positions regardless of their ordination status.

The minister of religious education furthermore represents a presence of female clergy on parish staffs in a manner that does not directly compete with the parish minister's position. Parishes with budgets sufficiently large to hire more than one ordained clergy disproportionately have senior parish ministers who are male, which results in lopsided female gender representation in positions subordinate to men. Additionally, as ministers of religious education can be "home schooled" through denominational study programs, parishes have the flexibility to identify, support, and supervise a woman's educational preparation through independent study for ordained U.U.A. fellowship. The result can minimize possibilities of women holding or developing conflicting perspectives with those of the parish, or becoming a serious threat intellectually or occupationally to predominately male parish ministers.

Episcopal Church

In the Episcopal Church, two alternative ordination tracks to the traditional priesthood have proliferated over the last two decades. They are the permanent diaconate and the Canon 9 priesthood.

PERMANENT DIACONATE   The permanent diaconate was formally established in 1952 for men to serve the church as ordained deacons while remaining in secular employment.[53] Argued to have been an office of the early church that was being reinstated, ecclesially it has been asserted to be a separate yet equal order,[54] although hierarchically it functions in a subordinate relationship to priesthood. For instance, while priests are first ordained to the transitional diaconate and therefore can perform all diaconate roles, deacons cannot perform all of the sacramental rites of priests. As with ministers of religious education, permanent deacons are subordinate both in pay and prestige to priests, particularly as most permanent deacons work on a volunteer, nonstipendiary basis.[55] Both education and ordination requirements for the permanent diaconate are far less demanding than those for priesthood.

The number of permanent deacons in the church had remained constant until the late 1960s, a point when pressure for women's ordination was intensifying. In 1970, the year in which women's ordination to the diaconate was granted, the church canons were revised to specifically establish the permanent diaconate as an unpaid clergy ministry residing primarily outside the church.[56] While a significantly greater percentage of women than men have been ordained to the permanent rather than to the transitional diaconate for each cohort year in the data of this analysis, the overall majority of permanent deacons ordained annually were primarily male until the mid-1980s, a point when the annual ratio of all clergy ordained—to either the transitional or permanent diaconate—reached about 30 percent female which, as discussed earlier, has tended to be a generally acknowledged tipping point where effects of occupational feminization become visible (Figure 7.1). By 1985, candidates ordained as permanent deacons had become predominately female, which concurs with a 1984 denominational study identifying students in permanent deacon training programs being 56 percent female, up

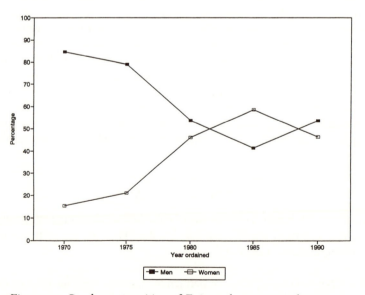

Figure 7.1 Gender composition of Episcopal permanent deacons ordained 1970–1990.

from 39 percent two years earlier.[57] By 1994 women represented 44 percent of the 1,567 permanent deacons ordained in the church.[58]

Given the elimination of the church's lay deaconess order in 1970 by regularizing deaconesses as ordained deacons, the concentration of women in the permanent diaconate during the early 1970s is not surprising. But the increasing ratio of female permanent deacons over recent years, well after women have been granted ordination to the priesthood and have been increasingly accepted as priests within the church, suggests that other issues may be involved, such as a heightened interest among bishops both in the permanent diaconate and in encouraging women to pursue this track, as well as a plethora of opportunities available for permanent deacons.

The growth of the permanent diaconate addresses several organizational concerns that relate directly to women clergy.[59] First, it offers a means to increase job segregation between men and women, minimizing the percentage of women priests likely to present a serious competitive occupational threat to men. The occupational overlap between permanent deacons and female priests that wasn't evident for male priests, discussed in chapters 3 to 5, has deleterious implications for the suppression of occupational opportunities for women priests. With women priests in the 1985 and 1990 cohorts being more than twice as likely as men to have held an entry job title of *deacon*, and their disproportionate sharing of second and subsequent job titles with titles held by permanent deacons, the conflation of opportunities between women priests and permanent deacons accentuates the growing difference between the opportunity structures of female and male priests.

Second, the permanent diaconate offers a way to meet affirmative action pressures without risking substantive changes in traditional views on women's roles. Smith and Grenier argue that hiring practices in secular occupations tend to select individuals with socialization experiences similar to those of an organization, which minimizes the risk of challenge and disruption to organizational operations.[60] It is not improbable that religious organizations might choose candidates on a similar basis, with congregations self-selecting and training female lay leaders who hold congruent perspectives on women's roles, gender, and sexuality-related issues. With recent attention paid to theologically articulating the permanent diaconate as an icon of servanthood,[61] women ordained as permanent deacons retain their service-oriented roles within the church, remaining subordinate to priests in sacramental and liturgical responsibilities. Furthermore, less stringent educational requirements that include provisions for "home schooling" or diocesan training programs rather than seminary education can result in limited or absent exposure to contemporary critical scholarship, liberation or feminist theologies, and controversial social and sexuality-related issues, particularly those which may be disquieting to the status quo. Thus, an objective of *structural* pluralism may be accomplished through increasing female clergy representation without risking the controversy wrought by *functional* pluralism.[62]

Third, when female permanent deacons and female priests hold markedly different perspectives on gender-related issues, tensions emerge that can serve to mitigate pressure for negotiating occupational and other gender-related concerns. For instance, the counterpositioning of women or minorities holding traditionalist versus progressive views can allow organizational leaders to express perplexity over what it should do, given the divided constituency, and absolve itself from having to take any specific action. Cockburn has noted men's tendency to play women off against each other in secular work as a means to inhibit the development of solidarity.[63] From interviews with women priests and conversations with permanent deacons, the differing views they tend to hold on gender roles were evident. Women priests observed that the permanent deacons, often viewing their diaconal ordination as a fulfillment of Christian servanthood, tend to align much more comfortably with traditional denominational perspectives than with their efforts to seek social change. Some female priests commented that female permanent deacons actually hindered their struggle for gender equality in opportunities, affirmative action, and inclusive language, with one priest anecdotally observing that one of the female deacons in her diocese didn't believe that women should be ordained to the priesthood. The few feminist permanent deacons tended to be either seminary trained or have a close female relative or friend who had been to seminary. Additionally, several women who sought ordination in the mid-1980s reported pressure from their bishop and diocese to enter the permanent diaconate rather than the priesthood. One woman anecdotally reported being told that as a deacon she too could "wear a collar." Disproportionate counseling of women toward alternative ordination tracks not only implies coerced rather than free choice, but suggests that the permanent diaconate may be consciously used to develop a cadre of women more likely holding traditionalist perspectives that can serve to divide women clergy on gender-related issues. Furthermore, placement opportunities for permanent deacons, even if nonstipendiary, are approved by bishops who are overwhelmingly male and to whom permanent deacons may report despite their parish affiliation. One can ask to what extent conscious strategic deployment decisions are being made for utilizing women deacons at the expense of women priests, which could serve to explain the occupational conflation between permanent deacons and women priests found in the data.

Fourth, the growth of the permanent diaconate may represent an organizational response to the declining ratio of young men, who resultantly are concentrated in the priesthood track. This not only maximizes their occupational opportunities but conserves whatever vestige remains in the church of a young and virile male priesthood. The significantly lower level of education ($p < .0001$) and older age ($p < .0001$) of permanent deacons, despite controls for gender and ordination year, further accentuate the contrast between ordination tracks. The heightened differentiation between male permanent deacons and male priests contrasts markedly from the conflation that has occurred since 1980 among permanent deacons and female priests. Furthermore, the continuing formalization of ordination requirements over the past decade[64] has decreased the fluidity by which permanent deacons previously could become ordained priests. Such trends serve to reinforce the distinctiveness of male priests from male deacons and from all female clergy.

CANON 9 PRIESTHOOD   A second alternative ordination track gaining momentum in the Episcopal Church with a potentially negative occupational impact on women priests is the *Canon 9 priesthood*, clergy ordained to serve as priests at a single location only. As an ordained order, it was first permitted in 1970 (Title III Canon 9), ironically the year that women's ordination to the diaconate was approved. The objective was to ordain lay leaders in locations where seminary-trained priests weren't available so that remote congregations could have a full and constant sacramental life. As a movement, it had begun in Alaska as a means to serve isolated Native American congregations. Since the early 1990s, Canon 9 priests have been used more frequently in the eastern as well as western United States, not only for isolated congregations but also for ethnic communities and in urban settings. Canon 9 priests, like permanent deacons, hold primarily nonstipendiary and part-time positions. Dugan points out that Canon 9 priests represent a possibility for large parishes needing additional clergy, yet adds the disclaimer that it shouldn't be used as a means to add staff where finances are tight.[65] Although the data in this analysis did not separate traditional priests from those ordained under Canon 9, an informal examination of a subsample verified as Canon 9 through the *Journal of the General Convention* suggests that the gender ratio may be disproportionately male, that Canon 9 priests tend to be ordained at an older age, and that they have substantially lower levels of education, usually "home schooled" in local or diocesan study rather than seminary trained, and that they typically hold part-time or nonstipendiary positions.[66]

The proliferation of these alternative ordination tracks in the Episcopal Church suggests a restructuring of job opportunities over coming years that holds serious implications for gender segregation. Given indications that Canon 9 priests have been ordained in metropolitan areas, and that their orders have been recognized beyond single locations, both it and the permanent diaconate may represent an organizational restructuring and co-optation of positions traditionally held by priests, especially paid positions at level 5 and below—parish assistant and associate positions, interim positions, and vicarships—the very job pool for the first three placements of women priests according to the data of this analysis. Furthermore, given the enthusiasm expressed by several dioceses over the possibilities represented in the Canon 9 priesthood, there is little evidence that diocesan deployment processes are conscientiously monitored in a manner that would assure that clergy in these alternative tracks do not replace traditional priests—male or female—who might be able or willing to accept a placement. That the Episcopal Church already has a surplus of active clergy,[67] as well as a cadre of retired clergy willing to serve in part-time, interim, or nonstipendiary situations, suggests that the proliferation of Canon 9 priests may be strategically *flooding the market* in a manner that those who cannot find appointments simply may *give up*, either to become inactive or to relinquish their ministry altogether. Women priests, who from the data of this analysis more frequently hold part-time and lower level placements, are the most vulnerable to occupational crowding, particularly by clergy willing to work on a nonstipendiary or part-time basis. These trends are least likely to affect young male priests given the evidence of their occupational advantages for upward mobility and attainment, particularly among the most recent cohorts in the data.

Thus, the growth of the Canon 9 priesthood may be serving as a means to enhance the distinctiveness, prestige, and consequent attractiveness of the traditional male priesthood as a relatively small, elite group; to dilute career opportunities for women clergy without denying them access to ordination; to create a two-tier priesthood interdependent with a dual-status labor market, where younger men are disproportionately concentrated in the primary sector consisting of fewer full-time denominational positions, with women, older second-career men and Canon 9 priests consolidated in the secondary sector consisting of lower level, part-time and nonstipendiary placements; and to gain a low-cost or free secondary labor supply that is compliant, committed, and obedient through the vow of ordination. Effectively such a strategy redistributes control of the religious organization in a manner that gives far more opportunity for conservative constituencies to resist exposure to controversial ideas, feminist clergy, and the threat of liberal social change, particularly that related to gender and sexuality.

An Interdenominational Analysis

The expansion of ordination tracks in these two denominations suggests that they may be serving multiple utilities, as occupational responses to organizational concerns. Not only do they offer lower cost solutions to budget constraints, but they serve to alleviate increased pressures of occupational feminization through the disproportionate concentration of men in the primary track. Strong similarities between the development of alternative ordination tracks in these two religious organizations include the timing of their emergence and proliferation in relation to increased pressure of women's ordination and the growing ratio of women clergy overall. That the minister of religious education is a solidly female gender-segregated status and that the permanent diaconate is becoming more so than the priesthood tend to support the argument that feminization and the denominational development of these newer ordination statuses are related phenomena. Furthermore, the similarities between these two denominations despite differences in theology, polity, and histories of women clergy suggest that the formation of such tracks may have at least a passive role in structural backlash against women.

While the Canon 9 priesthood does not appear to be rapidly feminizing, it nonetheless represents a labor supply competitive with women priests. Furthermore, results from the data of this analysis have pointed out that the newer ordination tracks appear to be having a negative effect on the careers of women but not men in the primary track, occupationally concentrating and crowding women in lower level positions. Since the first five years after ordination were identified in chapter 5 to be crucial for developing an upwardly mobile career trajectory, the concentration of women ministers and priests in a job pool shared by those in alternative ordination tracks during the early years predicts greater difficulty for their chances of attaining positions similar to those of their male counterparts. For men in both denominations, the ordination tracks have become ever more discrete, implying a distinctively subordinate status for the more recent tracks that serve to enhance the occupational prestige of men in the primary track.

The growth of alternative ordination tracks, including pressure to change consecrated lay diaconates into ordained orders, have affected other religious organizations over the last two decades as well. For instance, the Roman Catholic Church instituted a permanent diaconate in U.S. parishes beginning in 1968[68] as the shortage of priests was becoming evident. It also provided an alternative to women's ordination by allowing married men to assist in sacramental duties, a move that has frustrated female opportunities for ministry.[69] The United Methodist Church changed its lay diaconal ministry, which is predominantly female, to an ordained order in 1996. Since (lay) diaconal ministers tended to work in areas similar to Episcopal permanent deacons such as Christian education, evangelism, music, administration, and health and welfare,[70] United Methodist women ministers likely will face many of the occupational conflicts that their Episcopal counterparts have with the permanent diaconate, particularly if the itinerant appointment system of clergy deployment becomes modified toward a call system. Additionally, like the Episcopal Canon 9 priesthood, sectors of the United Methodist Church are increasingly relying on licensed lay pastors to fulfill a perceived need similar to that for which Canon 9 priests have been utilized. And like Canon 9 priests, they also tend to be "home schooled" rather than seminary educated.

Similarly, the Evangelical Lutheran Church in America (E.L.C.A.) approved a lay diaconal ministry in 1993, but rejected its task force's recommendation that it be an ordained order. The E.L.C.A. also has had a lay deaconess tradition within its merged denominational constituencies, although the number of deaconesses had declined over the years, partly a result of increased requirements for professionalism, the low status of deaconesses compared to pastors, a lack of training for specializations within the order, and women with pastoral aspirations choosing the same ordination track as men.[71] According to an interviewee, female Lutheran deaconesses—like female Episcopal permanent deacons—have tended to be more conservative on gender issues and view their ministry from the traditional understanding of servanthood. This also has been the case for lay deaconesses in both the Church of England (Anglican) and the Church of Sweden (Lutheran).

Additionally, the Anglican Church of Canada's newly restored permanent diaconate as of 1993 had become 52 percent female.[72] Since the Canadian Anglican Church's history of women priests closely resembles that of the U.S. Episcopal Church, the prospects for occupational conflation between Canadian permanent deacons and women priests should result in similar effects as those found in the data of this analysis.

Gender, Backlash, and Educational Inflation

Lieberson observed in stratification research that if educational disparities were eliminated, other dynamics would assume responsibility for producing similar economic results.[73] While there was virtually no educational disparity between men and women priests in the data of this analysis, gender differences were acutely significant in entry placements as well as overall attainment, which concurs with earlier findings on men and women clergy. The gender inequalities in placements, net of similar education, support the evidence in secular occupations that women get far less occupational return from their educational credentials than men.[74] Roos had found that education was the most important factor contributing to occupational prestige and held particular significance for women, but education also yielded 11 percent lower return in wages for women than men.[75] Furthermore, jobs held primarily by women characteristically have required a well-educated but inexpensive labor supply.[76]

The occupational conflation of well-educated women ministers and priests with clergy in alternative ordination tracks who might neither hold a theological degree nor have ever attended seminary not only suggests that the educational disparities between ordination tracks reinforce both the discrete nature and lower status of the newer tracks but also suppress the value of educational credentials held by women in the traditional tracks. For example, 65 percent of the male and 44 percent of the female permanent deacons in the Episcopal sample had not listed any formal theological education—either at a seminary or through a diocesan school—prior to ordination. Accentuating the educational differences by ordination track has been the rising educational level over time among clergy within the primary track, a trend that became particularly evident when comparing clergy ordained in 1950 and earlier and those ordained in 1970 or more recently ($p <$ .0001).[77] The deployment of clergy in the alternative tracks with less requisite education has presented a cost-effective alternative to hiring well-educated women ministers and priests.[78] Since education has been considered one of the most important objective resources for women,[79] those with theological and other advanced degrees who are forced into the same job pool as clergy who may not have even attended seminary effectively cannot utilize their education as a resource for occupational attainment.

There is yet another education-related trend that may imply structural backlash against women clergy, particularly for Episcopal priests and women in denominations that also ordain or license pastors for local-only ministry. The increase in local and regional study programs for candidates in these alternative tracks compete with seminary programs. With the seminary growth of the early 1980s having plateaued, competitive pressure is being felt by many mainline seminaries struggling to maintain enrollment levels. With denominational struggles between progressive and traditionalist factions also affecting internal decisions over which seminaries to support, they can exert considerable pressure on the viability of seminaries perceived as not in line with the strategic interests of those holding denominational power. Particularly vulnerable are seminaries that traditionally have affirmed women clergy, progressive scholarship, and the exploration of controversial social issues.[80] Those with modest endowments that cannot make the transition to concurrent sponsorship of lay, interdenominational, and continuing education programs as a means to broaden their educational base could be pressured to merge or close over the next decade. The effects of such consolidations could be particularly disruptive to scholarship on gender-related and other controversial social issues that challenge the status quo.

The Deconstruction of Full-Time Work

Chafetz observed for secular occupations that where the size of an eligible working-age group expands relative to the number of paid positions, the result is either underemployment or unemployment.[81] Accompanying the emergence of multiple ordination tracks has been an increase in part-time positions over the past two decades. While the U.U.A. has managed to maintain a closer ratio of clergy supply to demand than the Episcopal Church, the data nevertheless show some evidence of an increase in part-time positions within both denominations. Yet in contrast to the Episcopal data, women ministers were found increasingly to hold full-time placements, at least in their entry position, while men were more likely to have part-time or secular work. Given men's higher average level of educational credentials ($p < .001$), and given women's somewhat greater likelihood to hold full-time appointments that was significant for the most recent job held ($p < .05$) despite the lower level of these placements, then it is likely that men may be finding or retaining more lucrative opportunities outside the denomination while combining these with their denominational appointment, as chapter 4 pointed out. This especially may be the case where men fail to attain mid-level or higher placements with an attractive salary and congregational resources.

The trend toward part-time work is very different in the Episcopal data, where women have a significantly greater propensity than men to both part-time and lower level placements. The Church Pension Fund data support the results of this analysis, showing that between 1986 and 1989, 30 percent of women but only 5 percent of men held part-time positions.[82] Based on coding the data, there was some indication that former full-time positions may have been partitioned into part-time and nonstipendiary placements in recent years. If so, the deconstruction of full-time placements mirrors secular workforce trends over the past decade toward increased part-time and temporary employment,[83] which not only controls wages but can eliminate employee benefit costs. With a shrinking pool of full-time work, occupational crowding typically has resulted in the marginalization of women rather than men, whether in the clergy or in secular work.[84] The Church Pension Fund research also noted that 75 percent of parish part-time assistant placements were held by women.[85] While the increase in part-time positions might be the result of congregations faced with tightened budgets needing to cut labor costs,[86] job partition also increases the number of positions available and consequently opportunities for denominational placements. A denominational study also found that 83 percent of the permanent deacons it surveyed did not receive pay for their church work, which, for half of those responding, averaged at least fifteen hours per week.[87]

The deconstruction of clergy placements in the Episcopal Church has a structural backlash outcome in its disproportionate effect on women priests. It has resulted in the proliferation of a two-tier labor market structure differentiated by proportionately fewer full-time, higher level positions occupied predominately by well-educated male clergy, and a secondary sector consisting of part-time and nonstipendiary positions, with few if any benefits, held more frequently by women priests and clergy in the alternative ordained tracks. Furthermore, clergy interviews and anecdotal data, as well as other research, lend evidence to the part-time nature of these placements for women priests being in compensation only, not in hours worked.[88]

"The clergy needs to adjust for more part-time arrangements . . ." declares the 1993 vision statement of one of the largest Episcopal dioceses. It then discusses "growing support among some clergy and laity" for an interactive ministry of part-time clergy and laity, and rationalizes that "[t]hen the part-time phenomenon can be viewed as an opportunity rather than a curse."[89] This may be so, but only if the "growing support" as well as the "part-time arrangements" are evenly spread among all the affected constituencies. Otherwise, the outcome will not be unlike the volunteer pattern of traditional women's work in the church, with ordination primarily offering prestige rather than occupational economic viability. As Connell has observed, Western countries share a tendency to transfer welfare functions to local constituencies, and consequently onto women's unpaid work.[90]

Gender Segregation in the Clergy

Gender and age traditionally have been crucial career contingencies utilized to accomplish occupational differentiation, stratification, and segregation. Occupational differentiation may occur horizontally, where newer positions have equivalent status with the range of traditional jobs, or vertically, where they are clustered either at higher or lower occupational levels. Hierarchical differentiation has facilitated greater spatial control of job occupants,[91] including the maintenance of sexual division of labor patterns and the resulting subordination of women either through complete gender segregation or by integrating their labor but grouping them in lower level positions. Gender segregation, whether by exclusion or by status subordination, not only reinforces definitions of what is appropriately thought of as men's versus women's work but it can be utilized as a structural backlash mechanism against competitive pressure from female workers.[92]

Not surprisingly, gender segregation is one of the most persistent characteristics of the labor market, whether in the United States and other industrialized nations or in Third World countries.[93] According to Chafetz, as long as the supply of men is sufficient to meet the demand for traditional work roles, gendered divisions of labor will remain static, with women unlikely to displace men. Women may gain opportunities as the demand for workers increases, but as negative economic changes diminish both the quality and quantity of job opportunities, women disproportionately experience underemployment or segregation into lower level and deskilled jobs.[94] In the case of the clergy, the cyclical expansion and contraction of denominational needs have provided both opportunities for women's ministry and a basis for its marginalization.

Both multiple ordination tracking and job partition into part-time and nonstipendiary placements have been shown to serve as mechanisms for both horizontally and vertically segregating women clergy as well as for fast- tracking young men into higher level positions. The effects of job differentiation in facilitating gender segregation become apparent when comparing job titles that clergy hold. For instance, of 27 distinct Unitarian Universalist job titles found in the data, 78 percent are at least two-thirds or totally gender-segregated.[95] Similarly, 83 percent of the 69 distinct Episcopal job titles in the data are at least two-thirds or totally gender-segregated. When weighting is utilized to account for the fewer number of women clergy, the percentages do not change significantly. Table 7.1 illustrates how women clergy in both denominations, on the basis of their job title, are both segregated and disproportionately concentrated in lower level placements. Close to

Table 7.1. Percentage of Gender-Segregated Job Titles by Job Level for Episcopal and Unitarian Universalist Clergy, 1930–1993.

Job level	Episcopal		Unitarian Universalist	
	Men (%)	Women (%)	Men (%)	Women (%)
Six or higher	34	19	50	14
Five	23	10	14	29
Four or lower	43	71	36	57
(N segregated titles)	(35)	(21)	(14)	(7)

Only job titles at least 67 percent gender-segregated are included. When weighting is utilized to account for the overall lower number of women clergy, the concentration of women in lower level placements increases only slightly (6% or less). One segregated Episcopal job title could not be assigned a job level and consequently has been excluded.

three-fourths of the female-segregated Episcopal titles are at level 4 or lower. Additionally, the only female-segregated U.U.A. job title above level 5 is *co-minister*, a position normally shared with one's spouse. Horizontal as well as vertical job-title segregation by gender has been characteristic of other denominations as well. For instance, in some African-American Pentecostal churches male ministers are called *preachers* while females are *teachers*; although both titles may have the same job tasks, the latter carries less prestige.[96]

Job segregation has been perceived as the primary way that occupational discrimination becomes enacted.[97] Although several mainline denominations have developed equal opportunity and affirmative action programs to facilitate integration, their voluntary nature owing to First Amendment guarantees of church and state separation has resulted in more of a goodwill gesture than an effective means for assuring that women are able to gain access to higher level placements.[98] Some U.U.A. women clergy interviewed had claimed that they valued their denomination's initial affirmative action plan, which they believed actually had helped women to gain access to viable entry-level placements. But they didn't sense denominational support for "second level" affirmative action to facilitate their movement into higher level positions.

Denominational deployment practices, gatekeeping control, and selective information networks also have contributed to the maintenance of gender-segregated job opportunities. Since clergy normally obtain job prospects through intra-denominational deployment, opportunities are the easiest mechanism to manipulate in backlash movements against women. Congregations that hire clergy normally seek names or recommendations from personal contacts, from regional or denominationwide deployment officers, through advertising in denominational publications, or by means of computerized denominational placement services. Deployment officers may act as placement brokers by either informing clergy about job openings and encouraging them to apply or by withholding such information. As such, they have considerable gatekeeping power.

While U.U.A. deployment processes are congregational, the denomination's Department of Ministry has maintained an internal gatekeeping control by "seek[ing] to facilitate the appropriate matching" of clergy and congregations.[99]

Some U.U.A. clergy interviewed had intimated that this process, which had been traditionally dominated by men, can hinder women's opportunities for equal consideration, especially for senior-level appointments in larger suburban parishes offering higher salaries. The career paths of U.U.A. women in this analysis tend to support such concerns. In the Episcopal Church, men typically are responsible for employing newly ordained clergy and staffing most lower level positions. Since women are overwhelmingly concentrated at lower levels, men effectively control their employment opportunities. Only in the United Methodist Church, with its centralized appointment system and, originally, a handful of men committed to affirmative action, have women moved into higher level positions in any significant number—as district superintendents and bishops—where they in turn are able to positively influence the job opportunities of other women clergy. Yet even there, internal resistance to women sharing leadership in areas traditionally considered to be male oriented has continued to be an issue.[100]

As noted in chapter 3, men interviewed for this analysis benefited from extra-denominational networks such as college fraternity and boarding school colleagues who held lay positions of influence in obtaining rectorships (level 6 positions), while no women claimed to have obtained a placement as a result of these types of networks. Fox and Hesse-Biber point to women's exclusion from informal circles of communication that cut them off from professional information, resulting in women having to rely on more limited, formal processes for deployment. The impact of gender-segregated information networks, given the importance of personal male contacts for higher status positions, illustrates not only women's restricted modes of access to opportunities but their consequent dependency upon men.[101] Furthermore, Lehman's evidence among American Baptists suggest that women initiating informal contacts can have negative results in terms of deployment, with women who "play by the rules," relying on formal deployment processes controlled primarily by men, being more successful in obtaining positions.[102] Women not only are disadvantaged, then, from a lack of powerful informal networks but also can be penalized if they attempt to utilize the same job-seeking flexibility as men. Consequently, few women make choices from a position completely free of male dependency. At the same time, some women clergy interviewed for this analysis felt they had not been taken seriously by deployment officers because of gender bias when they sought consideration for mid-level placements in more desirable urban and suburban congregations.

One means of objectifying the deployment process has been the development of denominationwide computerized national clergy employment services where, for a substantial fee, clergy profiles are matched to qualifications requested by congregations and denominational agencies with job openings. Although a computerized process offers an advantage to female and minority-race male clergy of circumventing dependency upon the traditional European-American male-controlled networks, the viability of such services depends on the commitment that employers give them. Obtaining positions through computerized searches has yielded a mixed result, especially for higher level positions. For instance, a comparison of results from Episcopal clergy registered with the Church Deployment Office (C.D.O.) and an earlier wave (1988) of this analysis suggests either that those registered with the C.D.O. were more recently ordained or that clergy moving into high-level placements were not necessarily registered.[103] The deployment officer of a large diocese affirmed in an interview that local congregations were encouraged to review clergy profiles registered with the C.D.O., as well as the recommendations of candidates gathered through more subjective and traditional networks, but then remarked, "None of our parishes have hired a 'computer priest' yet." In Lehman's American Baptist research, however, despite conversations with deployment staff doubting the efficacy of computerized placement, women using it were more successful in finding placements than those who did not.[104]

In addition to women's disadvantage in both formal and informal denominational networks for obtaining job opportunities, they also are less likely to be mentored from those within their denominations who hold deployment influence,[105] or taught negotiating processes for salary, benefits, or job title. As Cook and Moorehead observed, congregations have found that they can pay women less.[106] Several women interviewed had said that they simply accepted the package that was offered, unaware at the time that their male colleagues were expected to negotiate for more attractive packages. While this might partially explain gender differences in salaries for similar placements in a manner that displaces overt discrimination from the hiring organization, attributing it to personal initiative of the job candidate or at best to passive socialization processes, male hegemony nonetheless can be assured by paying men more for the same work.[107] Although the data for this analysis didn't include compensation figures, Episcopal Church Deployment Office research has pointed to a consistent salary differential of 15 to 20 percent between men and women priests holding similar positions, with the disparity slightly greater among those more recently ordained.[108] For instance, women ordained to the priesthood in 1977—the first year women priests were admitted—who had become vicars or rectors by 1990 made 97 percent of what their male counterparts did, but women ordained to the priesthood in 1986, holding such positions, made only 73 percent of their male counterparts' salary—men who had been ordained the same year. In other types of clergy jobs, women averaged 13 to 20 percent less than men in the same position. An Episcopal Church report suggests that priests over time reach a "de facto ceiling" for average stipends,[109] although another interpretation may be the manifestation of a tokenism effect. Where relatively few women compete with men for similar placements, those who do succeed are more likely to be compensated well. As the ratio of women increases, the novelty or tokenism effect wears off and gender inequalities are more likely to arise. Similarly, Reskin argues that the primary cause of income disparities is men's interest and ability in maintaining an advantaged position by developing ways that distribute occupational resources to their benefit. The implications that Reskin draws are that men will find value in preserving gender-related job segregation as a primary means by which they maintain dominance,[110] which supports a fluidity observed by Weber between economic and authoritarian dominance.[111] Male mentoring processes or the withholding thereof to women, including salary negotiation, can serve as additional strategic mechanisms for ensuring disparity and therefore dominance.

Women's occupational impact upon the clergy, or the lack thereof evident by their job mobility and attainment patterns, suggests that ongoing occupational changes tend to be ones that facilitate the co-optation and concentration of women's labor into lower level subordinate or mid-level positions, commonly referred to in secular occupations as beneath the "glass ceiling."[112] That women clergy regardless of ordination year tended to hold lower level positions than men, from entry job to their most recent placement, implies that their occupational patterns are ancillary to the traditional career paths that have given men opportunities to hold authority as denominational leaders. Gender segregation mechanisms at work in the two denominations under analysis point to male clergy continuing to have disproportionately greater opportunities for higher level attainment, as has been the case in feminized secular occupations such as teaching, librarianship, nursing, and public relations.[113]

Crompton and Jones have explicitly linked men's opportunities in secular occupations with the maintenance of barriers denying those same opportunities to women.[114] Job segregation by gender provides an alternative labor supply that not only supports those in leadership but maintains men's noncompetitive access to occupational privilege and dominance. Concern over potential opposition from male colleagues has been a major reason in secular occupations for suppressing the level of women's placements.[115] It also can be crucial during periods of backlash against women. Since internal church conflict can result in membership and contribution losses, clergy have had a tendency to minimize the potential for severe dissension.[116] Related to gender, Lehman made a twofold observation that affluent Presbyterian congregations were more likely to discriminate against women ostensibly out of concern for avoiding conflict with their membership, and that congregations were more likely hire men when they perceived financial or organizational viability to be involved.[117] Nonetheless, job segregation effectively controls the political opportunities of women while exploiting their labor, subtly reenacting the division of labor traditionally represented by lay women and ordained men.

The Mixed Blessings of Tokenism

The career paths of women clergy tend to illustrate what Carroll et al. describe as the third stage in American women's religious leadership, where women may participate visibly but often in ways that are marginal to organizational authority and direction.[118] The positions of authority that women have come to hold, according to the data of this analysis, either aren't placements that threaten to destabilize men's opportunities, or the frequency of women occupying them has not risen above marginal, or *token*, levels. Tokenism, according to Kanter, arises when members of a nondominant group in ratio or status are appointed as symbolic representatives of their category.[119] When the ratio of a token constituency threatens to contend for more than marginal status, it is likely to incur backlash.

While tokenism offers the theoretical possibility of upward mobility for women, it also provides an effective means of social control. Tokenist positions can be costly to the women who take them. First, if women are breaking fresh organizational ground they must surmount substantial opposition and hostility prior as well as subsequent to their appointment. They risk the consequences of "breaking the rules," as did the fifteen Episcopal women ordained to the priesthood prior to the denomination's official sanction. Of the original eleven women irregularly ordained, only two have had primarily parish careers.[120] Furthermore, the elite men who support women moving into fresh occupational territory do so at considerable risk of hostility from male colleagues. Consequently they are more likely to support women with charisma and strong prophetic commitments in the Weberian sense, who can withstand the hostility and the subtle yet pervasive pressures of tokenism. The Rt. Rev. Barbara Harris, known as a prophetic writer and strong advocate for social justice prior to her election as the first female Episcopal bishop, was supported in part because of such commitments.[121] Typically, the first women moving into male occupational territory are likely to outperform their male colleagues,[122] which can exacerbate internal friction and resentment.

Second, a token's visibility magnifies whatever she says or does as representative of her entire status group. Tokenist women may feel the added weight of representing women—or women of color—in a manner that European-American men attaining such positions do not. Nason-Clark, in a study of British and American women ministers, found that more than half of the women had a sense of constant pressure to "prove their personal worth," and of greater time demands placed upon them than their male colleagues.[123]

Third, tokens through their isolation and consequent vulnerability are subject to discrimination, overt hostility, and passive resistance by those opposed to their constituency holding such positions, in a way that European-American men are not. Furthermore, direct challenges to a token's qualifications or credentials for attaining a position are usually accompanied by a mythology that unqualified members of that status group are being promoted, which may serve to fuel the potential mobilization of a backlash movement.[124] Tokens are evaluated concurrently by behavioral standards expected not only of the dominant group in leadership positions but also by those of their status group. In the case of women, the result becomes a double bind: their leadership style may be perceived as insufficiently authoritative or, if utilizing assertive behaviors similar to their male colleagues, they may be perceived as authoritarian.

Fourth, a token's power is usually far more limited than her or his visibility. Women clergy in leadership positions often have limited opportunity to utilize their visibility and their voice to work for substantive social change within their denomination, owing to structural or procedural blockages facilitated by the resistance of those uncommitted or in opposition to their presence. For assertive women with transformative agendas, the erosion of opportunity to be more than figureheads can be psychically corrosive. As Acker notes for secular organizations, as long as male-gendered imagery dominates an organization's language and metaphors, women remain disadvantaged in such a work environment.[125] Occasionally token women may clash with former male mentors or supporters when they overstep unspoken boundaries, or when men move on to other ground-breaking causes.[126] Where tokenist women are dependent on male supervision and support, they are continually vulnerable to having their efficacy undermined. While some women clergy who have finally succeeded in moving into positions of power may in turn be overtly indifferent or hostile to assisting other women, such scenarios usually are characterized by a continued dependency on men who can affect their long-term career security. Others have less optimistically claimed that women who reach high-level positions were carefully chosen, had demonstrated loyalty to a male-dominant structure and its accompanying values, and thereby were compromised from working in the interest of women.[127] Yet Cockburn argues that men in elite positions explicitly seek to maintain women's loyalty to them and the status quo while discouraging women from identifying with other women at lower levels in an organization.[128]

Chafetz argues that while women's equal representation at decision-making levels is the key to movement toward gender equality, it is the most difficult step to achieve.[129] Yet even if as tokens, the visibility of women leaders can provide an important incentive to other women or their daughters either to seek ordination or, as laity, to struggle for social and ideological change in ways that affirm women. While the exceptionally high occupational attainment of women priests in the original cohort of Episcopal women clergy can be regarded as another manifestation of tokenism, they have served as important role models for women who have subsequently been ordained.[130] United Methodist minister Lucia Guzman, who also serves as executive director of the Colorado Council of Churches, admitted in an interview for this research that what had convinced her to seek ordination was a week spent with United Methodist bishop Leontine Kelly, who was a powerful role model and source of inspiration. Stevens's research also has emphasized the importance of female role models for younger women considering ordination.[131]

Despite the costs of tokenism for women who willingly undertake movement into elite positions, their presence has facilitated some cracks in the proverbial glass ceiling for other women. The United Methodist appointment system of clergy deployment, where pastors periodically are sent to different congregations regardless of either's interest in a change, has facilitated the promotion of women into leadership positions at a pace far ahead of other episcopal or congregational denominations.[132] The first female bishop of any denomination, Marjorie Matthews, not surprisingly was elected in the United Methodist Church (1980). Seven more United Methodist female bishops have since been elected, more than any other mainline denomination.

Women denominational leaders subsequently emerged in other religious organizations. Barbara Harris was the first woman bishop in a denomination claiming Apostolic succession, elected an Episcopal suffragan bishop in 1988.[133] The first female Anglican diocesan bishop was elected two years later, Penelope Jamieson, in New Zealand. Subsequently, five more U.S. Episcopal women bishops have been elected, two suffragan and three diocesan bishops. Canada also has elected an Anglican female suffragan bishop (1994). In the Lutheran tradition, the first female bishop was Maria Jepsen, elected in Germany (1992). Female Lutheran bishops subsequently have been elected in the United States (1992), in Norway (1993), in Denmark (1995), and in Greenland (1995). Although these various denominations are predominately European American in race and culture, two of the female bishops elected in these traditions have been African American—one United Methodist and one Episcopalian.

Lay women are being elected to lead in other denominations, such as Donella Clemens (1993), the first female moderator of the Mennonite Church, which represents a two-year leadership post. Those within the Mennonite Church admit that Clemens's election wasn't random, but partly the result of a concentrated effort by the denomination to widen its leadership base,[134] a pattern not dissimilar to the concerted efforts within the Episcopal Church to elect a female bishop for nearly a decade prior to Harris's consecration.[135] Such efforts, necessarily supported by a progressive male leadership, by their ground-breaking nature tend to be tokenist. So tends to be the pattern of laywomen preceding clergywomen into high-level positions,[136] as they represent less potential competition with clergymen.

The critical challenge to the efficacy of women's impact on organizational leadership is likely to emerge if women should approach a 30 percent annual ratio of all who are attaining senior-level placements. At this point their concentration not only would make them visible beyond token levels, but collectively they would have sufficient leverage to press audibly for social change particularly in relation to ideology and practices that would benefit women. As Chafetz has pointed out, "[t]he equitable sharing of elite roles clearly involves the redistribution of power and perquisites and is, therefore, more likely than virtually any other goals sought by gender-conscious groups to elicit hostile reactions."[137]

Backlash to the influx of women clergy has taken several forms: from overt attacks on the legitimacy of women's ordination itself to more passive processes with deleterious effects such as the proliferation of multiple ordination tracks, the devaluation of women's educational credentials, the growth of gender-related job segregation as the ratio of women clergy increases, the use of tokenism as a means to grant ideological concessions to supporters of gender equality while isolating tokens in a manner so as to limit their opportunity to make substantive change, and the strategic deployment of women with traditionalist views so as to counter those with progressive commitments in terms of feminist ideological and social change. The very gender-conscious nature of backlash mechanisms suggests that change already has occurred in the influence women have had on how gender relations are constituted, sanctioned, and maintained by organized religion. The extent to which backlash movements prevail in reversing change toward gender equality depends not only on the dominance of resistant men and complicity of women dependent on them, but also on external economic factors putting pressure upon religious organizations to transform their structure and how they deploy their clergy. As Chafetz points out, where men hold most of the rule and policymaking, the gatekeeping and opportunity distribution, as well as the primary social definitional power, they can readily reverse gains made in gender equality. Consequently, the stability of change in women's ordination and opportunities for movement into the full range of clergy positions depends on women being equally represented in senior-leadership placements responsible for policy, ideology, and deployment decisions.[138] Yet the momentum of women's influx into the clergy could be sufficient to resist backlash movements provided the resistance is as organized as the backlash movements themselves.

Faludi, in *Backlash: The Undeclared War Against American Women*, compares the illusion of gender equality to the actual erosion of gains toward women's equality in recent decades.[139] Some religious organizations, particularly those perceived to be more conservative or traditionalist, have dispensed with illusionism in attempting to constrain or halt either women's ordination or their opportunities for ministry. Although more moderate and liberal denominations have retained a veneer of acceptance toward women clergy, strong undercurrents of occupational change and restructuring have served to erode the opportunities that women clergy have had, according to the data of this analysis. The proliferation of alternative ordination tracks, with women priests and ministers more often conflated with clergy in the alternative tracks, effectively devaluing their educational resources and facilitating more staff and part-time positions, are prime indicators of such occupational change. Although since 1980 women have been elected to denominational leadership positions, their scant number does not yet represent a significant, gender-related challenge to the male-dominant authority structure.

In sum, while chapter 6 illustrated how occupational change in the clergy may have facilitated the ordination and deployment of women, this chapter has shown how occupational mechanisms can be utilized in backlash movements, or otherwise be employed to control the extent of occupational change represented by women's influx, so as to maintain a male-dominant leadership. The utilization of such mechanisms as multiple-ordination tracking, job differentiation, and deconstruction of full-time work serve to support the first hypothesis, that *similarities are evident in women clergy careers across very different types of religious organizations*; the fifth hypothesis, that *the careers of women clergy are more adversely sensitive to the increasing influx of women than are men's careers*; and the sixth hypothesis, that *trends toward occupational feminization in the clergy are consistent with feminization trends in secular occupations*. The next chapter will show further how the influx of women clergy interacts with ongoing structural change in religious organizations themselves.

⌣· Eight ·⌢

Structural Change
in the Ministry

At the turn of the century, Universalist women were discouraged from enrolling in Bachelor of Divinity programs less for religious reasons than for pater-
nal concern over whether women clergy would have viable careers. As the president of Tufts responded to an applicant,

> The ministry is not a profession for women. . . . The women who have
> entered the profession in the Universalist denomination at any rate have met
> with only a scanty measure of success, so scanty I should think it must be to
> them a continual disappointment. The best that a woman can hope for in the
> ministry is a fifth or sixth rate parish, generally a parish which cannot afford to
> hire a man, and is in an apologetic attitude because it has a woman.[1]

The data for this analysis have shown that career opportunities for U.U.A. women
ministers in the 1990s are not entirely inconsistent with those of their sisters a
century ago. Besides various *causal* attributions, such as discriminatory preferences
for men, gatekeeping, and other backlash processes; and *personal* attributions, such
as individual choice in which opportunities to pursue, structural changes within
religious organizations themselves have affected women's careers. The 1961 Unitarian Universalist merger opened up a wider assortment of potential congregational job opportunities, but men have appeared to benefit occupationally more
than women. Similarly, the addition of new job titles and new ordination tracks
appear to have substantively improved men's occupational opportunities relative to
women's.

While substantial fluctuations over the past fifty years in church membership
and clergy supply were shown in chapters 5 and 6 to have affected occupational
opportunities and attainment, particularly for men, the data have suggested that
these have been maintained through both controlling the supply of men entering
the traditional ordination track and segregating women in lower level placements.

Combined, these two trends have concentrated men disproportionately in mid- to senior-level positions. Structural changes, then, ultimately have tended to conserve men's occupational attainment—and by implication their opportunity structure—at the expense of women's parity.

Weber believed that people struggle for dominance to the extent of their available resources, and that when their resources change so will the structure of domination.[2] From chapter 6 it is evident that the low ratio of young men being ordained today indicates not only that the composition of human resources available to religious organizations has changed substantially, but the influx of women and second-career clergy represents a high potential for modification of the norms, theological values, and practices of the religious organization that men, ordained at an early age, traditionally have controlled. In their effort to maintain not only what has been historically normative for clergy but also what has been a standard range of belief and practice for their denominations, male backlash against women clergy can be perceived as an expression of the disparity between ensuring future control of the religious organization and the current resources for achieving it.[3]

How institutions adapt to changing physical circumstances, political conditions, and technological breakthroughs may hold implications for the survival of certain groups and for the culling of others, according to Featherman.[4] Wider socioeconomic changes that create disparities in labor demand and supply, trends toward job deskilling, and the emergence of issues related to professionalization and deprofessionalization are crucial to concerns involving occupational feminization. As a result, the contemporary state of many religious organizations reflects a dynamic tension between how they may seek to hold onto a predominately male clergy constituency while utilizing the needed labor, skills, and talent that female clergy bring.

As noted in chapter 6, men may reject occupations or specialties for a variety of reasons besides relatively low salary. Other motivations may include declines in autonomy, fewer opportunities for entrepreneurial efforts, decreased availability of full-time positions, routinization of job tasks, or declining usage of the occupation as a means for upward social mobility.[5] Concurrently, male leadership may perceive that the encouragement and deployment of women clergy hold strategic economic benefit for their religious organization—benefit that does not necessarily infer equality of opportunity and attainment. Cockburn argues that, "cost-efficiency in service organizations depend[s] on the sex-specific exploitation of women."[6] Indeed, the influx of women has been accompanied by a concurrent reorganization of work tasks so as to maintain some advantageous jobs—those which traditionally have attracted men—while women have been disproportionately deployed in those positions where the cost-effectiveness of their labor may represent an important asset, especially in positions that are part-time or nonstipendiary.

Over the past fifty years, widespread socioeconomic change has markedly affected religious organizations and consequently the clergy. Older buildings have faced major maintenance and capital repair costs; many structures built at a time when energy was relatively cheap and plentiful have encountered high fuel expenditures as well as retrofitting costs. Newer congregations as well as those having completed major renovations have taken on large construction debt and interest payments. Clergy salaries, pension, medical, and other insurance costs have risen substantially. Administrative demands include increased paperwork required by denominational judicatories. In most situations, growing budgets to cover such costs have exceeded growth in membership. Some congregations have encountered a loss of both substantial and reliable contributors as elderly long-time members have died and haven't been replaced in number by prosperous, middle-aged families. Consequently many congregations have faced a loss of real income over the last twenty years while expenses have continued to mount.[7]

Tight budgets have affected denominations themselves, as well as their constituent congregations. Denominational contributions declined at an estimated $2.8 billion, adjusted for inflation, between 1968 and 1991.[8] Sizable insurance and liability increases, litigation, settlement, and internal programming costs resulting from clergy sexual abuse have also weighed heavily on denominational resources. As litigation continues to cost religious organizations, one of two outcomes may be likely. The first, which already is evident, involves new limitations and exclusions by insurers that may necessitate congregations and clergy carrying their own malpractice insurance. This would further strain already constricted budgets, adding to clergy overhead costs and additionally placing pressure on minimizing the number of hired clergy. The status of nonstipendiary clergy involved in abuse has yet to be litigated; if the religious organization is deemed responsible by virtue of ordaining and identifying clergy in "good standing," the implications could be significant for those denominations that increasingly rely on a nonstipendiary workforce. The second alternative would be to rely more upon women clergy as a cost-effective resource in terms of potential abuse cases, since inappropriate sexual contact with lay members of congregations is a much rarer occurrence among women clergy.[9] To date, the growing concern over clergy sexual abuse has yet to benefit women clergy occupationally.

Mainline religious organizations for the past several years have cut budgets, restructured services, and downsized their staffs. The Presbyterian Church (U.S.A.), with a $7 million deficit for 1994 alone, developed a restructuring plan to reduce national staff by 25 percent.[10] The Episcopal Church by 1994 faced a $5 million deficit, attributed to reduced support from local congregations.[11] One official interviewed for this analysis also expressed wariness over the possible removal of tax-exempt status for property owned by religious organizations, a concern which was realized in a 1996 Colorado ballot measure. The Colorado Episcopal diocese has estimated that the tax assessment would be $130,000 greater than the entire 1996 diocesan budget. With many properties already strapped for maintenance and capital repair costs, the increased tax liability would result in a downsizing and restructuring that could accelerate movement toward a small, paid clergy denominational leadership and a large part-time or nonstipendiary workforce. Since it has been shown that women clergy disproportionately hold part-time and nonstipendiary positions, it is likely that such displacements would marginalize women further.

Occupationally, constricted budgets have resulted in the compression of clergy positions offering substantive financial and labor resources for developing sizable ministerial programs. As shown in chapter 5, the proportion of high-level placements has lagged well behind the ratio of experienced clergy. Tight finances have contributed to a shortage of paid denominational work overall. In 1993 there were an estimated 6,200 full-time positions compared to more than 14,000 Episcopal priests.[12] The formation of "cluster ministries" where several congregations share a single priest or minister, a practice reminiscent of the turn of the century, not only has sought to resolve strained budgets of adjacent congregations by consolidating two or more financially marginal positions or those receiving denominational financial support[13] but as a trend has contributed to the constriction of full-time work, eliminating the very types of placements that, according to the data, have been critical to women clergy seeking opportunity for congregational responsibility, autonomy, and influence despite financial marginality.

Simultaneously, congregations have faced losses in voluntary labor. The percentage of married women with children under age 6 working outside the home had doubled from 30 percent in 1970 to 62 percent by 1994; similarly, married women with children between ages 6 and 17 working outside the home had climbed from 49 percent in 1970 to 76 percent by 1994.[14] With an increased number of middle and upper middle-class women below retirement age in the workforce, long working hours per week for both men and women, a rise in single-parent families—up from 11 percent of all family households with children in 1970 to 24 percent by 1994[15]—competing demands and growing opportunities for ever-shrinking free time, such trends have pressured not only the amount of volunteer labor available but also on the type of work commitments that members have been willing to undertake. According to Gillespie's study of Episcopal lay women, the traditional commitment of older women to fill in where needed contrasts with that of younger women who both experience severe time constraints and make selective choices for volunteer work in ways that maximize individual self-fulfillment, such as projects with specific time limitations. Even church attendance is considered to be part of their volunteer commitment. Consequently, selective volunteering has contributed to dislocations in work allocation within the congregation. Traditional churchwomen's work is either tending to disappear or is being substantially restructured, according to Gillespie.[16]

Yet another trend currently affecting religious organizations involves the consumerization of the church. Geographic mobility has facilitated a consumerist approach to religion, with denominational affiliation becoming a rational, voluntaristic choice whereby those new to a community or unhappy with their current congregation may "shop around" for desired programs or specialized ministries. Nemeth and Luidens point out that the consumerization trend has substantively increased congregational competition and altered contribution patterns to denominations nationally.[17] But as members of religious communities have become increasingly like clients or customers in evaluating the extent of their religious participation, commitment, and financial contribution, so have their expectations shifted on what the clergy role should entail.[18] Furthermore, increases in civil lawsuits have emphasized that clergy have responsibilities and limitations commensurate with secular professional providers. Religious consumerism consequently has acted as a counterweight to both clergy and denominational authority.

Besides structural socioeconomic change, attitudinal conflicts have contributed to financial shortfalls. Where persuasion of liberal European-American male leadership to participate in backlash movements appears to break down, the social control of the clergy and their egalitarian commitments has been implemented through the selective application of measures designed to economically strangle their efforts. Congregations, unhappy with what they perceive as a more liberal position by their denomination on matters related to gender and sexuality, have held back contributions to denominational overhead in organizations where congregational assessments are ultimately noncompulsory. Voluntary organizations are vulnerable to member withdrawal of participation and financial support where policies or organizational direction goes contrary to their needs or wishes, as Lehman and others have pointed out.[19] Predictably, issues related to gender and sexuality have been the most divisive in recent years.

Much of the grassroots movement to reduce national denominational structure in favor of congregational empowerment has in common a concurrent backlash against liberalized gender roles and attitudes toward sexuality, manifested in complaints that the domination at the national level is issue-driven.[20] For instance, the Episcopal Church's leadership, which as a body has been supportive of women's ordination and consecration to the episcopate, as well as willing to study the use of more gender-inclusive language for liturgies and to reconsider its position on matters of sexual orientation, has incurred grassroots accusations that it is out of touch and, according to Todd Wetzel a priest and executive director of the conservative movement, Episcopalians United, "it's time to make a theological statement with our checks."[21] At the core of such critique is a push to move the denomination's national leadership away from "issue-centered" programs—many which have promoted egalitarian and inclusive participation with regard to gender and race.[22] The sector of grassroots discontent also has been a major force behind a movement to restructure the denomination, including its senior leadership. Similarly, other denominations have been challenged by conservative politicized factions seeking to renounce inclusive language and liberal teachings on gender; to reduce financial support for the national denomination, staff, boards, and agencies; and to redirect monies to the local level. For the United Methodist Church, such rationale has been articulated for increasing "mission and ministry," despite the denomination's Board of Global Ministry being part of the targeted structure. Liberal seminaries also have been targeted.[23]

But denominations are little different from secular bodies in their reorganization and reallocation of human resources as a cost-effective means of ensuring their survival. The combination of an expanded demand for work vacated by a decline of volunteer labor and too few economic resources to pay for the full value of that work have resulted in direct labor supply redistributions. Additionally, the accompanying issues of changing lay commitment and expectations, shifting professional self-understanding, reemergence of clericalism, increases in nonstipendiary clergy, and tensions surrounding the prospect of clergy choosing to leave the profession all hold gender-related implications.

Shortage or Surplus: The Supply and Demand of Clergy Labor

Reskin and Roos link both occupational restructuring and increased demand for labor with shifts toward occupational feminization. [24] As they have pointed out for secular occupations, changed attitudes were less critical to hiring women than were both labor shortages and the economic prospect of acquiring women's labor more inexpensively than men's. Not only is it known that many denominational reforms have occurred in response to changes in clergy supply, [25] but such dislocations have had a long interrelationship with women's ordination and consequently with occupational feminization.

Just as concerns over the decline in occupational prestige afflicted the clergy for at least a century if not substantially longer prior to the influx of women, as was noted in chapter 6, so have concerns over clergy shortages. Chronic shortages of clergy, for instance, plagued the Unitarian and Universalist Churches in the latter decades of the nineteenth century, the very period when ordination was opened to women. [26] Clergy supply dislocations also were material to women's ordination movements during the 1950s. Following World War II, the number of men entering the ministry had not kept pace with the rapid growth in families and church membership, a period that saw a 50 percent rise in U.S. population claiming church membership. [27] Such growth sorely strained supplies of existing clergy, a pattern similar in secular occupations where shortages in male workers relative to the available jobs became a formative condition for influxes of women into the workforce. [28] Clergy supply concerns during the 1950s were particularly critical to women's ordination being granted in the Presbyterian (U.S.A.) Church. [29] Although the Episcopal Church had clergy surpluses rather than shortages during the period in which ordination was opened to women, the need for part-time or nonstipendiary labor was already being acknowledged. [30]

The issue of clergy shortages has arisen again in recent years. [31] Declines in seminary enrollments also have been cited to justify shortage theories. Admittedly, growth in seminary enrollments during the 1970s and early 1980s, infused with both a proliferation of women and older men, leveled off during the late 1980s but then increased to some extent again during the early 1990s. [32] Additionally, the modest growth that is projected for the occupation overall—involving a 9 percent increase in clergy from 1990 to 2005 [33]—is seldom addressed in shortage discussions. More likely, the shortages involve the growing need for training prospective clergy willing to hold part-time or nonstipendiary positions.

Unlike at mid-century, however, mainline denominations are not growing at an unprecedented rate. The end of the 1950s growth spurt was followed by a decline in membership less than a decade later, without a comparable decrease in clergy. Although the number of candidates being ordained dipped in the mid-1970s and early 1980s, the overall annual number ordained in the mid-1980s and early 1990s was not inconsistent with that of the 1960s. For instance, Unitarian Universalist clergy increased by 46 percent between 1961—the year of the merger—and 1991, despite declines of 3 percent in membership and 2 percent in the number of congregations during that period. [34] Additionally, the number of candidates for denominational fellowship has increased sharply, resulting in lengthy waiting queues, a condition that contributed to pressure for development of the nonstipendiary community minister ordination track.[35] Similarly, in the Episcopal Church, not only was the annual number of clergy ordained to the diaconate in 1990 approximately at its 1960 level, but the overall number of clergy has risen 64 percent between 1960 and 1990 despite a 4 percent decline in the number of congregations and a 20 percent decline of confirmed communicants in good standing.[36] Table 8.1, illustrating the denominational growth in clergy, congregations, and membership over much of this century, presents a poignant contrast of supply relative to the structural needs for clergy services.

Not surprisingly, anxieties over clergy shortages have also been met with concerns about clergy oversupply, a debate that has been particularly acute within the Episcopal Church.[37] The data in Table 8.1 raise a serious question regarding the extent to which concern over clergy shortages is really the core issue. Put simply, if shortages were a serious problem, the results of this analysis would have shown an increasing opportunity structure in recent years for female as well as

Table 8.1. Changes in Episcopal Church and U.U.A. Membership, Congregations and Clergy Supply, 1920–1991.

	Episcopal		
Year	Total Clergy	Congregations	Communicants
1990	14,878	7,354	1,698,240
1980	13,089	7,591	2,018,870
1970	11,963	7,417	2,269,627
1960	9,079	7,657	2,123,110
1950	6,654	7,784	1,688,611
1940	6,335	7,995	1,489,384
1930	8,253	6,304	1,287,431
1920	5,987	9,031	1,096,895

	Unitarian Universalist[a]		
Year	Total Clergy	Congregations	Adult Members
1990-1[b]	1,250	1,020	147,256
1980	970	989	136,192
1970	887	1,038	164,270
1961	856	1,035	151,557
1950	830	775	78,470[c]
1940	994	894	172,287
1930	1,012	1,002	109,077
1920	1,090	1,150	43,242[c]

a Figures prior to the 1961 Unitarian Universalist merger are combined from separate Unitarian and Universalist documents.

b 1990–91 figures were used for comparison with 1961, the year of the merger.

c Figure represents Unitarian membership only. No Universalist membership figures are provided in the *Universalist Year Book* or the *Universalist Register* for these years.

Source: *The Episcopal Church Annual* 1953–1993; *The Living Church Annual* 1921–1952; *Journal of the General Convention* 1922–1991; *Unitarian Universalist Association Directory* 1961–1993; *Universalist Year Book* 1931–1952; *Universalist Register* 1920; *Unitarian Year Book* 1920–1951.

male priests.[38] That marital and parenthood status do not affect either women's placements or overall mobility suggest that the demand for priests is being met with an adequate supply of first and second-career male priests and perhaps the recent ordination of Canon 9 local priests.

The data of this analysis further suggest that whatever Episcopal clergy shortages may exist tend to be localized to particular geographic settings such as rural areas, where small congregations socioeconomically may not be able to support full-time clergy or where job opportunities for clergy spouses might be limited.[39] Such shortages are not new to religious organizations, although the increasing frequency of two-income families, heightened geographic mobility, and urbanization trends in the population have aggravated these dislocations.

Implicit in the concern over what Soule calls the "shortage of clergy to exercise ministry as we know and cherish it now"[40] may be an expectation of maintaining an occupational structure reminiscent of a 1950s "golden age" of mainline denominational membership growth. That the ramifications of occupational feminization are obliquely touched upon in discussions about shortages suggests that part of the concern may involve nostalgia for a constituency of clergy that understands and exercises its vocation in a manner characteristic of a bygone era, a time when its view of the religious organization, its theology and practices, were primarily uncontested. Indeed, relative to the substantive change that the more recent alternative clergy constituencies—namely, women and second-career men— might bring if reaching positions of influence and leadership beyond token levels, a *strategic* clergy shortage can be said to exist. The recognition that the potential for occupational feminization to create significant change, juxtaposed with discussions of shortages,[41] suggests that the prospect of increasing divergence from traditional notions of clergy and church may be a primary concern. Thus, it can be argued that the only substantive shortage seems to consist of *young male seminary-trained clergy*. Rather, the title of Steinfels's 1989 *New York Times* article, "Shortage of Qualified New Clergy Causing Alarm for U.S. Religions . . . Loss of Clergy Is Seen as Moral Threat to Nation"[42] suggests that the national moral threat may be perceived to lie in the loss of clergy who are young and male, especially given the comparative influx of females.

There is a conflict embedded within the structure of religious tradition itself that is crucial to the issue of clergy shortages: the desire for a greater supply of young men who can be easily socialized to uphold the traditional beliefs and practices of the religious organization despite an existential reality that current organizational needs may be requiring radical change from what has served the status quo. Tighter budgets and finances sharply affect the number of full-time salaried positions and consequently the available opportunities. Decreased occupational attractiveness among young men may serve to increase congregational concerns over difficulties in offering appealing compensation packages for entry-level clergy. Conversely, a proportionally larger ratio of older and female candidates being ordained may more suitably serve the pastoral and spiritual needs of an older membership. The integration of secular specializations, such as administration, management, social work, or counseling, with ministerial positions has been shown to advantage entering second-career clergy having such skills, according to the Episcopal data in chapters 3 and 6. Similarly, the feminization of the clergy may signal the need for rethinking traditional religious views on gender and sexuality in relation to more recent scientific knowledge and changing sociocultural norms on gender role ideology, particularly in ways that are more affirmative of women. In short, the realities of current labor-supply demographics well may accord with the actual shifts that religious organizations as well as the wider society have undergone over the last four decades. Occupational and organizational nostalgia, then, would suggest concerns related more to the loss of dominance and control by a particular constituency.

In sum, clergy shortages and surpluses appear to work in tandem. While shortages increase pressure that facilitates women's entry into the occupation, surpluses—which the influx of women may augment—serve to facilitate occupational gender segregation for women and opportunity reconstruction for men. The shortage discussions serve to call attention to the need for young male entrants, whether to secure a balanced clergy labor supply or to assure male dominance and control of the religious organization and its tradition. But where acute shortages of both young men and well-paid positions occur in relation to a surplus of ordained clergy, women are disproportionately likely to become crowded into the more marginal positions, as shown in the more recent Episcopal cohorts of this analysis.[43] Such dislocations hold important implications for job opportunities among women clergy.

Alternative Clergy Labor Supplies

Chafetz argues that given gender inequality in the division of labor, no change will result as long as the supply of qualified men is sufficient to meet the demand, with labor shortages alternatively met by recruiting men from other sectors, particularly those who are discrete and ultimately noncompetitive, in lieu of recruiting women.[44] There seems to be some evidence to support this prospect in the Episcopal Church's recruitment and deployment of Canon 9 local priests. Also, the severe priest shortages experienced by the Roman Catholic Church, particularly in the United States and other First World countries, have directly contributed to the revival of the ordained permanent diaconate open to married men as an alternative labor supply, a move that has been widely recognized as yet another organizational response to pressure by religious and lay women for ordination.[45] Schoenherr and Young have predicted that the number of Roman Catholic diocesan priests in the United States will have dropped by 40 percent between 1966 and 2005, while the lay membership is expected to grow by 65 percent during that period.[46] Yet while shortages may have opened up opportunities for women lay pastors as an alternative labor supply—according to Wallace, 2 percent of U.S. Roman Catholic parishes are headed by women[47]—they have been deployed in a manner that has kept their labor discrete and noncompetitive with that of any ordained men.

While the relationship of women's influx to their deployment as a lower level labor source has been discussed in previous chapters, little attention has been given to the large wave of clergy retirements as yet another alternative source of clergy labor. This surge for some denominations has been sizable. For instance, the

United Methodist Church had predicted in 1989 that 42 percent of its then active clergy would be retired by 1995.[48] The slightly higher level entry jobs, more full-time and more normative positions of men ordained in 1985 and 1990, evident in the Episcopal data, likely have been the result of vacancy chains[49] created by this generation of retirements. The trickle-down effect, however, has not trickled across gender lines.

Complicating even further the lack of equal benefit to men and women from retirement vacancies is the increased number of clergy engaging in postretirement work. For example, of clergy listed as retired in the data of this analysis, 17 percent of the U.U.A. ministers and 25 percent of the Episcopal priests subsequently held positions other than emeritus. Such placements were primarily interim appointments averaging about one year for U.U.A. ministers, while retired priests most frequently held part-time assistant positions. Of those who worked after retirement, priests averaged 1.3 positions compared to 2.75 positions for U.U.A. ministers. Although the retirement dates in both samples ranged from 1959 through 1992, 37 percent of Episcopal placements and *all* of U.U.A. positions held by retired clergy had begun after 1984. This trend would suggest a shortage of active clergy to meet the need for available positions, which from the data of this analysis certainly does not seem to be the case. More likely it represents a growing interest by both retiring clergy and their denominations to utilize their accumulated experience as an alternative labor supply.

One of the crucial factors involving retiree interest in continued work is the growth of male longevity over the last several decades, which has added five years to men's life expectancy just since 1970,[50] as well as an increased likelihood of good health for a greater portion of later life. Another factor may involve identity maintenance. Parsons observed that since occupational status depends on holding a specific job, abrupt retirement can leave men feeling "functionless."[51] According to a U.U.A. report, some retired ministers perceive that they have much yet to offer.[52] Postretirement work resolves both the abrupt loss of occupational status and prestige when clergy retire from their congregations particularly if, through lack of other vocational interests, their job has been their primary status identity. Yet another factor may involve needed supplemental income that interim or part-time positions can provide. Furthermore, that the retired ministers and priests in the data who continued to work were at least 98 percent male, ordained at a median age of 29 or lower, and whose average career attainment had been at least level 6 (rector or minister of a self-supporting parish), suggests that they may constitute an alternative labor supply—overwhelmingly male and ordained young—that is likely to uphold traditional clergy values as well as denominational norms. According to an Episcopal deployment officer interviewed, retirees are appreciated for particular types of jobs such as interim placements not only because of their extensive experience but also because they have no interest in making the job permanent.[53]

The deployment of retirees on either a part-time or a nonstipendiary basis yields a sizable source of experienced, well-socialized, and often mobile labor that is more cost-effective than regular salaried clergy, as a result of savings on costly portions of employee benefits—pension contributions and medical insurance. Occupational restructuring, in terms of both ordination tracking and the utilization of retired clergy as an alternative labor supply competing in the same job pool as women priests, is particularly evident in the Episcopal Church, according to both statistical data and interviews for this analysis. The Church Pension Fund also has sought to modify the restriction against retirees earning more than $16,600 annually from church-related positions and keeping their pensions. Despite a 1988 Episcopal General Convention resolution that urged "the placement of women and people of color as interim pastors,"[54] the use of retired male priests for interim positions, as well as other lower to mid-level stipendiary jobs, increases the likelihood of occupational marginalization for women by crowding them into ever fewer paid placement opportunities.

In sum, emergent alternative clergy labor supplies have included women, second-career men, retirees, and those interested the less traditional ordination tracks. Given the economic stringencies that religious organizations currently face, as well as the dwindling supply of young first-career male clergy who have traditionally supplied the occupation, organizational resources are being reallocated to meet needs in creative ways that do not threaten the control of male denominational leadership or the maintenance of the religious tradition. The positions that women, as an alternative labor supply, have held are those that tend to offer less autonomy or opportunities for upward mobility. According to Cohn, such positions in secular occupations are constructed to be less desirable so as to encourage greater turnover and thereby reduce pressure for higher compensation and benefits.[55] Oversupplies of women tend to increase labor inequalities, according to Almquist, with women's occupational value and their likelihood of integrating into more advantageous positions inversely related to their numbers.[56] Consequently, the continued influx of women clergy is likely to provide an increased source of alternative clergy labor for deployment in positions marginal to those traditionally linked to denominational influence and authority, with the deployment of retirees and clergy in alternative ordination tracks further presenting a competing labor resource for the occupational opportunities of women ministers and priests.

Clergy versus Laity: The Emergence of Clericalism

Clericalism—the process of preserving or expanding the power of an ordained religious hierarchy—tends to measure one's religious authenticity by having attained status as an ordained leader.[57] The secular experience of second-career clergy, the increased ratio of women, and the scarcity of young male clergy serve to undermine the welfare of a traditional *clergy class* with its particular ideological framework and occupational self-understanding that has bolstered a legacy of the clergy as a set-apart, priestly body. As a response, clericalism has been manifested through occupational and organizational restructuring that has included a proliferation of clergy jobs and ordination tracks that have effectively abraded occupational opportunities for women ordained in the primary track, as discussed in earlier chapters.

Several factors have contributed to the increasing social pressure for clericalism movements. The first involves a basic resistance to the erosion of privileged entitlement. As Ranson et al. argue, those in more prestigious positions are likely to hold values appropriate to maintaining the basis of that prestige.[58] Those positions with a surplus of prestige, such as at the senior leadership level, may be more flexible in affirming pluralistic interests and constituencies such as women clergy. This would concur with a tendency in secular work for senior executive management to be more socially liberal in organizational issues, more willing to take risks, and less authoritarian than upper-middle management.[59] It also would explain the tendency for senior religious leadership to have been more supportive of women's ordination movements—and of women clergy—than male clergy at lower levels who have been the most resistant of all constituencies to women's ordination and deployment—a constituency who also is the most affected by occupational competition from women.[60] Additionally, where clergy still aspire to upward job mobility or where their aspirations have become frustrated, their occupational interests would suggest resistance to changes that facilitate democratic values and practices that, by their nature, erode aristocratic privilege.

A second, related factor has to do with declines in member participation and a resultant decrease in clergy influence over laity. An emphasis on sacraments in some traditions has strengthened the distinctiveness and professional importance of a clergy role set apart from laity, irrespective of the latter's educational level. Stendahl attributes the rise of high-church clericalism in the (Lutheran) Church of Sweden to an establishment response resulting from declines in church participation induced by a geographic transition to urban location and lifestyle, and compounded by the popular folk-church movement in the early decades of the twentieth century.[61] Church services had become primarily a gathering of priests, resulting in the Church of Sweden increasingly becoming defined by liturgy and sacraments rather than by the community of participants, with clergy attention fixed upon the proper interpretation of the priestly role and its responsibilities as distinct from laity. Potential parallels with American mainline religious organizations become particularly evident when comparing the twofold decline in membership and rise in Episcopal and U.U.A. clergy over the last thirty years (cf. Table 8.1).

Nonsacramental traditions have utilized an emphasis on sin and repentance, including the importance of clergy mediation through preaching and a style of worship facilitating personal penitence and conversion, to accentuate the subtle import of clergy-laity distinctions. Some traditions such as the U.S. Episcopal Church have developed both "high church" sacramentalist and "low church" evangelical factions, emphasizing clergy roles as set apart from laity either through sacramental ritual or facilitating "renewal." Stewart and West attribute the proliferation of the Episcopal permanent diaconate to the high-church Liturgical Movement, during the 1950s and 1960s.[62] Predictably, movements toward women's ordination have encountered higher tension among denominational factions where strong distinctions are made between clergy and laity.

A third factor in the growth of clericalism reflects both membership declines and the growing shortage of volunteer labor. The vow of obedience—for example, in the Episcopal ordination rite—can be an effective means to sustain a commitment of both time and labor in a way that may alleviate dislocations in both the quantity and the growing selectivity of lay volunteer work. The current tendency to devalue traditional women's work in congregations among women under age 60[63] raises a question of whether alternative ordination tracks might be serving as replacements for lay ministry. For instance, the permanent diaconate has been justified as "provid[ing] an opportunity to experience more rewarding ministry than that which they previously exercised as lay leader. . . . "[64] An Episcopal Church study showed that those encouraged to seek ordination as permanent deacons had substantial lay church experience, had been involved in congregational and diocesan governing bodies, had taught Sunday School, and had been involved as lay readers during worship. Occupationally, permanent deacons and laity were found to have similar backgrounds in small business and middle management, teaching, social work, and paraprofessions.[65] As such, alternative ordination tracks can serve as clerical orders to which laity can enter without substantial disruption to their secular lives. The proliferation of clergy, then, may be a pragmatic, clerical response to the demand for ongoing commitment to a multitude of congregational tasks, as well as bolstering the prestige of such work. As such, ordained orders offer a more effective means to control the religious organization's workforce.

An economic advantage to increased clericalism, in addition to extensive low-cost or voluntary clergy labor to replace the loss of lay volunteers, is the likelihood that clergy will contribute more financial resources to the church than as laity. Although not all religious organizations insist on an annual tithe of 10 percent of gross income, most do hold it as an explicit goal. Clergy are encouraged to set an example for laity in this regard. With the average Protestant church member giving 2 to 3 percent of income annually, and Roman Catholic laity averaging less than 1 percent annually,[66] a greater pool of clergy increases the twofold prospect of higher annual giving and that it will be sustained.

Organizational restructuring in a way that facilitates the growth of clericalism can serve as a means to rebuild or enrich the existing authority of the clergy. In 1992, the quadrennial United Methodist Church's General Conference narrowly defeated a motion to make the denomination's lay diaconate an ordained order as a means to enhance its prestige, then passed it in 1996. In the Episcopal Church and the U.U.A., ordination and fellowship processes have been increasingly formalized, clarified, and objectified, with tightened requirements for access, as well as the addition of newer discrete ordination tracks. In the Episcopal Church, the national canons have been revised to not only define discrete roles and responsibilities for bishops, priests, and deacons, but also to regulate lay participation by requiring training and licensing for activities such as lay reader (if also leading a public worship service), preacher, catechist, pastoral leader, and eucharistic minister.[67] This formalization effectively has decreased the permeability of nontraditional routes for ordination to the priesthood, including *trading up* from the permanent diaconate, although nontraditional entries have continued to occur on a situational basis. For instance, Canon 9 local priests, although theoretically ordained and licensed for a single location, are granted mobility with their bishop's approval, thus making them potentially less distinguishable from traditionally ordained priests. Permanent deacons also have subsequently been ordained either as Canon 9 local priests or as traditional priests.

Alternative ordination statuses also reflect a trend toward increased clericalism in congregationally oriented denominations. The U.U.A.'s implementation of certification and then ordination for its *minister of religious education* status, with extensive study required for denominational fellowship recognition, reflects an effort to raise the occupational prestige of religious education. One minister of religious education interviewed for this analysis claimed that her ordained status did make a difference. "It was as if they had said, 'finally we can call you a minister.'" Additionally, the presence of a minister of religious education can relieve pressure on the parish minister to handle educational tasks that, in most denominations, have been considered less prestigious as well as associated with women's work.[68] While the two ordination tracks theoretically are discrete, more permeability was shown in previous chapters to exist for men than women. Women holding dual ordination status were disproportionately concentrated in religious education positions while men holding the same credentials were more likely to be parish ministers.

The proliferation of ordination tracks and lay certification programs also directly enhance the relative prestige of clergy in the primary track and, in Episcopal denominations, ultimately of the bishop. Alternative ordination tracks that are distinct and specialized effectively secure a discrete hierarchical labor supply, as well as provide male ministers and priests with an additional source of subordinate, noncompetitive clergy colleagues—those more likely to hold traditionalist perspectives on gender-related issues, especially given their parochial training. Episcopal permanent deacons, for instance, allow a rector to delegate more traditional and routine, but relatively less prestigious responsibilities, such as home, hospital, and care-facility visitation, and labor-intensive ministry with the poor and disenfranchised. Interestingly, both permanent deacons and Canon 9 local priests have been assigned in some Episcopal dioceses to report to the bishop, despite functional supervision by a priest.[69] Unlike priests holding assistant or associate positions, permanent deacons are not necessarily required to offer their resignation when a new rector comes. Consequently, their placement gives bishops fresh, direct authority linkages into congregations, particularly those that are self-supporting and heretofore had maintained a financial supplier relationship to the denomination. This structural move effectively undermines parish autonomy and the authority of both parish clergy and lay leadership. Where several permanent deacons per parish and increased reliance on Canon 9 local priests are envisioned, with ordination to the traditional priesthood continuing only on a limited basis, the authority of the episcopate effectively becomes consolidated without controversial constitutional or canonical change.

The clericalism movement may not only serve to provide and maintain a labor supply for the work of the church and to bolster clergy prestige, but it also may represent a grassroots movement to retain a traditionalist control of the church as yet another backlash response to occupational feminization and a changing consciousness on gender-related issues. Clericalism consolidates authority and social control much more than lay movements. By inflating the overall number of clergy who hold traditionalist perspectives or are not likely to challenge the authority, ideology, or practices of their clergy leaders, pro-feminist clergy effectively can be outnumbered, outvoted, and marginalized without a direct confrontation over affirmative action, equal opportunity, inclusive language, or other gender-related concerns. Furthermore, the occupational conflation of women in the primary ordination track with those in the alternative tracks minimizes women's potential impact on the occupation and the religious organization, and serves to set apart male ministers and priests from all others—preserving as much as possible a male professional image at the core of the clergy occupation.

A tension emerges, however, between expectations of clergy in the alternative tracks and those of clergy in the primary, or traditional, track. For instance, about one-third of students in Episcopal permanent diaconate training programs and of ordained permanent deacons surveyed in a denominational study said that they were at least somewhat likely to seek ordination to the priesthood within the next ten years.[70] Not only do diaconal aspirations support a thesis of clericalism—whereby the measure of religious authenticity resides in attaining an ever-higher ordained status—but they raise a further concern about potential occupational competitiveness with priests.

Concurrent with the rise of clericalism has been a movement to affirm lay ministry. Opponents of alternative ordination tracks have pointed out that Episcopal permanent deacons, for instance, sacramentally cannot do any more than laity can do when a deacon is not present,[71] and fears have been expressed that ordaining large numbers of laity will undermine lay ministry through the development of distinctive ordained roles and responsibilities that may resemble what Wortman calls "rungs on a corporate ladder."[72] Some Episcopal dioceses have refused to ordain permanent deacons for that reason.[73] Ironically, concerns over protecting lay ministry also have had some anti-feminist undercurrents.

The implications of the clericalism movement and its congregationalist countermovement are critical for the viability and future of women clergy. At their worst, both of these movements have strains that are anti-feminist. As manifested in the proliferation of alternative ordination tracks trained within the local congregation or judicatory, they also risk the dangers of parochialism and of impairing seminaries that have affirmed feminist and innovative scholarship.[74] They well may not only embody an attempt to bolster the authority and prestige of the clergy, as well as to secure a committed, economical labor supply for the work of the church, but also represent grassroots backlash attempts to undermine opportunities for feminist clergy—male as well as female—to make substantive change in gender-related ideology and practices in their religious organizations.

Professionalism and Deprofessionalization

Not only has professionalism been accused of facilitating clericalism by differentiating and stratifying religious roles,[75] but it also has served as a means of marginalizing ordained women. Resultingly, women have had a tenuous relationship with professionalization movements. Such movements, where skill requirements are increased and hierarchical differentiation sharpened, effectively serve as a twofold attempt to raise occupational prestige and attract men.[76] In medicine and ministry, as in other professions, movements toward professionalization historically have marginalized and segregated women practitioners from the central positions of authority, if not excluding them altogether.[77] In this context, professionalization can be regarded as a process by which those producing special services seek to develop and control the market for their expertise.[78]

Professionalization movements typically occur where a substantial concentration of women exists whose training has been informal and where men could benefit by making distinctions between those who have been formally credentialed and those who have not. Those who are informally trained become a lower paid, supportive labor supply if not excluded altogether. The proportionally fewer women with formal credentials may support the movement so as to preserve or enhance their own standing relative to other women even though, as was noted in the preceding chapter, educational credentials hold a lower payoff for women than men.[79]

Most large denominations have formalized and upgraded ordination requirements as part of professionalization processes over the last two decades, particularly as concentrations of women clergy have increased. While some steps ostensibly benefit women, such as objectifying the ordination process and moving away from informal networks as the normative means by which clergy once were recruited, the very clarification of the process has added bureaucratic layers that not only have made ordination a more rigorous rite of passage but the objective nature of the formal requirements can be utilized to legitimately exclude unwanted candidates, including women. At the same time, denominational gatekeepers have retained some ability to modify or short-circuit the process for particularly desirable candidates.

The Unitarian Universalist ministerial fellowship process has grown increasingly exacting, particularly after the annual concentration of women ordained surpassed 50 percent. Added requirements for U.U.A. fellowship status include psychological interviews, required clinical pastoral education experience, supervised internships, demonstrated competence in several academic areas, and demonstrated preaching expertise.[80] For predominately female ministers of religious education, professionalization steps have distinguished "qualified" women and men through the development of the certification program and then the procedures for ordained fellowship. At the same time, however, professionalization has not removed the hierarchical and economic status separation from parish ministers, nor have women holding dual ordination occupationally benefited to the same extent as men.

The linkage between women's ordination and the clergy professionalization movement is yet more explicit in the Episcopal Church. The ordination process has been objectified and considerably tightened since 1970, when women were first granted access to ordination. That year, a denominationwide General Ordination Examination was instituted as a requirement of all Episcopal candidates (permanent deacons and Canon 9 local priests were excluded). Each diocese, however, was allowed to decide how to interpret the results of its candidates, including whether to ordain those not passing all areas of the exam. While the exam has helped some women to objectively demonstrate their qualifications in dioceses where women's ordination has been highly controversial, the examination also has been argued to screen for feminist biases. Ordination steps for the transitional diaconate and priesthood, like those for U.U.A. fellowship, now also typically include physical and psychological examinations, clinical pastoral education experience, supervised internships, a Master of Divinity degree, and periodic meetings with diocesan commissions and committees.

Professionalization also has been linked to rising educational levels,[81] evident in the changing forms of clergy address. In various denominational publications, clergy more frequently are being referred to as "Reverend Mr.," "Reverend Ms.," or "Reverend Dr.," making visible a distinction between those with or without doctoral credentials, although distinctions among types of doctorates are not yet being made. While educational inflation has benefited seminary and university doctoral programs, three intriguing questions remain:

1. To what extent does doctoral status significantly advance professional standards?
2. How might it be serving to bolster occupational prestige?
3. What aim might it have in making sharp internal status distinctions among clergy?

Educational inflation puts women in a double bind. Educational credentials have long been an important objective indicator of women's professional competency,[82] and the data show that U.U.A. women ministers and Episcopal women priests with doctorates have tended to equalize significant attainment disparities that had been evident between men and women ordained with master's degrees (Table 8.2). For instance, a master's degree resulted in significantly higher career attainment for men relative to women ministers ($p < .05$) and priests ($p < .00001$) among clergy ordained in 1970 or later; but among those with doctorates, men's higher relative attainment was not statistically significant.[83]

One of the crises that was articulated to be facing the ministry in mainline religious organizations during the early 1970s was the increased need for professional specializations, provoked by the encroachment of other occupations—particularly the helping professions.[84] Traditional clergy functions as community healer, teacher, scholar, writer, orator, psychologist, and social worker subsequently have reemerged as specialties in pastoral counseling, education and supervision, preaching and homiletics, religious education, administrative management, urban ministry, fund-raising, agency program development, and various specialized chaplaincies in hospitals, colleges, prisons, and ethnic communities. This professionalization trend has been particularly evident in conservative Protestant denominations, as higher educational requirements for ordination increasingly are being stipulated. Electronic technology, having come to have a greater role in worship and evangelism, also has encouraged clergy to develop professionalized technological expertise.

Two pervasive yet little foreseen effects on occupational professionalization trends have involved the proliferation of litigation involving clergy sexual misconduct and the increased difficulty for clergy engaged in formal pastoral counseling to negotiate third-party (insurance) payments unless dually licensed in a related secular specialty, such as social work or clinical psychology. Litigation has pressured denominations into developing standards specifically for clergy engaged in pastoral

Table 8.2. Highest Average Attainment of Episcopal Priests and U.U.A. Ministers Ordained 1970–1990, Based on Educational Credentials.

	Job level			
Degree	1–3	4–6	7–9	(N)
	Episcopal			
No degree				
Men	38%	63%	0%	(8)
Women	100	0	0	(3)
Any degree through master's				
Men	16	76	9	(556)
Women	42	56	2	(264)
Doctorate				
Men	27	59	15	(82)
Women	36%	60%	4%	(25)
	Unitarian Universalist			
Any degree through master's				
Men	2%	94%	4%	(47)
Women	21	79	0	(53)
Doctorate				
Men	7	72	21	(29)
Women	0%	100%	0%	(8)

Percentages may not total 100% owing to rounding off.

counseling or spiritual direction. Candidates seeking dual training in religion and social work to facilitate credentialization for such specialties have proliferated since 1990, presenting an ongoing illustration of how professionalization may both act as a defensive response to external influences and seek the renegotiation of diminishing occupational power. Professionalization movements also facilitate a growing attention to professional boundaries between clergy and laity, increasing the professional distance as well as contributing to the growth of both clericalist and consumerist perspectives within the religious organization.

Interestingly, professionalization trends have developed concurrently with tendencies toward occupational deprofessionalization. Douglas points to a deprofessionalization trend neatly embedded in liberal Protestantism by the middle of the nineteenth century, with the split of the theological and pastoral dimensions of the occupation, a trend toward anti-institutionalism, and ministerial virtue becoming located in the character of the incumbent rather than professional role activities that had lent the occupation distinct power and privilege.[85] This movement shortly preceded the ordination of the first women ministers. By the end of the century, a reprofessionalization movement undergirded with remasculinizing the notion of ministry fed into the backlash against women ministers who had become increasingly visible in number. In its more recent manifestation, during the mid-twentieth century, Kleinman hypothesizes that deprofessionalization had been induced both by competition from secular occupations and by change in the occupation's self-understanding of clergy authority, from a traditionally elite clericalist perspective as being *set apart* from laity through ordination to a humanistic perspective of clergy as enablers or facilitators for developing ministerial skills among all religious participants. Kleinman perceived these occupational shifts to be occurring in the 1960s and early 1970s, the period immediately preceding the sharp influx of women clergy.[86] A shift in focus to enablement, for Kleinman, posed a concern over the clergy's continued status as a profession: if clergy were charged with enabling the ministry of all, then what remained professionally distinctive about the clergy? Both clericalization and professionalization movements since 1970 could be considered as responses to such concerns.

Accompanying deprofessionalization concerns has been evidence from this analysis over the relative decline in opportunities for male upward mobility into leadership positions or their maintenance through controlling male ordinations and limiting women's opportunities. Trends toward diminishing occupational authority, social status, and prestige also were discussed in chapter 6.[87] Although the proliferation of more recently created specialized positions found in the data could be a professionalization response to secular occupational encroachment, in secular occupations the trend toward specialized lower level positions has been argued to represent evidence of deprofessionalization.[88] Applying Pavalko's observation of greater age diversity occurring in lesser skilled secular occupations with truncated career lines, it is possible to hypothesize that the growing age diversity among those entering the ministry may be indicative of an occupational redefinition and restructuring not incomparable to what has been regarded as semiprofessional work—nursing, teaching, or social work—with correspondingly more limited authority and autonomy than is traditionally characteristic for the profession.[89] If so, the wide age diversity at ordination may be symptomatic of compressed occupational opportunities, skill requirements, authority, and status relative to other professions. Evidence of the utilization of retirees as an alternative labor supply would further support this prospect.

Deprofessionalization and professionalization trends meet in the emergence of the alternative nonretiree labor supplies that have been facilitated through clericalist movements. These newer alternative tracks, with less stringent requirements, also have experienced internal professionalism movements. Roles and responsibilities have undergone scrutiny, and both training and entry requirements have been formalized, resulting for the permanent diaconate in a rhetorical transformation from clergy who "mostly 'suit[ed] up on Sunday mornings' . . . to help with the worship service" or assisted in home visitation,[90] into a social service orientation much like the early deaconess movement.[91] At the same time, occupational de-skilling has emerged within the permanent diaconate, particularly as the concentration of women clergy has increased. This has been illustrated by the shift in placements that permanent deacons held since 1970, which had included assistant, associate, or denominational administrative staff positions, with specialized responsibilities, to primarily nonstipendiary positions with generalized responsibilities, typically with the job title of *deacon*, according to the data of this analysis. Similar evidence of de-skilling entry jobs for those ordained to the priesthood was found to occur over the 1980s and 1990s, primarily as the normative entry job title of *assistant* was replaced by that of *deacon*, especially for women.

Feminization has long been associated with de-skilling tendencies in secular occupations. Not only is de-skilling more likely to occur in positions held by women but where it does occur in male-dominant jobs, women are more likely to replace men if higher skilled alternatives are available for the latter.[92] Additionally, as Reskin has pointed out, the devaluation of women's work relative to men's leads to an assessment of whatever women do as being less skilled.[93] The occupational conflation that occurred between permanent deacons and women priests, as male priests became ever more sharply differentiated from them, suggests an interaction between occupational de-skilling and gender segregation, offering yet another illustration of how women become disadvantaged as professionalization and de-professionalization trends intersect.

The professionalism-deprofessionalization dialectical tension has cut to the heart of the Roman Catholic Church in its struggle to find alternatives to women's ordination. The deprofessionalization of the priest's role, particularly as parish pastor, to a series of parish administrative and pastoral roles that can be filled by lay or religious women and men has served to reduce clericalism and at the same time open the way for new professional opportunities for women. Yet because of the denomination's tight sacramental control by men, including the maintenance of a priestly class as set apart through ordination, which is the basis of both occupational and organizational authority, women's participation remains peripheral and ultimately expendable should clergy supply problems ever be resolved.

Wilson has argued that the devaluation of clergy professional status has aided the growth of the ecumenical movement as a means to reassert clergy authority and privilege.[94] Ironically, the ecumenical movement has taken two different turns, sharply differentiated by gender. Urban church councils representing predominantly mainline denominations remain largely male. Similarly, alliances in conservative Protestant groups such as the Christian Coalition are overwhelmingly male in their leadership. However, feminist theological and spirituality movements also have developed an ecumenical solidarity, poignantly evident in the women-church movement, seeking to minimize occupational as well as denominational authority and privilege.[95]

In sum, while deprofessionalization may be associated with both increasingly larger concentrations of women clergy and occupational conflation among women despite objective educational credentials, professionalization movements also negatively affect women relative to men by facilitating gender-related job segregation and the suppression of women's opportunities as the occupation is restructured in ways to attract and secure a male labor supply. Either way, women suffer greater inequalities than men. As Chafetz puts it, only when the demand for *skilled* labor exceeds the supply of men do women occupationally benefit.[96]

A Future of Nonstipendiary Clergy

Another crisis facing the clergy that surfaced more than two decades ago was the decreasing ability of mainline denominations to support full-time positions, with the consequent increase in part-time and nonstipendiary placements. Clergy in most religious organizations traditionally have been expected to work full time in local congregations or on denominational staffs, although there has been a long history of clergy whose ministry was to socioeconomically poor congregations and therefore concurrently worked at a secular job.

The growth of nonstipendiary clergy may be considered an effect of occupational specialization produced by the interaction of professionalization and deprofessionalization trends. The development of formalized clergy pay scales and compensation packages including health insurance, pension, housing, and more often than not a cash allowance for charitable purposes known as a discretionary fund, have had exacerbating pressure on congregational budgets. Professionalization, according to Schaller, has "priced thousands of congregations 'out of the preacher market.'"[97] One denominational deployment officer interviewed for this analysis foresees the clergy becoming primarily a *tentmaker* occupation,[98] warning that "clergy will have to be more flexible." One Episcopal diocese has predicted that only 20 percent of its annual ordinands can expect to have full careers in parish ministry, with the remainder required to spend some time working on a nonstipendiary basis.[99]

The turn to part-time and nonstipendiary clergy has been seen as an important alternative, particularly where losses in lay volunteer labor have severely stretched congregational resources. Carroll and Wilson observed that between 1966 and 1974 Episcopal nonstipendiary clergy increased by more than 300 percent.[100] The "hard times" thesis has been utilized to argue for both the proliferation of Canon 9 priests and the revival of the permanent diaconate, clergy who overwhelmingly are nonstipendiary or part-time.[101] Of those permanent deacons in the data of this analysis who hold current appointments or whose most recent placements ended in 1990 or later, 50 percent of the men and 77 percent of the women were estimated to be part-time or nonstipendiary. As a trend, part-time and nonstipendiary placements were found to have increased significantly over time, especially for the more recent female ($p < .001$) and male ($p < .01$) cohorts. This trend is chronologically associated with the feminization of the permanent diaconate during the mid-1980s. Since the data represent a conservative estimate of part-time or nonstipendiary employment, the actual figures are likely much higher.[102] Where permanent deacons are usually not paid for their work, which can average as many hours as a part-time job, evident by a 1991 denominational study,[103] it underscores the economic importance of these alternative labor supplies. The deployment of voluntary permanent diaconal labor is not without critics. Leidel has raised concerns about both the lack of seminary training and the absence of wages, as a justice issue, for the work deacons perform. In his diocese, deacons have resorted to part-time *secular* jobs so as to provide time for their diaconal ministry.[104]

According to the Episcopal Church Pension Fund, women constituted 18 percent of all nonstipendiary clergy in 1990, even though they represented only about 12 percent of all clergy in the denomination. A denominational report concluded that women clergy were disproportionately involved in the "'voluntary' work of the Church," continuing a tradition of lay women's disproportionate volunteerism.[105] The disproportionate allocation of female labor to part-time and nonstipendiary positions regardless of women's marital status as found in the data of this analysis resembles secular occupations where the use of women's unpaid labor has been observed both to be in the interest of men, who rely upon it, and to inhibit female competition for desirable positions.[106] Writes Chafetz, "if men continue to possess superior resource power, they can coerce heretofore voluntary behavior from women. Women may seek nontraditional work roles, but if male elites refuse to make opportunities available, women will probably not acquire them."[107] Thus, the relative lack of opportunities for women clergy within the church tends to perpetuate traditionally gendered labor patterns.

The use of lay local pastors in the United Methodist Church provides yet another example of the growing overall movement toward part-time and non-stipendiary labor. Not being ordained elders, United Methodist local pastors have no claim on the denomination for a full-time placement. Much of the discussion over eliminating the itineracy system, which could result in phasing out about 17,000 appointments according to Schaller, has to do with removing denominational subsidies for clergy salaries.[108] It has been argued that the competition for full-time placements would attract and keep talented clergy, while other placements could utilize nonstipendiary pastors, retirees, and others interested in positions offering less than full-time compensation.[109] If the experience of the Episcopal Church and of other denominational studies cited in this analysis are indicators, young men likely will be overrepresented in the full-time placements while women will become disproportionately segregated into the secondary constituency.

The nonstipendiary trend is also occurring outside the United States. For instance, the British Methodist church has commonly utilized "'sector' ministries," where clergy work for a living outside the denomination.[110] The estimate of clergy holding secular positions has averaged only about 7 percent in the Church of England compared to more than 20 percent in the U.S. Episcopal Church. The lack of stipendiary work has severely afflicted Church of England women priests; up to 500 of the 1,400 women ordained since 1994 do not hold paid church positions.[111]

An intriguing variation on the nonstipendiary trend is the tendency to work across denominational lines, or to hold a part-time or nonstipendiary appointment in another judicatory within a denomination. These tendencies illustrate both greater geographic and denominational mobility, and organizational changes increasingly have facilitated such opportunities.[112] Augmented by growing demands of two-career households, and with men's occupational earning power greater than women's, career relocation decisions still tend to favor men, however, while the relocated spouses occupationally fend for themselves. Another contributing factor is the prospect that clergy, particularly men, may find greater socioeconomic opportunities outside of their own diocese or judicatory. Furthermore, mobility across denominational lines suggests a professionalization trend whereby clergy are recognized for normative skills extending well beyond organizational boundaries, which would serve to enhance both professional prestige and occupational opportunities. It also might represent yet more competition for women. Since men aren't faced with the problem of some geographic locations being resistant to their presence in a way that women are, the organizational and geographic flexibility would be expected to work more to men's than to women's advantage.

Nonstipendiary status holds potential drawbacks for clergy, such as not accumulating denominational experience and seniority, and the inability to participate in most denominational pension, medical, or other insurance plans. Clergy piecing together two or more part-time positions or relying upon denominational supply work (i.e., hired and paid on a daily basis) seldom have access to insurance benefits and other protections. Although denominational discussions with prospective ministerial candidates more recently are including nonstipendiary interests, there was some evidence through interviews that denominational encouragement toward nonstipendiary ministries tends to be made selectively. Furthermore, Episcopal priests who had been nonstipendiary for part or much of their careers spoke in interviews of being given little attention by diocesan officials, and of being somewhat looked down upon by parochial (i.e., congregationally employed) clergy. They did not seem discontent with their nonstipendiary status itself, or with their occupational choice, which supports other research on nonstipendiary clergy. For instance, a 1989 Presbyterian study found that only 14 percent of those clergy not working as parish pastors said they would probably or definitely consider returning to parish employment.[113]

However, long-time parochial male clergy anecdotally and in interviews have spoken of "nonstipes" as clergy who would prefer to hold denominational jobs but lacked competence or had some deficiency. Some comments were harsh: "they're loose cannons," "they oughtn't have the same privileges as parochial clergy," and in two dioceses the feeling was expressed that "they should have no vote." According to one priest, "nonstipendiary priests are responsible to no one. There's no way to control them. Why should they have a vote that affects diocesan policy for the rest of us?" Although the speakers were referring to male nonstipendiary clergy, it is not unlikely that such comments would comparably be applied to females. Similarly, Lowery found the tendency to regard dual-occupation priests as "second-class citizens" and the negative regard for nonstipendiary clergy to be both widespread and international. They also have been perceived as a threat in that they "question prevailing clericalism and understandings of the Church and ministry in general."[114]

Ironically, neither female nor male priests in the data of this analysis who had spells of nonstipendiary employment appeared to suffer ill occupational effects when returning to denominational employment. This finding contradicts the attitude expressed in some of the interviews that nonstipendiary clergy are somehow inferior to parochial clergy. Since those interviewed who held this attitude tended to have mid-level placements (job levels 5 and 6) and had been ordained young, it's possible that this group may feel competitive pressure with nonstipendiary male colleagues. If so, it would partly explain attempts to differentiate between the prestige of parochial and nonstipendiary clergy, and would suggest why they might seek to minimize the permeability between parochial and nonstipendiary status. For those parochial clergy with no secular occupational skills, concerns over occupational deprofessionalization would add to increased competitive tension and strategic interest in maintaining prestige differentials.

With the growth of nonparochial clergy approaching or exceeding the numbers of parish clergy in some denominations, tension over the traditional "one vote per clergy" policy at regional governing meetings is likely to increase. One Episcopal diocese, for example, abolished automatic clergy votes in favor of requiring every voting delegate to be elected from a congregation.[115] Schaller phrases the concern in terms of rights: "Who should have the right to vote on issues that may have a major impact on the role of parish pastors?"[116] which echoes some of the long-time male clergy concerns expressed in interviews. A danger of calling explicit attention to voting rights based on stipendiary status is the risk of alienating nonstipendiary labor supplies that religious organizations are coming to depend upon. Furthermore, in the case of the Episcopal Church, nonstipendiary permanent deacons and Canon 9 local priests are more likely to hold traditionalist perspectives owing in part to the type of training they have received. Where they report directly to the bishop, they represent strategically important voting constituencies. As Lowery has observed, both bishops and laity are far less anxious over nonstipendiary ministry than parochial clergy.[117]

Given the increasing tendency for denominations to turn toward nonstipendiary ministry to resolve structural socioeconomic challenges, the tension between parochial and nonstipendiary clergy is likely to persist. It also suggests that a two-tier prestige system may become even more explicit, particularly as nonstipendiary clergy begin to outnumber parochial clergy holding full-time placements. More likely, the prestige hierarchy will develop through more subtle means than voting status. As the proportion of full-time positions continues to constrict, the consequent competition likely will contribute to the prestige value of full-time clergy who, from the results of this analysis, are disproportionately likely to remain predominately male and ordained young.

Occupational Feminization and Male Exodus

Clergy exodus, like occupational decline, has been lamented as a dreaded consequence of occupational feminization. But like declines in prestige, salary, and leadership opportunities, exodus was a denominational concern prior as well as subsequent to the large influx of women. A wave of concern over clergy exodus had swept religious organizations during the 1960s, during a time of occupational quandary over roles, authority, leadership, and compensation.[118] In perhaps the most well-known study of its time, Jud, Mills, and Burch's examination of United Church of Christ male clergy who had left the occupation altogether identified no single reason or trend for clergy departures. The three most common motivations were a sense of personal or professional inadequacy (17%), inability to relocate when it was necessary for them to do so (15%), and family concerns (13%).[119] Similarly, in a more recent multidenominational study of men and women clergy "drop-outs," Lummis found the inability to control boundaries, role conflicts over church and family or private life, and low professional self-understanding to contribute to the likelihood of seriously considering leaving the ministry.[120] And men and women asked to consider why they might leave the rabbinate have cited a diversity of reasons, from inability to accomplish one's goals to career dissatisfaction and financial concerns.[121]

Fear of male exodus had been one of several anxieties expressed to thwart women's ordination in the Episcopal Church.[122] Yet based on the data of this analysis, among Episcopal male clergy ordained between 1950 and 1975 who subsequently left the occupation, only 17 percent departed within two years after women's ordination to the diaconate (1970) and priesthood (1976) was granted—a pattern that shows only marginally more clustering around these dates than the overall distribution of departure years. This suggests that women's ordination likely added at most only slightly to the array of individual reasons for departure. Similarly, despite dire predictions by Church of England conservatives that up to 4,000 male priests might leave after women's ordination to the priesthood began in 1994, less than 250 had departed by the end of 1995.[123]

In the data of this analysis, while Episcopal and U.U.A. clergy who subsequently left the ministry altogether could be identified but not subsequently tracked or interviewed, few differences were observed between those who remained and those who ultimately left the occupation. The most striking contrast was that leavers were disproportionately male and European American—86 percent of Episcopal and 95 percent of U.U.A. leavers. Interestingly, between the first (1988) and second (1993) wave of this data, Episcopal women clergy departures had risen from 3 percent to 11 percent of all those in the "leaver" sample, surpassing the ratio of men leaving since 1985. This trend was not evident in the U.U.A. data. Furthermore, of Episcopal women leaving the clergy, 60 percent have exited within the first five years after ordination. All women in the sample who departed within this period had been ordained in 1985 or later, which suggests, in addition to the results discussed in the preceding chapters, that the ordained ministry is growing less hospitable as a career choice for Episcopal women.

One other clear trend was evident: most exits, female or male, are relatively recent. Although there was some tendency for clergy to leave between their sixth and tenth year despite the year of ordination, the more striking pattern was for nearly two-thirds of all Unitarian Universalist and over half of all Episcopal clergy to have exited since 1980, with over 40 percent departing since 1985. Although this trend is timed in relation to occupational feminization in these two denominations, more likely it is related to the pattern of diminished high-level opportunities for Episcopal male clergy and even fewer opportunities for female clergy, and sharp competition for substantive opportunities among U.U.A. male clergy—trends which began to take shape well before the large influx of women.

Occupational Change and Organizational Response

Nearly two decades ago Ranson et al. pointed out that the clergy was an occupation in flux, residing in denominations "whose secular relevance is questioned from without and whose traditions are threatened from within."[124] Substantial structural change has since occurred within religious organizations, the socioeconomic milieu in which they operate, and in how they deploy clergy. But organizational responses to dislocations in clergy supply and demand appear to have affected men less than women. Furthermore, the development and implementation of alternative sources of clergy labor have exacerbated job segregation by gender and facilitated the occupational marginalization of women clergy. The emergence of clericalism, while serving as a convenient if not totally necessary response to concerns facing religious organizations in terms of declining occupational prestige and volunteer time commitments, has created barriers that further differentiate male clergy ordained in their youth from all others, especially women. Likewise, while professionalism movements have objectified ordination processes that have helped to qualify and deploy women, they also have been used to control or inhibit women's progress. Deprofessionalization movements, including job de-skilling, have further reinforced gender-related job segregation, especially where women also become disproportionately represented in part-time and nonstipendiary positions regardless of their marital status. In the Episcopal Church, the recent exodus of women clergy reflects the impact that these structural shifts have had on their career opportunities.

It is important to remember that these socioeconomic effects upon religious organizations had developed prior to and independently of the substantial influx of women into the clergy. While their effects may have facilitated the trend toward occupational feminization, they also transcend it in both substance and significance. That men's careers were more negatively affected by changes preceding rather than following the large influx of women is significant in relation to how religious organizations have structurally responded in a manner that has sought to preserve the structure of male opportunities. Although part of structural reorganization and clergy redeployment may be attributed as an explicit backlash response to the sharply increased ratio of women clergy, alternatively women have been disproportionately caught in an impersonal net of solutions that religious organizations have developed to meet these socioeconomic and structural crises.

Chafetz proposed that where great economic challenges are encountered, elite decision makers are both less inclined to develop policies that support gender equity and more inclined to cut existing programs.[125] That such decisions are made with few women clergy at an occupational level sufficient to be influential in developing the proposed solutions becomes yet another illustration of the history of women's participation in organized religion where the men decide what is best for the common good while ignoring the difficult questions of who disproportionately benefits and who occupationally pays. In terms of outcomes, benign neglect of such consequences is little different than actions deliberately calculated toward gender discrimination and exclusion. Consequently, occupational feminization if anything is symptomatic of complex organizational and occupational responses to an array of socioeconomic and structural shifts in wider society. But what, then, bodes for the future of women clergy, particularly in an occupation that demographically is continuing to become heavily feminized?

Clergy Feminization

Controlled Labor or Liberationist Change?

Occupational feminization not only suggests change in the ordained ministry itself but has been shown to be part of larger socioeconomic concerns that involve organizational shifts and restructuring. Although structures may have changed in response to pragmatic socioeconomic need, the processes have held constant the dominance of those currently in power. Women's labor has been grafted into the clergy, but as it has taken root, breaking new social ground, the occupational and denominational structures have shifted. In the Episcopal Church, such shifts appear to involve intentional occupational crowding, the proliferation of multiple ordination tracks, and gender-based job segregation to the extent that women effectively cease to make much headway in gaining legitimate access to positions of significant authority or influence. Generalized, such shifts resemble a series of mirrors whereby shapes of occupational and organizational change ripple across the face of many denominations at once, all the while belying the apparent intransigence of "women's place" within each of these illusions.

If women were to participate in the ordained leadership of their religious organizations in the same percentage as the female concentration in denominational membership, substantive pressure likely would be brought for change in female dependency on male authority to determine and control not only their opportunity structure but also matters of doctrine, religious language, and liturgical practices that have legitimated male dominion and the suppression of female status. Yet, as Hargrove has warned, "No decision to push the inclusion of women into leadership positions should be expected to be without consequences. One change is likely to create others."[1] But to date, women leaders remain challenged by both continued passive and active pressures against the successful articulation of their voice and influence within the stable network of male leadership.

The Future of Women Clergy

Reskin and Roos conclude from their analysis of recently feminized secular occupations that women benefited little if at all occupationally by entering them. By the time substantial numbers of women gained access, the occupations not only had lost their attractiveness to men but were offering tangibly fewer advantages to women.[2]

The data of this analysis have pointed to antecedent and ensuing effects of occupational feminization on clergy careers in a highly diverse pair of American mainline religious organizations. While differences in organizational design do affect opportunities and attainment, such as the greater availability of sole pastorates relative to the number of ministers in the U.U.A., or the prevalence of part-time and nonstipendiary positions in the Episcopal Church, the pattern of gender inequality in career outcomes shows alarming consistencies. The results demonstrate that secular trends accurately depict what has been occurring for women in these two denominations. However, since secular work doesn't have the prospect of ideological influence over large sectors of women, as does organized religion, the clergy becomes strategically more critical as a battleground for occupational feminization and its implications.

Given women's apparently greater occupational attainment when their ratio does not exceed token levels,[3] it could be argued that women clergy might improve their occupational opportunities by voluntarily controlling their influx. This would mean discouraging other women from seeking ordination. Based on the strategically positive occupational effect for U.U.A. men as the annual number of new male ordinands declined, discussed in chapter 6, the short-term effect for women would alleviate some crowding in the pool of placements realistically available to them, enhancing opportunities for higher level placements relative to the number of women, and would mitigate some of the backlash against occupational feminization.[4] But while evidently effective for male clergy ordained in their youth, who categorically have been the most prestigious constituency for religious organizations to attract and retain, such strategies would alter neither the structure of gender subordination and discrimination nor the relative paucity of opportunities for women in denominational leadership, as the occupational histories of U.U.A. women clergy ordained prior to 1975 attest.

Schlegel contends that gender-segregated work is unimportant provided the myths and rituals of a society value women as highly as men.[5] Since myth and ritual are manifested in language and imagery, the male bias of these become crucially important in understanding the coercive processes that underlie the persistence of occupational inequality between men and women clergy, and the consequences of the strife over inclusive language in religious organizations. In secular structures, the use of male sexual imagery for organizational metaphors and work tasks has been linked to the maintenance of male dominance and the marginalization of women.[6] Similarly in religious organizations, attitudes toward liturgical language have been connected with attitudes on authority, women's ordination, and leadership.[7]

Where the structure of gender inequality remains embedded and perpetuated within religious imagery, practices, and discourse, men remain disproportionately empowered. The use of inclusive language has been a source of intense friction within the Episcopal Church. The gender bias in the U.U.A., however, has resided primarily in the notion of *fellowship*, a concept that theoretically has been argued to be gender inclusive in its plural form, like *men*, while remaining male exclusive in the singular: a female would not be described as a "good man" or an "amiable fellow." While perplexity has been expressed over the lack of inclusive synonyms in denominational circles where *fellowship* is used in a religious context, the gender bias in the concept underlying the word has yet to be seriously dealt with: how effectively do women measure up as "fellows"? The possibility that women might reconstruct the fundamental notion that fellowship has expressed, in a manner that transforms the core ethos of the concept, would represent a substantial risk for those who benefit from the current language and imagery.

What actions, then, can be taken besides reconceptualizing myth, imagery, language, and ritual to assure that occupational opportunities are more equitable between men and women? Those in religious organizations who are concerned about creating a more inclusive climate for women clergy need to explicitly monitor gender differences in entry and subsequent placements, and to evaluate the conflationary effects that structural occupational or organizational changes might have. They also must be willing to submit to conscious role reversal: what would it mean for men to be disproportionately represented in hands-on religious education, youth ministry, and various part-time placements connoted primarily with service while women were groomed for denominational leadership? Abolishing gender-related job segregation and unequal opportunities means that large numbers of men must agreeably undertake the same meager job placements and responsibilities that have sufficed for women.

Agassi has argued that to break the ties that sustain gender inequalities, traditional work patterns must be altered.[8] In religious organizations, the costs to the male-dominant status quo will not be effectively challenged until women clergy collectively press issues as to why their labor and status are worth less than men's. The ethos of individuality in opportunity and treatment facilitates occupational segregation by isolating women with the deceptive assumption that their opportunities are based on merit, when the data show this not to be the case. The proliferation of part-time and nonstipendiary positions has served to divide women occupationally, as well as politically. Where their energies are compromised by the need to hold concurrent secular employment, in addition to their denominational work and the disproportionate share of domestic and family responsibilities that they continue to hold, their abilities to organize effectively are weakened. Denominational trends such as formalized expectations for clergy compensation based on the type of position, length of time in the placement, and congregational resources are positive steps, but as shown in the previous chapter, objectification does not necessarily translate to equality.

Cockburn suggests for transformative practice in secular organizations that energy and resources must be committed to an internal women's movement that can support female efforts at all occupational levels.[9] But networks and coalitions tend to fracture along the fault lines of what members perceive they may have to lose, what they are willing to risk, or simply their diverse competing agendas. Nonetheless, coalitions not only can be important sources for sharing information and for various internal constituencies to work collectively to raise issues of inequity but can be a means of publicly holding to account those who perpetuate the dialectical structure of privilege and marginalization.

Reskin argues that those who benefit from hierarchical systems will give up their privilege only when the consequences of not doing so become too costly. For change to occur, either the costs to hold onto the status quo must become escalated or those who are privileged must receive rewards for dividing their resources more equitably.[10] Men who have sought equity for women typically have incurred the reward of increased prestige from public visibility over their leadership of such movements. However, such rewards lose currency when a movement decelerates and subsequently encounters widespread structural resistance.

Some women, frustrated with a lack of access, will continue to establish their own religious groups, congregations, and feminist *base communities* like those that have developed around the women-church movement,[11] or will found new religious movements, which have long been the tradition for women seeking religious leadership in both European-American and African-American traditions.[12] Exodus, however, does little to change the structure of inequality embedded in religious organizations or the influence they maintain on large constituencies of lay women. Exodus also has been linked with a rise in misogynism.[13] Additionally, women leaders of autonomous sect or cult movements risk social persecution depending upon the radicality of their beliefs and practices, particularly those pertaining to gender and sexuality.[14] Such movements also face problems of survival beyond the founding generation.

Most likely, women will continue to enter mainline denominations, preferring to work for change internally as best they can. Yet as long as greater social esteem resides with male gender attribution, and where religious organizations do not have a surplus of economic resources, membership likely will remain politically hesitant to entrust women with positions of power and leadership[15] despite historical and contemporary evidence that women have capably built congregational memberships and improved their financial circumstances.[16] The rational qualities, as well as experiential evidence of ability and achievement, apparently will have little to do with the prospect of improving attainment possibilities for women clergy.

In sum, the future of women clergy realistically appears to be one increasingly crowded with female colleagues in lower to mid-level placements as the occupation continues to feminize. Although some women will attain positions of religious leadership, it is doubtful that they will increase beyond a token level in either number or influence unless current gender-segregation practices in placements and opportunities are mitigated. In short, women will continue to labor in the vineyard while the masters reap the fruits of their harvest. Over the longer term, however, suggested by the intensity of the backlash movement, a more pervasive, gender-related social transformation may be taking root that should bode a more optimistic future for women clergy and ultimately for their religious organizations.

Women and the Future of the Clergy

Imagining that the clergy were to become predominately a female occupation with full access and opportunities to attain positions of denominational authority, how might both the clergy and their religious organization be transformed? Some evidence suggests that women generally tend to be more drawn to the relational than the ideological aspects of religion.[17] Definitive gender differences in clergy leadership styles were documented by Lehman at the senior level only, however. Men were more likely to use coercive power over the congregation, to seek positions of formal authority, to prefer rationally structured decision making and to manifest ethical legalism, while women utilized a more personal and congregationally empowering style.[18] Given the importance of those in senior leadership to shape the ethos as well as influence organizational policy or practice, it can be hypothesized that lay women as well as men would experience decreased authoritarian ideological control and more relational empowerment to live affirmatively in religious and social relationship.

According to Fitzpatrick, national coordinator of the Women's Ordination Conference (W.O.C.), should the Roman Catholic Church decide to ordain women, female priests and bishops are likely to bring about significant structural changes.[19] Many women have stated that their vision of a female priesthood is markedly different from the status quo. Already, the persistent exclusion of Roman Catholic women from ordination has served to redistribute the occupational workload of the priesthood such that the division of labor between clergy and laity is blurring in all but sacramental tasks. As of 1991, of the parishes administered without priests, 63 percent were being led by religious sisters.[20] Furthermore, Wallace found that the women pastors developed, partly out of necessity due to their lay status, a new paradigm that rejected a status of being set apart for one of collaborative leadership, with a resultant increased sense of community and empowerment among the laity, which included feminist commitments to gender equality. This internal occupational restructuring, combined with a widespread rejection of recent traditionalist Vatican proclamations relating to women's ordination, gender, and sexuality[21] hold far more significant implications for the prospect of radical occupational and organizational change than shifts that have occurred in other mainline religious organizations where women have been ordained, co-opted, job segregated, and to some extent pacified, mollified or frustrated.

Women Clergy and the Future of Liberationist Change

While religion has been utilized as an agent of social control it also holds the potential for empowerment among those who have been subject to its strictures. *Liberation* in a religious context has promulgated radical social transformation by giving greater social resources to those who have been socioeconomically oppressed and politically marginalized. Liberation theologies have reinterpreted traditional religious scripture and doctrine in a manner so as to inspire and empower marginalized groups to engage in sociopolitical conflict for the renegotiation of a more equitable distribution of resources.[22] Feminist liberation theology, normally interpreted as the struggle of white women against marginalization by a white male authority structure, has provoked the development of racial and cultural counterparts. Womanist liberation theology has affirmed African-American women's struggle against both racism and sexism; the *mujerista* movement similarly has affirmed the struggle of Latin-American women against these oppressive forces. According to Gilkes, the theological issues that such perspectives have wrought are generating ongoing crises over traditional understandings of divinity within religious organizations—not only through language and imagery but also in interracial and cross-cultural self-critiques that challenge racial as well as sexual hegemony.[23] As European-American women clergy recognize that their sisters of color face a shared yet significantly different constellation of issues—namely, the interaction of racism and sexism—the transformative agenda represented by liberationist change becomes both more complex and far-reaching.

Movements for liberationist change, then, are to a great extent dependent on social location. A major drawback to such movements persistently has involved divisiveness within women's constituencies. Those who hold traditionalist understandings of gender often may benefit from their dependency arrangements, as discussed in chapter 7. Women also can become placated or co-opted by their religious organizations, where inequalities no longer are perceived as intolerable or are relativized within a context of injustice. When the illusion of access to senior leadership can be maintained through tokenism, with carefully selected women attaining visible placements even though socially constrained from taking significant action, or women are rewarded in little ways although remaining structurally dependent upon male approval and authority, solidarity with women who are unrewarded or marginalized by the status quo can easily disintegrate. Even within those constituencies pressing for change, conflict over how reform should be defined and shaped can generate substantial internal dissension. This has been a particular dilemma for women taking seriously changes that are racially and culturally inclusive as well as gender inclusive. Internal dissension, however, can serve as a process of clarification and ensurance that one type of oppression simply doesn't replace another. But according to Chafetz, factionalism and internal conflict ultimately can result in an apathy that is antithetical to continued social change.[24] Substantial internal strife can result in a movement's loss of momentum and eventual standstill, especially if external backlash elements have been encouraging internal dissension while overtly working against these movements. Dissension, then, must be balanced with sustained internal commitment if pressure for change is likely to continue.

Within the context of liberationist change it might be prudent to reflect on the extent to which women's ordination might be utilized as a tactic of social control over lay women. Where newer ordination tracks draw directly from women experienced in lay ministry, such as the Episcopal permanent diaconate, not only can status differentials be created through aspirations toward ordination but the act of ordination exerts more direct control over women's voice and activities, which can have the consequence of gutting the latent power that lay ministry holds. The prospect of status mobility that increased clericalism facilitates through aspirancy to hierarchically differentiated orders can result in individualistic rather than collective expectations, with consequently greater difficulty in building alliances across status lines. While men concerned over the social control of women may observe rifts between lay and clergywomen, or between women in traditional and newer ordination tracks, women also need to be aware of these fractures and where they strategically occur if they are to assertively minimize differences and enhance mutual support. Where women priests strive to develop strong collegial relations with female permanent deacons, for example, and permanent deacons with lay women, such alliances can facilitate communication on issues concerning women's welfare and more effectively resist manipulation, dominance, and control by men threatened by the prospect of women's equality.

Women clergy cannot generate social change alone. The secular feminist literature on organizational change emphasizes the importance of senior management or elites in setting the tone, as well as affirmative action policies, if transformation toward gender equality is to occur.[25] As Cockburn notes, men pay attention to other men more willingly than to women.[26] In hierarchical religious organizations, the leadership of bishops on matters of gender equality has been decisive on the extent of inclusiveness that women clergy experience, including support for women's ordination itself.[27] Whatever change that has occurred in a liberationist direction can be interpreted as the interactive consequence of women laity, women clergy, and women theologians with shared commitments, supported by male elites who have believed in the justness of such causes. Elites have been better able to afford the risks while the grassroots, with relatively little to risk, have provided the energy, creativity, and radical vitality necessary for empowering social change.

But women's movements also can be co-opted by male elites who quickly support some concerns while overlooking others, with the consequence of defusing momentum so that they never reach their maximum potential, according to Chafetz.[28] A historical comparison of feminist theology generated from denominations that have ordained women and from Roman Catholic women systemically excluded from ordination serves to illustrate the difference that the potential for co-optation can make. By the early 1980s, many Roman Catholic women conceptually had moved beyond working for a gender-inclusive ordination process toward transforming the nature of priesthood, questioning the need for ordination at all, and the need for church as it is now institutionally configured.[29]

Chafetz argues that women's movements achieve change not only by applying pressure on elites but also by shaping public opinion.[30] Where women or minorities are underrepresented in population or power, their placement in leadership holds considerable symbolic power, or charisma, for followers, which can thereby serve to inspire widespread support for a liberationist agenda despite coercive dynamics of tokenism[31] or dissention among women. This transformative effect has been demonstrated at the congregational level by the attitude change that women clergy have stimulated in lay women.[32] Mobilizing a widespread grassroots constituency is central to a movement's likelihood of success, as the grassroots can apply more pressure for radical change than can women in leadership positions who may be particularly vulnerable to organizational scrutiny and control.

The interdenominational nature of women's religious movements is one of the most important assets for an agenda of liberationist change. As Schüssler Fiorenza observed, "My experience of feminist liturgies and theological dialogue, moreover, has taught me that feminist theology is truly *ecumenical.* . . ."[33] Roman Catholic and post-Catholic feminist theology has had a radicalizing impact on feminists in other denominations. Similarly, activist groups such as the Women's Ordination Conference (W.O.C.) have worked concertedly for the ordination of women in other religious organizations, and have received reciprocal support for their own efforts. For instance, an ecumenical group of women clergy, supporting the W.O.C. during the 1993 World Youth Day Conference, held prayer vigils, a march, and an ecumenical communion service celebrated by United Methodist bishop Mary Ann Swenson and women clergy from various denominations, during which they affirmed Roman Catholic women's call to ordination. One Catholic woman anecdotally recounted, "I expected to see an aging, balding, stern male bishop preceded by all these male priests. Instead, the bishop was young, with long blond hair, and was smiling. And all the clergy were women!" The next day, following the World Youth Day Sunday Mass, the women clergy and others supporting the W.O.C. coincidentally came face-to-face with Pope John Paul II in central Denver. Recalled Nan Hobart, a U.U.A. minister, "He blessed us. What else could he do!" Women who participated in the events recalled feeling reinvigorated to continue their struggle for gender equality in their own religious organizations, an awareness similar to that women and men in various denominations have expressed repeatedly after experiencing gender-related ground-breaking events.[34]

While ecumenism is an important resource for women's religious empowerment, it also represents one of the more significant threats to both the denominational hierarchicalization and differentiation that have benefited male clerics. Hierarchies are gendered, argues Acker, because of the assumptions upon which they are based.[35] Where religious hierarchies are based on foundational presumptions about male gender—in divinity and in role identity or responsibility—their deconstruction entails a loss of legitimation for male dominance. Dedifferentiation also directly threatens male privilege. The growth of movements such as women-church that transcend boundaries not only of Catholic-Protestant Christianity but also Christian perimeters by affirming spiritualities of other religious movements or traditions where women have been valued present an extreme challenge to differentiation and hierarchicalization. So do allied New Age and Wiccan spiritualities. Such noninstitutionalized movements, energized by women disenfranchised from their own denominations and traditions, have attempted to create a theological and ethical basis for reconstituting community and social relations that are more equitable across religious, cultural, racial, gender, and sexual orientation boundaries. The architecture of new forms and processes of community also represent new paradigms in the distribution and utilization of authority and the power it sanctions.[36]

Besides ecumenism, another threat of women's liberationist movements is their potential for transforming those mores that circumscribe not only women's behavior but sexuality itself, including traditional concepts of family, kinship, and patrilineal inheritance patterns. As Roberts points out, episodes of backlash and vilification of women, including witchcraft-persecution frenzies, have occurred in periods when women were becoming more independent of male dominance.[37] Since the strife over sexuality manifests issues that go to the core of gender identity, herein may lie the heart of the struggle within religious organizations. Some theorists have argued that gender inequality is predicated not only on the need to control sexuality but also on mandatory heterosexuality,[38] where men potentially can dominate and control women as both a political and a sexual constituency. Furthermore, the use of natural law ethics to justify the subordination of women has depended on the universality of the heterosexual paradigm. Maintaining its ubiquity also serves to legitimate status differentials. Millet and others have maintained specifically that male political power over women is the central division of social organization.[39]

Heterosexual-based gender roles have been utilized as defining criteria for an essentialist organizing principle of gender differences, such as female ability to give birth delimiting women as a community's nurturers and caregivers, entitling men to authority and social power as compensation for their inability to do so. Such arguments have been used to absolve men from responsibility for nurturing roles and to evaluate women's social worth as to how well they perform their childbearing role. Race and class are other categories where physiological or moral attributes have been defined and evaluated in relation to religious precepts that in turn have been utilized as justifications for the formation and enactment of social dominance and subordination.

European-American men have depended on the labor market in terms of hierarchical position and salary as important components of their social status.[40] In instances where their social understandings of manhood interact with the need for male role identification to be discrete from what is signified for women, the holding of higher level positions that pay well becomes an important component of that social construction. The situation for men of color in a European-American male-dominant organizational culture is yet more complex, with the overlayment of European-American gender-role expectations on those of their own racial or cultural constituency. Where men have constructed, defined, and justified the concept of gender as well as gender-differentiated vocational roles through religious authority and ideology, their understandings of what constitutes essential manhood and womanhood become grounded in terms of ultimate virtue, good, or worth.[41]

Men's negative response to feminist concerns, then, involves both anger and distress, according to Cockburn, because of their dependence on women holding a subordinate status.[42] In short, if a man believes that to be a good follower of his religion he must protect and provide for women, then women who seek equality not only represent a threat to his occupational competitive ability but also embody a potential hinderance of his attempt to fulfill his religious obligation, thus threatening perceived existential worth as well as social esteem. Such a linkage of occupational expectations, male gender-role identity, and eschatology may help to explain why men who potentially face strong competition from women may place high value on hierarchical organization and maximization of their occupational opportunities while allowing passive forces to hinder or undermine women's prospects. The interactive nature of the conservative critiques of both feminism and homosexuality in many arenas of the New Christian Right illustrate the utilization of gender organization for a source of social authority.

The intensity of debates over sexual orientation that came to the fore in mainline religious organizations during the 1970s, as the number of women clergy sharply increased, suggests that concerns over gender and human sexuality are more than coincidentally linked. Nonheterosexual men historically had been ordained without fuss provided they remained discrete about their sexual orientation, and were either celibate or heterosexually married.[43] While male hostility toward lesbian women might seem more readily apparent where heterosexual male identity is socially understood and justified in relation to dominance over women, gay men represent a deeper threat in their perceived betrayal of those dominance patterns, including the increased potential for erosion of the gender-differentiated distinctions on which gender-based hierarchicalization has been justified.

The relationship of gender identity, sexual orientation, and social control is illustrated in backlash movements within organized religion against women clergy, homosexuality, and feminism. The amount and intensity of backlash, which form perhaps the most visible barometer of the actualizing effect of a liberationist social reality against the subordination and social control of women and other marginalized constituencies also can be assessed as a measure of the traditionalist vitality that remains. The conservative theological movement gaining momentum at the outset of the 1980s may be interpreted partly as a response to the potential impact of women's movements in both theology and ordination, and the capacity for transformation in authority and ensuing social power that they represent. Fueling the intensity of backlash movements may be a realization that the traditional methods of social control have diminished in their effectiveness. The extent to which the social construction and justification of male gender identity is integral to the control of women's opportunities suggests that liberationist work faces deep-seated psychological as well as socioeconomic challenge.

The nature of authority has been central to issues involving liberationist change, since the intersection of gender and religious authority has constituted the locus where injustice against women has been theologically formulated, maintained, and perpetuated. Kleinman argues that because clergy authority traditionally has been associated with male status, women will have a difficult challenge proving their competency until this linkage is broken.[44] Any transformation of gender relations therefore necessarily must involve a radical analysis, rearticulation, and reappropriation of authority. Feminist theology and gender equality, defying the legitimacy of male-dominant divine ordinance and natural law theology, have discredited the articulation of universal and absolute divine authority as it has been perceived and promulgated by men.[45] Yet the legitimation of women's access to authority involves not only the renegotiation of unilateral male guardianship and control but also creative opportunities to reconceptualize the meaning of clergy, church, tradition, and human relational roles and responsibilities with values grounded in the transcendent.

The bottom-line concern of religious leaders resistant to gender-related change essentially appears to reside in an apprehension that if one lets go of scriptural literalism and a universalized perception of tradition as twin bases for authority and the legitimation of social control particularly over matters of gender and sexuality, what is left but relativism? An inherent weakness of relativism is its vulnerability to the ongoing renegotiation of power and privilege as a consequence of the flexibility of its appropriation and formulation of authority. As a complex web of intentionality or spirit-centeredness underlying words, actions, and relationality across diverse human community, the open exploration and negotiation of ultimate values, the assessment of the ensuing results from historical tradition and human experience, and attentiveness to the voids or silences as well as those vocal or visible constituencies who have tended to dominate the interpretation of discourse and resulting doctrine, relativism theologically represents a relational listening and openness to reevaluate particular human understandings of divine will or purpose. In this manner, it defies the granting of unilateral authority to any single perspective or constituency. But extreme relativism can result in tolerance for any attitude or behavior including prejudice, thereby defeating the transformative intent of liberationist movements. In order to avoid this pitfall, the multiplicity of voices from different liberationist constituencies becomes crucial to the articulation of a basis of authority grounded in the negotiation of values that affirm equity without concurrently legitimating injustice.

Passive support and assertive strategies to preserve a male authority structure for the maintenance of ideological control and empowerment of men in relation to women, and heterosexual men in relation to all others, manifested in backlash against inroads these other constituencies have made, should not be surprising. In accord with the results of this analysis, the prospect of liberationist change is at best on the distant horizon. As Cockburn warns for secular organizations, women may reach positions of power and may influence leadership styles, but there is little likelihood of feminists, womanists, *mujeristas*, and others gaining sufficient control to change an organization's structure, its goals, or its nature,[46] owing to the importance of these for legitimating and supporting those who hold cultural, political, and economic dominance. Short of transformation, women remain either exploited or expendable.

Social change involves "period effects," a process whereby the influence of one generation interpenetrates another over time.[47] Such generational effects are neither linear nor cumulative. Rather, they are selective and critical, challenging but also refining the advocacy and change of the previous era to fit contemporary exigencies. As generational critique is applied, a retrograde or cyclical pattern may become apparent. Furthermore, when both internal dissention and external backlash produced by those resistant to a movement are combined with a generational critique, direct losses can eradicate gains that previously had been made. For women, such losses in some religious organizations over the past decade have involved occupational status, ordination rights, religious language, and legitimating theology.

Young postfeminists critiquing the collectivist movements of their feminist predecessors as ineffective and inappropriate for the current generation are tending to opt for individualized solutions. While they risk the dangers of privatization, such as inertia, lack of communication linkages, transitory community constituencies, and ease by those in authority to circumvent or block change on a case-by-case basis, an individualized grassroots approach can provide an intriguing strategy for social change in the 1990s—each woman working situationally and contextually—provided that communication linkages are maintained and resources and experiences are shared with one another. Such strategies are less vulnerable to backlash attacks than organized coalitions and movements, and are sufficiently flexible to accommodate the contingent formation of alliances among diverse liberationist constituencies.

Chafetz argues that prospects for occupational equality also reside in forces outside women's control.[48] External economic shifts toward prosperity or decline influence the prospect for social movements, as do political climates generating wider social activism and reform. Chafetz has proposed that declining support for gender equality occurs in times of economic downturn and sociopolitical conservatism.[49] However, wider trends involving increased education among women, the informational effects of mass media and computer networks, and expanded female interaction across denominational and secular boundaries manifested through unparalleled numbers of women in the labor force, suggest a high probability of continued periodic change toward more egalitarian empowerment of women despite socioeconomic fluctuations. As United Methodist Bishop Mary Ann Swenson has observed,

> What I have experienced is that once people have lived with and embraced a vision for that change, they do not want to go back. They want to make sure that change continues to happen. . . . Certainly, we may have setbacks, but then we try again and eventually the vision takes hold.[50]

Given the mutually empowering effect of diverse liberationist-oriented movements interacting over time, more likely than not there will be a transformative consequence for traditional gender arrangements in both religious and secular institutions.

A periodic perspective presents an important reminder that over the past century sizable changes have occurred in religious understandings of gender roles. In most mainline religious organizations, strides have been made to minimize at least some male-biased language and imagery in scriptural translations, liturgical language, and hymnody. Recovery and exposition of women's religious history have made some inroads in religious education. In Episcopal dioceses vehemently opposed to women clergy a decade ago, softening steps have been taken, such as recognizing women priests ordained in other dioceses or moving to ordain women priests outright.[51] Furthermore, in 1995 the House of Bishops overwhelmingly endorsed a resolution declaring women's ordination to be mandatory in all dioceses of the church, and thereby disaffirming the "conscience clause" that had protected bishops opposed to women's ordination since the 1976 vote validating women in the priesthood.[52] Other facets of transformation are occurring under the auspices of women's spirituality and women's Bible study, where these are taught as means of spiritual, social, and political empowerment.[53] In traditionally more conservative religious organizations, despite recent waves of backlash that have suppressed opportunities for women pastors, some strides continue to be made toward more equitable participation, such as the Mennonite Church's 1993 election of a female denominationwide moderator. The Mennonite church historically has had gender-segregated roles with leadership being the male domain.[54] Additionally, three Seventh-Day Adventist women were ordained in 1995 despite the denomination's repeated rejection of women's ordination, reasserted earlier that year.[55]

For women with a transformative agenda, time is on their side if they utilize it wisely. Over the long term, they have the potential to catalyze change within the clergy as an occupation and within religious organizations in ways likely to mitigate clericalism and denominationalism, replacing them with more relational and democratically empowering alternatives, if the evidence on gender-related leadership styles is any indicator.[56] Central to the success of this prospect would be women's conscious refusal to merely accept the male-dominant paradigms as the basis of their own internal and external authority structure. As Episcopal bishop Barbara Harris has preached,

> Justice, the Bible tells us, is a sorting out of what belongs to whom and returning it to them. That must be at the essence of restoring God's creation to wholeness. It is time, past time, for women in the church to do the kind of holistic analysis that will move us away from treating symptoms of problems to attacking root causes.[57]

Rethinking and articulating freshly the authoritative basis for their understanding of leadership, of clergy and church, grafting elements of male-dominant paradigms that have supported inclusive justice with understandings coming from their social location and those of others who have been marginalized, women can offer a spiritually creative infusion to how organized religion is practiced in the twenty-first century. But women also need to anticipate backlash from those who fear the erosion of their power or their access to privilege over others.

Yet whether widespread resistance to the social change that liberationist women represent may lessen over time, to the extent that women can move more expeditiously beyond tokenism, may depend upon two key elements: first, reconstructing a widespread shared understanding of what it means to be a gendered human within a religious context; and second, a cooperative willingness both to renounce any perceived entitlement to privilege over others and to transform the structures that have created and maintained such privilege. But whether change may be the result of radical transformation from within or of shifts and relocations of ideological power and its grounding authority structure to organizations outside contemporary religious denominations remains to be seen. If the latter, women may attain leadership and transformative power within their religious organizations, while the locus of the legitimating authority for male dominance and privilege has moved elsewhere.

A Concluding Unscientific Postscript on Gender and Organized Religion

Some men tend to perceive all-female groups as anti-male or somehow engaged in plotting against them, as Kleinman noticed in interviews of seminarians. Kleinman's later observations revealed that these same all-female groups, rather, were overwhelmingly focused on issues of female inclusion and not on male exclusion.[58] Years ago, a senior professional colleague advised me that too many women talking together would incite concern among our male colleagues that we were talking about them, as if there were no other significant topics or agendas. Male preoccupation with critical masses of women seeking to disempower them as men is illustrative of similar anxieties on a wider scale over the disproportionate concentration of female clergy and laity in religious organizations and what their critical mass might represent: the treatment of men as they have historically treated women. Ignoring that a female liberationist agenda might not necessarily strive to replace one hierarchical paradigm with another, perhaps because of paucity of imagination, some men have felt cornered into "fight or flight" decisions.

Options to fight are sharply evident in waves of backlash against women manifested explicitly in religious neofundamentalism, where selective scriptural literalism is applied to justify traditional male-dominant family values regarding appropriate gender roles and behavior. Restructuring both the clergy as an occupation and the religious organization, not unlike the "poison pill" concept utilized by corporations during the 1980s to ward off hostile takeovers, represents another alternative.

Flight options include the possibility that men might abandon religious organizations altogether, favoring instead alternative structures such as capitalism, Congress, and the courts for asserting moral suasion as the cornerstone of the secular social institutions they dominate. It's been predicted that national denominational structures will become extinct by the middle of the next century.[59] To what extent might the sector of socioeconomically elite male power within various religious organizations abandon denominationalism altogether as the traditional means of morally legitimating and upholding hegemonic social arrangements from which it has benefited, especially those related to gender? More diffuse networks situated in secular structures, such as those devoted to organizational ethics, represent one possibility. A rich tradition of Enlightenment thought stemming from Rousseau and Kant forms the rationale for such a possibility. Lyman Beecher and Horace Bushnell enthusiastically had supported the formation of moral societies that, free of explicit religious expression, could exert the necessary political pressure on certain social causes with whose socioeconomic interests they disagreed.[60] Secular ethics organizations—led, staffed, and servicing a predominately upper-middle-class European-American male population—have garnered the energy and commitment of many socioeconomically elite businessmen, government officials, and educators since the mid-1970s. Most such programs in the United States have tended to be pragmatic and utilitarian in their assumptions, circumventing issues involving gender and human diversity. Rather than serving as a foundation for a radical restructuring of moral understanding through serious commitments to equality, which would shift the power bases of most organizations, diversity, if addressed at all, typically has been perceived strategically: how to placate the disenfranchised with the least cost or disruption. This contemporary approach to U.S. business ethics has been biased toward preserving the establishment, with an emphasis on "playing by the rules" but without questioning whose rules, or why this game.

If *flight* should be the case, then have American mainline denominations essentially *seen their day*, terminally ill as institutions with women and other disenfranchised constituencies composing the twilight membership while secular organizations absorb organized religion's former fervor? Perhaps sociologist David Riesman may be correct in suggesting to me that my interest in clergy feminization may represent "going up the elevator while the building is crumbling."[61] However, much of the twentieth century has witnessed mainline religion's self-preoccupation with its prospective decline, often amid a resurgence of religious conservativism and fundamentalism and the proliferation of diverse religious sects, cults, spirituality, and New Age movements. In short, the impetus to religiosity, whether hierarchicalist or liberationist, is vigorous and healthy. If anything, occupational feminization of the clergy may add fresh data and perhaps vitality to the debate.

The prospective exodus from organized religion and shift toward ethics organizations as moral reinforcement for American social institutions among socioeconomically elite men is unlikely to replace organized religion, for several reasons. First, religion is the only social institution with access to the divine, the transcendent, or the notion of immortality. Second, religion is the only social institution where individual and collective conscience can be examined and absolved, new beginnings sanctioned, and reconciliation exhorted. And third, it offers for some the means to manipulate the ultimate: to attempt to speak for, and thereby ostensibly to control, the divine. Furthermore, as long as there is significant opportunity to utilize the religious ideology of "church spiritual" to further the economic and political self-interest of "church organizational," not only will religious organizations remain viable contenders for public community and control but internal political strife over justice issues, especially those related to gender, is likely to continue.

Schaller argues that most Christian congregations "are structured to attract women and repel men,"[62] adding that with men composing less than 40 percent of adult Protestant Sunday morning worshippers, and with women now dominating those lay positions that once were the prerogative of men, congregations will need to create "all-male enclaves" for attracting and retaining male members. Such enclaves, if formed to support traditional understandings of masculinity legitimated through religious tenets and acted out in the arena of negotiating power and dominance as symbols of male potency, will ultimately seek to assert their dominance over women. Male spirituality groups, without concurrently transforming their understandings of gender identity and exploring the religious basis for that transformation, tend to use as their traditional bargaining chip their presence—whether in the family or in church—in return for a renewed right to dominance and control.

The fatal flaw of deconstructive analysis is its failure to offer radical reconstructive alternatives while at the same time acknowledging that what is proposed needs ongoing reexamination and transformation in relation to external socioeconomic and political shifts, generational critique, and the creative influence of constituencies outside the mainstream. Acknowledging that the reconstructive task is to a large extent situational, the prospect of women authentically able to share in religious leadership, in interconnected collaboration with the grassroots, involves several possibilities:

1. A radical social reconstruction of gender identity and understanding, including flexible interpretations of role identity, would bring about greater inclusivity with regard to sexual orientation.

2. There would be a more relational, interconnected understanding of religious authority and divine immanence, socially from women's experience on the margin of power and essentialistically from women's differing biological experience connected with menstruation and childbearing.

3. Given the linkage of women's biological functions—menstruation and childbirth—to concerns of purity in various religious traditions, as well as any increased emphasis on relationality and the authentication of diversity that women might bring, it's not unrealistic that women's full inclusion might either radically reconstitute notions of purity or diminish their traditional importance, with a consequent reconfiguration of the meaning of "sacred" or "holy."

4. Women may increase tolerance for emotional expressions of fear and vulnerability, and for a wider legitimation of socialization experiences. Marder, for instance, noted that some male rabbis have spoken optimistically about occupational feminization as an opportunity for men to participate in the values and issues of concern to female rabbis. [63]

5. Although women have been traditionally forced into dependency relationships because of gender, their self-reliance and resilience in face of personal devastation exemplify opportunities for additional paradigms of interdependency.

6. Women's differing interpretations of the quest for immortality have yet to be taken seriously, legitimated, and integrated into religiocultural understandings of various religious traditions. They include less dichotomization between the immanent and transcendent, between life and notions of afterlife, and more integrative emphasis on biological chains linking all living creation. The nascent ecofeminist movement illustrates important applications of feminist theologies in this direction. [64]

7. There would be a transformation of traditional relationships between religion and politics. Those women who affirm that the personal is both the political and the spiritual can add an energizing force to those committed to social action without the risk of breaking action apart from spiritual reflection, a bifurcation that has characterized the critiques of activist streams within mainline Protestantism.

A liberationist ideal would involve movement beyond gender parity to an inclusivity that would break down the exclusivity of particular roles, races, cultures, orientations, abilities, and socioeconomic status in religious organizations, as microcosms of what could be possible in human society. But most likely religious organizations will remain composed of a small elite male clergy leadership that will give liberationist constituencies a long leash if pressures for diversity and for the consequent redistribution of power do not become too intense.

However, we appear to be in the midst of a long-range social transformation. How far it goes will depend partly on external factors, involving a sufficient degree of economic security that can facilitate the building of trust relationships, including the mitigation of male wariness that women won't do to them what they historically have done to women, and partly on a brave willingness to explore both how gender has been constituted and how it might be recomposed—gender assignment, attribution, identity, and roles associated with those attributions[65]—and how these have been utilized to privilege or marginalize peoples. A conscious reconstitution of gender understanding, done concurrently with close exegetical and theological reflection, can open new directions for fresh understandings of commonality and appreciation for diversity that facilitate a functional religious, as well as cultural, pluralism in a global community. This is a long-range possibility for the occupational feminization of religious leadership, an outcome that might truly offer—across gender, racial, cultural, and orientation lines—both the vision and the guidance toward a holistic and humanitarian transformation of both our religious communities and the wider society with which they interconnect.

Clergy Job Titles Aggregated by Job Level

Clergy positions differ widely in requisite skills and prestige. They also vary by the amount of autonomy and by the extent of authority to influence or make substantive change in policy, practices, and direction of a religious organization. Based on such differences, a job ladder of nine hierarchical levels has been constructed for each denomination, depending on the job titles that appeared in the clergy occupational biographical data. The levels are not exhaustive of all possible titles within these denominations, and some specific overlapping titles have been aggregated to a title category. Where clergy hold more than one job title concurrently, only the placement that represented the highest level, the most time commitment, or association with a larger parish was coded for this analysis. Titles were assigned to hypothetical job levels, then verified with knowledgeable clergy. Both Episcopal and U.U.A. job ladders contain similar types of positions at each level, which makes cross-denominational comparisons possible.

Some positions require expertise beyond proficiency normally expected for clergy—for example, as a denominational financial officer, hospital administrator, or librarian. While they may involve substantially more prestige than other jobs at their assigned level, they share similar critical criteria: amount of autonomy and authority to influence the religious organization. Such specialized positions tend to be atypical of normative career progression and involve only a few cases. Another specialized situation involves emeritus titles, which are not bestowed automatically upon retirement and consequently represent some prestige. Since emeritus clergy continue to be associated with the authority they held at retirement, and many such positions still hold some influence within the denomination as well as with their former congregation, emeritus titles have been aggregated at the level equal or only slightly below that of the last nonretirement title. Additionally, the Episcopal title *honorary canon*, bestowed in special situations of high respect for clergy upon their movement to another job title, may subsequently be included in their title of address (ex. The Reverend Canon J. Doe) and consequently carries some residual authority, especially when the next placement may be a lateral or downward move. Therefore, this honorary title has been attributed to the same hierarchical level as *canon*, if the position held concurrently is not at a higher level.

For each job level, those titles with the greatest proportion of clergy and that have been considered to be traditional to the occupation have been starred (*). These jobs tend to be considered normative to the clergy in their respective denomination, in contrast to positions that have been recently created. Normative jobs also are typical of the traditional expected path of career development and attainment. The total occurrences of each job title in the data are represented by the numbers in parentheses.

Level 1

Jobs are characteristic of entry placements, with close supervision and tightly constricted autonomy. They occur primarily on parish staffs, with general duties or tasks that may be assigned at will by the supervisor. Some positions may be held by laity as well as ordained clergy.

| *Episcopal* | *Unitarian Universalist* |

Parish Level

*Deacon, deacon in-residence,
   in-training, intern (259)
Priest, priest in-residence,
   intern (27)
Parish staff, misc. (24)
Team minister (4)
Sacristan (2)
Pastoral affiliate (2)
Seminarian, intern (1)

Diocesan, Regional, or Seminary Level

Postulant or novice, religious
   order (5)
Administrative assistant (2)
Clinical pastoral education
   resident (1)
Teaching fellow (1)

Level 2

Jobs at this level are still characteristic of entry placements in terms of authority and autonomy, with authority constricted but with some opportunities for autonomy.

First, there are the part-time, nonstipendiary, or supply positions that otherwise would be a higher level if full-time. Such clergy don't necessarily have an economically dependent relationship with a single work site. Second are the specialist positions, responsible for particular programs or aspects of a congregation or a local ministry. Third are denominational staff positions. All three types of jobs normally are supervised at the work site.

Episcopal	*Unitarian Universalist*
Parish Level	
*Part-time assistant, associate or interim rector (77)	*Part-time minister (16)
*Director of religious education, youth, music, or outreach (23)	*Director/minister of religious education (23)
Supply priest (15)	Supply minister (6)
Deputy for grants (1)	
Liturgics officer (1)	
Circuit rider (1)	

Diocesan, Regional, or Denominational Level

Tutor, instructor in
    Episcopal seminary/institu-
    tion (21)
Professed, religious order (1)
Assistant editor (1)
Part-time spiritual director,
Episcopal seminary/institution (1)

Level 3

Jobs typically represent parish or denominational staff positions with broad responsibilities yet limited authority and autonomy. Presumably these are full-time jobs, although the data on congregation size, number of clergy listed, and, for U.U.A. parishes, total expenditures, suggest that some positions may be less than full-time. Based on this information, a separate variable has been included to control for whether a position likely is part-time. Other types of positions include urban ministry or missionary work, where autonomy may be substantial but authority to influence denominational policy and practice is limited. Clergy in denominational or regional staff positions typically may be in charge of a program or administrative function, but are supervised at the work site and generally have no clergy supervisory responsibilities of their own. Atypical jobs include editors of a denominational publication where autonomy and authority are controlled by processes of content review; staff administration; assistant professors at denominational seminaries—positions with some responsibility yet proportional limitation of denominational authority.

Episcopal	*Unitarian Universalist*

Parish/Cathedral Level

*Assistant or associate rector, curate (1,259)	*Assistant or associate minister (19)
*Canon, diocesan staff (91)	

Diocesan, Regional, or Denominational Level

Administrator (2)	Professional staff (5)
	Minister administrator (1)
Assistant professor, Episcopal seminary (8)	Assistant professor, U.U.A. seminary (1)
	Community minister (1)
Project coordinator, deployment officer, director of church relations, assistant to bishop, (diocese); admissions officer, registrar, assistant to dean, Episcopal seminary (9)	
Computer manager (diocese) (1)	
Assistant/associate director of a national church program (4)	
Assistant superintendent, Indian missions (1)	
Assistant director/administrator Episcopal institution (7)	
Assistant superior, religious order (1)	

Level 4

Jobs have substantial autonomy but some limitations on authority. For both denominations, the most common titles at this level are *chaplain* and *interim*, the latter usually temporarily in charge of a congregation. Such clergy are not directly supervised at the work site, but seldom do they supervise other clergy. Or, if so, their opportunities for authoritative influence are limited either by the temporary character of their position or, in the case of chaplains, by the transitory nature of their constituency. Atypical jobs include those such as denominational consultants, with substantial autonomy and indirect influence but limited direct authority to make change.

Episcopal	*Unitarian Universalist*

Parish Level

*Interim rector, priest in-charge, acting vicar (461)	*Interim or acting minister (68)
Deacon in-charge (26)	
Locum tenens (12)	

Diocesan, Regional, or Denominational Level

*Chaplain, Episcopal institution or affiliation (62)	*Chaplain, U.U.A. affiliation (1)
	Legal ministries, U.U.A. affiliation (1)
Missionary, canon missioner (17)	
Spiritual director, Episcopal institution (3)	
New church developer (1)	

Level 5

Positions at this level typically have in common a lack of direct supervision at the work site. The most common titles are U.U.A. *extension minister* and Episcopal *vicar*, both typically appointed by a denominational executive or bishop, in charge of a congregation that is financially dependent on denominational assistance. Such positions don't have a fixed time duration, as do similar jobs at level 4. Financial dependency does limit clergy authority and autonomy through denominational supervision. In some cases, clergy may be supervised at the work site but also have substantial autonomy and influence over a constituency, and may supervise other clergy.

Episcopal	*Unitarian Universalist*

Congregational Level

*Vicar (472)	*Extension minister (9)
Canon pastor, chancellor, senior canon, subdean (cathedral) (11)	
Pastor, co-pastor (2)	

Diocesan, Regional, or Denominational Level

Archdeacon (8)	Denominational consultant/ Associate executive officer (8)
Associate professor, Episcopal seminary (97)	Associate professor, U.U.A. seminary (2)
	Senior librarian, U.U.A. seminary (1)

Episcopal	*Unitarian Universalist*
Editor, managing editor, denominational publication (4)	Editor, managing editor, U.U.A. publication (1)
Executive director, continuing education, Episcopal seminary	
National coordinator, denominational program (4)	
Deputy to presiding bishop (2)	
Superintendent, Indian missions (1)	
CPE director, Episcopal hospital (1)	
Vice president, finance, Episcopal institution (1)	

Level 6

U.U.A. ministers or Episcopal rectors hired to lead self-supporting parishes of less than 500 members are the normative positions at this level. The authority relationship of these clergy with their denomination is functional rather than direct. While the congregation holds authority over the clergy leader, most limitations on authority and autonomy are negotiable with substantial opportunities for clergy to exert influence over time. Since parishes provide funds for denominational budgets, clergy essentially hold a supplier relationship with their denomination and consequently hold greater sway than those in lower level jobs. *Co-minister* or *co-rector* positions usually although not always are held by clergy couples.

Episcopal	*Unitarian Universalist*
Parish Level	
*Rector (815)	*Minister (senior clergy in parish) (241)
Co-rector (6)	Co-minister (7)
*Rector emeritus (honorary) (14)	*Minister emeritus (honorary) (9)
Diocesan, Regional, or Denominational Level	
Executive director, Episcopal institution (local/diocesan) (10)	District executive (14)
Director emeritus, Episcopal institution (local/diocesan) (2)	
Dean, principal, parish or diocesan school (4)	

Level 7

A distinction has been made on the basis of parish size between level 6 ministers or rectors and those who oversee parishes of substantial size, wealth, or influence. Both denominations have proportionally few parishes of more than 500 members (U.U.A.) or communicants (Episcopal). Large parishes, where there may be several clergy on staff, offer added autonomy through the ability to delegate tasks and pursue leadership activities. These parishes are likely to contribute more to the diocesan or denominational budget, and resultantly often carry more influence and prestige. Other positions equated with this level include headmasters of denominational schools that are not part of a parish and full professors at denominational seminaries with their commensurate influence as top scholarly resources for development or revision of denominational policy and practice.

Episcopal	*Unitarian Universalist*

Parish Level

*Rector (137)	*Minister (9)

Diocesan, Regional, or Denominational Level

Episcopal	*Unitarian Universalist*
Headmaster, Episcopal school (private) (6)	
Professor, Episcopal seminary (10)	Professor, U.U.A. seminary (1)
Executive director, national church department/program (2)	
Executive officer, national Episcopal Church (3)	

Level 8

All titles at this level hold substantial authority, autonomy, and prestige. While Episcopal cathedral deans and suffragan or assistant bishops have limited authority by supervision of the diocesan bishop, these positions entail substantial amounts of autonomy and prestige, and in the case of cathedral deans, often a sizable subordinate staff. Since all bishops are voting members in the House of Bishops, this title grants an important degree of policy-making autonomy and influence.

Episcopal	*Unitarian Universalist*
*Dean, Episcopal college or seminary (4)	*Dean/president, U.U.A. seminary (1)
*Cathedral dean (15)	
Dean emeritus (honorary) (2)	
*Assistant or suffragan bishop (6)	

Level 9

The limitation on authority and autonomy at level 9 rests in the collegial relationship with peers at the leadership level or in voting bodies of laity and subordinate
clergy.

Episcopal	*Unitarian Universalist*
*Diocesan bishop, bishop co-adjutor (16)	*Executive vice president (1) *U.U.A. president (1)

Demographic Variables

The following demographic variables consist of raw percentages for all men and women in the data. Variables in the following form should be regarded as categorical rather than continuous. For noncategorical use in the analysis, categories were either collapsed or constructed as a series of dummy variables. For the summary below, some categories in the data have been collapsed. Percentages don't always total 100 percent because of rounding off. Where a category is listed, 0 percent may also indicate that cases were too few for rounding up to 1 percent.

	Episcopal		U.U.A.	
	Men	Women	Men	Women
Total sample (N)	(974)	(399)	(119)	(77)
Cohort year				
1990	15%	38%	14%	25%
1985	15	32	15	30
1980	16	19	11	33
1975	17	10	19	8
1970	18	3%	16	3
1950	13		14	1
1940	3		7	0
1930	3		4%	1%
1920	1%			
Clerical status				
Active	85%	96%	77%	99%
Deceased	5	2	7	0
Left the ministry	10%	3%	16%	1%

	Episcopal		U.U.A.	
	Men	Women	Men	Women
Biographical information				
Current	69%	72%	98%	100%
Not current but traced and verified	29	27	1	
Not current, traced but unverifiable	3%	1%	1%	
Age at ordination (mean years)	35	43	32	38
				(estimated)
Clergy parent(s)				
None	94%	96%		
Reverend	6	3		
Right Reverend	0%	1%		
Prestige of undergraduate or first degree				
No degree or certificate listed	9%	6%	1%	1%
Two-year degree/certificate program	1	6	0	1
Denominational extension school/ seminary	2	1	3	3
Public four-year college	4	1	3	14
Nonelite private four-year college	20	23	18	13
Public state university	34	31	31	35
Nonelite private university	13	9	20	18
Private elite four-year college/academy	5	10	8	9
Private elite university	10	7	3	1
Other	2%	2%	3%	1%
Theological degree				
None	17%	18%	0%	0%
Attended but no degree	7	5	2	7
Denominational certificate/license	1	3	0	12
Degree from other denominational school	6	9	24	34
Degree from own denominational school	58	53	51	31
Degree from elite school	9	10	21%	17%
Degrees from denominational school and another institution	2%	1%		
Education at ordination				
No education beyond high school listed	4%	3%	0%	0%
Less than bachelor's degree	5	3	4	5
Bachelor's degree (other than B.D.)	13	13	5	5
Bachelor's degree plus certification	2	2	1	4
Master's degree (other than religion)	3	5	2	10
Master's degree (religion-related, other than M.Div.)	5	5	8	4
Master of Divinity (B.D.)	47	43	45	47
More than one master's degree	11	19	14	16
Doctoral degree preceding religion-related degree	5	5	3	5
Doctoral degree, religion applied (D.Min., S.T.D., D.Rel., D.D.)	1	0	17	4
Doctoral degree, religion academic	1	0	0	0
Other	0	0	0	0

	Episcopal		U.U.A.	
	Men	Women	Men	Women
Missing	2%	2%	2%	0%
Total education				
No education beyond high school listed	3%	3%	0%	0%
Less than bachelor's degree	7	5	1	4
Bachelor's degree (other than B.D.)	9	11	1	1
Bachelor's degree plus certification	2	2	1	4
Master's degree (other than religion)	4	5	0	10
Master's degree (religion-related, other than M.Div.)	5	4	8	13
Master of Divinity (B.D.)	40	40	41	49
More than one master's degree	16	24	13	17
Doctoral degree preceding religion-related degree	5	5	3	5
Doctoral degree, religion applied (D.Min., S.T.D.,D.Rel.,D.D.)	4	1	22	7
Doctoral degree, religion academic	5	2	8	0
Other	0%	3%	2%	0%
Ordination status				
Deacon	14%	25%		
Priest	86	75		
Bishop	1%	0%		
Minister			98%	86%
Minister of religious education			0	8
Community minister			2	0
Dual ordination			1%	7%
Race (estimated)				
European American	93%	97%	92%	100%
African American	2	2	4	
Native American	0	0	0	
Latin American	2	1	3	
Asian/Asian American	1	1	1%	
Polynesian/Philippino	2	0		
Other	0%	0%		
Religious orders				
None	88%	88%		
1	10	11		
2 or more	3%	2%		
Marital status				
Single	13%	25%		
Married	81	66		
Remarried	4	4		
Legally separated/divorced	0	2		
Widowed	1%	3%		
Number of children				
None	22%	36%		
1	11	10		
2	30	26		

	Episcopal		U.U.A.	
	Men	Women	Men	Women
3	19	18		
4 or more	7%	11%		
Clergy couple				
No	98%	90%	97%	95%
Yes	2%	10%	3%	5%
Former occupation				
None listed	81%	73%	90%	82%
Not religion-related:				
Labor/hourly	1	0		
Clerical	0	0		
Technical	0	1		
Semi-professional	4	4		
Professional	4	8	3	
Administrative	1	3		
Managerial	2	3		
Religion-related	8%	10%	7%	18%
Publications				
None listed	80%	85%		
Printed	21	15		
Music	0	0		
TV/video/film	0%	0%		
Academic honors				
None listed	92%	91%	98%	99%
Postgraduate fellowship	3	2	0	1
Honorary doctorate(s)	0	0	1	0
Research award	0	1	0	0
Honor from college/university/seminary	0	1	1%	0%
Grant/sponsorship recipient	0	1		
Degree with honors	2	3		
Honorary societ(ies)	2	2		
Other	0%	1%		
Other honors				
None listed	94%	96%		
One or more	6%	4%		

Percentages may not total 100% owing to rounding off.

Mean (average) Career Trajectory

	Episcopal priests		U.U.A. ministers	
	Men	Women	Men	Women
Age at ordination (mean)	33 yrs.	41 yrs.	32 yrs.	37 yrs.
				(estimated)
Denominational job duration (mean)				
Job 1	3.0 yrs.	2.8 yrs.	4.6 yrs.	5.2 yrs.
2	4.7	3.6	6.3	3.7
3	5.4	3.7	6.6	2.7
4	5.6	3.2	4.7	2.9
5	5.4 yrs.	3.3 yrs.	4.1 yrs.	4.2 yrs.
Denominational job level (mean)				
Job 1	3.5	2.8	5.4	4.7
2	4.6	3.7	5.6	4.4
3	4.9	3.8	5.6	4.7
4	5.0	4.3	5.5	4.9
5	5.0	4.0	5.2	5.3
Percentage who have one or more breaks in denominational employment	53%	44%	56%	41%
Number of breaks in denominational work (mean, for those with more than one break)	1.7	1.5	2.1	1.3
Duration of break away from denominational work (mean per break)	12 yrs.	6 yrs.	13 yrs.	6 yrs.

Notes

Preface

1. Mary Lin Hudson, "'Shall Women Preach?' Louisa Woosley and the Cumberland Presbyterian Church." *American Presbyterians* 68 (Winter 1990): 221.

2. Rosemary S. Keller, "Women and the Nature of Ministry in the United Methodist Tradition." *Methodist History* 22 (January 1984): 100–102. Susanna's sons, John and Charles, became cornerstones of the emergent Methodist movement.

Introduction

1. *The Letters of the Rev. John Wesley*, ed. John Telford (London: Epworth Press, 1931), vol. 7, pp. 8–9; cf. vol. 6, p. 24. This quotation also is cited in Jacqueline Field-Bibb, *Women Towards Priesthood: Ministerial Politics and Feminist Praxis* (Cambridge, England, and New York: Cambridge University Press, 1991), p. 11.

2. Albert Brown Lawson, *John Wesley and the Christian Ministry* (London: SPCK, 1963), p. 178.

3. Field-Bibb, *Women Towards Priesthood*, pp. 12–14; Rosemary S. Keller, "Women and the Nature of Ministry in the United Methodist Tradition." *Methodist History* 22 (January 1984): 101–103; Jean Miller Schmidt, "Denominational History When Gender Is the Focus: Women in American Methodism," in *Reimagining Denominationalism: Interpretive Essays*, eds. Robert Bruce Mullin and Russell E. Richey (New York: Oxford University Press, 1994), pp. 203–221; Lawson, *John Wesley and the Christian Ministry*.

4. Bucklee has pointed out how the perception of decreased vitality in her denomination, the Episcopal Church, outside the United States has been attributed to the presence of women clergy. She also noted that women's ordination in Canadian and New Zealand Anglican Churches wasn't blamed to the same extent as in the United States, which suggests that the United States may be internationally perceived as dispro-

portionately influential in religious trend-setting. Sally Bucklee, "Let's Spread the Good News About the U.S. Church." *Episcopal Life* August 1991, p. 31.

5. Ann Douglas, *The Feminization of American Culture* (New York: Alfred A. Knopf, 1977).

6. The impetus for inclusive language is not new within the past three decades. The incendiary furor that Elizabeth Cady Stanton's *The Woman's Bible* generated when it was first issued illustrates the widespread anxiety over language's power to affect beliefs or ideologies. The pressure on religious organizations to move toward androgynous or inclusive language has increased significantly as the influx of women clergy has grown since 1970.

7. Telephone interview December 1990; reaffirmed September 1995.

8. *Resource Sharing Book: Programmes/Projects and Services* (Geneva: World Council of Churches, 1988), p. 125.

9. Jackson W. Carroll, Barbara Hargrove, and Adair T. Lummis, *Women of the Cloth: A New Opportunity for the Churches* (San Francisco: Harper & Row, 1983); Barbara Brown Zikmund, Adair T. Lummis, and Patricia M. Y. Chang, *An Uphill Calling: Ordained Women in Contemporary Protestantism* (Louisville, Ky.: Westminster/John Knox Press, forthcoming 1997). See also Edward C. Lehman, Jr., *Gender and Work: The Case of the Clergy* (Albany: State University of New York Press, 1993); Rita J. Simon, Angela J. Scanlan, and Pamela S. Nadell, "Rabbis and Ministers: Women of the Book and the Cloth," in *Gender and Religion*, ed. William H. Swatos, Jr. (New Brunswick. N.J.: Transaction, 1993), pp. 45–52; Eric. C. Lincoln and Lawrence H. Mamiya, *The Black Church in the African American Experience* (Durham, N.C.: Duke University Press, 1990); Juanne N. Clark and Grace Anderson, "A Study of Women in Ministry: God Calls, Man Chooses," in *Yearbook of American and Canadian Churches*, ed. Constant H. Jacquet, Jr. (Nashville, Tenn.: Abingdon Press, 1990), pp. 271–278; Martha Long Ice, *Clergy Women and their World Views: Calling for a New Age* (New York: Praeger, 1987); Susan Kwilecki, "Contemporary Pentecostal Clergywomen: Female Christian Leadership, Old Style." *Journal of Feminist Studies in Religion* 3 (Fall 1987): 57–75.

10. For example, O. John Eldred, *Women Pastors: If God Calls, Why Not the Church?* (Valley Forge, Pa.: Judson Press, 1981); Edward C. Lehman, Jr., "Organizational Resistance to Women in Ministry." *Sociological Analysis* 42 (Summer 1981): 101–118; Edward C. Lehman, Jr. and the Task Force on Women in Ministry, *Project SWIM: A Study of Women in Ministry* (Valley Forge, Pa.: The Ministry Council, American Baptist Churches, 1979).

11. For example, Sarah Frances Anders and Marilyn Metcalf-Whittaker, "Women as Lay Leaders and Clergy: A Critical Issue," in *Southern Baptists Observed: Multiple Perspectives on a Changing Denomination*, ed. Nancy Tatom Ammerman (Knoxville: University of Tennessee Press, 1993), pp. 201–221; Nancy Tatom Ammerman, *Baptist Battles: Social Change and Religious Conflict in the Southern Baptist Convention* (New Brunswick. N.J.: Rutgers University Press: 1990).

12. For example, see collection of studies in Juanita Evans Leonard, ed., *Called to Minister . . . Empowered to Serve: Women in Ministry and Missions in the Church of God Reformation Movement* (Anderson, Ind.: Warner Press, 1989).

13. For example, *Report of the Executive Council's Committee on the Status of Women* (New York: The Episcopal Church, May 1991); Pamela Ann Mylet, "Dogmatism and Acceptance of Women Priests in the Episcopal Church." Ph.D. dissertation. Northwestern University, 1988; Mary S. Donovan, *Women Priests in the Episcopal Church: The Experience of the First Decade* (Cincinnati, Ohio: Forward Movement,

1988); John H. Morgan, *Women Priests: An Emerging Ministry in the Episcopal Church* (1975–1985) (Bristol, Ind.: Wyndham Hall Press, 1985).

14. The United Methodist Church's General Commission on the Status and Role of Women regularly studies the comparative ratio and placement of its women clergy. Also see George E. Schreckengost, "The Effect of Latent Racist, Ethnic and Sexual Biases on Placement." *Review of Religious Research* 28 (June 1987): 351–366.

15. For example, *Presbyterian Clergywomen Survey 1993: Final Report* (Louisville, Ky.: Presbyterian Church (U.S.A.), Congregational Ministries Division, 1993); *The Presbyterian Placement System*, Presbyterian Panel Report (Louisville, Ky.: Presbyterian Survey Magazine, 1989); Edward C. Lehman, Jr., *Women Clergy: Breaking Through the Gender Barriers* (New Brunswick. N.J.: Transaction, 1985).

16. For example, Janet Marder, "How Women Are Changing the Rabbinate." *Reform Judaism* 19 (Summer 1991), pp. 4–8, 41; Jennifer R. Cowan, "Survey Finds 70% of Women Rabbis Sexually Harassed." *Moment* 18 (October 1993): 34–37; Elaine Shizgal Cohen, "Rabbis' Roles and Occupational Goals: Men and Women in the Contemporary American Rabbinate." *Conservative Judaism* 42 (Fall 1989): 20–30.

17. For example, Lesley Stevens, "Different Voice/Different Voices: Anglican Women in Ministry." *Review of Religious Research* 30 (March 1989): 262–275.

18. For example, Edward C. Lehman, Jr., *Women in Ministry: Receptivity and Resistance* (Melbourne, Australia: The Joint Board of Christian Education, 1994). Lehman reviews several other Australian studies involving ordained women.

19. For example, Per H. Hansson, "Female Ministers in the Church of Sweden: Resistance and Progress." Paper presented at the Annual Meeting of the Association for the Sociology of Religion. Miami, Fla., 1993; Brita Stendahl, *The Force of Tradition: A Case Study of Women Priests in Sweden* (Philadelphia: Fortress Press, 1985); Edward C. Lehman, Jr., *Women Clergy in England: Sexism, Modern Consciousness, and Church Viability* (Lewiston, N.Y.: Edwin Mellen Press, 1987); Nancy Nason-Clark, "Are Women Changing the Image of Ministry? A Comparison of British and American Realities." *Review of Religious Research* 28 (June 1987): 330–340; Nancy Nason-Clark, "Ordaining Women as Priests: Religious vs. Sexist Explanations for Clerical Attitudes." *Sociological Analysis* 48 (1987): 259–273.

20. For example, Virginia Celmer and Jane L. Winer, "Female Aspirants to the Roman Catholic Priesthood." *Journal of Counseling & Development* 69 (November–December 1990): 178–183; Fran Ferder, CSPA, *Called to Break Bread?* (Mt. Ranier, Md.: Quixote Center, 1978).

21. For example, Ruth A. Wallace, "The Social Construction of a New Leadership Role: Catholic Women Pastors," in *Gender and Religion*, ed. William H. Swatos, Jr. (New Brunswick. N.J.: Transaction, 1993), pp. 15–26; Ruth A. Wallace, *They Call Her Pastor: A New Role for Catholic Women* (Albany: State University of New York Press, 1992).

22. For example, Kari Elisabeth Børresen, "Women's Ordination: Tradition and Inculturation." *Theology Digest* 40 (Spring 1993): 15–19; Jennifer Chapman, *The Last Bastion: Women Priests—The Case For and Against* (London: Methuen, 1989); Carroll Stuhlmueller, ed., *Women and Priesthood: Future Directions* (Collegeville, Minn.: Liturgical Press, 1978); Robert J. Heyer, ed., *Women and Orders* (New York: Paulist Press, 1974); Emily C. Hewitt and Suzanne R. Hiatt, *Women Priests: Yes or No?* (New York: Seabury Press, 1973); Rosemary Radford Ruether, *Women-Church: Theology and Practice of Feminist Liturgical Communities* (San Francisco: Harper & Row, 1985); Rosemary Radford Ruether, *Sexism and God-talk: Toward a Feminist Theology* (Boston:

Beacon Press, 1983); Mary Daly, *Beyond God the Father: Toward a Philosophy of Women's Liberation* (Boston: Beacon Press, 1973).

23. For example, Board for Clergy Deployment, *Their Call Answered: Women in Priesthood* (New York: The Episcopal Church, 1979). For example of call to voluntary affirmative action, see *Journal of the General Convention of the Episcopal Church in the United States of America* (New York: The Episcopal Church, 1985, 1991); *Report of the Executive Council's Committee on the Status of Women*. Also see chapter 7 of this analysis.

24. For example, David M. Scholer, "Women in Ministry." Four-part series, *The Covenant Companion* 1 December 1983, pp. 8–9; 15 December 1983, pp. 14–15; January 1984, pp. 12–13; February 1984, pp. 12–16; Edward L. Kessel, "A Proposed Biological Interpretation of the Virgin Birth." *Journal of the American Scientific Affiliation*, September 1983, pp. 129–136; Virginia Ramey Mollenkott, "An Evangelical Feminist Confronts the Goddess." *The Christian Century* 20 October 1982, pp. 1043–1046; Paul K. Jewett, *The Ordination of Women* (Grand Rapids, Mich.: William. B. Eerdmans, 1980).

25. Cf. Constance H. Buchanan, "The Anthropology of Vitality and Decline: The Episcopal Church in a Changing Society," in *Episcopal Women: Gender, Spirituality, and Commitment in a Mainline Denomination*, ed. Catherine M. Prelinger (New York: Oxford University Press, 1992), pp. 310–329; Carroll, et al., *Women of the Cloth*, pp. 116, 157; James L. Lowery, Jr., *Peers, Tents and Owls: Some Solutions to Problems of the Clergy Today* (New York: Morehouse-Barlow, 1973); William E. Hulme, *Your Pastor's Problems: A Guide for Ministers and Laymen* (Garden City, N.Y.: Doubleday, 1966).

26. Janet Saltzman Chafetz, *Gender Equity: An Integrated Theory of Stability and Change* (Newbury Park, Calif.: Sage, 1990), p. 122.

27. For example, Hans A. Baer, "The Limited Empowerment of Women in Black Spiritual Churches: An Alternative Vehicle to Religious Leadership," in *Gender and Religion*, ed. William H. Swatos, Jr. (New Brunswick. N.J.: Transaction, 1993), pp. 75–92. Also see Lincoln and Mamiya, *The Black Church in the African American Experience*; Ari L. Goldman, "Black Women's Bumpy Path to Church Leadership." *The New York Times* 29 July 1990, pp. 1, 28; Jacquelyn Grant, "Black Theology and the Black Woman," in *Black Theology: A Documentary History, 1966–1979*, eds. Gayraud S. Wilmore and James H. Cone (Maryknoll. N.Y.: Orbis, 1979), pp. 418–433.

28. In some Episcopal dioceses, application procedures have been accused of discouraging or turning away aspirants, either explicitly or implicitly, for gender-related reasons.

29. Cf. Benny Kraut, "A Wary Collaboration: Jews, Catholics, and the Protestant Goodwill Movement," in *Between the Times: The Travail of the Protestant Establishment in America*, ed. William R. Hutchison (Cambridge, England, and New York: Cambridge University Press, 1989), pp. 193–230.

30. Cf. William R. Hutchison, "Discovering America," in *Between the Times: The Travail of the Protestant Establishment in America*, ed. William R. Hutchison (Cambridge, England, and New York: Cambridge University Press, 1989), pp. 303–309; Kraut, "A Wary Collaboration"; Richard John Neuhaus, *The Naked Public Square: Religion and Democracy in America* (Grand Rapids, Mich.: William B. Eerdmans, 1984); Sacvan Bercovitch, *The American Jeremiad* (Madison: University of Wisconsin Press, 1980); Douglas, *The Feminization of American Culture*.

31. See Barbara F. Reskin and Patricia A. Roos, *Job Queues, Gender Queues: Explaining Women's Inroads into Male Occupations* (Philadelphia: Temple University Press, 1990).

Chapter 1

1. Alexis de Tocqueville, *Democracy in America*, ed. J. P. Mayer (New York: Doubleday, 1969), pp. 293, 295; cf. Sacvan Bercovitch, *The American Jeremiad* (Madison: University of Wisconsin Press, 1980), p. 169.

2. As Durkheim observed, religion provides the moral substance for social cohesion. See Emile Durkheim, *The Elementary Forms of the Religious Life* (New York: The Free Press, 1965); W. S. F. Pickering, ed., *Durkheim on Religion: A Selection of Readings with Bibliographies and Introductory Remarks* (London and Boston: Routledge and Kegan Paul, 1975), p. 147.

3. Durkheim believed that the gendered division of labor, by which family and social relations have been organized, was the consequence of natural evolution, and that equality defined through the interchangeability of gender roles would have a deleterious effect on society. Jennifer M. Lehmann, *Durkheim and Women* (Lincoln: University of Nebraska Press, 1994), pp. 53–73.

4. Cf. Keith A. Roberts, *Religion in Sociological Perspective*, 1st ed. (Homewood. Ill.: Dorsey Press, 1984), pp. 74, 76, 371; Max Weber, *The Protestant Ethic and the Spirit of Capitalism* (New York: Charles Scribner's Sons, 1958). Also see discussions on Catharine Beecher's A *Treatise on Domestic Economy* (1841), ed. Kathryn Kish Sklar (New York: Schoken Books, 1977) in Bercovitch, *The American Jeremiad*, pp. 157–158; and in Daniel T. Rodgers, *The Work Ethic in Industrial America 1850–1920* (Chicago: University of Chicago Press, 1978), pp. 186–189.

5. For instance, many African-American women have side-stepped conspicuous leadership aspirations in order to support African-American men obtaining the social esteem denied them elsewhere in society, although accusations of sexism have been made at those points where other African-American women and men have come into conflict over entitlement to preaching and ministerial leadership. Cf. Cheryl Townsend Gilkes, "Mother to the Motherless, Father to the Fatherless: Power, Gender, and Community in an Afrocentric Biblical Tradition." *Semeia* 47 (1989): 57–85; Hans A. Baer, "The Limited Empowerment of Women in Black Spiritual Churches: An Alternative Vehicle to Religious Leadership," in *Gender and Religion*, ed. William H. Swatos, Jr. (New Brunswick. N.J.: Transaction, 1993), pp. 75–92; C. Eric Lincoln and Lawrence H. Mamiya, *The Black Church in the African American Experience* (Durham, N.C.: Duke University Press, 1990); Jacquelyn Grant. "Black Theology and the Black Woman," in *Black Theology: A Documentary History, 1966–1979*, eds. Gayraud S. Wilmore and James H. Cone (Maryknoll. N.Y.: Orbis, 1979), pp. 418–433; Ari Goldman, "Black Women's Bumpy Path to Church Leadership." *The New York Times* 29 July 1990, pp. 1, 28.

6. Max Weber, *The Sociology of Religion* (Boston: Beacon Press, 1963), p. 104.

7. Cf. Lynn Davidman and Arthur L. Greil, "Gender and the Experience of Conversion: The Case of 'Returnees' to Modern Orthodox Judaism," in *Gender and Religion*, ed. William H. Swatos, Jr. (New Brunswick. N.J.: Transaction, 1993), pp. 85, 94–96; Carolyn Braun, "Equality of Ordination for Women at JTS?" *Sh'ma* 31 May 1985, p. 113; Rita Gross, "Female God Language in a Jewish Context," in *Womanspirit Rising: A Feminist Reader in Religion*, eds. Carol P. Christ and Judith Plaskow (San Francisco: Harper & Row, 1979), pp. 167–173.

8. For example, 1 Cor. 14:34, Col. 3:18, Eph. 5:23–24, 1 Tim. 2:11–22, 1 Pet. 3:1.

9. Seyyed Hossein Nasr, *Ideals and Realities of Islam* (London: George Allen & Unwin, 1985), p. 110.

10. Nasr, *Ideals and Realities of Islam,* p. 111.

11. For example, James Dobson, founder of the conservative Christian organization Focus on the Family, blames feminism as the core threat to American families. Ward Harkavy, "War is Heck." *Westword* 15–21 September 1993, p. 24.

12. Marty has defined *mainline* in the context of Protestantism as a normative style of American religiosity. He and other scholars have regarded the term as problematic, but have been unable to settle on a more effective way to distinguish between denominations with dominant cultural authority and others. Martin E. Marty, "If It's Not Mainline, What Is It?" *The Christian Century* 8 November 1989, p. 1031; Martin E. Marty, *A Nation of Behavers* (Chicago: University of Chicago Press, 1976), p. 53; William R. Hutchison, "Discovering America," in *Between the Times: The Travail of the Protestant Establishment in America,* ed. William R. Hutchison (Cambridge, England, and New York: Cambridge University Press, 1989), p. 308.

13. Cf. Ann Douglas, *The Feminization of American Culture* (New York: Alfred A. Knopf, 1977); Barbara Welter, *Dimity Convictions: The American Woman in the Nineteenth Century* (Athens. Ohio: Ohio University Press, 1976).

14. Usage of *nonrational* is based on Otto's explication. Rudolph Otto, *The Idea of the Holy: An Inquiry into the Non-rational Factor in the Idea of the Divine and its Relation to the Rational* (London, Oxford, England, and New York: Oxford University Press, 1982). For a discussion of the mystical, see Weber, *The Sociology of Religion.*

15. Similarly, other cultures not heavily dependent upon western Enlightenment rational consistency have granted women religious leadership, based for instance on the belief that a particular woman is a reincarnation of a spiritual leader or is otherwise filled with a male's spirit. Postmenopausal women also have been appointed to be spiritual healers while maintaining traditional gender role circumscriptions in daily life.

16. Kwilecki identified mixed feelings about the prescribed ideal of biblical patriarchy among younger Pentecostal women clergy having substantial exposure to more liberal gender mores of wider society. Susan Kwilecki, "Contemporary Pentecostal Clergywomen: Female Christian Leadership, Old Style." *Journal of Feminist Studies in Religion* 3 (Fall 1987): 74.

17. Nancy Nason-Clark, "Are Women Changing the Image of Ministry? A Comparison of British and American Realities." *Review of Religious Research* 28 (June 1987): 332.

18. Nason-Clark, "Are Women Changing the Image of Ministry?" p. 332; cf. Edward C. Lehman, Jr., "Research on Lay Church Members Attitudes Toward Women Clergy: An Assessment." *Review of Religious Research* 28 (June 1987): 319–329.

19. Schaller subsequently raises the rhetorical question, "is this the hand of God at work in the world?" Lyle E. Schaller, *It's a Different World: The Challenge for Today's Pastor* (Nashville, Tenn.: Abingdon Press, 1987), p. 165.

20. Howard W. Stone, "The New Breed of Minister." *The Journal of Pastoral Care* 47 (Fall 1993): 286–297; cf. Edward C. Lehman, Jr., "Placement of Men and Women in the Ministry." *Review of Religious Research* 22 (September 1980): 27; Edward C. Lehman, Jr., *Gender and Work: The Case of the Clergy* (Albany: State University of New York Press, 1993), p. 84.

21. The assumption that women will act in the interests of their status group, at least to the extent of affirming women's efficacy and right to opportunities, depends on the rational consistency model of knowledge construction and utilization. Cf. Judith Lorber, "Dismantling Noah's Ark," in *The Social Construction of Gender,* eds. Judith Lorber and Susan A. Farrell (Newbury Park, Calif.: Sage, 1991), p. 365.

22. Lehman, *Gender and Work.* Cockburn's observations of the British Civil

Service suggest that white women attaining positions of authority develop a more relational style of management that facilitates collegiality across racial lines. She also noted a feeling among white men that "it was no longer [*their*] place," indicating both a difference in management styles and the latter's interest in hegemony. Cynthia Cockburn, *In the Way of Women: Men's Resistance to Sex Equality in Organizations* (London: ILR Press, 1991), p. 65.

23. Cf. Dirk Johnson, "Mormon Church Views New Threat." [*The New York Times*], *The Denver Post* 2 October 1993, p. 16A; Harkavy, "War is Heck"; Virginia Culver, "Pope Unlikely to Resolve Rifts with U.S. Catholic Protesters." *The Denver Post* 11 July 1993, pp. 1A, 10A.

24. Weber, *The Sociology of Religion*.

25. For example, Declaration of the Sacred Congregation for the Doctrine of the Faith, "The Ordination of Women. Inter Insigniores, Vatican Doctrinal Congregation's Declaration on the Question of Admission of Women to the Ministerial Priesthood." *The Pope Speaks* 15 October 1976, pp. 108–122; cf. Ida Raming, "The Twelve Apostles Were Men . . ." *Theology Digest* 40 (Spring 1993): 21–25.

26. Weber, *The Sociology of Religion*, p. 104.

27. Denise Lardner Carmody, *Women and World Religions* (Nashville, Tenn.: Abingdon Press, 1979), pp. 48–50.

28. For example, Paul mentions Junia as an apostle (Rom. 16:7 NRSV). Mary Magdalene has been considered to be an apostle in New Testament apocryphal writings and in Eastern Orthodox Christianity. Also see Barbara J. MacHaffie, *Her Story: Women in Christian Tradition* (Minneapolis, Minn.: Fortress Press, 1986), pp. 30–31; Elisabeth Schüssler Fiorenza, *Discipleship of Equals: A Critical Feminist Ekklesia-logy of Liberation* (New York: Crossroad, 1993), pp. 80–90; Judith Johnson, "Mary Magdalene: Priest, Prostitute or a Model for the Post-Priesthood of Catholic Women?" *New Women, New Church* 16–17 (November 1993–June 1994): 22–23.

29. Weber, *The Sociology of Religion*, p. 150; Randall Collins, "A Conflict Theory of Sexual Stratification." *Social Problems* 19 (Summer 1971): 14–15.

30. Carmody, *Women and World Religions*, p. 140.

31. Weber, *The Sociology of Religion*, p. 105; Carmody, *Women and World Religions*; Georgia Harkness, "Pioneer Women in the Ministry." *Religion in Life* 39 (Summer 1970): 263–264.

32. Weber, *The Sociology of Religion*, p. 104.

33. Carmody, *Women and World Religions*, pp. 48–50, 140–141.

34. Constance F. Parvey, "The Theology and Leadership of Women in the New Testament," in *Religion and Sexism: Images of Woman in the Jewish and Christian Traditions*, ed. Rosemary Radford Ruether (New York: Simon and Schuster, 1974), p. 146.

35. Declaration of the Sacred Congregation for the Doctrine of the Faith, "The Ordination of Women," p. 110.

36. The first women's convent is believed to have been opened about 320 C.E.; William E. Hopke, ed., *The Encyclopedia of Careers and Vocational Guidance* (Chicago: J. F. Ferguson, 1981), p. 57.

37. Cf. Keith A. Roberts, *Religion in Sociological Perspective*, 2nd ed. (Belmont, Calif.: Wadsworth, 1990), pp. 294–299.

38. John Paul II, "Reserving Priestly Ordination to Men Alone: *Ordinatio Sacerdotalis.*" Apostolic Letter (Washington, D.C.: Office for Publishing and Promotion Services, United States Catholic Conference, 26 May 1994). For priest shortages, see Richard A. Schoenherr and Lawrence A. Young, *Full Pews and Empty Altars: Demo-*

graphics of the Priest Shortage in United States Dioceses (Madison: University of Wisconsin Press, 1993).

39. Jackson W. Carroll, Barbara Hargrove, and Adair T. Lummis, *Women of the Cloth* (San Francisco: Harper & Row, 1983), p. 20f.

40. Max Weber, "Charismatic Authority and its Routinization," in *Religion and the Sociology of Knowledge: Modernization and Pluralism in Christian Thought and Structure*, ed. Barbara Hargrove (New York: Edwin Mellen Press, 1984), pp. 155–165.

41. Wrote Puritan historian Edward Johnson, "the Congregation of the people of God began to be forsaken, and the weaker Sex prevailed so farre, that they set up a Priest of their own Profession and Sex, who was much thronged after. . . ." Edward Johnson, "Wonder Working Providence of Sions Savior," in *The Puritans: A Sourcebook of their Writings*, vol. 1. eds. Perry Miller and Thomas H. Johnson (New York: Harper & Row, 1963), p. 156. Also see John Winthrop's account of Hutchinson (John Winthrop. "Journal: the Antinomian Crisis," pp. 129–143, in the same volume); cf. Perry Miller and Thomas H. Johnson, "The Puritan Way of Life," p. 10, in the same volume.

42. Carroll Smith-Rosenberg, "Women and Religious Revivals: Anti-Ritualism, Liminality, and the Emergence of the American Bourgoisie," in *The Evangelical Tradition in America*, ed. Leonard I. Sweet (Macon, Ga.: Mercer University Press, 1984).

43. Rosabeth Moss Kanter, *Commitment and Community: Communes and Utopias in Sociological Perspective* (Cambridge, Mass.: Harvard University Press, 1972), p. 115. At Amana, other than Heinemann, women held no temporal or spiritual authority. Charles Nordhoff, *The Communistic Societies of the United States: From Personal Visit and Observation* (New York: Dover, 1966), pp. 27–37.

44. Cf. Carroll et al., *Women of the Cloth*, p. 21.

45. Andrew J. Kaslow, "Saints and Spirits: The Belief System of Afro-American Spiritual Churches in New Orleans." *Perspectives on Ethnicity in New Orleans* (New Orleans, La.: Committee on Ethnicity, 1981), pp. 61–68, cited in Baer, "The Limited Empowerment of Women," p. 71.

46. Webber also notes the lack of sexism in slave communities. Thomas Webber, *Deep Like the Rivers: Education in the Slave Quarter Community, 1831–1865* (New York: W. W. Norton, 1976); cited in Gilkes, "Mother to the Motherless," p. 74.

47. Page Smith, *Daughters of the Promised Land: Women in American History* (Boston: Little, Brown and Co., 1970), p. 177.

48. See Carolyn G. Heilbrun, *Reinventing Womanhood* (New York: W. W. Norton, 1979), p. 203. Eddy also had proposed an androgynous Godhead; cf. Mary Daly, "After the Death of God the Father: Women's Liberation and the Transformation of Christian Consciousness," in *Womanspirit Rising: A Feminist Reader in Religion*, eds. Carol P. Christ and Judith Plaskow (New York: Harper & Row, 1979), p. 59; David G. Roebuck, "Pentecostal Women in Ministry: A Review of Selected Documents." *Perspectives in Religious Studies* 16 (Spring 1989): 40; Charles H. Barfoot and Gerald T. Sheppard, "Prophetic vs. Priestly Religion: The Changing Role of Women Clergy in Classical Pentecostal Churches." *Review of Religious Research* 22 (September 1980): 2–16; Virginia Lieson Brereton and Christa Ressmeyer Klein, "American Women in Ministry: A History of Protestant Beginning Points," in *Women of Spirit: Female Leadership in the Jewish and Christian Traditions*, eds. Rosemary Ruether and Eleanor McLaughlin (New York: Simon and Schuster, 1979), pp. 302–332.

49. The Millennial Church, or United Society of Believers in the First and Second Appearing of Jesus Christ, known as Shakers, was founded in 1787, three years after Ann Lee's death. She and a group of English immigrants had formed a community in 1775, a year after reaching the American colonies. Lee herself had been a member of a fervent

sect of English Quakers known as the "Shaking Quakers" founded in 1747. She ideologically claimed that Jesus Christ and herself were the perfect male and female patterns of an androgynous God (Nordhoff, *The Communistic Societies*, pp. 118–120, 132f; June Sprigg, *By Shaker Hands* [New York: Alfred A. Knopf, 1975], p. 87).

50. Cf. Barfoot and Sheppard, "Prophetic vs. Priestly Religion"; Edith Blumhofer, "The Role of Women in the Assemblies of God." *A/G Heritage*, Winter 1987–88, p. 14.

51. Keller notes that the deaconess movement served as an alternative to alleviate pressure for women's ordination. Rosemary S. Keller, "Women and the Nature of Ministry in the United Methodist Tradition." *Methodist History* 22 (January 1984): 111.

52. Smith, *Daughters of the Promised Land*, p. 181.

53. For instance, Heideman writes that by the end of the nineteenth century, it was generally acknowledged that women in the Reformed Church were better organized in their missionary work than men. Eugene P. Heideman, *A People in Mission: Their Expanding Dream* (New York: Reformed Church Press, 1984); cited in Edwin G. Mulder, "Full Participation—A Long Time in Coming!" *Reformed Review* 42 (Spring 1989): 227; cf. Cynthia Grant Tucker, *Prophetic Sisterhood: Liberal Women Ministers of the Frontier, 1880–1930* (Boston: Beacon Press, 1990), pp. 122–124.

54. Mary S. Donovan. *A Different Call: Women's Ministries in the Episcopal Church, 1850–1920.* (Wilton, Conn.: Morehouse-Barlow, 1986), pp. 1f; Pamela W. Darling, *New Wine: The Story of Women Transforming Leadership and Power in the Episcopal Church* (Cambridge, Mass., and Boston: Cowley, 1994), pp. 26–28, 47–49, 54–64.

55. Virginia L. Brereton, "United and Slighted: Women as Subordinated Insiders," in *Between the Times: The Travail of the Protestant Establishment in America*, ed. William R. Hutchison (Cambridge, England, and New York: Cambridge University Press, 1989), pp. 147, 156; cf. Sara J. Myers, "Women's Missionary Societies in the Methodist Episcopal Church, South." Paper presented at the Faculty Colloquium, Iliff School of Theology, May 1994, pp. 23–24.

56. See Barfoot and Sheppard, "Prophetic vs. Priestly Religion"; David G. Roebuck, "Pentecostal Women in Ministry," p. 40; cf. Rosemary Ruether and Eleanor McLaughlin, eds., *Women of Spirit: Female Leadership in the Jewish and Christian Traditions* (New York: Simon and Schuster, 1979); Donovan, *A Different Call*, p. 3.

57. Robert S. Lynd and Helen Merrell Lynd, *Middletown in Transition: A Study in Cultural Conflicts* (New York: Harcourt Brace, 1937), pp. 295, 308.

58. For instance, Brereton writes that the United Church women vexed the male–dominant Federal Council of Churches and its successor, the National Council of Christian Churches, because of the women's denominational inclusivity of Unitarian and Universalist members; Brereton, "United and Slighted," p. 157.

59. *Annual Report of the NWCTU* (1877, p. 136), cited in Joseph R. Gusfield, *Symbolic Crusade: Status Politics and the American Temperance Movement* (Urbana: University of Illinois Press, 1970), p. 77.

60. Cf. Donovan, *A Different Call*; Fredrica Harris Thompsett, *Christian Feminist Perspectives on History, Theology and the Bible* (Cincinnati, Ohio: Forward Movement, 1986); Carmody, *Women and World Religions*; Douglas, *The Feminization of American Culture*; Julia O'Faolain and Lauro Martines, eds., *Not in God's Image: Women in History from the Greeks to the Victorians* (New York: Harper & Row, 1973).

61. In the Episcopal Church, for example, see David E. Sumner, *The Episcopal Church's History 1945–1985* (Wilton, Conn.: Morehouse, 1987); Christine Camilla Gaylor, "The Ordination of Women in the Episcopal Church in the United States: A Case Study." Ph.D. dissertation, St. John's University, 1982; Heather Ann Huyck, "To

Celebrate a Whole Priesthood: The History of Women's Ordination in the Episcopal Church." Ph.D. dissertation, University of Minnesota, 1981.

62. The use of *frontier* is the descriptive term used by European-American immigrants for land that was populated by indigenous groups.

63. Cf. Miller and Johnson, "The Puritan Way of Life," p. 17.

64. Cf. Tucker, *Prophetic Sisterhood.*

65. Douglas, *The Feminization of American Culture.* Douglas notes that Tocqueville had thought that separation of church and state would be beneficial to Roman Catholicism in America because priests, like Protestant clergy, would need to attract and maintain parish support on a voluntary rather than state-funded basis; cf. Tocqueville, *Democracy in America.*

66. Douglas, *The Feminization of American Culture,* pp. 20, 45–48, 69. Douglas also cites Tocqueville's observation that both women and ministers have authority only within the domestic and personal spheres, careful not to trespass beyond them (pp. 10–11, 43); cf. Welter, *Dimity Convictions;* Carroll et al., *Women of the Cloth,* p. 41.

67. Douglas, *The Feminization of American Culture,* pp. 105–111.

68. Mary S. Donovan, "Women as Priests and Bishops." Paper presented at University of Arkansas—Little Rock History Seminar, 7 November 1989; Donald W. Dayton and Lucille Sider Dayton, "Women as Preachers: Evangelical Precedents." *Christianity Today* 23 May 1975, p. 5.

69. Donovan, *A Different Call,* p. 174.

70. For example, Donovan, *A Different Call;* cf. Brereton and Klein, "American Women in Ministry," pp. 314–315; Darling, *New Wine.* Also, when women were first seated as voting participants at the Episcopal Church's 1970 General Convention, leaders of the separate Episcopal Church Women (E.C.W.) organization believed that it would be integrated at all levels into the church structure and so it suspended its bylaws. The General Division of Women's Work also closed. "Instead, we lost ground," stated 1991 E.C.W. President Marjorie Burke. Julie A. Wortman, "Triennial Still a Necessity for Church Women." *Episcopal Life* July 1991, p. 11.

71. Elisabeth Schüssler Fiorenza, *Bread Not Stone: The Challenge of Feminist Biblical Interpretation* (Boston: Beacon Press, 1984); cf. Rudolph Bultmann, *Jesus Christ and Mythology* (New York: Charles Scribner's Sons, 1958).

72. The Conference also included representation from the National Council of Jewish Women, attesting to women's shared commitments across religious boundaries. Smith, *Daughters of the Promised Land,* pp. 175–177. Also see MacHaffie, *Her Story,* pp. 113–116; Elizabeth Cady Stanton, *The Woman's Bible* (New York: Arno Press, 1972).

73. See Valerie Saiving, "The Human Situation: A Feminine View." *The Journal of Religion* 40 (April 1960): 100–112; reprinted in *Womanspirit Rising,* eds. Christ and Plaskow, pp. 25–42. Also see Carol P. Christ and Judith Plaskow, "The Essential Challenge: Does Theology Speak to Women's Experience?" pp. 19-24, in the same volume.

74. Kari Elisabeth Børresen, "Women's Ordination: Tradition and Inculturation." *Theology Digest* 40 (Spring 1993): 15–19; MacHaffie, *Her Story;* George H. Williams, "The Ministry in the Later Patristic Period (314–451)," in *The Ministry in Historical Perspectives,* eds. H. Richard Niebuhr and Daniel D. Williams (New York: Harper & Row, 1956), pp. 64–65.

75. See Barbara Brown Zikmund, "Winning Ordination for Women in Mainstream Protestant Churches," in *Women and Religion in America 1900–1968,* eds. Rosemary Radford Ruether and Rosemary Skinner Keller (San Francisco: Harper &

Row, 1986), p. 193; Gary B. McGee, "Three Notable Women in Pentecostal Ministry." *A/G Heritage* 6 (Spring 1985–86): 3; Edith L. Blumhofer, "The Role of Women in Pentecostal Ministry. *A/G Heritage* 6 (Spring 1985–86): 14; Blumhofer, "The Role of Women in the Assemblies of God."

76. For example, Douglas, *The Feminization of American Culture.* As a contemporary example, the U.S. Episcopal Church resolution granting women's ordination to the priesthood nearly passed in 1970, rather than six years later, but failed in the clergy vote. Recently, the Church of England's long struggle to ratify women's ordination to the priesthood met the greatest resistance among the clergy. The Anglican Church in Wales rejected women's ordination in 1994; the measure had been approved by laity and bishops but was rejected by clergy. This also was the case nearly four decades earlier in the Church of Sweden. For example, Brita Stendahl, *The Force of Tradition: A Case Study of Women Priests in Sweden* (Philadelphia: Fortress Press, 1985); Darling, *New Wine*; "Welsh Anglicans Reject Women Priests," *The Woman's Pulpit* July–September 1994, p. 4.

77. Hewitt and Hiatt, *Women Priests*; Carmody, *Women and World Religions*; Huyck, *To Celebrate a Whole Priesthood.*

78. Declaration of the Sacred Congregation for the Doctrine of the Faith. "The Ordination of Women"; Catherine Mowry LaCugna, "Catholic Women as Ministers and Theologians." *America* 10 October 1992, p. 247.

79. Mulder, "Full Participation," pp. 228–229.

80. Kenneth Escott Kirk, *Beauty and Bands and Other Papers* (Greenwich, Conn.: Seabury Press, 1957), p. 182, quoted in Emily C. Hewitt, "Anatomy and Ministry: Shall Women Be Priests?" in *Women and Orders*, ed. Robert J. Heyer (New York: Paulist Press, 1974), pp. 52, 55.

81. Laura Kerr, *Lady in the Pulpit* (New York: Woman's Press, 1951), cited in Harkness, "Pioneer Women," pp. 264–267; Elsie Gibson, *When the Minister is a Woman* (New York: Holt, Rinehart and Winston, 1970), p. 18.

82. Smith, *Daughters of the Promised Land*; Dorothy Emerson, "Feminists and Religious Trailblazers." *The World* March–April 1992, p. 29.

83. Brown believed that suffrage was both a political and moral statement, and a means to community betterment. Emerson, "Feminists and Religious Trailblazers," p. 29; Dana Greene, ed., *Suffrage and Religious Principle: Speeches and Writings of Olympia Brown* (Metuchen, N.J.: Scarecrow Press, 1983).

84. E. Wilbur Bock, "The Female Clergy: A Case of Professional Marginality." *American Journal of Sociology* 72 (March 1967): 534–535; Nason-Clark, "Are Women Changing the Image of Ministry?" pp. 330–331; cf. Joseph A. Hill, *Women in Gainful Occupations 1870 to 1920* (New York: Johnson Reprint Corp., 1972); Carroll et al., *Women of the Cloth*, p. 102.

85. For example, *The Proceedings of the Unitarian Universalist Historical Society*, 20, ed. Richard E. Myers (Boston: Unitarian Universalist Association, 1984).

86. Keller, "Women and the Nature of Ministry," p. 113.

87. Myers, "Women's Missionary Societies in the Methodist Episcopal Church, South," p. 23.

88. Bock, "The Female Clergy," p. 534; Hill, *Women in Gainful Occupations*, p. 182.

89. Barfoot and Sheppard, "Prophetic vs. Priestly Religion," p. 8; Blumhofer, "The Role of Women in the Assemblies of God," p. 14.

90. Deaconesses, considered a lay order, had been instituted in the U.S. Episcopal Church in 1885; Hewitt and Hiatt, *Women Priests*, p. 102.

91. Margaret Lamberts Bendroth, "Fundamentalism and Femininity: Points of Encounter Between Religious Conservatives and Women, 1919–1935." *Church History* June 1992, pp. 221–223.

92. Cf. Tucker, *Prophetic Sisterhood*, pp. 227–228; Blumhofer, "The Role of Women in the Assemblies of God," p. 16.

93. See John D. Krugler and David Weinberg-Kinsey, "Equality of Leadership: The Ordinations of Sarah E. Dickson and Margaret E. Towner in the Presbyterian Church in the U.S.A." *American Presbyterians* 68 (Winter 1990): 255; Carroll et al., *Women of the Cloth*, pp. 37–38; Gibson, *When the Minister is a Woman.*

94. Catherine F. Hitchings, *Universalist and Unitarian Women Ministers* (Boston: Unitarian Universalist Historical Society, 1985), p. 6; cf. Tucker, *Prophetic Sisterhood.*

95. Blumhofer, "The Role of Women in the Assemblies of God," p. 16.

96. Episcopal News Service, "The Entire Anglican Communion Mourns the Death of the Rev. Florence Li Tim Oi, First Woman Ordained a Priest." *The Episcopal Times* (Diocese of Massachusetts) April 1992, p. 11. Also see Donovan, "Women as Priests and Bishops," pp. 15–16.

97. See "Czech Priests Defrocked." *The Christian Century* 13 May 1992, p. 513; Dolly Pomerleau, *Journey of Hope: A Prophetic Encounter in Czechoslovakia* (Mt. Ranier, Md.: Quixote Center, 1992).

98. Carroll et al., *Women of the Cloth*, p. 102; Gibson, *When the Minister is a Woman*, p. 21; Hewitt and Hiatt, *Women Priests*, p. 80; Donovan, *A Different Call*, p. 4; Nancy Tatom Ammerman, *Baptist Battles: Social Change and Religious Conflict in the Southern Baptist Convention* (New Brunswick, N.J.: Rutgers University Press, 1990), p. 91.

99. Hewitt and Hiatt, *Women Priests*, p. 81.

100. *The Documents of Vatican II*, cited in Stendahl, *The Force of Tradition*, p. 151. It was through the efforts of women's organizations plus a plea from Cardinal Suenens (Belgium) that resulted in seventeen women being invited as observers. This sentence was only added in the final draft of the document (p. 150). Also see Ruth A. Wallace, "The Social Construction of a New Leadership Role: Catholic Women Pastors," in *Gender and Religion*, ed. William H. Swatos, Jr. (New Brunswick. N.J.: Transaction, 1993), pp. 15–17.

101. Carroll et al., *Women of the Cloth*, p. 4.

102. The Congregational Church merged with the Evangelical and Reformed Church to form the U.C.C. Statistics are from Hewitt and Hiatt, *Women Priests*, p. 124n; and Carroll et al., *Women of the Cloth*, pp. 5–7.

103. Susan Bailey and Barbara Burrell, *A Report on the Careers of the Graduates of the Harvard Divinity School* (Cambridge: Office of Institutional Policy and Research on Women's Education, 1980); "Summary Affirmative Action Plan, Harvard University 1987." *Harvard University Gazette* 3 April 1987, p. 9.

104. Ed. Gail Buchwalter King, *Fact Book on Theological Education 1990–91* (Pittsburgh, Pa.: The Association of Theological Schools, 1991).

105. For instance, nearly half of those applying to Reform rabbinic programs have been female (Janet Marder, "How Women Are Changing the Rabbinate." *Reform Judaism* Summer 1991, pp. 4–8, 41).

106. Cf. Table 1.7. in Barbara F. Reskin and Patricia A. Roos, *Job Queues, Gender Queues: Explaining Women's Inroads into Male Occupations* (Philadelphia: Temple University Press, 1990). By 1990, women constituted about 10 percent of the clergy in the Presbyterian (U.S.A.), United Methodist, and the Episcopal Churches. Women

constituted about 7 percent of Evangelical Lutheran Church in America (E.L.C.A.) clergy, although they represented about 42 percent of E.L.C.A. seminarians; Linda-Marie Delloff, "Still Pioneers." *The Lutheran* 3 (28 November 1990), p. 9.

107. Women rabbis now total over 400; Maggie Jones, "25 Hottest Careers for Women." *Working Woman*, July 1995, p. 40.

108. Information on international ordinations comes from *The Woman's Pulpit*, a quarterly journal of The International Association of Women Ministers.

109. Per H. Hansson, "Female Ministers in the Church of Sweden: Resistance and Progress." Paper presented at the Annual Meeting of the Association for the Sociology of Religion, Miami, Fla., 1993.

110. Among the more widely known Protestant groups in the United States that don't ordain women are the Missouri Synod Lutheran and the Seventh-Day Adventist Churches. Similarly, in the Mormon Church (L.D.S.), women cannot be priests or bishops.

111. Ethelbert D. Warfield, "May Women Be Ordained in the Presbyterian Church?" *The Presbyterian* 99 (14 November 1929): 6; cited in Krugler and Weinberg-Kinsey, "Equality of Leadership," p. 245.

112. Cf. Reskin and Roos, *Job Queues, Gender Queues*; Carolyn Garrett Cline et al., *The Velvet Ghetto: The Impact of the Increasing Percentage of Women in Public Relations and Business Communication* (San Francisco: International Association of Business Communicators Foundation, 1986); Jane Lewis, "The Debate on Sex and Class." *New Left Review* 149 (January–February 1985): 113; Michael J. Carter and Susan Bostego Carter, "Women's Progress in the Professions Or, Women Get a Ticket to Ride After the Gravy Train Has Left the Station." *Feminist Studies* 7 (Fall 1981): 479; Margaret Power, "The Making of a Woman's Occupation." *Hecate* January 1975, pp. 25–34.

113. Douglas's argument of both the privatization and the interaction of domestic and religious spheres would support the "logical transition" argument; Douglas, *The Feminization of American Culture*.

114. Although the impetus for inclusive language is not new, the most notable early effort being Stanton's *The Woman's Bible*, the pressure on religious organizations to move toward androgynous language has increased significantly with the influx of women clergy since 1970. For example, Sherryl Kleinman, *Equals Before God: Seminarians as Humanistic Professionals* (Chicago: University of Chicago Press, 1984), p. 90; Isabel Carter Heyward, *The Redemption of God: A Theology of Mutual Relation* (Washington, D.C.: University Press of America, 1982).

115. Cf. Reskin and Roos, *Job Queues, Gender Queues*; Joanna Brenner and Maria Ramas, "Rethinking Women's Oppression." *New Left Review* 144 (March–April 1984): 33–71. Also, by contrasting Kwilecki, "Contemporary Pentecostal Clergywomen," to Kleinman, *Equals Before God*, an interesting point can be raised as to the potential linkage of socioeconomic status to the direction of occupational change: deprofessionalization for middle- and upper-class mainline denominations and professionalization in the traditionally lower and middle-class evangelical and Pentecostal groups. Concurrently, professionalization attempts in mainline denominations have been identified as the ratio of women clergy has increased, perhaps as a means to raise professional esteem and thereby attract more desirable candidates, especially those who are male. Chapters 6 and 8 further explore this possibility.

116. Cf. Ammerman, *Baptist Battles*; Mary S. Donovan, *Women Priests in the Episcopal Church: The Experience of the First Decade* (Cincinnati, Ohio: Forward Movement, 1988); Carroll et al., *Women of the Cloth*; Edward C. Lehman, Jr., "Sex-

ism, Organizational Maintenance and Localism." *Sociological Analysis* 48 (Fall 1987): 274–282; Edward C. Lehman, Jr., *Women Clergy: Breaking Through the Gender Barriers* (New Brunswick, N.J.: Transaction, 1985); Edward C. Lehman, Jr. and The Task Force on Women in Ministry, *Project SWIM: A Study of Women in Ministry* (Valley Forge. Pa.: The Ministry Council, American Baptist Churches, 1979); E. M. (Bud) Rallings and David J. Pratto, *Two-Clergy Marriages* (Lanham, Md.: University Press of America, 1984); Gibson, *When the Minister is a Woman.*

Chapter 2

1. Cf. Denise Lardner Carmody, *Women and World Religions* (Nashville, Tenn.: Abingdon Press, 1979); Jackson W. Carroll, Barbara Hargrove, and Adair T. Lummis, *Women of the Cloth: A New Opportunity for the Churches* (San Francisco: Harper & Row, 1983).

2. Collins argues that historically religious organizations have been responsible for the transmission of culture, as well; Randall Collins, "A Conflict Theory of Sexual Stratification." *Social Problems* 19 (Summer 1971): 15. Also see Talcott Parsons, *Essays in Sociological Theory*, rev. ed. (New York: The Free Press, 1954), p. 167; Carroll et al., *Women of the Cloth*, p. 210; Edwin M. Leidel, Jr., "Bishop Priest or Deacon?" Unpublished paper (New Brighton, Minn.: The [Episcopal] Diocese of Minnesota, n.d.), p. 20.

3. Walter W. Skeat, *A Concise Etymological Dictionary of the English Language* (New York: G.P. Putnam's Sons, 1980), p. 360; cf. E. Dale Dunlap, "Consecration or Ordination: A Critical Look at the Proposal." *Circuit Rider* November 1991, p. 8.

4. Elsie Gibson, *When the Minister is a Woman* (New York: Holt, Rinehart and Winston, 1970), p. xvi. Both of these groups have a lengthy history of women's leadership; the Salvation Army was co-founded by preacher Catherine Mumford Booth and her husband William Booth; Georgia Harkness, "Pioneer Women in the Ministry." *Religion in Life* 39 (Summer 1970): p. 264.

5. Cf. Seyyed Hossein Nasr, *Ideals and Realities of Islam* (London: George Allen & Unwin, 1985), pp. 161–162.

6. Vocation is based on the Latin verb *uocāre*, which means "to call" (Skeat, *A Concise Etymological Dictionary of the English Language*, p. 595). The Vulgate *vocatio* is a translation of the New Testament Greek, which means "the call of the Gospel to eternal salvation"; Max Weber, *The Protestant Ethic and the Spirit of Capitalism* (New York: Charles Scribner's Sons, 1958), p. 205n. Weber notes theological differences in how a *calling* is interpreted: Luther viewed it as a divinely mandated condition that oughtn't be rebelled against, while the Calvinistic view saw it as a personal choice made with religious responsibility and commitment. Across various denominations, it is normative for those seeking ordination to claim a *divine call* prompting their commitment. Similarly, in selecting aspirants for the ordination process, the nature of one's call to ministry typically is probed and discussed.

7. The variation of names is particular to each religious organization, but all represent an equivalent status derived from the Greek πρεσβυτέρους.

8. Mary Frank Fox and Sharlene Hesse-Biber, *Women at Work* (Palo Alto, Calif.: Mayfield, 1984), pp. 128–129; also see Stewart Ranson, Alan Bryman, and Bob Hinings, *Clergy, Ministers and Priests* (London: Routledge & Kegan Paul, 1977).

9. Cf. Aage B. Sørensen, "Social Structure and Mechanisms of Life-Course Processes," in *Human Development and the Life Course: Multidisciplinary Perspectives,*

eds. Aage B. Sørensen, Franz E. Weinert and Lonnie R. Sherrod (Hillsdale. N.J.: Lawrence Erlbaum, 1986), p. 181.

10. Mary S. Donovan, *Women Priests in the Episcopal Church: The Experience of the First Decade* (Cincinnati, Ohio: Forward Movement, 1988), p. 161.

11. Parsons, *Essays in Sociological Theory*, p. 426.

12. For example, William R. Hutchison, "Discovering America," in *Between the Times: The Travail of the Protestant Establishment in America*, ed. William R. Hutchison (Cambridge, England, and New York: Cambridge University Press, 1989); Richard John Neuhaus, *The Naked Public Square: Religion and Democracy in America* (Grand Rapids: William B. Eerdmans, 1984); Sacvan Bercovitch, *The American Jeremiad* (Madison: University of Wisconsin Press, 1980); Robert Bellah, *The Broken Covenant: American Civil Religion in the Time of Trial* (New York: Seabury Press, 1975).

13. Cf. Carroll et al., *Women of the Cloth*, pp. 116, 157; James L. Lowery, Jr., *Peers, Tents and Owls: Some Solutions to Problems of the Clergy Today* (New York: Morehouse-Barlow, 1973); Fred Wolf, "Moving into the Episcopate: Resources for New Bishops". Unpublished report prepared for the Presiding Bishop and the House of Bishops Committee on Pastoral Development, The Episcopal Church, New York, 1978; William E. Hulme, *Your Pastor's Problems: A Guide for Ministers and Laymen* (Garden City, N.Y.: Doubleday, 1966).

14. Cf. Tony R. Nester, "Doubts that Eat Away at Morale." *Circuit Rider* March 1991, p. 9; Stan Purdum, "A Response . . . What is Success? *Circuit Rider* March 1991, pp. 7–8; Janet Marder, "How Women Are Changing the Rabbinate." *Reform Judaism* Summer 1991, pp. 4–8, 41; Audrey Chapman, *Faith, Power and Politics: Political Ministry in Mainline Churches* (New York: Pilgrim Press, 1991); Edward C. Lehman Jr., "Status Differences Between Types of Ministry: Measurement and Effect," in *Research in the Social Scientific Study of Religion: A Research Annual 2.*, eds. Monty L. Lynn and David O. Moberg (Greenwich, Conn.: JAI Press, 1990), p. 99; Charles William Stewart, *Person and Profession: Career Development in the Ministry* (Nashville, Tenn.: Abingdon Press, 1974).

15. For example, Cynthia Grant Tucker, *Prophetic Sisterhood: Liberal Women Ministers of the Frontier, 1880–1930* (Boston: Beacon Press, 1990); Gibson, *When the Minister is a Woman*.

16. For example, Ellis L. Larson and James M. Shopshire, "A Profile of Contemporary Seminarians." *Theological Education* 24 (Spring 1988): 10–136; Edward C. Lehman, Jr., *Women Clergy: Breaking Through the Gender Barriers* (New Brunswick, N.J.: Transaction, 1985); Edward C. Lehman, Jr. and the Task Force on Women and Ministry, *Project SWIM: A Study of Women in Ministry* (Valley Forge, Pa.: The Ministry Council, American Baptist Churches, 1979); Carroll et al., *Women of the Cloth*; for secular occupations cf. Ruth Ann Erdner and Rebecca F. Guy, "Career Identification and Women's Attitudes Toward Retirement." *International Journal of Aging and Human Development* 30 (1990): 132; Carolyn Garrett Cline et al., *The Velvet Ghetto: The Impact of the Increasing Percentage of Women in Public Relations and Business Communication* (San Francisco: International Association of Business Communicators Foundation, 1986).

17. Edward C. Lehman Jr., *Gender and Work: The Case of the Clergy* (Albany: State University of New York Press, 1993), p. 101.

18. Reskin and Roos cite several studies on this topic. Barbara F. Reskin and Patricia A. Roos, *Job Queues, Gender Queues: Explaining Women's Inroads into Male Occupations* (Philadelphia: Temple University Press, 1990), p. 38.

19. Ralf Dahrendorf, *Life Chances: Approaches to Social and Political Theory* (London: Widenfeld and Nicolson, 1979), pp. 28–33.

20. Sørensen, "Social Structure and Mechanisms of Life-Course Processes"; Harrison C. White, *Chains of Opportunity: System Models of Mobility in Organizations* (Cambridge: Harvard University Press, 1970).

21. Cf. Joseph A. Hill, *Women in Gainful Occupations 1870 to 1920* (New York: Johnson Reprint Corp., 1972), p. 42; U.S. Bureau of the Census. *Census of Population and Housing, 1990: Equal Employment Opportunity File* (Washington, D.C.: Bureau of the Census, Data User Services Division, 1990).

22. Jerald C. Brauer, ed., *The Westminster Dictionary of Church History* (Philadelphia: Westminster Press, 1971), pp. 32, 835–837; John C. Godbey, "Unitarian Universalist Association," in *The Encyclopedia of Religion*, 15., ed. Mircea Eliade (New York: Macmillan, 1987), pp. 144–146.

23. Wade Clark Roof and William McKinney, *American Mainline Religion: Its Changing Shape and Future* (New Brunswick, N.J.: Rutgers University Press, 1987), p. 110f; Bellah et al., *Habits of the Heart: Individualism and Commitment in American Life* (New York: Harper & Row, 1986), p. 225.

24. For instance, 24 percent of all U.U.A. congregations are located in New England states. The Episcopal Church has developed a wider geographic base, with only 9 percent of its congregations now located in New England (Province I); *Unitarian Universalist Association Directory 1994* (Boston: Unitarian Universalist Association, 1994) and *The Episcopal Church Annual 1993* (Wilton, Conn.: Morehouse-Barlow, 1993).

25. *Unitarian Universalist Association Directory 1994*, Bylaws, Article II, Section C-2.3, p. 443.

26. For an overview of the struggle toward women's ordination, see Heather Ann Huyck, "To Celebrate a Whole Priesthood: The History of Women's Ordination in the Episcopal Church." Ph.D. dissertation, University of Minnesota, 1981; Christine Camilla Gaylor, "The Ordination of Women in the Episcopal Church in the United States: A Case Study." Ph.D. dissertation, St. John's University, 1982; Donovan, *Women Priests*; David E. Sumner, *The Episcopal Church's History: 1945–1985* (Wilton, Conn.: Morehouse-Barlow, 1987); Emily Hewitt and Suzanne Hiatt, *Women Priests: Yes or No?* (New York: Seabury Press, 1973).

27. For a comparative explication of the evangelical low-church and the clerical high-church elite coalition over women's ordination in the Church of Sweden (Lutheran), see Brita Stendahl, *The Force of Tradition: A Case Study of Women Priests in Sweden* (Philadelphia: Fortress Press, 1985). Behaviorally, the effects of these forces inside the Episcopal Church are not dissimilar to what Lehman observed as a relationship between conservatism on the issue of women clergy and attitudes held by a less educated socioeconomic constituency in his Presbyterian study; Edward C. Lehman, Jr., *Women Clergy: Breaking Through the Gender Barriers* (New Brunswick. N.J.: Transaction, 1985).

28. There are some sample differences when compared to an earlier version of this study developed through 1987, primarily owing to the addition of a few names to the 1985 cohort and changes in ordination status. While these changes do affect the statistical results, they don't change them substantively; cf. Paula D. Nesbitt, "Dual Ordination Tracks: Differential Benefits and Costs for Men and Women Clergy," in *Gender and Religion*, ed. William H. Swatos, Jr. (New Brunswick: Transaction, 1993), pp. 27–44.

29. The 1990 Episcopal cohorts were selected from a list of all ordained that year; *Journal of the General Convention of the Episcopal Church in the United States of America* (New York: The Episcopal Church, 1991). The 1920 to 1985 cohorts were selected from those listed in the *Episcopal Clerical Directory 1987* (New York: The Church Hymnal Corp., 1987). Clergy ordained but subsequently leaving the ministry were identified by comparison with those ordained for a particular year listed in *Journal of the General Convention* for that triennium. Discrepant names were then tracked through subsequent issues of the clerical directory to discern the date of departure. While the advantage of an alphabetic rotation formula was the ability to capture clergy families (father/son, siblings, etc.), its other disadvantages led to the shift toward random number selection in 1990. Male clergy biographies not selected for the 1950 to 1985 cohorts were spot-checked to verify that the alphabetic method hadn't introduced significant bias into the sample.

30. Each Episcopal biography constructed from the *Episcopal Clerical Directory* was cross-referenced with the triennial *Journal of the General Convention* to verify ordination year, and with various years of *The Episcopal Church Annual* to verify or correct placement data. About 70 percent of the sample were current, and another 26 percent either were at the same placement or could be traced and updated. Those with name changes were identified through parents' names. The *Unitarian Universalist Association Directory*, from which U.U.A. clergy biographies were constructed, had less extensive data although placements could be verified through comparison with clergy listed at each parish, in another section of the directory. U.U.A. clergy contacts assisted in gender identification of names in the sample.

31. *The Presbyterian Placement System*, Presbyterian Panel Report (Louisville, Ky.: Presbyterian Church [U.S.A.], September 1989); cf. Lehman, *Gender and Work*; Patrick M. Horan and Thomas A. Lyson, "Occupational Concentration of Work Establishments." *Sociological Forum* 1 (1986): 428–449.

32. Reskin and Roos in *Job Queues, Gender Queues* (p. 76) cite several studies pointing to African-American women being the last to benefit from opportunities to enter previously male-dominated occupations.

33. Subjective estimations were made based upon whether clergy had attended educational institutions or participated in organizations with primarily a non-European-American racial composition, by personal knowledge, or knowledge by clergy interviewed.

34. Cf. Carroll et al., *Women of the Cloth*; Emily C. Hewitt, "Anatomy and Ministry," in *Women and Orders*, ed. Robert J. Heyer (New York: Paulist Press, 1974), pp. 39–55; Hewitt and Hiatt, *Women Priests*.

35. Bylaws, Article XI, "Ministry," *Unitarian Universalist Association Directory 1994*, p. 453. Ministers can be removed from fellowship through due process by the U.U.A. Ministerial Fellowship Committee.

36. Forrest Whitman, "Women Liberal Religious Pioneers." An Earth Room Talk. Unpublished (Boulder, Colo.: Boulder Unitarian Universalist Church, 1991).

37. Tucker, *Prophetic Sisterhood*.

38. Cf. John E. Booty, *The Servant Church: Diaconal Ministry in the Episcopal Church* (Wilton, Conn.: Morehouse-Barlow, 1982); James Monroe Barnett, *The Diaconate: A Full and Equal Order* (New York: Seabury Press, 1981).

39. Sumner, *The Episcopal Church's History*, p. 17; James B. Simpson and Edward M. Story, *The Long Shadows of Lambeth X: A Critical, Eye-Witness Account of the Tenth Decennial Conference of 462 Bishops of the Anglican Communion* (New York: McGraw-Hill, 1969), p. 184.

40. A new canon was adopted allowing inclusive interpretation of the male pronouns in canons dealing with ordination.

41. Sumner, *The Episcopal Church's History*, p. 28.

42. *Journal of the General Convention*, 1979, p. B–202. Also see Sumner, *The Episcopal Church's History*, p. 29. A similar clause was adopted in the Church of Sweden when women were granted ordination to the priesthood (1958), which allowed resistance against women clergy to continue until it was dropped in 1982; Stendahl, *The Force of Tradition*, p. 7.

43. Julie A. Wortman, "One (sort of) in Christ Jesus." *The Witness* January–February 1993, p. 23.

44. Sumner, *The Episcopal Church's History*, pp. 154f, 159f.

45. The breakaway faction became the Episcopal Missionary Church, cf. Jeffrey Penn, "Traditionalist 'Missionary Diocese' Forms New Denomination." *The Episcopal Times* (Diocese of Massachusetts) December 1992–January 1993, p. 13.

46. The annual ratio of U.U.A. women ordained first exceeded 50 percent in 1978.

47. The comparative data are from the 1972 and 1989 editions of *The Episcopal Church Annual*. Church *communicants* were selected as a more conservative estimate of church participation than membership, as they imply active members who utilize clergy services, and therefore are more indicative of the demand for numbers of clergy.

48. Cf. Myra Strober, "Toward a General Theory of Occupational Sex Segregation: The Case of Public School Teaching," in *Sex Segregation in the Workplace: Trends, Explanations, Remedies*, ed. Barbara F. Reskin (Washington, D.C.: National Academy Press, 1984), pp. 144–145.

49. Cf. Reskin and Roos, *Job Queues, Gender Queues*; Barbara F. Reskin and Patricia A. Roos, "Status Hierarchies and Sex Segregation," in *Ingredients for Women's Employment Policy*, eds. Christine Bose and Glenna Spitze (Albany: State University of New York Press, 1987), pp. 3–21; Michael J. Carter and Susan Bostego Carter, "Women's Recent Progress in the Professions Or, Women Get a Ticket to Ride After the Gravy Train Has Left the Station." *Feminist Studies* 7 (Fall 1981): 477–504.

Chapter 3

1. For example, Jackson W. Carroll, Barbara Hargrove, and Adair T. Lummis, *Women of the Cloth: A New Opportunity for the Churches* (San Francisco: Harper & Row, 1983), p. 101; Edward C. Lehman, Jr., *Women Clergy: Breaking Through the Gender Barriers* (New Brunswick, N.J.: Transaction, 1985).

2. Cf. Carroll et al., *Women of the Cloth*, pp. 116, 157; Constance H. Buchanan, "The Anthropology of Vitality and Decline: The Episcopal Church in a Changing Society," in *Episcopal Women: Gender, Spirituality, and Commitment in a Mainline Denomination*, ed. Catherine M. Prelinger (New York: Oxford University Press, 1992), pp. 310–329; Mary S. Donovan, *Women Priests in the Episcopal Church: The Experience of the First Decade* (Cincinnati, Ohio: Forward Movement, 1988); p. 109; James L. Lowery, Jr., *Peers, Tents and Owls: Some Solutions to Problems of the Clergy Today* (New York: Morehouse-Barlow, 1973); William E. Hulme, *Your Pastor's Problems: A Guide for Ministers and Laymen* (Garden City, N.Y.: Doubleday, 1966).

3. Edward C. Lehman, Jr., "Status Differences Between Types of Ministry: Measurement and Effect," in *Research in the Social Scientific Study of Religion: A Research*

Annual 2., eds., Monty L. Lynn and David O. Moberg (Greenwich, Conn.: JAI Press, 1990), p. 99.

4. Suzanne R. Hiatt, "Women in Research: A Subject's Reflections." *Review of Religious Research* 28 (June 1987): 387.

5. Edward C. Lehman, Jr., *Gender and Work: The Case of the Clergy* (Albany: State University of New York Press, 1993), p. 65.

6. The process and the challenge of developing an occupational hierarchy are illustrated by the Episcopal positions of parish *assistant* and *associate*. Both are supervised by clergy of higher authority at the work site. Some parishes may have either or both positions. Where parishes have both, reference to the clergy biographical data suggest that the *associate* tends to be the more experienced and is listed in *The Episcopal Church Annual* next or closer to the senior clergy. Such distinctions are important in examining whether one job rather than another is part of an upwardly mobile career track. Cook and Moorehead similarly have noted that associate positions tend to be more secure; J. Keith Cook and Lee C. Moorehead, *Six Stages of a Pastor's Life* (Nashville, Tenn.: Abingdon Press, 1990), p. 24. But since an assistant may progress to a higher job title such as *rector* without holding an associate position, the nuances are minimal when evaluating gross job mobility over career trajectories. Consequently, both job titles are aggregated at the same occupational level.

7. As Leidel notes, clergy overseeing large parishes function in ways similar to bishops; Edwin M. Leidel, Jr., "Bishop Priest or Deacon?" Unpublished paper (New Brighton, Minn.: The [Episcopal] Diocese of Minnesota, n.d.), p. 22.

8. The measure for full-time positions beyond the first clergy listed at a job site was the ratio of clergy to congregational membership (1:150), unless other data suggested that the congregation could financially support more than one full-time. Such exceptions include the few parishes in large cities known by name to have wealthy endowments despite a moderate congregational size, such as Trinity Episcopal Church in the Wall Street district of New York.

9. Unitarian Universalist men ordained in 1950 and earlier had a wide variance in waiting time that wasn't characteristic of men ordained later. Women ordained in 1950 and earlier appeared to have no time lag between ordination and first placement.

10. While there have been geographical differences in how long women have had to wait for ordination to the priesthood, owing to some dioceses refusing to ordain women, these dioceses typically have been situated near other dioceses open to women. Occasionally women have established residency in an open diocese and entered the ordination process there.

11. U.U.A. *minister* represents job level 6 (cf. Appendix A), which is substantially higher than the Episcopal *assistant*, at level 3. This implies that U.U.A. clergy overall have more opportunity to exercise professional autonomy and authority earlier in their careers. The reason appears to be threefold. First, the U.U.A.'s smaller and more decentralized structure yields fewer parishes of a sufficient size to afford assistant positions. Decentralization also means fewer jobs available on denominational staffs. Second, the supply and demand for clergy seems to be well balanced, indicated by the relatively low mean waiting times between ordination and first placement. And third, most placements are full time.

12. Cf. Barbara F. Reskin and Patricia A. Roos, *Job Queues, Gender Queues: Explaining Women's Inroads into Male Occupations* (Philadelphia: Temple University Press, 1990); Barbara F. Reskin and Patricia A. Roos, "Status Hierarchies and Sex Segregation," in *Ingredients for Women's Employment Policy*, eds. Christine Bose and Glenna Spitze (Albany: State University of New York Press, 1987), pp. 3–21.

13. The sample shows some disparities with data compiled by Stewart and West on the population of permanent deacons, suggesting that male permanent deacons either may be under-represented in my 1980 and 1985 cohorts or men are much more likely to move between the permanent diaconate and the priesthood. From tracking denominational publications, as well as *Diakonos*, published by the North American Association for the Diaconate (N.A.A.D.), the latter may be the case. Additionally, there is only a 1 percent difference between my sample and their population figures for the 1990 cohort, which supports the likelihood that men more likely than women move into the priesthood track; cf. Alexander D. Stewart and Margaret S. West, "The Diaconate: A Call to Serve." Unpublished report, The Church Pension Fund, New York, 1991. The 1994 statistics are from N.A.A.D.

14. For educational effects on attainment see Peter M. Blau and Otis Dudley Duncan, *The American Occupational Structure* (New York: The Free Press, 1978); Patricia A. Roos, *Gender and Work: A Comparative Analysis of Industrial Societies* (Albany: State University of New York Press, 1985). For effects on upward mobility see Aage B. Sørensen and Hans-Peter Blossfeld, "Socioeconomic Opportunities in Germany in the Post-War Period," in *Research in Social Stratification and Mobility*, ed. Arne E. Kalleberg (Greenwich, Conn.: JAI Press, 1989), pp. 85–106.

15. Roof and McKinney show that the average level of education is highest for U.U.A. members (15.7 years), followed by Jews (13.9 years) and Episcopalians (13.8 years); Wade Clark Roof and William McKinney, *American Mainline Religion: Its Changing Shape and Future* (New Brunswick, N.J.: Rutgers University Press, 1987), pp. 112–113.

16. This particularly has been the case since 1970. For clergy ordained earlier, the Bachelor of Divinity, normally earned after college graduation, has been equated with the Master of Divinity degree.

17. Roof and McKinney, *American Mainline Religion*, p. 65; Dennis Gilbert and Joseph A. Kahl, *The American Class Structure: A New Synthesis* (Homewood, Ill.: Dorsey Press, 1982), p. 183; Robert M. Hauser and David L. Featherman, *The Process of Stratification: Trends and Analyses* (New York: Academic Press, 1977), pp. 130–131. The increase in education over time found in the data is net of the change from the B.D. to M.Div. degree, which occurred around 1970 as the normative preparation for ordination.

18. Elizabeth M. Almquist, "Labor-Market Gender Inequality in Minority Groups," in *The Social Construction of Gender*, eds. Judith Lorber and Susan A. Farrell (Newbury Park, Calif.: Sage, 1991), p. 190.

19. When separate equations were run, different variables influenced men's and women's entry job level. This suggests that an interaction effect is occurring between education and gender which influences entry level placements. As Lehman found in earlier research on American Baptist seminary graduates, women may earn higher grades in seminary but men are more successful in obtaining placements; Edward C. Lehman, Jr., "Placement of Men and Women in the Ministry." *Review of Religious Research* 22 (September 1980): 25.

20. Meadville/Lombard seminary has added an M.A. program in religious education. It also has planned to add a religious education track to its Master of Divinity program, and a doctoral program as well. Cf. *Our Professional Ministry: Structure, Support and Renewal* (Boston: Unitarian Universalist Association, Commission on Appraisal, 1992), p. 18.

21. Jay D. Teachman and Karen A. Polonko, "Marriage, Parenthood and the College Enrollment of Men and Women." *Social Forces* 67 (December 1988): 512–523;

Karl L. Alexander and Thomas W. Reilly, "Estimating the Effects of Marriage Timing on Educational Attainment." *American Journal of Sociology* 87 (July 1981): 143–156.

22. Cf. *The Presbyterian Placement System*, Presbyterian Panel Report (Louisville, Ky.: Presbyterian Survey Magazine, 1989).

23. It's important to note that prior occupational experience and age at ordination had low correlations for both U.U.A. men (.009) and women (.096) ministers. Diagnostics testing for possible collinearity between these two variables showed no relationship.

24. *Semiprofessional* includes nursing, recreational supervision, general consulting in business or government, social work, and social agency work involving counseling, consulting, or as a specialist. Psychologists and psychotherapists are included in the professional category.

25. Various types of prior occupational experience were treated as dummy variables within the regression equations. For other research, see Janet F. Fishburn and Neill Q. Hamilton, "Seminary Education Tested by Praxis." *The Christian Century* February 1–8, 1984, pp. 108–112; cf. Cook and Moorehead, *Six Stages of a Pastor's Life*, pp. 18–19.

26. Cf. Stewart Ranson, Alan Bryman, and Bob Hinings, *Clergy, Ministers and Priests* (London: Routledge & Kegan Paul, 1977).

27. Sørensen has pointed out that organizational structures with closed-position systems develop certain expectations over the relationship of various resources to rewards (such as occupational attainment); Aage B. Sørensen, "Social Structure and Mechanisms of Life-Course Processes," in *Human Development and the Life Course: Multidisciplinary Perspectives*, eds. Aage B. Sørensen, Franz E. Weinert, and Lonnie R. Sherrod (Hillsdale, N.J.: Lawrence Erlbaum, 1986), pp. 177–197.

28. Blau and Duncan, *The American Occupational Structure*; Sherryl Kleinman, *Equals Before God: Seminarians as Humanistic Professionals* (Chicago: University of Chicago Press, 1984), pp. 93–94; cf. O. John Eldred, *Women Pastors: If God Calls, Why Not the Church?* (Valley Forge, Pa.: Judson Press, 1981), pp. 93–103; Charles William Stewart, *Person and Profession: Career Development in the Ministry* (Nashville, Tenn.: Abingdon Press, 1974), p. 94f; Hulme, *Your Pastor's Problems*.

29. Pentecost's (1964) research had suggested that ministers' wives were averaging 40 hours per week of volunteer church involvement; Dorothy Harrison Pentecost, *The Pastor's Wife and the Church* (Chicago: Moody Press, 1964). For a review of studies on this topic, see Liz Greenbacker and Sherry Taylor, *Private Lives of Ministers' Wives* (Far Hills, N.J.: New Horizon Press, 1991), p. 48f; cf. June McConnell and Taylor McConnell, "The Impact of Culture on Clergy Marriages," in *The Interface of Marriage and the Ministry: Findings of the Consultation on Clergy Marriages*, ed. Miriam Herin (Lake Junaluska, N.C.: Intentional Growth Center, 1981), p. 35; Charlotte Ross, *Who Is the Minister's Wife: A Search for Personal Fulfillment* (Philadelphia: Westminster, 1980), p. 30f.

30. Kleinman, *Equals Before God*, p. 94; cf. Eldred, *Women Pastors*, p. 93.

31. Cf. Donovan, *Women Priests*; Kleinman, *Equals Before God*, pp. 93, 95; Frederick W. Schmidt, "Transcending Bureaucratic and Cultural Linkages: Women and the Church." Paper presented at the Annual Meeting of The Society for the Scientific Study of Religion and The Religious Research Association, Washington, D.C., 1992, p. 42; Eldred, *Women Pastors*.

32. For data analysis, married and remarried clergy were collapsed. In preliminary analyses, no significant differences had appeared between married and remarried status. Women priests ordained in the 1970s were significantly more likely to have never married than women ordained subsequently ($p < .005$).

33. Cf. Nancy E. Betz and Louise F. Fitzgerald, *The Career Psychology of Women* (Orlando, Fla.: Academic Press, 1987); Roos, *Gender and Work.*

34. Cf. Paula D. Nesbitt, "Marriage, Parenthood, and the Ministry: Differential Effects of Marriage and Family on Male and Female Clergy Careers." *Sociology of Religion* 56 (Winter 1995): 397–415.

35. In the regression models depicted in Table 3.6, prior occupational experience, gender, marital status, ordination status, and year of ordination (i.e., cohort) were treated as dummy variables.

36. Donald J. Treiman and Heidi I. Hartmann, eds., *Women, Work and Wages: Equal Pay for Jobs of Equal Value* (Washington, D.C.: National Academy Press, 1981).

Chapter 4

1. Cf. Harrison C. White, *Chains of Opportunity: System Models of Mobility in Organizations* (Cambridge: Harvard University Press, 1970).

2. By the research cutoff date (1993), only two U.U.A. clergy ordained in 1990 had moved into their second placement.

3. For example, Marjorie Harding Royle, "Using Bifocals to Overcome Blindspots: The Impact of Women on the Military and the Ministry." *Review of Religious Research* 28 (June 1987): 344.

4. Jacob Mincer and Solomon Polachek, "Family Investments in Human Capital: Earnings of Women." *Journal of Political Economy* 82 (March–April 1974): S76–S108; also see Mary Corcoran, Greg J. Duncan, and Michael Ponza, "Work Experience, Job Segregation, and Wages," in *Sex Segregation in the Workplace: Trends, Explanations, Remedies,* ed. Barbara F. Reskin (Washington, D.C.: National Academy Press, 1984), pp. 171–191; Ronald M. Pavalko, *Sociology of Occupations and Professions* (Itasca, Ill.: F. E. Peacock, 1971), pp. 162–163.

5. William H. Sewell, Robert M. Hauser, and Wendy Wolf, "Sex, Schooling, and Occupational Status." *American Journal of Sociology* 86 (November 1980): 551–583; Patricia A. Roos, *Gender and Work: A Comparative Analysis of Industrial Societies* (Albany: State University of New York Press, 1985), p. 94.

6. Aage B. Sørensen, "Social Structure and Mechanisms of Life-Course Processes," in *Human Development and the Life Course: Multidisciplinary Perspectives,* eds. Aage B. Sørensen, Franz E. Weinert, and Lonnie R. Sherrod (Hillsdale, N.J.: Lawrence Erlbaum, 1986), pp. 177–197; White, *Chains of Opportunity.*

7. Episcopal Church Deployment Office data cited in *Report of the Executive Council's Committee on the Status of Women* (New York: The Episcopal Church, May 1991), p. 13.

8. For example, Jackson W. Carroll, Barbara Hargrove, and Adair T. Lummis, *Women of the Cloth: A New Opportunity for the Churches* (San Francisco: Harper & Row, 1983), pp. 130–132; *Presbyterian Clergywomen Survey 1993: Final Report* (Louisville, Ky.: Presbyterian Church (U.S.A.), Congregational Ministries Division, 1993); Frederick W. Schmidt, "Transcending Bureaucratic and Cultural Linkages: Women and the Church." Paper presented at the Annual Meeting of The Society for the Scientific Study of Religion and The Religious Research Association, Washington, D.C., 1992.

9. Forced resignation upon marriage traditionally was typical for women in various secular occupations; cf. Reskin and Roos, *Job Queues, Gender Queues: Explaining Women's Inroads into Male Occupations* (Philadelphia: Temple University Press, 1990),

pp. 12–13. One of the objectives of the massive waves of corporate downsizing during the 1980s and early 1990s was to reduce compensation overhead for highly paid long-time employees. The secondary labor market historically has used high turnover to keep down wage expense.

10. The small U.U.A. sample size combined with controls for other variables could explain the lack of significant effect.

11. For a brief discussion of such problems, see Paul D. Allison, *Event History Analysis* (Beverly Hills, Calif.: Sage, 1984), p. 1of.

12. The censoring variable in the Cox models was constructed as a dummy variable, with a positive difference between first and second job level indicating that upward mobility had occurred. Though it is possible in this data to refine a test for whether lateral movement actually represents an increased opportunity in terms of parish size and wealth, preliminary tests on membership size, total expenditures, and geographic location (e.g., metropolitan, urban, suburban, small town, rural) yielded no discernable patterns that improved upon the original variable construction. Lateral and downward moves were treated as censored observations (i.e., not having experienced upward mobility). For discussion of Cox modeling, see Allison, *Event History Analysis*, p. 34f and Appendix A.

13. The data in most cases listed only the year in which a job change was made.

14. This suggests that the small size of the U.U.A. sample was affecting the potential significance of trends evident in the data.

15. Cf. Roos, *Gender and Work*; Aage B. Sørensen and Hans-Peter Blossfeld, "Socioeconomic Opportunities in Germany in the Post-War Period," in *Research in Social Stratification and Mobility*, ed. Arne L. Kalleberg (Greenwich, Conn.: JAI Press, 1989), pp. 85–106.

16. Carroll is quoted by Paul Wilkes, "The Hands That Would Shape Our Souls." *The Atlantic Monthly* December 1990, p. 81.

17. Carroll et al., *Women of the Cloth*, p. 127.

18. For example, Judith Buber Agassi, "Theories of Gender Equality: Lessons From the Israeli Kibbutz," in *The Social Construction of Gender*, eds. Judith Lorber and Susan A. Farrell (Newbury Park, Calif.: Sage, 1991), p. 324.

19. Mincer and Polachek, "Family Investments in Human Capital"; cf. Corcoran et al., "Work Experience, Job Segregation, and Wages."

20. Male gender was a significant predictor of higher job level ($p < .005$) in U.U.A. O.L.S. regression models when both year ordained and time out between second and third placement were controlled, and with previous job level omitted from the model.

21. Age normally was used in the regression equations as a continuous variable. A series of dummy variables were constructed in order to discern if the age effect becomes curvilinear at a particular point. In this case, the negative effect became more pronounced for those ordained over age 50.

22. The actual average was 5.4 positions, which would total 34 years. Since most clergy were ordained prior to age 30 in 1950 and earlier, retirement would average between age 59 and 64. While some clergy continued to work past retirement, others died prior to retirement, resulting in substantial variance.

23. For example, *Presbyterian Clergywomen Survey 1993*; Schmidt, "Transcending Bureaucratic and Cultural Linkages"; Juanne N. Clark and Grace Anderson, "A Study of Women in Ministry: God Calls, Man Chooses," in *Yearbook of American and Canadian Churches*, ed. Constant H. Jacquet, Jr., (Nashville, Tenn.: Abingdon Press, 1990), pp. 271–278; Carroll et al., *Women of the Cloth*; Mary S. Donovan, *Women*

Priests in the Episcopal Church: The Experience of the First Decade (Cincinnati, Ohio: Forward Movement, 1988); Edward C. Lehman, Jr., *Women Clergy: Breaking Through the Gender Barriers* (New Brunswick, N.J.: Transaction, 1985); Barbara Brown Zikmund, Adair T. Lummis, and Patricia M. Y. Chang, *An Uphill Calling: Ordained Women in Contemporary Protestantism.* Louisville, Ky.: Westminster/John Knox Press, forthcoming 1997.

24. Elsie Gibson, *When the Minister is a Woman* (New York: Holt, Rinehart and Winston, 1970), p. xvi. Cf. Cynthia Grant Tucker, *Prophetic Sisterhood: Liberal Women Ministers of the Frontier, 1880–1930* (Boston: Beacon Press, 1990); *The Proceedings of the Unitarian Universalist Historical Society,* ed. Richard E. Myers (Boston: Unitarian Universalist Association, 1984); Catherine Hitchings, *Universalist and Unitarian Women Ministers* (Boston: Unitarian Universalist Historical Society, 1985).

25. Jennifer R. Cowan, "Survey Finds 70% of Women Rabbis Sexually Harassed." *Moment* 18 (October 1993): 34–37.

Chapter 5

1. Opportunities, in this manner, can be defined as access points between one's personal resources, such as education or experience, and various assets offered by particular placements.

2. *The Presbyterian Placement System.* Presbyterian Panel Report (Louisville, Ky.: Presbyterian Survey Magazine, 1989), pp. A-12–A-14.

3. Alan Kerckhoff, "The Status Attainment Process: Socialization or Allocation?" *Social Forces* 55 (December 1976): 368–381; Edward C. Lehman, Jr., "Placement of Men and Women in the Ministry." *Review of Religious Research* 22 (September 1980): 24.

4. Sørensen points out that the longer incumbents are in the secular labor force, the less likely is further attainment (or upward mobility, since these concepts are used synonymously); Aage B. Sørensen, "Social Structure and Mechanisms of Life-Course Processes," in *Human Development and the Life Course: Multidisciplinary Perspectives,* eds. Aage B. Sørensen, Franz E. Weinert, and Lonnie R. Sherrod (Hillsdale, N.J.: Lawrence Erlbaum, 1986), pp. 177–197.

5. Since priests normally do not move into a rectorship until their second or subsequent placement, the data are incomplete for the 1990 cohort owing to the 1993 research cutoff date. When attainment of level 5 or higher positions was substituted for level 6, the gender gap was 30 percent, suggesting that this cohort likely will develop a pattern similar to that of earlier cohorts.

6. *Report of the Executive Council's Committee on the Status of Women* (New York: The Episcopal Church, May 1991): 14.

7. Analysis of an earlier version of this data was made in 1988, showing only twenty-seven women priests in the sample attaining level 6 or higher positions compared to seventy-seven in this analysis.

8. Data for U.U.A. ministers ordained in 1990 are incomplete because the average duration of the entry placement extends beyond the 1993 research cutoff date.

9. Nancy E. Betz and Louise F. Fitzgerald, *The Career Psychology of Women* (Orlando, Fla.: Academic Press, 1987).

10. Cf. Brent B. Benda and Frederick A. DiBlasio, "Clergy Marriages: A Multivariate Model of Marital Adjustment." *Journal of Psychology and Theology* 20 (Winter 1992): 368; Miriam Herin, "Issues and Recommendations," in *The Interface of Marriage*

and the Ministry: Findings of the Consultation on Clergy Marriages, ed. Miriam Herin (Lake Junaluska, N.C.: Intentional Growth Center, 1981), p. 5; Mary S. Donovan, *Women Priests in the Episcopal Church: The Experience of the First Decade* (Cincinnati, Ohio: Forward Movement, 1988), p. 53.

11. Cf. *Presbyterian Clergywomen Survey 1993: Final Report* (Louisville, Ky.: Presbyterian Church [U.S.A.], Congregational Ministries Division, 1993), p. 9; Donovan, *Women Priests*, p. 88; Jackson W. Carroll, Barbara Hargrove, and Adair T. Lummis, *Women of the Cloth: A New Opportunity for the Churches* (San Francisco: Harper & Row, 1983), pp. 135–137; Charlotte Ross, *Who is the Minister's Wife: A Search for Personal Fulfillment* (Philadelphia: Westminster Press, 1980), p. 120.

12. *Presbyterian Clergywomen Survey 1993*, pp. 2, 9; cf. Carroll et al., *Women of the Cloth*, pp. 135–137.

13. J. Keith Cook and Lee C. Moorehead, *Six Stages of a Pastor's Life* (Nashville, Tenn.: Abingdon Press, 1990), p. 37.

14. E. M. (Bud) Rallings and David J. Pratto, *Two-clergy Marriages: A Special Case of Dual Careers* (Lanham, Md.: University Press of America, 1984). Sawtell found similar patterns among U.C.C. clergy couples; Peter S. Sawtell, *Clergy Couples in the United Church of Christ: A Statistical Survey* (Sioux City, Iowa: First Congregational United Church of Christ, 1988), pp. 15, 34.

15. Cf. Edward C. Lehman, Jr., *Gender and Work: The Case of the Clergy* (Albany: State University of New York Press, 1993), p. 96f; Herbert Lunt Robinson, Jr., "Hazards of the Ministry for Dual-Clergy Couples." Ph.D. dissertation, Fuller Theological Seminary, 1988; Sawtell, *Clergy Couples*; Laura Deming and Jack Stubbs, *Men Married to Ministers* (Washington, D.C.: Alban Institute, 1986); Carroll et al., *Women of the Cloth*; Rosemary Salem and Douglas C. Stange, "Clergywomen of Ohio: Roles, Restraints, Recommendations." *Journal of Women and Religion* 7 (Winter 1988): 43.

16. *The Presbyterian Placement System*, p. 21; cf. Robinson, *Hazards of the Ministry for Dual-Clergy Couples*, p. 50f; Donovan, *Women Priests*, pp. 53, 55; Rallings and Pratto, *Two-clergy Marriages*; Carroll et al., *Women of the Cloth*.

17. Sawtell, *Clergy Couples*; *Presbyterian Clergywomen Survey 1993*, p. 6.

18. In both the Episcopal and U.U.A., two-thirds of the clergy couple members were women. While most of their spouses were not ordained in the cohort years selected for each sample, there were a few Episcopal and U.U.A. couples where both spouses were included, either in the same or different cohorts.

19. Sawtell, *Clergy Couples*.

20. Not all positions are necessarily full time; Herb Gunn, "Building Ministry for a New World: The Commission on Ministry." *The Record* (Episcopal Diocese of Michigan) 44 (May 1995): 6; Loren Mead, executive director of the Alban Institute, in 1990 had estimated about 5,000 paid positions; Marjorie Hyer, "Church Tackles Clergy 'Crisis' Head On." *Episcopal Life* July 1990, pp. 20–21.

21. Although eleven women were irregularly ordained to the priesthood in July 1974, neither their ordinations nor their priesthood were officially recognized by the church until after the 1976 General Convention.

22. Ruth Tucker, "Colorizing Church History." *Christianity Today* 20 July 1992, p. 21.

23. For example, *Presbyterian Clergywomen Survey 1993*; Frederick W. Schmidt, "Transcending Bureaucratic and Cultural Linkages: Women and the Church." Paper presented at the Annual Meeting of The Society for the Scientific Study of Religion and The Religious Research Association, Washington, D.C., 1992. Janet Marder, "How Women Are Changing the Rabbinate." *Reform Judaism* Summer 1991, pp. 4–8, 41;

Lehman, *Women Clergy: Breaking Through the Gender Barriers* (New Brunswick, N.J.: Transaction, 1985); cf. "Fifth GCSRW Survey Polls 1,000 Churches." *The Flyer* (The General Commission on the Status and Role of Women in the United Methodist Church) 12 (Fall–Winter 1991–92): 1–2. Similar disparities have been documented in the Church of Sweden (Lutheran). Cf. Per D. H. Hansson, "Female Ministers in the Church of Sweden." Paper presented at the Annual Meeting of the Association for the Sociology of Religion, Miami, Fla., August 1993; Brita Stendahl, *The Force of Tradition: A Case Study of Women Priests in Sweden* (Philadelphia: Fortress Press, 1985).

24. Carroll et al., *Women of the Cloth.*

25. Cf. Ivana Edwards, "A New Life: Parish Minister Margot Campbell-Gross," *The World*, March–April 1991, p. 63; Lehman, *Women Clergy.*

26. Lehman, *Women Clergy*, p. 38.

27. *The Presbyterian Placement System*, p. A-9. Lehman, "Placement of Men and Women in the Ministry."

28. Schmidt, "Transcending Bureaucratic and Cultural Linkages," p. 78.

29. Marjorie Harding Royle, "Women Pastors: What Happens After Placement?" *Review of Religious Research* 24 (December 1982): 116–126; cf. Marjorie Harding Royle, "Using Bifocals to Overcome Blindspots: The Impact of Women on the Military and the Ministry." *Review of Religious Research* 28 (June 1987): 341–350; Schmidt, "Transcending Bureaucratic and Cultural Linkages."

30. Barbara F. Reskin and Patricia A. Roos, *Job Queues, Gender Queues: Explaining Women's Inroads into Male Occupations* (Philadelphia: Temple University Press, 1990), p. 15

Chapter 6

1. Barbara F. Reskin, "Bringing the Men Back In: Sex Differentiation and the Devaluation of Women's Work," in *The Social Construction of Gender*, eds. Judith Lorber and Susan A. Farrell (Newbury Park, Calif.: Sage, 1991), pp. 151–152; Barbara F. Reskin and Patricia A. Roos, *Job Queues, Gender Queues: Explaining Women's Inroads into Male Occupations* (Philadelphia: Temple University Press, 1990), pp. 14–15, 44–48.

2. Cf. Theodore Caplow, *The Sociology of Work* (New York: McGraw-Hill, 1964); David O. Moberg, *The Church as a Social Institution: The Sociology of American Religion* (Englewood Cliffs, N.J.: Prentice-Hall, 1962), p. 503.

3. Ann Douglas, *The Feminization of American Culture* (New York: Alfred A. Knopf, 1977).

4. Hutchison was referring to Lynd and Lynd's famous study *Middletown.* William R. Hutchison, "Protestantism as Establishment," in *Between the Times: The Travail of the Protestant Establishment in America*, ed. William R. Hutchison (Cambridge, England, and New York: Cambridge University Press, 1989), p. 13; Robert S. Lynd and Helen Merrell Lynd, *Middletown: A Study in American Culture* (New York: Harcourt, Brace, 1929).

5. Jones notes that World War II was a turning point in declining status among English clergy, including loss of clergy discounts, excused bus fares, preferences to the head of a line, and other perquisites. Alan Jones, *Sacrifice and Delight: Spirituality for Ministry* (San Francisco: Harper SanFrancisco, 1992). Also see Stewart Ranson, Allen Bryman, and Bob Hinings, *Clergy, Ministers and Priests* (London: Routledge and Kegan Paul, 1977); cf. Stendahl, *The Force of Tradition.*

6. Ellis L. Larsen, "A Profile of Contemporary Seminarians Revisited." *Theological Education* 31 (Supplement 1995), pp. 9–11, 87; cf. Ellis L. Larsen and James M. Shopshire, "A Profile of Contemporary Seminarians." *Theological Education* 24 (Spring 1988), pp. 10–136; Jackson W. Carroll, Barbara Hargrove, and Adair T. Lummis, *Women of the Cloth: A New Opportunity for the Churches* (San Francisco: Harper & Row, 1983); H. Newton Malony and Richard A. Hunt, *The Psychology of Clergy* (Harrisburg, Pa.: Morehouse, 1991); David E. Sumner, *The Episcopal Church's History: 1945–1985* (Wilton, Conn.: Morehouse-Barlow, 1987); Constance H. Buchanan, "The Anthropology of Vitality and Decline: The Episcopal Church in a Changing Society," in *Episcopal Women: Gender, Spirituality, and Commitment in a Mainline Denomination*, ed. Catherine M. Prelinger (New York: Oxford University Press, 1992), pp. 310–329.

7. James M. Gustafson, "The Clergy in the United States," in *The Professions in America*, eds. Kenneth S. Lynn and the editors of *Daedalus* (Boston: Houghton Mifflin, 1965), pp. 70–90.

8. Bryan R. Wilson, *Religion in Secular Society* (Baltimore, Md.: Penguin Books, 1969).

9. David L. McKenna, "A Second 'Calling.'" *Christianity Today* 5 February 1988, p. 62.

10. Personal discussion with Reform and Conservative seminarians (1986). Cf. Rita J. Simon, Angela J. Scanlan, and Pamela S. Nadell, "Rabbis and Ministers: Women of the Book and the Cloth," in *Gender and Religion*, ed. William H. Swatos, Jr., (New Brunswick, N.J.: Transaction, 1993), pp. 45–52.

11. Schein has defined stage six of the career life cycle as the *mid-career crisis*, affecting men ages 35 to 45 with issues such as career reassessment and possible career change, balancing work with other aspects of one's life, and coming to terms with needs to mentor others. Edgar Schein, *Career Dynamics: Matching Individual and Organizational Needs*. (Reading, Mass.: Addison-Wesley, 1978).

12. Seymour B. Sarason, *Work, Aging, and Social Change: Professionals and the One Life-One Career Imperative* (New York: Free Press, 1977), p. 242.

13. Peter Costa, "A Conversation With Ronald Thiemann." *Harvard University Gazette* 21 October 1988, pp. 6–7. Thiemann is Dean of Harvard Divinity School. Cf. remarks of Constance Buchanan, Associate Dean for Academic Affairs at Harvard Divinity School, in Paul Wilkes, "The Hands That Would Shape Our Souls." *The Atlantic Monthly* December 1990, p. 66.

14. Larsen and Shopshire, "A Profile of Contemporary Seminarians," p. 45; Larsen, "A Profile of Contemporary Seminarians Revisited," pp. 18–19.

15. Cf. Wilkes, "The Hands That Would Shape Our Souls."

16. Sarason, comparing the rate of career change among those listed in *Who's Who* in 1934 and 1975, found it to be virtually constant over the years, at 8 to 9 percent, which suggests that while the norm for European-American men overwhelmingly has been a single career beginning by one's mid-twenties, voluntary career change is not a new—or generational—phenomenon. Vocational research also has pointed out that satisfaction with one's initial career choice typically is low, although opportunities for voluntary change may be limited or impractical. Sarason, *Work, Aging and Social Change*; cf. Judith Waldrop, "Making a Career of it." *American Demographics* 11 (April 1989): 14; Fred W. Vondracek, Richard M. Lerner, and John E. Schulenberg, *Career Development: A Life-span Developmental Approach* (Hillsdale, N.J.: Lawrence Erlbaum, 1986).

17. Gary Blonston, "New Twist on Recession: White-collar Blues." *The Denver Post* 19 September 1991, pp. 2A, 15A.

18. Malony and Hunt, *The Psychology of Clergy*, pp. 122–123; cf. D. E. Super, *The Psychology of Careers* (New York: Harper & Brothers, 1957).

19. Cf. Charles William Stewart, *Person and Profession: Career Development in the Ministry* (Nashville, Tenn.: Abingdon Press, 1974), p. 78; Paula D. Nesbitt, "First and Second Career Clergy: Influences of Age and Gender on the Career-Stage Paradigm." *Journal for the Scientific Study of Religion* 34 (June 1995): 142–171.

20. Matilda White Riley and John W. K. Riley, Jr., "Longevity and Social Structure: The Potential of the Added Years," in *Our Aging Society: Paradox and Promise*, eds. Alan Pifer and D. Lydia Bronte (New York: W. W. Norton, 1986), pp. 53–77; Matilda White Riley, Marilyn Johnson, and Anne Foner, *Aging and Society* (New York: Russell Sage Foundation, 1972).

21. Carroll, et al., *Women of the Cloth*; cf. Riley et al., *Aging and Society*; Ronald M. Pavalko, *Sociology of Occupations and Professions* (Itasca, Ill.: F. E. Peacock, 1971).

22. Buchanan, "The Anthropology of Vitality and Decline," pp. 319–320; cf. Pavalko, *Sociology of Occupations and Professions*, pp. 159–160. Additionally, while observing a diocese select a new bishop, I noted that substantial concerns were raised over not electing one who was much over age 50. Given a certain amount of expected occupational experience prior to being nominated as a candidate, the age bias against those ordained over age 40 becomes pivotal.

23. Patricia A. Roos, *Gender and Work: A Comparative Analysis of Industrial Societies* (Albany: State University of New York Press, 1985), p. 140.

24. Larsen, "A Profile of Contemporary Seminarians Revisited," pp. 14–15. This trend was consistent with the 1986 study; Larsen and Shopshire, "A Profile of Contemporary Seminarians," pp. 28–29.

25. Cf. Roos, *Gender and Work*, p. 141; Inge Powell Bell, "The Double Standard: Age," in *Women: A Feminist Perspective*, ed. Jo Freeman (Palo Alto, Calif.: Mayfield, 1979), pp. 233–244; Pavalko, *Sociology of Occupations and Professions*.

26. Cf. Nesbitt, "First and Second Career Clergy."

27. For example, Larsen, "A Profile of Contemporary Seminarians Revisited"; Carroll et al., *Women of the Cloth*.

28. Cf. Mary Frank Fox and Sharlene Hesse-Biber, *Women and Work* (Palo Alto, Calif.: Mayfield, 1984); Pavalko, *Sociology of Occupations and Professions*. In secular occupations, gender-related conflicts with normative career expectations resulted in popularization of the "mommy track," where advancement is delayed until child-rearing commitments are ended. A counterpart "daddy track" has been poorly received by men. See Felice Schwartz, "Management Women and the New Facts of Life." *Harvard Business Review* 67 (January–February 1989): 65; Keith A. Hammonds, "Taking Baby Steps Toward a Daddy Track." *Business Week* 15 April 1991, pp. 90–92. Cf. Nesbitt, "First and Second-Career Clergy."

29. Cf. Dorothy Harrison Pentecost, *The Pastor's Wife and the Church* (Chicago: Moody Press, 1964).

30. Data included Episcopal, U.U.A., United Methodist, and Lutheran clergy involved in deployment, and an interdenominational clergy counseling center utilized by several religious organizations for vocational assessment and counseling. Even those deployment officials who supported second-career clergy agreed that the stigma of having failed in their first career existed. Cf. Wilkes, "The Hands That Would Shape Our Souls"; George Hodges Soule, "We're Not Keeping the Clerical Pipeline Full." *The Episcopalian* March 1987, pp. 16–17; Carroll et al., *Women of the Cloth*.

31. Wilkes, "The Hands That Would Shape Our Souls," p. 61.

32. Peter Steinfels, "Shortage of Qualified New Clergy Causing Alarm for U.S. Religions." *The Sunday New York Times* 9 July 1989, p. 22.

33. Carroll et al., *Women of the Cloth*; cf. Permanent Diaconate Evaluation Committee and Adair T. Lummis, *Raising Up Servant Ministry* (New York: The Episcopal Church, 1985).

34. Organizations also may argue that they get more overall productivity from younger workers per investment dollar. For a review of studies on this topic, see Anne Foner and Karen Schwab, "Work and Retirement in a Changing Society," in *Aging in Society: Selected Reviews of Recent Research*, eds. Matilda White Riley, Beth B. Hess, and Kathleen Bond (Hillsdale, N.J.: Lawrence Erlbaum, 1983), p. 84; cf. Charles Handy, *The Age of Unreason* (Boston: Harvard Business School Press, 1989); Riley et al., *Aging and Society*; Malcolm. H. Morrison, "Work and Retirement in an Older Society," in *Our Aging Society*, eds. Pifer and Bronte (New York: W. W. Norton, 1986) pp. 341–365.

35. Larsen, "A Profile of Contemporary Seminarians Revisited," pp. 22–23, 44–45; Larsen and Shopshire, "A Profile of Contemporary Seminarians," p. 97.

36. Howard W. Stone, "The New Breed of Minister." *The Journal of Pastoral Care* 47 (Fall 1993): 291.

37. Ranson et al., *Clergy, Ministers and Priests*.

38. Cf. Edward C. Lehman, Jr., *Women Clergy in England: Sexism, Modern Consciousness, and Church Viability* (Lewiston, N.Y.: Edwin Mellen Press, 1987); Edward C. Lehman, Jr., *Women Clergy: Breaking Through the Gender Barriers* (New Brunswick, N.J.: Transaction, 1985).

39. Harris T. Schrank and Joan M. Waring, "Aging and Work Organizations," in *Aging in Society*, eds. Riley et al., pp. 60–61.

40. The struggle over women's ordination in the Episcopal Church received much greater support by bishops and laity, for instance, than the clergy—a trend which has been observed in other denominations as well. Cf. Sumner, *The Episcopal Church's History*; Lehman, *Women Clergy*; Nancy Tatom Ammerman, *Baptist Battles: Social Change and Religious Conflict in the Southern Baptist Convention* (New Brunswick, N.J.: Rutgers University Press: 1990), pp. 96–97.

41. Over half of the women in the 1991 and 1986 A.T.S. studies identified themselves as "liberal" or "very liberal." Larsen, "A Profile of Contemporary Seminarians Revisited," pp. 22–23; cf. Stone, "The New Breed of Minister."

42. Handy, *The Age of Unreason*; cf. Charles F. Hendricks, *The Rightsizing Remedy: How Managers Can Respond to the Downsizing Dilemma* (Alexandria, Va. and Homewood, Ill.: Society for Human Resource Management and Business One Irwin, 1992).

43. Larsen, "A Profile of Contemporary Seminarians Revisited"; cf. Malony and Hunt, *The Psychology of Clergy*, p. 44; Wilkes, "The Hands That Would Shape Our Souls."

44. Cf. Richard A. Schoenherr and Lawrence A. Young, *Full Pews and Empty Altars: Demographics of the Priest Shortage in United States Dioceses* (Madison: University of Wisconsin Press, 1993), p. 156.

45. In both the 1991 and 1986 A.T.S. studies, *church influence* was the second of the three top motivations for entering seminary regardless of age. Larsen, "A Profile of Contemporary Seminarians Revisited," pp. 18–19.

46. For comparison, average weekly earnings for lawyers, engineers, physicians, noncollege teachers, and clergy in 1994 were $1,116, $897, $996, $839, and $536,

respectively. U.S. Bureau of Labor Statistics. *Employment and Earnings* (Washington, D.C.: Government Printing Office, January 1995), p. 209.

47. National Association of Student Financial Aid Administrators. Cf. "National Study of Theological Student Indebtedness." Unpublished study, Auburn Theological Seminary, New York, 1991.

48. Cf. John F. Rice, "So You Think Your Rector Is Paid Too Much. . . ." *The Episcopal Times* (Diocese of Massachusetts) October 1993, p. 16; Timothy J. Gilbride, Mearle L. Griffith, and C. David Lundquist, *The Survey of United Methodist Opinion* (Dayton, Ohio: The United Methodist Church, General Council on Ministries, The Office of Research, 1990), p. 4; Harold C. Warlick, Jr., *How to Be a Minister and a Human Being* (Valley Forge, Pa.: Judson Press, 1982), p. 91.

49. The study also compared U.U.A. minister compensation with clergy of other denominations. Heading the list were Jewish Reform rabbis, at $50,000. Episcopal compensation was fifth, at $32,479, just ahead of U.U.A. clergy. "Compensation Matters." *Prospectus* (U.U. Office of Church Finances) Winter–April 1990, cited in *Our Professional Ministry: Structure, Support and Renewal* (Boston: Unitarian Universalist Association, Commission on Appraisal, 1992), p. 74.

50. Cf. Carroll et al., *Women of the Cloth*, pp. 116, 157; James L. Lowery, Jr., *Peers, Tents and Owls: Some Solutions to Problems of the Clergy Today* (New York: Morehouse-Barlow, 1973); William E. Hulme, *Your Pastor's Problems: A Guide for Ministers and Laymen* (Garden City, N.Y.: Doubleday, 1966).

51. For example, Candace Waldron, "Women and Resources Audit." Unpublished report, Episcopal Diocese of Massachusetts, Boston, 1986; cf. Charles Prestwood, *The New Breed of Clergy* (Grand Rapids, Mich.: William B. Eerdmans, 1972), p. 78.

52. Buchanan, "The Anthropology of Vitality and Decline." Tucker notes that the Unitarian masculine revitalization movement was intended to recover a perceived decline in "institutional vigor." Cynthia Grant Tucker, *Prophetic Sisterhood: Liberal Women Ministers of the Frontier, 1880–1930* (Boston: Beacon Press, 1990).

53. Tony R. Nester, "Doubts That Eat Away at Morale." *Circuit Rider* March 1991, p. 9.

54. Steinfels, "Shortage of Qualified New Clergy Causing Alarm for U.S. Religions."

55. Elite schools were identified as Ivy League or those whose student S.A.T. scores averaged 600 or higher.

56. When only those priests belonging to academic honor societies are examined, the percentages are similar. While Stone noted a drop in Phi Beta Kappa members from 4 percent in the 1940s to 1 percent in the early 1980s at one Disciples of Christ seminary he studied, the Episcopal cohort data do not support that as an overall trend (cf. Stone, "The New Breed of Minister," p. 288).

57. This has been evident in the U.U.A. as well as in Protestant denominations (e.g., *Our Professional Ministry*, pp. 13, 30; Stone, "The New Breed of Minister," p. 296).

58. Larsen, "A Profile of Contemporary Seminarians Revisited;" Larsen and Shopshire, "A Profile of Contemporary Seminarians."

59. As Catanzarite and Strober have observed, male representation is directly related to an occupation's return on human capital investments and relative decline in compensation or promotion opportunities for other occupations. Lisa M. Catanzarite and Myra H. Strober, "Occupational Attractiveness and Race-Gender Segregation, 1960–1980." Paper presented at the Annual Meeting of the American Sociological

Association, Atlanta, Ga., August 1988; cited in Reskin and Roos, *Job Queues, Gender Queues*, p. 35.

60. Cf. Peter T. Kilborn, "Good Pay Drawing More Men into Nursing." *(The New York Times) The Denver Post* 29 November 1992, p. 2A.

61. Cf. Margaret Power, "The Making of a Woman's Occupation." *Hecate* January 1975, p. 28.

62. U.S. Bureau of Labor Statistics, *Occupational Projections and Training Data.* Bulletin 2401 (Washington, D.C.: U.S. Department of Labor, May 1992), p. 18.

63. Cf. Gene R. Hawes, *The Encyclopedia of Second Careers* (New York: Facts on File Publications, 1984), p. 246.

64. Francine D. Blau, "Occupational Segregation and Labor Market Discrimination," in *Sex Segregation in the Workplace: Trends, Explanations, Remedies,* ed. Barbara F. Reskin (Washington, D.C.: National Academy Press, 1984), pp. 117–143; Paula England, "The Failure of Human Capital Theory to Explain Occupational Sex Segregation." *Journal of Human Resources* 17 (Summer 1982): 358–370; Patricia A. Roos, "Sexual Stratification in the Workplace: Male-Female Differences in Economic Returns to Occupation." *Social Science Research* 10 (September 1981): 195–224.

65. Reskin and Roos, *Job Queues, Gender Queues*, pp. 14, 101–102.

66. Robert W. Peterson and Richard A. Schoenherr, "Organizational Status Attainment of Religious Professionals." *Social Forces* 56 (March 1978): 794–822; Edward C. Lehman, Jr., "Status Differences Between Types of Ministry: Measurement and Effect," in *Research in the Social Scientific Study of Religion: A Research Annual 2.,* eds. Monty L. Lynn and David O. Moberg (Greenwich, Conn.: JAI Press, 1990), p. 98.

Chapter 7

1. For a review of studies documenting men's resistance, see Barbara F. Reskin and Patricia A. Roos, *Job Queues, Gender Queues: Explaining Women's Inroads into Male Occupations* (Philadelphia: Temple University Press, 1990), p. 36; cf. Patricia A. Roos and Barbara F. Reskin, "Institutional Factors Contributing to Sex Segregation in the Workplace," in *Sex Segregation in the Workplace: Trends, Explanations, Remedies,* ed. Barbara F. Reskin (Washington, D.C.: National Academy Press, 1984), pp. 235–260; Jane Lewis, "The Debate on Sex and Class." *New Left Review* 149 (January–February 1985): 113; Michael J. Carter, and Susan Bostego Carter, "Women's Recent Progress in the Professions or, Women Get a Ticket to Ride After the Gravy Train Has Left the Station," *Feminist Studies* 7 (Fall 1981): 479.

2. Frederick Wilcox Dupee, *Henry James: His Life and Writings,* 2nd ed. (Garden City, N.Y.: Doubleday, 1956), p. 11; cited in Ann Douglas, *The Feminization of American Culture* (New York: Doubleday, 1977), p 17; cf. pp. 12–13, 18.

3. Douglas further argues that concurrent cultural feminization essentially guaranteed that male hegemony would persist; Douglas, *The Feminization of American Culture.* Cf. Cynthia Grant Tucker, *Prophetic Sisterhood: Liberal Women Ministers of the Frontier, 1880–1930* (Boston: Beacon Press, 1990); Margaret Lamberts Bendroth, "Fundamentalism and Femininity: Points of Encounter Between Religious Conservatives and Women, 1919–1935." *Church History* 61 (June 1992): 228–229.

4. Tucker, *Prophetic Sisterhood*, p. 6.

5. Tucker, *Prophetic Sisterhood*, p. 6.

6. Charles H. Barfoot and Gerald T. Sheppard, "Prophetic vs. Priestly Religion: The Changing Role of Women Clergy in Classical Pentecostal Churches." *Review of*

Religious Research 22 (September 1980): 2–16; cf. Margaret Poloma, *Assemblies of God at the Crossroads: Charisma and Institutional Dilemmas* (Knoxville: University of Tennessee Press, 1989).

7. For a contemporary example of apprehension over the efficacy of female leadership at congregational crisis points, see Edward C. Lehman, Jr., *Women Clergy: Breaking Through the Gender Barriers* (New Brunswick, N.J.: Transaction, 1985).

8. Barfoot and Sheppard, "Prophetic vs. Priestly Religion," p. 14.

9. Elsie Gibson, *When the Minister is a Woman* (New York: Holt, Rinehart and Winston, 1970), p. 90; cf. Tucker, *Prophetic Sisterhood*, p. 28; Catherine F. Hitchings, *Universalist and Unitarian Women Ministers* (Boston: Unitarian Universalist Historical Society, 1985), p. 6.

10. Bendroth, "Fundamentalism and Femininity," p. 231.

11. Barfoot and Sheppard, "Prophetic vs. Priestly Religion," p. 15.

12. Donald W. Dayton and Lucille Sider Dayton, "Women as Preachers: Evangelical Precedents." *Christianity Today* 23 May 1975, p. 7; "Wesleyan-Holiness Women Clergy Confer in New Mexico." *The Woman's Pulpit* October–December 1994, p. 5.

13. Cf. Nancy Tatom Ammerman, *Baptist Battles: Social Change and Religious Conflict in the Southern Baptist Convention* (New Brunswick, N.J.: Rutgers University Press: 1990); Frederick W. Schmidt, "Transcending Bureaucratic and Cultural Linkages: Women and the Church." Paper presented at the Annual Meeting of The Society for the Scientific Study of Religion and The Religious Research Association, Washington, D.C. 1992, pp. 57–60; Edward C. Lehman, Jr., *Women in Ministry: Receptivity and Resistance* (Melbourne, Australia: The Joint Board of Christian Education, 1994), pp. 23–25; "Latvian Lutherans Halt Ordination of Women." *The Woman's Pulpit* July–September 1995, 7.

14. Opposition to women's ordination was a central issue in the new formation of the Australian Evangelical Lutheran Church ("Resistance to Ordaining Women." *The Woman's Pulpit* October–December 1993, p. 7). The most notable U.S. Episcopal Church schisms followed the 1976 decision to ordain women to the priesthood when an estimated 20,000 members broke away to form other groups such as the Anglican Catholic Church of North America, or be received into the Roman Catholic Church; David E. Sumner, *The Episcopal Church's History: 1945–1985* (Wilton, Conn.: Morehouse-Barlow, 1987), pp. 158–162. Cf. Heather Ann Huyck, "To Celebrate a Whole Priesthood: The History of Women's Ordination in the Episcopal Church." Ph.D. dissertation, University of Minnesota, 1981; Christine Camilla Gaylor, "The Ordination of Women in the Episcopal Church in the United States: A Case Study." Ph.D. dissertation, St. John's University, 1982. Another recent schism occurred in 1992, when the Episcopal Missionary Diocese of America dissolved its relationship with the Episcopal Church over issues stemming from denominational support of women's ordination.

15. Erdey, reporting on the convention, recounted that after one bishop had complained about the difficulty of getting consent from the church's dioceses because of his stand against women's ordination, Barbara Harris, the first woman bishop in the church, responded, "If you'll recall, my consent process wasn't exactly a piece of cake!" Susan Erdey, "A Reporter's Notebook from General Convention." Special NEWS Section. *The Episcopal Times* (Diocese of Massachusetts) October 1994, p. 5; cf. Jerry Hames, "Convention Validates Two Views on Women Priests." *Episcopal Life* October 1994, p. 12; James Solheim, Jeffrey Penn, and Michael Barwell, "Report: General Convention

1994." Special NEWS Section. *The Episcopal Times* (Diocese of Massachusetts) October 1994, pp. 2–6.

16. Joyce McCarl Nielsen, *Sex and Gender in Society: Perspectives on Stratification*, 2nd ed. (Prospect Heights, Ill.: Waveland Press, 1990), p. 231.

17. Janet Saltzman Chafetz and Anthony Gary Dworkin, "In the Face of Threat: Organized Antifeminism in Comparative Perspective," in *The Sociology of Gender: A Text-Reader*, ed. Laura Kramer (New York: St. Martin's Press, 1991), pp. 471, 476–477.

18. Cynthia Cockburn, *In the Way of Women: Men's Resistance to Sex Equality in Organizations* (London: ILR Press, 1991), p. 46. Cf. Martha Long Ice, *Clergy Women and Their World Views: Calling for a New Age* (New York: Praeger, 1987), p. 9.

19. Cf. Chafetz and Dworkin, "In the Face of Threat," p. 482.

20. Cynthia Cockburn, *Machinery of Dominance: Women, Men, and Technical Know-How* (Boston: Northeastern University Press, 1988), p. 204.

21. Jennifer R. Cowan, "Survey Finds 70% of Women Rabbis Sexually Harassed." *Moment* October 1993, p. 35.

22. *Report of the Executive Council's Committee on the Status of Women* (New York: The Episcopal Church, 1991), p. 16.

23. R. W. Connell, *Gender and Power: Society, the Person and Sexual Politics* (Stanford, Calif.: Stanford University Press, 1987), p. 263.

24. The clause stated that, "No bishop, priest, or lay person should be coerced or penalized in any manner" for acting in accord with personal convictions on the matter of women's ordination. *Journal of the General Convention of the Episcopal Church in the United States of America*, 1979, p. B-202; Sumner, *The Episcopal Church's History*, p. 29. A number of male clergy nevertheless moved into different positions, dioceses or monastic orders where they would be free of the presence of women clergy.

25. Brita Stendahl, *The Force of Tradition: A Case Study of Women Priests in Sweden* (Philadelphia: Fortress Press, 1985), p. 7. In 1994 the Church of Sweden approved a measure that would keep those opposed to women clergy from being ordained. "Church of Sweden Drops 'Conscience Clause.'" *The Christian Century*, 16 November 1994, p. 1072.

26. Resolution A018a, 1994 General Convention.

27. Peter Fishburn, Janet Fishburn, and Arthur Hagy, "Are There Better Ways to Elect Bishops?" *Circuit Rider*, July–August 1992, pp. 11–12.

28. See female clergy comment, *Presbyterian Clergywomen Survey 1993: Overview of Respondents' Comments* (Louisville, Ky.: Presbyterian Church (U.S.A.), Congregational Ministries Division, Research Services), p. 4.

29. Jackson W. Carroll, Barbara Hargrove, and Adair T. Lummis, *Women of the Cloth: A New Opportunity for the Churches* (San Francisco: Harper & Row, 1983). Note the virtual absence of preference for women as pastor in *The Presbyterian Placement System*. Presbyterian Panel Report (Louisville, Ky.: Presbyterian Survey Magazine, 1989).

30. Lehman, *Women Clergy*.

31. Cockburn found that both white men in support or clerical grades and men of color have felt the most resistant to women's equality; Cockburn, *In the Way of Women*, p. 67. Evidence from secular occupations points to men's reticence over the prospect of working for women. For example, Margaret Power, "The Making of a Woman's Occupation." *Hecate* January 1975, 30; Theodore Caplow, *The Sociology of Work* (New York: McGraw-Hill, 1964); Helen Weinreich-Haste, *The Sexual Metaphor* (Cambridge: Harvard University Press, 1994), p. 271.

32. For example, Lehman, *Women Clergy*; Schmidt, "Transcending Bureaucratic and Cultural Linkages," p. 77; Lesley Stevens, "Different Voice/Different Voices: Anglican Women in Ministry." *Review of Religious Research* 30 (March 1989): 265–266.

33. Edward C. Lehman, Jr., "Sexism, Organizational Maintenance and Localism: A Research Note." *Sociological Analysis* 48 (Fall 1987): 274–282; Edward C. Lehman, Jr., *Women Clergy in England: Sexism, Modern Consciousness and Church Viability* (Lewiston, N.Y.: Edwin Mellen Press, 1987); Lehman, *Women Clergy*.

34. For an illustration of how such an objective appeal to scripture undergirded the changes in the Southern Baptist Convention's policy on women's ordination, see Ammerman, *Baptist Battles*, pp. 93–94, 223–224.

35. Cf. Stendahl, *The Force of Tradition*, p. 99.

36. Cf. Chafetz and Dworkin, "In the Face of Threat," p. 480.

37. Cockburn, *In the Way of Women*, p. 223.

38. Bendroth, "Fundamentalism and Femininity," p. 230.

39. Ammerman, *Baptist Battles*, p. 95.

40. Chafetz and Dworkin, "In the Face of Threat," p. 483.

41. James Solheim, "Jubliant [sic] Vermonters Welcome Woman as Diocesan Bishop," *Episcopal Life* December 1993, pp. 1, 6.

42. Carroll et al., *Women of the Cloth*. Cf. Lehman's discussion of the "contact hypothesis" in *Women Clergy*.

43. For example, Mary S. Donovan, A *Different Call: Women's Ministries in the Episcopal Church, 1850–1920* (Wilton, Conn.: Morehouse-Barlow, 1986).

44. Janet Saltzman Chafetz, *Gender Equity: An Integrated Theory of Stability and Change* (Newbury Park, Calif.: Sage, 1990), p. 140.

45. For example, Edward C. Lehman, Jr., "Research on Lay Church Members Attitudes Toward Women Clergy: An Assessment." *Review of Religious Research* 28 (June 1987): 325; Lehman, "Sexism, Organizational Maintenance, and Localism," pp. 275, 279; Lehman, *Women Clergy*; Edward C. Lehman, Jr., "Organizational Resistance to Women in Ministry." *Sociological Analysis* 42 (Summer 1981): 101–118.

46. Max Weber, *The Sociology of Religion* (Boston: Beacon Press, 1963), p. 217.

47. Cf. Barbara F. Reskin, "Bringing the Men Back In," in *The Social Construction of Gender*, eds. Judith Lorber and Susan A. Farrell (Newbury Park, Calif.: Sage, 1991), pp. 143–149.

48. Gender ratios for both community ministers and ministers of religious education are approximations owing to a few cases where gender could not be inferred by name or other directory information.

49. *Our Professional Ministry: Structure, Support and Renewal* (Boston: Unitarian Universalist Association, Commission on Appraisal, 1992), p. 55.

50. *Unitarian Universalist Association Directory* (Boston: Unitarian Universalist Association, 1981), p. 194.

51. Dorothy Jean Furnish, *DRE/DCE: The History of a Profession* (Nashville: Christian Educators Fellowship, The United Methodist Church, 1976), pp. 37–41, 76–82, 89, 95. For the feminization statistic, Furnish cites Otto Mayer, "A Study of Directors of Religious Education and Their Profession." *International Journal of Religious Education* 15 (October 1938): 12.

52. Cf. *Our Professional Ministry*, p. 76.

53. Edward R. Hardy, "Deacons in History and Practice," in *The Diaconate Now*, ed. Richard T. Nolan (Washington: Corpus Books, 1968), pp. 11–36.

54. Cf. John E. Booty, *The Servant Church: Diaconal Ministry in the Episcopal*

Church (Wilton, Conn.: Morehouse-Barlow, 1982); James Monroe Barnett, *The Diaconate: A Full and Equal Order* (New York: Seabury Press, 1981); Permanent Diaconate Evaluation Committee and Adair T. Lummis, *Raising Up Servant Ministry* (New York: The Episcopal Church, 1985).

55. Cf. Permanent Diaconate Evaluation Committee and Lummis, *Raising Up Servant Ministry*.

56. Julie A. Wortman, "Deacons' Revival Brings Servant Ministry to Fore." *Episcopal Life* June 1991, p. 7.

57. Permanent Diaconate Education Committee and Lummis, *Raising Up Servant Ministry*, p. 100f.

58. The 1994 statistics are from the North American Association for the Diaconate.

59. I had argued these concerns in earlier research based on 1988 data and which was again borne out in this analysis. Cf. Paula D. Nesbitt, "Dual Ordination Tracks: Differential Benefits and Costs for Men and Women Clergy," in *Gender and Religion*, ed. William H. Swatos, Jr., (New Brunswick, N.J.: Transaction, 1993), pp. 27–44.

60. Howard L. Smith and Mary Grenier, "Sources of Organizational Power for Women: Overcoming Structural Obstacles." *Sex Roles* 8 (July 1982), pp. 733–746; also see Roos and Reskin, "Institutional Factors Contributing to Sex Segregation in the Workplace," pp. 235–260.

61. Cf. Robert B. Slocum, "The Diaconate: Barrier or Catalyst for Lay Ministry?" *St. Luke's Journal of Theology* 33 (March 1990), p. 137. *Deacon*, based on the Greek word *diakonos*, is commonly defined as "one who serves." Cf. Booty, *The Servant Church*.

62. Functional pluralism entails developing whatever structure of diversity may be necessary so that divergent perspectives are fully represented and weighted.

63. Cockburn, *In the Way of Women*, pp. 70, 219.

64. Cf. Slocum, "The Diaconate." The triennial General Conventions from 1985 onward have been concerned with tightening and formalizing requirements for ordination to the various orders, ironically coinciding with a 30 percent or higher female gender ratio of ordinands in the 1985 and subsequent cohorts.

65. Michael H. Dugan, "What are 'Canon Nine' Clergy?" *The Mountain Echo* (Episcopal Diocese of Vermont) 57 (August 1992): 4.

66. For example, Ross writes that the first "local priest" in the diocese of Arizona was 57 years old, a sales administrator for the U.S. Forest Service; Nan Ross, "Bishop Ordains First 'Local Priest.'" *The Arizona Episcopalian* (Diocese of Arizona) 12 (June–July 1992): 1, 3. In another diocese, "teams of lay people" have been ordained since 1990 as Canon 9 deacons and priests to hold responsibility for congregations; Julie A. Wortman, "Dioceses Redefining Roles of Deacons, Priests." *Episcopal Life* May 1991, p. 1.

67. Cf. Marjorie Hyer, "Church Tackles 'Clergy Crisis' Head On." *Episcopal Life* July 1990, pp. 20–21.

68. Vatican II provided for the institution of the permanent diaconate (Lumen Gentium, 1964); *De Ecclesia: The Constitution on the Church of Vatican Council II Proclaimed by Pope Paul VI, November 21, 1964*, ed. Edward H. Peters (Glen Rock, N.J.: Paulist Press, 1965); Francis J. Dunigan, "Perception of the Laity of the Restored Permanent Diaconate, Archdiocese of Boston: An Attitude Measurement and Analysis." Ph.D. dissertation, Catholic University of America, 1986.

69. The permanent diaconate has thwarted substantial lay ministry efforts in Latin-

American base communities, particularly those strongly dependent on female leadership.

70. Carroll et al., *Women of the Cloth*, pp. 35–36; Marjorie H. Royle, "Using Bifocals to Overcome Blindspots: The Impact of Women on the Military and the Ministry." *Review of Religious Research* 28 (June 1987): 345.

71. Cf. Carroll et al., *Women of the Cloth*, pp. 36–37.

72. North American Association for the Diaconate, "1993 Year-end Statistics." *Diakoneo* 16 (Epiphany 1994), p. 7.

73. Stanley Lieberson, *Making It Count: The Improvement of Social Research and Theory* (Berkeley: University of California Press, 1985), p. 164; cf. Reskin, "Bringing the Men Back In," p. 142.

74. Cf. Nancy E. Betz and Louise F. Fitzgerald, *The Career Psychology of Women* (Orlando, Fla.: Academic Press, 1987), p. 55; Patricia A. Roos, *Gender and Work: A Comparative Analysis of Industrial Societies* (Albany: State University of New York Press, 1985), p. 68; William H. Sewell, Robert M. Hauser, and Wendy Wolf, "Sex, Schooling, and Occupational Status." *American Journal of Sociology* 86 (November 1980): 551–583. Racial minorities also have been found to get less return on their education than European-American men; e.g., Nielsen, *Sex and Gender in Society*, pp. 103, 105.

75. Roos, *Gender and Work*, pp. 108, 148.

76. Valerie K. Oppenheimer, "Demographic Influences on Female Employment and the Status of Women." *American Journal of Sociology* 78 (January 1973): 946–961; cf. Roos, *Gender and Work*; Nielsen, *Sex and Gender in Society*, pp. 68–72.

77. The rise in education takes into account the change from Bachelor of Divinity to Master of Divinity degrees. All B.D. degrees in the data, regardless of year, are treated as M.Div. degrees. The upgrading in educational attainment includes a higher concentration of clergy with additional master and doctoral degrees, and supports similar evidence of educational upgrading in stratification research. Cf. Wade Clark Roof and William McKinney, *American Mainline Religion: Its Changing Shape and Future* (New Brunswick, N.J.: Rutgers University Press, 1987), p. 65; Dennis Gilbert and Joseph A. Kahl, *The American Class Structure: A New Synthesis* (Chicago: Dorsey Press, 1982), p. 183.

78. Schaller notes, for instance, that since the mid–1960s, seminary-trained specialists in religious education have been replaced "with a mature woman" presumably experienced but not seminary educated. Lyle E. Schaller, *It's a Different World: The Challenge for Today's Pastor* (Nashville, Tenn.: Abingdon Press, 1987), p. 202.

79. See Betz and Fitzgerald, *The Career Psychology of Women*, pp. 54–55, for a brief review on this topic. Cf. Roos, *Gender and Work*, p. 111.

80. Episcopal Divinity School, for example, known for its curricular inclusion of gender and controversial issues, including a doctoral program in feminist liberation theology, has been singled out by several conservative dioceses that haven't approved candidates to attend seminary there. Despite such strictures, the 1995 entering class was the seminary's largest in years.

81. Chafetz, *Gender Equity*, pp. 125, 127.

82. *Report of the Executive Council's Committee on the Status of Women*, 1991, pp. 14–15.

83. Cf. James Risen, "Part-time Jobs Rise While Security Drops." [*Los Angeles Times*] *The Denver Post* 15 February 1994, p. 6A.

84. Cf. *Presbyterian Clergywomen Survey 1993: Overview of Respondents' Comments*, p. 6; Chafetz, *Gender Equity*, pp. 126–127.

85. *Report of the Executive Council's Committee on the Status of Women,* 1991, pp. 14–15.

86. For instance, an amendment to the Colorado diocesan canons passed in 1995 that would grant missions parish status merely by demonstrating an ability to compensate a rector rather than to support a full-time rector. This step effectively removes the diocese from responsibility for overseeing congregational affairs or for clergy deployment, including possible salary supplement. It also weakens what can be considered the financial norm for rectorship positions, effectively setting up a two-tier rectorship—one for full-time paid professionals and another for clergy either who have other sources of nonemployment income or who must hold at least a part-time placement elsewhere. Cf. James L. Lowery Jr., *Peers, Tents and Owls: Some Solutions to Problems of the Clergy Today* (New York: Morehouse-Barlow, 1973).

87. Permanent Diaconate Evaluation Committee and Adair T. Lummis, *Raising Up Servant Ministry.*

88. As one part-time female priest who also is a secular teacher anecdotally commented, "I look forward to summer. Then I only have one 40-hour-a-week job." This trend has affected other religious organizations as well. For instance, a disproportionate number of female Reform and Conservative rabbis have been identified with part-time salaries but full-time responsibilities; Janet Marder, "How Women Are Changing the Rabbinate." *Reform Judaism* Summer 1991, p. 5; Elaine Shizgal Cohen, "Rabbis' Roles and Occupational Goals: Men and Women in the Contemporary American Rabbinate." *Conservative Judaism* 42 (Fall 1989): 25.

89. "Threshold '93: A Summary of the Study of the Organizational Structures of the Diocese as They Impact its Present and Future Mission and Ministry." *The Episcopal Times* (Diocese of Massachusetts), December 1993–January 1994, p. 13.

90. Connell, *Gender and Power,* p. 129.

91. Cf. Stewart Ranson, Alan Bryman, and Bob Hinings, *Clergy, Ministers and Priests* (London: Routledge and Kegan Paul, 1977), p. 11.

92. Chafetz, *Gender Equity,* pp. 80, 125, 132, 136. Cf. Roos and Reskin, "Institutional Factors Contributing to Sex Segregation in the Workplace"; Carter and Carter, "Women's Recent Progress in the Professions"; Cockburn, *Machinery of Dominance,* p. 234.

93. Reskin and Roos, *Job Queues, Gender Queues,* pp. 4, 10–11; cf. Barbara F. Reskin and Heidi I. Hartmann, eds. *Women's Work, Men's Work: Sex Segregation on the Job* (Washington, D.C.: National Academy Press, 1986); Cockburn, *Machinery of Dominance,* p. 17; Roos, *Gender and Work.*

94. Chafetz, *Gender Equity.*

95. Although forty-one Unitarian Universalist titles actually were listed, fourteen were functionally equivalent to other titles. Similarly, of the 153 total titles in the Episcopal data, sixty-nine were distinct from one another.

96. Melvin D. Williams, *Community in a Black Pentecostal Church: An Anthropological Study* (Pittsburgh: University of Pittsburgh Press, 1974); cf. Sheila Briggs, "Women and Religion," in *Analyzing Gender: A Handbook of Social Science Research,* eds. Beth B. Hess and Myra Marx Feree (Newbury Park, Calif.: Sage, 1987), p. 411.

97. Donald J. Treiman and Heidi I. Hartmann, eds., *Women, Work and Wages: Equal Pay for Jobs of Equal Value* (Washington: National Academy Press, 1981); cf. Edward C. Lehman, Jr., "Placement of Men and Women in the Ministry." *Review of Religious Research* 22 (September 1980): 23.

98. For instance, some Episcopal dioceses have been resistant to denominational

surveys assessing lay and clergy women's participation. *Report of the Executive Council's Committee on the Status of Women*, p. 10; cf. *Presbyterian Clergywomen Survey 1993*, "Discrimination Against Women." *Church & Society* July–August 1992, pp. 95–96.

99. *Unitarian Universalist Association Directory 1987*, p. 16.

100. The General Commission on the Status and Role of Women (GCSRW) randomly sampled 1,000 United Methodist churches. "Women's Participation in Local Churches Still Lags," *The Flyer* (GCSRW) 12 (Fall 1991–Winter 1992): 1–2.

101. Mary Frank Fox and Sharlene Hesse-Biber, *Women at Work* (Palo Alto, Calif.: Mayfield, 1984); cf. Roos and Reskin, "Institutional Factors Contributing to Sex Segregation," pp. 245–246; Margaret Hennig and Anne Jardim, *The Managerial Woman* (New York: Pocket Books, 1977).

102. Lehman, "Placement of Men and Women in the Ministry."

103. For Church Deployment Office data, see Mary S. Donovan, *Women Priests in the Episcopal Church: The Experience of the First Decade* (Cincinnati, Ohio: Forward Movement, 1988). Comparing Donovan's findings with the Episcopal data from this analysis, using priests from the 1980 and 1985 cohorts (N = 405) with a 1988 censoring date, similar results to the C.D.O. data were found in the percentages of female and male priests who moved into vicar and rector placements.

104. Lehman, "Placement of Men and Women in the Ministry," p. 31.

105. Edward C. Lehman, Jr., and The Task Force on Women in Ministry, *Project SWIM: A Study of Women in Ministry* (Valley Forge, Pa.: The Ministry Council, American Baptist Churches, 1979); cf. Lehman, "Placement of Men and Women in the Ministry"; Veronica F. Nieva and Barbara A. Gutek, *Women and Work: A Psychological Perspective* (New York: Praeger, 1981); Betz and Fitzgerald, *The Career Psychology of Women*, p. 164.

106. J. Keith Cook and Lee C. Moorehead, *Six Stages of a Pastor's Life* (Nashville, Tenn.: Abingdon Press, 1990), p. 18.

107. Reducing gender segregation doesn't effectively reduce the wage gap. See Reskin, "Bringing the Men Back In," p. 152; Cockburn, *In the Way of Women*, p. 63; Power, "The Making of a Woman's Occupation," p. 33. For the effects of women's socialization on wages in secular work, see Reskin and Roos, *Job Queues, Gender Queues*, p. 102; Reskin and Roos survey other research on the importance that women give to income (p. 38).

108. *Report of the Executive Council's Committee on the Status of Women*, p. 14.

109. *Report of the Executive Council's Committee on the Status of Women*, p. 14. The report argued that salary compression may be at work, limiting the upward range for rector salaries. This would partly explain the similarity in salaries between male and female rectors, ordained as priests in 1977. It also would make logical sense that clergy registered with the C.D.O. were those still interested in upward job mobility, suggesting that these may not represent the most socioeconomically desirable rectorships.

110. Reskin, "Bringing the Men Back In," p. 143. For a brief discussion of other research on this topic, see Judith Lorber and Susan A. Farrell, "Gender Construction in the Workplace," in *The Social Construction of Gender*, eds. Judith Lorber and Susan A. Farrell (Newbury Park, Calif.: Sage, 1991), p. 137.

111. Max Weber, *Economy and Society: An Outline of Interpretive Sociology*, eds. Guenther Roth and Claus Wittich (Berkeley: University of California Press, 1978), p. 946; Victoria Lee Erickson, *Where Silence Speaks: Feminism, Social Theory, and Religion* (Minneapolis, Minn.: Fortress Press, 1993), p. 100.

112. For notation of the glass ceiling in women clergy careers, see *Presbyterian Clergywomen Survey 1993*; Cohen, "Survey Finds 70% of Women Rabbis Sexually

Harassed"; Schmidt, "Transcending Bureaucratic and Cultural Linkages,"p. 78; Paul Wilkes, "The Hands That Would Shape Our Souls." *The Atlantic Monthly* December 1990, p. 81; Sally B. Purvis, *The Stained Glass Ceiling: Churches and Their Women Pastors* (Louisville, Ky.: Westminster/John Knox Press, 1995).

113. See Reskin and Roos, *Job Queues, Gender Queues*; Cockburn, *Machinery of Dominance*; Liliane Floge and Deborah M. Merrill, "Tokenism Reconsidered: Male Nurses and Female Physicians in a Hospital Setting." *Social Forces* 64 (June 1986): 925–947; Barbara Sinclair Deckard, *The Women's Movement: Socioeconomic and Psychological Issues* (New York: Harper & Row, 1975).

114. Rosemary Crompton and Gareth Jones, *White-Collar Proletariate: Deskilling and Gender in Clerical Work* (Philadelphia: Temple University Press, 1984); cf. Joan Acker, "Hierarchies, Jobs, Bodies: A Theory of Gendered Organizations," in *The Social Construction of Gender*, eds. Judith Lorber and Susan A. Farrell (Newbury Park, Calif.: Sage, 1991), p. 175; Cockburn, *In the Way of Women*, p. 216.

115. Ruth Milkman, *Gender at Work: The Dynamics of Job Segregation by Sex During World War II* (Urbana: University of Illinois Press, 1987); cf. Roos and Reskin, *Job Queues, Gender Queues*, p. 56.

116. Cf. Ann Douglas, *The Feminization of American Culture* (New York: Alfred A. Knopf, 1977); Mayer N. Zald and John D. McCarthy, "Religious Groups as Crucibles of Social Movements," in *Social Movements in an Organizational Society: Collected Essays*, eds. Mayer N. Zald and John D. McCarthy (New Brunswick, N.J.: Transaction, 1987), p. 82.

117. Lehman, *Women Clergy*. Cf. *Presbyterian Clergywomen Survey 1993*.

118. Carroll et al., *Women of the Cloth*.

119. Rosabeth Moss Kanter, *Men and Women of the Corporation* (New York: Basic Books, 1977), p. 208f.

120. Marcy Darin, "They Smashed the Mold and Wear the Collar." *Episcopal Life* June–July 1994, p. 14.

121. Shortly after her consecration Harris had commented, "Some of the men try to be very protective and that is nice of them, but I hope to retain enough of my own independence to share with them as an equal." Monica Furlong, "A Bishop to Break the Mold," [*The Guardian*] *The Episcopal Times* (Diocese of Massachusetts), February–March 1989, p. 10.

122. Cf. Reskin and Roos, *Job Queues, Gender Queues*, p. 49.

123. Nancy Nason-Clark, "Are Women Changing the Image of Ministry? A Comparison of British and American Realities." *Review of Religious Research* 28 (June 1987), p. 334.

124. Cf. Cockburn, *In the Way of Women*, p. 67.

125. Acker, "Hierarchies, Jobs, Bodies," pp. 173–174.

126. According to Cockburn, women who overstep boundaries considered to be male territory not only risk forfeiture of male approval and support but are penalized, as a means of men maintaining masculine hegemony. Cockburn, *In the Way of Women*, p. 218; cf. Stevens, "Different Voice/Different Voices," p. 265.

127. J. Long Laws, "The Psychology of Tokenism: An Analysis." *Sex Roles* 1 (1975): 51–67; cf. Judith Lorber, "Dismantling Noah's Ark," in *The Social Construction of Gender*, eds. Judith Lorber and Susan A. Farrell (Newbury Park, Calif.: Sage, 1991), p. 365.

128. Cockburn, *In the Way of Women*, p. 216.

129. Chafetz, *Gender Equity*.

130. For example, Sandra Hughes Boyd, "A Woman's Journey Toward Priesthood:

An Autobiographical Study from the 1950s Through the 1980s," in *Episcopal Women: Gender, Spirituality and Commitment in an American Mainline Denomination*, ed. Catherine M. Prelinger (New York: Oxford University Press, 1992), p. 274.

131. Stevens, "Different Voice/Different Voices," p. 265.

132. The appointment system not surprisingly is under attack from within the United Methodist Church. Cf. Jack M. Tuell, "Itineracy Revisited." *Circuit Rider*, November 1992, pp. 4–6; William Boyd Grove, "Appointment-Making in the West Virginia Area." *Circuit Rider* November 1992, pp. 7–8.

133. Apostolic succession is claimed to be an unbroken tradition of the laying on of hands as part of the ordination rite passed down to present day from the time of the Apostles. A suffragan bishop has limited authority and autonomy, reporting to the diocesan bishop.

134. Kristen E. Holmes, "A Mennonite first." [*Knight-Ridder News Service*] *The Denver Post* 27 November 1993, p. 10B; "Mennonites Elect Clemens First Woman Moderator." *The Woman's Pulpit* October–December 1993, p. 6.

135. Cf. Mary S. Donovan, "Women as Priests and Bishops." Paper presented to the University of Arkansas-Little Rock History Seminar, 2 November 1989.

136. For example, the first woman to head the Episcopal House of Deputies is laywoman Pamela Chinnis; the first two women elected as moderator of the Uniting Church's New South Wales Synod in Australia were laywomen.

137. Chafetz, *Gender Equity*, p. 221.

138. Chafetz, *Gender Equity*, p. 108; cf. Lehman, *Women in Ministry: Receptivity and Resistance* (Melbourne, Australia: The Joint Board of Christian Education, 1994).

139. Susan Faludi, *Backlash: The Undeclared War Against American Women* (New York: Doubleday, Anchor Books, 1991).

Chapter 8

1. President Hamilton wrote this letter to Elizabeth Murray Newman in February 1910. *The Proceedings of the Unitarian Universalist Historical Society*, ed. Richard E. Myers (Boston: Unitarian Universalist Association, 1984), p. 37.

2. Randall Collins, "A Conflict Theory of Sexual Stratification." *Social Problems* 19 (Summer 1971): 3–21.

3. Ranson et al., studying clergy in the British Methodist Church, the Church of England, and the Roman Catholic Church in Britain, suggest that the clergy crisis in England has arisen from the disjunction between denominational objectives and both the resources and means for achieving them, Stewart Ranson, Alan Bryman, and Bob Hinings, *Clergy, Ministers and Priests* (London: Routledge and Kegan Paul, 1977), p. 17.

4. David L. Featherman, "Biography, Society, and History: Individual Development as a Population Process," in *Human Development and the Life Course: Multidisciplinary Perspectives*, eds. Aage B. Søorensen, Franz E. Weinert, and Lonnie R. Sherrod (Hillsdale, N.J.: Lawrence Erlbaum, 1986), p. 109.

5. Barbara F. Reskin and Patricia A. Roos, *Job Queues, Gender Queues: Explaining Women's Inroads into Male Occupations* (Philadelphia: Temple University Press, 1990), p. 73, also see pp. 44–45, 85, 88; Jackson W. Carroll, Barbara Hargrove, and Adair T. Lummis, *Women of the Cloth: A New Opportunity for the Churches* (San Francisco: Harper & Row, 1983), pp. 52, 59.

6. Cynthia Cockburn, *In the Way of Women: Men's Resistance to Sex Equality in Organizations* (London: ILR Press, 1991), p. 61.

7. Nemeth and Luidens, in a comparative study of the Presbyterian Church (U.S.A.) and Reformed Church in America, compare fiscal trends with other mainline Protestant denominations having made cutbacks in programming and staff (Religious News Service, "Competition for Members Keeps More Money at Home." *Episcopal Life* December 1993, p. 27; Roger J. Nemeth and Donald A. Luidens, "Congregational vs. Denominational Giving: An Analysis of Giving Patterns in the Presbyterian Church in the United States and the Reformed Church in America." *Review of Religious Research* 36 (December 1994): 111–122. Cf. Edward C. Lehman, Jr., "Placement of Men and Women in the Ministry." *Review of Religious Research* 22 (September 1980): 19–20.

8. David Briggs, "Church Collection Plates in U.S. Very Light." *The Denver Post* 17 December 1993, p. 25A.

9. *Report of the Executive Council's Committee on the Status of Women* (New York: The Episcopal Church, May 1991), p. 4.

10. "Presbyterians Cut Staff, Reduce Ministry Units." *Episcopal Life* September 1993, p. 3; cf. Nemeth and Luidens, "Congregational Vs. Denominational Giving."

11. Michael Barwell, "Money Serves as Metaphor for How Church Ministers." *Episcopal Life* July 1994, p. 10.

12. Charles R. Wilson, "Cancel the Funeral: The Church is Quite Alive." *Episcopal Life* December 1993, p. 27. A 1995 estimate suggested 7,200 paid positions, although not all of these may be full-time; Herb Gunn, "Building Ministry for a New World: The Commission on Ministry." *The Record* (Episcopal Diocese of Michigan) 44 (May 1995): 6.

13. Cf. Jay Cormier, "Parish 'Cluster' Ministries: A Means of Survival May Be Source of New Life for Local Congregations." *The Episcopal Times* (Diocese of Massachusetts) September 1994, pp. 8–9; Ariel Miller, "Too Few Resources? Look Again: Northern Michigan Pioneers Mutual Ministry." *The Record* (Episcopal Diocese of Michigan) 43 (March 1994): 1, 11.

14. U.S. Bureau of the Census, *Statistical Abstract of the United States 1995* (Washington, D.C.: Government Printing Office, 1995), Tables 637–638, pp. 405–406.

15. U.S. Bureau of the Census, *Statistical Abstract of the United States 1995*, Table 76, p. 64.

16. Joanna B. Gillespie, "Gender and Generations in Congregations," in *Episcopal Women: Gender, Spirituality, and Commitment in a Mainline Denomination*, ed. Catherine M. Prelinger (New York: Oxford University Press, 1992), pp. 168, 191–196.

17. Religious News Service, "Competition for Members Keeps More Money at Home;" Nemeth and Luidens, "Congregational Vs. Denominational Giving."

18. Anecdotally, several clergy talked of parishes known informally among clergy networks as *minister* or *priest breakers*, sites where negotiations for authority, power, and sometimes economic remuneration, become untenable.

19. Edward C. Lehman, Jr., "Placement of Men and Women in the Ministry," pp. 19–20; cf. Ann Douglas, *The Feminization of American Culture* (New York: Alfred A. Knopf, 1977); Alexis de Tocqueville, *Democracy in America* (New York: Anchor Books, Doubleday & Co., 1969).

20. The Episcopal Church's national organization is accused of having a "political nature," with "politicized special interest groups tak[ing] away from the missionary focus of the church." Elliott Sorge, "Dioceses to National Church: Think Locally, Act Locally." *Episcopal Life* November 1993, p. 16.

21. Episcopal Presiding Bishop Edmond L. Browning acknowledged that part of

the denomination's financial stringency was the result of withholding funds because of differences of view that included issues related to gender and sexuality. For Browning and Wetzel's remarks, see Nan Cobbey, ed., "Voices of General Convention." *Episcopal Life* October 1994, pp. 18–19.

22. Stated the Diocese of Pittsburgh, "The impression is that the presiding bishop has become a political figure elected by a partisan process dedicated to the implementation of a party agenda . . . [that is] . . . irrelevant to the average parish." Nan Cobbey, "Dioceses Sound Alarm to National Staff." *Episcopal Life* November 1993, p. 16.

23. Cf. Joseph C. Hough, Jr., "Future Pastors, Future Church: The Seminary Quarrels." *The Christian Century*, 24–31 May 1995, pp. 564–567; "The Memphis Declaration." Adopted by 177 concerned United Methodists. Written in a meeting at Memphis, Tenn., 25 January 1992; cf. James H. Steele, "Confessionals Call UMs to Reclaim and Re-ignite Doctrinal Heritage." *The Vision* (Rocky Mountain Conference of the United Methodist Church), June–July 1995, p. 6.

24. Reskin and Roos, *Job Queues, Gender Queues*, pp. 11, 56.

25. Cf. L. Paul, *The Deployment and Payment of the Clergy* (London: Church Information Office, 1964) cited in Ranson et al., *Clergy, Ministers and Priests*.

26. *The Proceedings of the Unitarian Universalist Historical Society*, ed. Myers; cf. Cynthia Grant Tucker, *Prophetic Sisterhood: Liberal Women Ministers of the Frontier, 1880–1930* (Boston: Beacon Press, 1990).

27. Charles Prestwood, *The New Breed of Clergy* (Grand Rapids, Mich.: William B. Eerdmans, 1972), p. 56.

28. Both the need for female labor during World War II and the increase in lower level workforce positions following the war created job opportunities for older married, as well as single, women during the 1950s. For a brief comprehensive review, see Janet Saltzman Chafetz, *Gender Equity: An Integrated Theory of Stability and Change* (Newbury Park, Calif.: Sage, 1990), p. 127. Bock also observed the relationship between shortages and the deployment of women, as well as the professional marginality women experience where they do hold placements; E. Wilbur Bock; "The Female Clergy: A Case of Professional Marginality." *American Journal of Sociology* 72 (March 1967): 531.

29. John D. Krugler and David Weinberg-Kinsey, "Equality of Leadership: The Ordinations of Sara E. Dickson and Margaret E. Towner in the Presbyterian Church in the U.S.A." *American Presbyterians* 68 (Winter 1990): 250.

30. Cf. James L. Lowery, Jr., *Peers, Tents and Owls: Some Solutions to Problems of the Clergy Today* (New York: Morehouse-Barlow, 1973). The Church of England acknowledged clergy shortages during the late 1980s, a time when women's ordination to the diaconate was granted (1987) and women's ordination to the priesthood was being intensely debated.

31. For concerns over shortages, see Alexander D. Stewart, "Episcopal Clergy: Is There a Danger of a Shortage?" Unpublished report, The Church Pension Fund, New York, 1987); George Hodges Soule, "We're Not Keeping the Clerical Pipeline Full." *The Episcopalian* March 1987, pp. 16–17; cf. Council of Bishops of the United Methodist Church. "A Statement on the Quality and Education Ministry for the United Methodist Church," Unpublished paper, 3 May 1991; Peter Steinfels, "Shortage of Qualified New Clergy Causing Alarm for U.S. Religions." *The Sunday New York Times* 9 July 1989, pp. 1, 22.

32. Gail Buchwalter King, "Trends in Seminary Education 1987–1992," in *Yearbook of American and Canadian Churches 1993*, ed. Kenneth B. Bedell (Nashville, Tenn.: Abingdon Press, 1993), p. 261.

33. U.S. Bureau of Labor Statistics, *Occupational Projections and Training Data.* Bulletin 2401 (Washington, D.C.: U.S. Department of Labor, May 1992), p. 18.

34. Clergy are those holding fellowship status in the U.U.A. Membership figures are reported adult members. The 1994 *Unitarian Universalist Association Directory* also made available a more conservative membership estimate of "certified members," but comparable figures are not included in U.U.A. directories for earlier years. *Unitarian Universalist Association Directory,* 1961–1994 (Boston: Unitarian Universalist Association).

35. *Our Professional Ministry: Structure, Support and Renewal* (Boston: Unitarian Universalist Association, Commission on Appraisal, 1992), p. 101.

36. Confirmed communicants in good standing indicates participation within the past six months. As such it is a more accurate measure of those more likely to utilize clergy services than membership figures alone. *The Episcopal Church Annual* (New York: The Episcopal Church, 1962, 1992). Comparing the number of Episcopal clergy ordained between 1960 and 1970 suggests that the proliferation has been more a response to organizational growth in the 1950s than of political and social issues rising out of the 1960s. For instance, in 1950, 274 men were ordained; in 1960 the number had risen to 448 men but declined to 410 men in 1970. *Journal of the General Convention of the Episcopal Church in the United States of America* (New York: The Episcopal Church, 1952–1973).

37. For discussions of surplus, see Marjorie Hyer, "Church Takes Clergy 'Crisis' Head On." *Episcopal Life* July 1990, pp. 20–21; Dean R. Hoge, John E. Dyble, and David T. Polk, "Organizational and Situational Influences on Vocational Commitment of Protestant Ministers." *Review of Religious Research* 23 (December 1981): 136; Jackson W. Carroll and Robert L. Wilson, *The Clergy Job Market: Oversupply and/or Opportunity.* Multilithed report (Hartford, Conn.: Hartford Seminary Foundation, 1978); Harold C. Warlick, Jr., *How to Be a Minister and a Human Being* (Valley Forge, Pa.: Judson Press, 1982), pp. 96–97.

38. Reskin and Roos discuss how labor shortages in secular occupations can benefit lower ranked constituencies such as women; Reskin and Roos, *Job Queues, Gender Queues,* pp. 34–43.

39. Cf. Stewart, *Episcopal Clergy.*

40. Soule, "We're Not Keeping the Clerical Pipeline Full," p. 17.

41. Soule observes in his concern over clergy supply that as women become increasingly influential, "they will undoubtedly cause changes in expectations of what the stipend is to pay for"; Soule, "We're Not Keeping the Clerical Pipeline Full," p. 17. Steinfels also notes that the changing clergy gender composition is likely to bring differing attitudes on sex; Steinfels, "Shortage of Qualified Clergy Causing Alarm for U.S. Religions."

42. Steinfels, "Shortage of Qualified New Clergy Causing Alarm for U.S. Religions," pp. 1, 22.

43. Cf. Elizabeth M. Almquist, "Labor Market Gender Inequality in Minority Groups," in *The Social Construction of Gender,* ed. Judith Lorber and Susan A. Farrell (Newbury Park, Calif.: Sage, 1991), p. 186.

44. In this particular situation, Chafetz refers to the deployment of men from other societies, such as captured slaves or immigrants. The ministerial analogy to other discrete male populations can be made to retirees or, applied to the case of the Roman Catholic Church, married men; Chafetz, *Gender Equity,* p. 127.

45. Ruth Wallace, *They Call Her Pastor: A New Role for Catholic Women* (Albany: State University of New York Press, 1992), p. 112. Wallace found that some

dioceses have refused to ordain permanent deacons in order to maintain lay leadership roles for women. She also notes a controversy in Seattle over conservative Catholics charging that their liberal bishop had been using the "alleged priest shortage" as a means to support the ordination of women. As a result of the controversy, the bishop cancelled a deacon training program, stating that "the church first should review the possibility of including women." The quoted material is from a (untitled) *Seattle Post-Intelligencer* article (19 May 1990, p. A8), cited in Wallace, p. 189.

46. Richard A. Schoenherr and Lawrence A. Young, *The Catholic Priest in the United States: Demographic Investigations.* (Madison: University of Wisconsin-Madison Comparative Religious Organization Studies Publications); Richard A. Schoenherr, *Goodbye Father, Celibacy, and Patriarchy in the Catholic Church* (New York: Oxford University Press, 1996); cited with a preliminary title in Wallace, "The Social Construction of a New Leadership Role."

47. Wallace, "The Social Construction of a New Leadership Role"; Wallace, *They Call Her Pastor.*

48. Steinfels, "Shortage of Qualified New Clergy Causing Alarm for U.S." Also see Council of Bishops, "A Statement on the Quality and Education of Ministry for the United Methodist Church." Unpublished paper, 3 May 1991.

49. Cf. Harrison C. White, *Chains of Opportunity: System Models of Mobility in Organizations* (Cambridge: Harvard University Press, 1970).

50. Male life expectancy was 67.1 years in 1970, 72.3 years in 1992, and has been projected to be 76.7 years by the year 2000. U.S. Bureau of the Census, *Statistical Abstract of the United States 1994* (Washington, D.C.: Government Printing Office, 1994), Table 114, p. 87.

51. Man was used intentionally, since retirement has been shown to differentially affect men and women; Talcott Parsons, "Age and Sex in the Social Structure of the United States," in *Essays in Sociological Theory,* rev. ed. (Glencoe, Ill.: Free Press, 1954), pp. 89–103; cf. Ruth Ann Erdner and Rebecca F. Guy, "Career Identification and Women's Attitudes Toward Retirement." *International Journal of Aging and Human Development* 30 (1990): 130. According to Davidson and Kunze, as well as Fellenbaum, men's stronger attachment to the work role makes retirement a less attractive status; postretirement work then would allow prestige, achievement, or recognized needs to be met; W. Davidson and K. Kunze, "Psychological, Sociological, and Economical Meanings of Work in Modern Society: Their Effects on the Worker Facing Retirement." *Gerontologist* 5 (September 1965): 129–133, 159; also see G. Fellenbaum, "A Consideration of Some Factors Related to Work After Retirement." *Gerontologist* 11 (Spring 1971): 18–23; see Erdner and Guy, "Career Identification," p. 131.

52. *Our Professional Ministry,* pp. 78–79.

53. Cf. Paula D. Nesbitt, "First and Second-Career Clergy: Influences of Age and Gender on the Career-Stage Paradigm." *Journal for the Scientific Study of Religion* 34 (June 1995): 152–171.

54. Resolution (D080) passed in both the House of Deputies and the House of Bishops. *Journal of the General Convention of the Episcopal Church in the United States of America* (New York: The Episcopal Church, 1988), p. 699.

55. Samuel Cohn, *The Process of Occupational Sex-Typing: The Feminization of Clerical Labor in Great Britain* (Philadelphia: Temple University Press, 1985); Judith Lorber and Susan A. Farrell, "Gender Construction in the Workplace," in *The Social Construction of Gender,* eds. Judith Lorber and Susan A. Farrell (Newbury Park, Calif.: Sage, 1991), p. 137.

56. Almquist, "Labor Market Gender Inequality in Minority Groups," p. 186. Cf. Reskin and Roos, *Job Queues, Gender Queues.*

57. Cf. Brita Stendahl, *The Force of Tradition* (Philadelphia: Fortress Press, 1985).

58. Ranson et al., *Clergy, Ministers and Priests*, p. 11. Rationale might include dependency upon the prestige value of one's position for status identity, especially in religious organizations where membership is voluntary.

59. Cf. Michael Maccoby, "The Company Man," in *Organizational Shock*, ed. W. Clay Hamner (New York: John Wiley and Sons, 1980), pp. 67–74; Rufus E. Miles, Jr., "Miles's Six Other Maxims of Management," pp. 299–310 in the same volume.

60. This was explored in the context of backlash in chapter 7. Cf. Edward C. Lehman, Jr., *Women Clergy: Breaking Through the Gender Barriers* (New Brunswick: Transaction, 1985); Carroll et al., *Women of the Cloth*, p. 176f; Heather Ann Huyck, *To Celebrate a Whole Priesthood: The History of Women's Ordination in the Episcopal Church.* Ph.D. dissertation, University of Minnesota, 1981; Emily C. Hewitt and Suzanne R. Hiatt, *Women Priests: Yes or No?* (New York: Seabury Press, 1973), p. 12f.

61. Stendahl, *The Force of Tradition*, p. 54f.

62. Alexander D. Stewart and Margaret S. West, "The Diaconate: A Call to Serve." Unpublished report, The Church Pension Fund, New York, 1991, pp. 8–9.

63. Gillespie, "Gender and Generations in Congregations."

64. Stewart and West, "The Diaconate," pp. 8–9.

65. Permanent Diaconate Evaluation Committee and Adair T. Lummis, *Raising Up Servant Ministry* (New York: The Episcopal Church, 1985).

66. David Briggs, "Catholic Churches Note Drop in Giving." *The Denver Post* 17 December 1993, pp. 25A, 35A; Nemeth and Luidens, "Congregational Vs. Denominational Giving;" Dean R. Hoge, "Introduction: The Problem of Understanding Church Giving." *Review of Religious Research* 36 (December 1994), pp. 101–110; Dean R. Hoge and Fenggang Yang, "Determinants of Religious Giving in American Denominations: Data from Two Nationwide Surveys." *Review of Religious Research* 36 (December 1994), pp. 123–148; Peter A. Zaleski and Charles E. Zech, "Economic and Attitudinal Factors in Catholic and Protestant Religious Giving." *Review of Religious Research* 36 (December 1994), pp. 158–167.

67. Title 3 Canon 3(1)(a) and 3(2)(a) *Constitution and Canons for the Government of the Protestant Episcopal Church in the United States of America Otherwise Known as The Episcopal Church Adopted in General Conventions 1789–1991* (New York: The Episcopal Church, 1991). Cf. *The Journal of General Convention*, 1985 and 1988; "Convention Clears the Clutter From Road to Ordination." *The Episcopalian* September 1988, p. 8.

68. Cf. Dorothy Jean Furnish, *DRE/DCE The History of a Profession* (Nashville: The Christian Educator's Fellowship, The United Methodist Church, 1976); Dorothy Jean Furnish, "Women in Religious Education: Pioneers for Women in Professional Ministry," in *Women and Religion in America 1900–1968*, eds. Rosemary Radford Ruether and Rosemary Skinner Keller (San Francisco: Harper & Row, 1986), pp. 310–338.

69. Cf. Stewart and West, "The Diaconate."

70. Another 16 to 18 percent of the students said that they either were not sure or were somewhat unlikely to seek ordination to the priesthood in the next decade, indicating a receptivity toward the priesthood rather than a focused commitment to the permanent diaconate. Additionally, another 24 percent of permanent deacons were interested in priesthood but didn't believe it was a realistic or logistically possible choice, given

time, financial, or age constraints, or they doubted the approval of their candidacy. This leaves a very small constituency intrinsically committed to the permanent diaconate. Permanent Diaconate Evaluation Committee and Lummis, *Raising Up Servant Ministry*, pp. 104, 181.

71. For example, David Cochran, "Are deacons necessary? No." *Episcopal Life* August 1993, p. 14. Cf. J. Robert Wright, "Ministry in New York: The Non-Stipendiary Priesthood and the Permanent Diaconate." *St. Luke's Journal of Theology* 19 (December 1975): 45.

72. Julie A. Wortman, "Dioceses Redefining Roles of Deacons, Priests." *Episcopal Life* May 1991, p. 1.

73. For example, the Diocese of Newark does not ordain permanent deacons. Cf. Julie Wortman, "Deacon's Revival Brings Servant Ministry to Fore." *Episcopal Life* June 1991, p. 7; Robert B. Slocum, "The Diaconate: Barrier or Catalyst for Lay Ministry?" *St. Luke's Journal of Theology* 33 (March 1990): 132f.

74. Cf. Edwin M. Leidel, Jr., "Bishop Priest or Deacon?" Unpublished paper (New Brighton, Minn.: The [Episcopal] Diocese of Minnesota, n.d.), p. 4; Loren B. Mead, *The Once and Future Church: Reinventing the Congregation for a New Mission Frontier* (Washington, D.C.: Alban Institute, 1991).

75. Marlene Cohen, "An Abuse of Power: Clericalism and Roles within the Church." *Modern Churchman* 34 (1992): 34; Anthony Russell, *The Clerical Profession* (London: SPCK, 1980), p. 37.

76. Cf. Chafetz, *Gender Equity*, p. 135.

77. For the rise of the medical profession's effect on women, see Kristin Luker, *Abortion and the Politics of Motherhood* (Berkeley: University of California Press, 1984); Faye D. Ginsburg, *Contested Lives* (Berkeley: University of California Press, 1990).

78. Magali Sarfatti Larson, *The Rise of Professionalism: A Sociological Analysis* (Berkeley: University of California Press, 1977).

79. For example, Patricia A. Roos, *Gender and Work: A Comparative Analysis of Industrial Societies* (Albany: State University of New York Press, 1985), pp. 60–65, 156.

80. *Our Professional Ministry*, p. 100.

81. Prestwood, *The New Breed of Clergy*, p. 59.

82. Cf. Roos, *Gender and Work*, p. 94.

83. Although men with doctorates tended to have higher attainment than women, the trends were not statistically significant for U.U.A. clergy but nearly so ($p < .10$) for Episcopal clergy.

84. Lowery, *Peers, Tents and Owls*. Cf. Donald R. LaMagdeleine, "U.S. Catholic Church-Related Jobs as Dual Labor Markets: A Speculative Inquiry." *Review of Religious Research* 24 (June 1986), p. 322.

85. Douglas, *The Feminization of American Culture*, pp. 152–153, 158.

86. Sherryl Kleinman, *Equals Before God: Seminarians as Humanistic Professionals* (Chicago: University of Chicago Press, 1984). Cf. Bryan R. Wilson, *Religion in Secular Society* (Baltimore: Penguin Books, 1969).

87. For diminishment of professional authority, see Kleinman, *Equals Before God*; Howard Moody, "Toward a Religionless Church for a Secular World," in *Who's Killing the Church?*, ed. Stephen C. Rose (Chicago: Renewal Magazine and Association Press, 1966), pp. 82–92; James M. Gustafson, "The Clergy in the United States," in *The Professions in America*, eds. Kenneth S. Lynn and the editors of *Daedalus* (Boston: Houghton Mifflin, 1965). For loss of social status, cf. Edwin S. Gaustad, "The Pulpit and the Pews," in *Between the Times: The Travail of the Protestant Establishment in America*, ed. William R. Hutchison (Cambridge, England, and New York: Cambridge

University Press, 1989), pp. 21–47; Lowery, *Peers, Tents and Owls*; cf. Wilson, *Religion in Secular Society*. For declining prestige, see notes for chapter 6.

88. Cf. Mary Frank Fox and Sharlene Hesse-Biber, *Women at Work* (Palo Alto, Calif.: Mayfield, 1984).

89. Ronald M. Pavalko, *Sociology of Occupations and Professions* (Itasca, Ill.: F. E. Peacock, 1961), p. 161; Fox and Hesse-Biber, *Women at Work*, p. 132; cf. Nielsen, *Sex and Gender in Society*, p. 73.

90. Permanent Diaconate Evaluation Committee and Lummis, *Raising Up Servant Ministry*, p. 5f.

91. Cf. Permanent Diaconate Evaluation Committee and Lummis, *Raising Up Servant Ministry*; Wortman, "Diocese Redefining Roles of Deacons, Priests;" Mary P. Truesdell, "The Office of Deaconess," in *The Diaconate Now*, ed. Richard T. Nolan (Washington, D.C.: Corpus Books, 1968), pp. 143–168.

92. Cf. Chafetz, *Gender Equity*; Barbara F. Reskin and Patricia A. Roos, "Status Hierarchies and Sex Segregation," in *Ingredients for Women's Employment Policy*, eds. Christina Bose and Glenna Spitze (Albany: State University of New York Press, 1987); Michael J. Carter and Susan Bostego Carter, "Women's Recent Progress in the Professions or, Women Get a Ticket to Ride After the Gravy Train Has Left the Station." *Feminist Studies* 7 (Fall 1981): 477–504.

93. Barbara F. Reskin, "Bringing the Men Back In: Sex Differentiation and the Devaluation of Women's Work," in *The Social Construction of Gender*. eds. Judith Lorber and Susan A. Farrell (Newbury Park, Calif.: Sage, 1991), p. 153.

94. Wilson, *Religion in Secular Society*; cf. Ranson et al., *Clergy, Ministers and Priests*, p. 79; Larson, *The Rise of Professionalism*; Stendahl, *The Force of Tradition*.

95. Cf. Rosemary Radford Ruether, *Women-Church: Theology and Practice of Feminist Liturgical Communities* (San Francisco: Harper & Row, 1985).

96. Italics have been added for emphasis. Chafetz, *Gender Equity*, p. 135.

97. Lyle E. Schaller, *It's a Different World: The Challenge for Today's Pastor* (Nashville, Tenn.: Abingdon Press, 1987), p. 211.

98. Tentmaking refers to the Apostle Paul's secular occupation. Cf. Lowery, *Peers, Tents and Owls*. Douglas Smith, "The Tentmakers." *The Episcopal Times*, March 1991, p. 6.

99. "Ordinations on Hold." *Advocate* (Episcopal Diocese of Lexington) May 1991, p. 15. The news item was referring to the Diocese of Central Florida.

100. Carroll and Wilson, *The Clergy Job Market*, p. 10; cited in Hoge et al., "Organizational and Situational Influences," p. 136.

101. The permanent diaconate resolves the need for clergy "who are not on the church's payroll" but who are committed through their ordination vows to servant ministry. Wortman, "Dioceses Redefining Roles of Deacons, Priests." *Episcopal Life* May 1991, p. 1.

102. Unless "part-time" or "nonstipendiary" was explicitly stated in a job title, this status had to be estimated based upon the ratio of clergy at a parish relative to its membership size. Consequently, the bias underestimates the extent of the part-time and nonstipendiary trend.

103. Over 80 percent of the permanent deacon respondents worked part time (20 hours or less per week), while 9 percent worked more than 40 hours per week although they were not necessarily paid—88 percent of the respondents had never received a stipend for their work; Stewart and West, "The Diaconate: A Call to Serve."

104. Leidel, "Bishop, Priest, or Deacon?" p. 33.

105. Figures are for May 1990. *Report of the Executive Council's Committee on the Status of Women*, May 1991, p. 15.

106. For a brief literature review on this topic, see Judith Buber Agassi, "Theories of Gender Equality: Lessons from the Israeli Kibbutz," in *The Social Construction of Gender*, eds. Judith Lorber and Susan A. Farrell (Newbury Park, Calif.: Sage, 1991), p. 317; Chafetz, *Gender Equity*, p. 136.

107. Chafetz, *Gender Equity*, p. 104.

108. Lyle E. Schaller, "Suggestions for Change in the Itinerant System." *Circuit Rider* November 1992, p. 12; Lyle E. Schaller, "Who Is the Client? The Clergy or the Congregation?" in *Send Me? The Itineracy in Crisis*, ed. Donald E. Messer (Nashville: Abingdon Press, 1991), pp. 87–99.

109. Schaller, "Suggestions for Change in the Itinerant System," p. 12.

110. Ranson et al., *Clergy, Ministers and Priests*, pp. 52–53.

111. The Lusitanian Church claims a rate of nearly 100 percent bivocational clergy. James L. Lowery, Jr., "'Tentmaker Priests' Contend They Have Apostolic Vocation." *The Lambeth Daily* 21 July 1988, p. 3; cf. Neville Clark, "Servant of the Servants of God," in *Ministry in Question*, ed. Alec Gilmore (London: Darton, Longman and Todd, 1971), p. 26. For figures on women priests, see "One Year Later—Anglicans Accept Norm of Women Priests," *The Woman's Pulpit* 73 (October–December 1995):2.

112. For example, encouraging appointments across (regional) conferences to increase clergy mobility was approved as a change to United Methodist Discipline. Keith Pohl, "Ministry Study Referred to Bishops for 1996." *Daily Christian Advocate*. The General Conference of the United Methodist Church, 16 May 1992, p. 8.

113. *The Presbyterian Placement System*. Presbyterian Panel Report (Louisville, Ky.: Presbyterian Survey Magazine, 1989), pp. 20, A-17; cf. Prestwood, *The New Breed of Clergy*, p. 63.

114. Lowery, "'Tentmaker Priests' Contend They Have Apostolic Vocation," p. 3. Lowery was drawing upon two conferences that included British and American Anglican tradition churches, the United Reformed Church, the British Methodist Church, the Old Catholic Church, and the French priest-worker movement.

115. The Diocese of Northern Michigan. See Ormonde Plater, "To Cut Clericalism, Don't Target Deacons." Letter to Editor. *Episcopal Life*, December 1993, p. 24.

116. Cf. Schaller, *It's a Different World!*, p. 210.

117. Lowery, "'Tentmaker Priests' Contend They Have Apostolic Vocation," p. 3.

118. A 1962 article "Why I Left the Ministry" published in *The Saturday Evening Post* aroused substantial public interest and denominational comment, according to Paul; Robert S. Paul, *Ministry* (Grand Rapids, Mich.: William B. Eerdmans, 1965), p. 23.

119. Gerald J. Jud, Edgar W. Mills, and Genevieve Walters Burch, *Ex-Pastors: Why Men Leave the Parish Ministry* (Philadelphia: Pilgrim Press, 1970), p. 50f. A study by Donahoe and Blue found a different set of reasons for Protestant clergy departures: job dissatisfaction (63%), intellectual crisis (45%), frustration with denominational leaders (38%), and personal growth (38%). Michael Donahoe and Earl Blue, *The Earl Blue Report on Clergy Disaffection* (San Francisco: Earl Blue Associates, 1970); Robert L. Wilson, "Drop-Outs and Potential Drop-Outs from the Parish Ministry." A Study of the Alabama-West Florida Annual Conference (New York: The United Methodist Church, National Division of the Board of Missions, 1970).

120. Adair T. Lummis, "Paradigms of Disaffiliation, Dissonance, Equity, and Feminism in Illuminating Occupational Dropout Among Clergy Women and Men."

Paper presented at the Annual Meeting of the Association for the Sociology of Religion, Washington, D.C., August 1995.

121. Elaine Shazgal Cohen, "Rabbis' Roles and Occupational Goals: Men and Women in the Contemporary American Rabbinate." *Conservative Judaism* 42 (Fall 1989): 28.

122. Cf. Hewitt and Hiatt, *Women Priests: Yes or No?*

123. James Solheim, "Women's Ordination Controversy Simmers in Church of England, But causes No Mass Exodus." Episcopal News Service, File A0000009, MSG, 12 December, 1995. James M. Rosenthal, "'Mother Church' Opens Priesthood to its Women." *Episcopal Life* April 1994, p. 12. The Church of England has about 10,000 male clergy.

124. Ranson et al., *Clergy, Ministers and Priests*, p. 169.

125. Chafetz, *Gender Equity*, p. 217.

Chapter 9

1. Barbara Hargrove, "On Digging, Dialogue, and Decision-Making." *Review of Religious Research* 28 (June 1987): 400.

2. Barbara F. Reskin and Patricia A. Roos, *Job Queues, Gender Queues: Explaining Women's Inroads into Male Occupations* (Philadelphia: Temple University Press, 1990), pp. 87–88.

3. The results of this analysis supported secular findings of a critical threshold at about 30 percent female, which represents a point that for secular occupations negative effects of occupational feminization such as job segregation become more apparent. Cf. Reskin and Roos, *Job Queues, Gender Queues*; Barbara F. Reskin and Patricia A. Roos, "Status Hierarchies and Sex Segregation," in *Ingredients for Women's Employment Policy*, eds. Christine Bose and Glenna Spitze (Albany: State University of New York Press, 1987), pp. 3–21.

4. Cf. Margaret Power, "The Making of a Woman's Occupation." *Hecate* January 1975, pp. 25–34.

5. Alice Schlegel, ed., *Sexual Stratification: A Cross-Cultural View* (New York: Columbia University Press, 1977); Judith Buber Agassi, "Theories of Gender Equality: Lessons from the Israeli Kibbutz," in *The Social Construction of Gender*, eds. Judith Lorber and Susan A. Farrell (Newbury Park, Calif.: Sage, 1991), p. 317.

6. Cf. Helen Weinreich-Haste, *The Sexual Metaphor* (Cambridge: Harvard University Press, 1994), p. 249; Joan Acker, "Hierarchies, Jobs, Bodies: A Theory of Gendered Organizations," in *The Social Construction of Gender*, eds. Judith Lorber and Susan A. Farrell (Newbury Park, Calif.: Sage, 1991), p. 173; J. Hearn and P. W. Parkin, "Gender and Organizations: A Selective Review and a Critique of a Neglected Area." *Organizational Studies* 4 (1983): 219–242.

7. For example, The Committee for the Full Participation of Women in the Church, *Reaching Toward Wholeness: The Participation of Women in the Episcopal Church*, ed. Pamela W. Darling (New York: Episcopal Church Foundation, 1988); cf. *Report of the Executive Council's Committee on the Status of Women* (New York: The Episcopal Church, 1991), p. 19; Susan A. Farrell, "It's Our Church Too!" in *The Social Construction of Gender*, eds. Judith Lorber and Susan A. Farrell (Newbury Park, Calif.: Sage, 1991), pp. 338–354; Frederick W. Schmidt, "Transcending Bureaucratic and Cultural Linkages: Women and the Church." Paper presented at the Annual Meeting of The Society for the Scientific Study of Religion and The Religious Research Associa-

tion, Washington, D.C., 1992; Sheila Briggs, "Women and Religion," in *Analyzing Gender: A Handbook of Social Science Research*, eds. Beth B. Hess and Myra Marx Feree (Newbury Park, Calif.: Sage, 1987), pp. 417–418; Edward C. Lehman, Jr., "Placement of Men and Women in the Ministry." *Review of Religious Research* 22 (September 1980), pp. 28–29; Pamela P. Chinnis, "Full Participation of Women in the Church: Our Time Has Come?" *Journal of Women's Ministries* 4 (Summer 1988), p. 9.

8. Agassi, "Theories of Gender Equality," p. 333.

9. Cynthia Cockburn, *In the Way of Women: Men's Resistance to Sex Equality in Organizations* (London: ILR Press, 1991), p. 233.

10. Barbara F. Reskin, "Bringing the Men Back In: Sex Differentiation and the Devaluation of Women's Work," in *The Social Construction of Gender*, eds. Judith Lorber and Susan A. Farrell (Newbury Park, Calif.: Sage, 1991), p. 155; Janet Saltzman Chafetz, *Gender Equity: An Integrated Theory of Stability and Change* (Newbury Park, Calif.: Sage, 1990), p. 221. Cf. Rodney Stark and William Sims Bainbridge, *The Future of Religion: Secularization, Revival and Cult Formation* (Berkeley: University of California Press, 1985).

11. Cf. Farrell, "It's our Church, Too!" p. 351.

12. Cf. Richard A. Hutch, *Religious Leadership: Personality, History and Sacred Authority* (New York: Peter Lang, 1991); Hans A. Baer, "The Limited Empowerment of Women in Black Spiritual Churches: An Alternative Vehicle to Religious Leadership," in *Gender and Religion*, ed. William H. Swatos, Jr., (New Brunswick, N.J.: Transaction, 1993), pp. 75–92; Stark and Bainbridge, *The Future of Religion*.

13. Keith A. Roberts, *Religion in Sociological Perspective*, 2nd ed. (Belmont, Calif: Wadsworth, 1990), pp. 290–293; Vern L. Bullough, *The Subordinate Sex: A History of Attitudes Toward Women* (Urbana: University of Illinois Press, 1973).

14. The conflation of feminism, New Age, goddess worship, neopagan spirituality, Wicca, other witchcraft traditions, and Satanism in contemporary backlash movements has been prevalent in both the Protestant and Roman Catholic Religious Right. For example, Alan Cowell, "Fight Feminist Fringe, Bishops Told." [*The New York Times*] *The Denver Post* 3 July 1993, p. 3A; Katie Kerwin, "Women Will Keep Fighting for Power, Feminist Warns." *Rocky Mountain News* 15 August 1993, p. 28A. For a brief comparative historical overview, see Roberts, *Religion in Sociological Perspective*, 2nd ed., pp. 280–300.

15. Cf. Edward C. Lehman, Jr., *Women Clergy: Breaking Through the Gender Barriers* (New Brunswick, N.J.: Transaction, 1985); cf. Jackson W. Carroll, Barbara Hargrove, and Adair T. Lummis, *Women of the Cloth: A New Opportunity for the Churches* (San Francisco: Harper & Row, 1983).

16. For instance, an Episcopal congregation reported that following the resignation of their male priest a woman was hired and within three years attendance increased 20 percent and giving rose 35 percent even in a difficult economy. Jack Burleson, "A Female Priest Brings Blessings." Letter to editor. *Episcopal Life* April 1994, p. 20. This represents only one example of a contemporary as well as historical trend affirming the organizational capabilities of women clergy. Cf. Elsie Gibson, *When the Minister Is a Woman* (New York: Holt, Rinehart and Winston, 1970); Cynthia Grant Tucker, *Prophetic Sisterhood: Liberal Women Ministers of the Frontier, 1880–1930* (Boston: Beacon Press, 1990); Ruth A. Wallace, "For the Record: Women Pastoral Administrators, Reflections from Interviews," *Church* 7 (Fall 1991), pp. 45–46.

17. Cf. Lynn Davidman and Arthur L. Greil, "Gender and the Experience of Conversion: The Case of 'Returnees' to Modern Orthodox Judaism," in *Gender and Religion*, ed. William H. Swatos, Jr., (New Brunswick, N.J.: Transaction, 1993),

pp. 95–112; Martha Long Ice, *Clergy Women and their World Views: Calling for a New Age* (New York: Praeger, 1987); Sherryl Kleinman, *Equals Before God: Seminarians as Humanistic Professionals* (Chicago: University of Chicago Press, 1984).

18. Edward C. Lehman, Jr., "Gender and Ministry Style: Things Not What They Seem," in *Gender and Religion*, ed. William H. Swatos, Jr. (New Brunswick, N.J.: Transaction, 1993), pp. 3–14; Edward C. Lehman, Jr., *Gender and Work: The Case of the Clergy* (Albany: State University of New York Press, 1993).

19. Ruth McDonough Fitzpatrick, "Is There a Valid Basis for a Male Priesthood?" *The Denver Post* 15 August 1993, p. 5D.

20. Statistics, cited by Wallace, are from the *Official Catholic Directory* (New York: Kenedy, 1991). See Ruth A. Wallace, "The Social Construction of a New Leadership Role: Catholic Women Pastors," in *Gender and Religion*, ed. William H. Swatos, Jr., (New Brunswick, N.J.: Transaction, 1993), p. 15; cf. Ruth A. Wallace, *They Call Her Pastor* (Albany: State University of New York Press, 1992); Schmidt, "Transcending Bureaucratic and Cultural Linkages," pp. 63–64.

21. U.S. Roman Catholic bishops in 1992 rejected a Vatican pastoral letter reinforcing traditional gender teachings, defying Papal authority that bishops not even discuss the issue of women's ordination. According to a 1992 Gallup survey, two-thirds of the 802 Catholics polled thought that women should be ordained. Among those below age 35, 80 percent favored women's ordination. David Crumm, "Ordain Women, Catholics Say in Poll." *The Denver Post*, 19 June 1992, pp. 1A, 25A; David Crumm, "Bishops Reject Vatican Stance on Women." *The Denver Post* 19 November 1992, p. 1A. Cf. Fitzpatrick, "Is There a Valid Basis for a Male Priesthood?"; Virginia Culver, "Bishops Gripe at Vatican: Church Accused of Ignoring U.S. Issues. *The Denver Post* 16 August 1995, pp. 1A, 18A. Young altar servers, traditionally a source of recruitment for the priesthood, have been under Vatican scruitiny because of trends toward role feminization in parishes that have utilized girls as well as boys. Cf. Karen Abbott, "Banished From the Altar: Decision Against Catholic Girls Leaves Local Youngsters Hurt, Puzzled." *Rocky Mountain News*, 1 April 1992, pp. 60, 62.

22. The most widely known movement of this type has been in Latin America, with the resultant formation of socialized base communities. In the United States, black liberation theology has utilized similar principles to mobilize a political struggle for racial justice. Cf. Cornel West, *Prophesy Deliverance! An Afro-American Revolutionary Christianity* (Philadelphia: Westminster Press, 1982).

23. Cheryl Townsend Gilkes, "Mother to the Motherless, Father to the Fatherless: Power, Gender, and Community in an Afrocentric Biblical Tradition," *Semeia* 47 (1989): 73–74. For instance, the Episcopal Church's Committee on the Status of Women has taken as one of its key objectives to "incorporate women of color in all aspects of the Church's life," including the leadership (*Report of the Executive Council's Committee on the Status of Women*, pp. 3, 18).

24. Chafetz, *Gender Equity*, p. 214.

25. Chafetz, *Gender Equity*. For a brief review of other research, cf. Patricia A. Roos and Barbara F. Reskin, "Institutional Factors Contributing to Sex Segregation in the Workplace," in *Sex Segregation in the Workplace: Trends, Explanations, Remedies*, ed. Barbara F. Reskin (Washington, D.C.: National Academy Press, 1984), pp. 253; Cockburn, *In the Way of Women*, pp. 232–233.

26. Cockburn, *In the Way of Women*, p. 234.

27. Cf. Schmidt, "Transforming Bureaucratic and Cultural Linkages," p. 80. For example, David E. Sumner, *The Episcopal Church's History: 1945–1985* (Wilton,

Conn.: Morehouse-Barlow, 1987); Brita Stendahl, *The Force of Tradition: A Case Study of Women Priests in Sweden* (Philadelphia: Fortress Press, 1985).

28. Chafetz, *Gender Equity*, pp. 166, 214.

29. Cf. Catherine Mowry LaCugna, "Catholic Women as Ministers and Theologians," *America* 167 (10 October 1992): 238–248; Wallace, *They Call Her Pastor*; Wallace, "The Social Construction of a New Leadership Role;" Rosemary Radford Ruether, *Women-Church: Theology and Practice* (San Francisco: Harper & Row, 1986), pp. 75–95.

30. Chafetz, *Gender Equity*, p. 169.

31. Cf. Rosabeth Moss Kanter, *Men and Women of the Corporation* (New York: Basic Books, 1977).

32. Cf. Carroll et al., *Women of the Cloth*; Schmidt, "Transcending Bureaucratic and Cultural Linkages," p. 78; Lesley Stevens, "Different Voice/Different Voices: Anglican Women in Ministry." *Review of Religious Research* 30 (March 1989): 270; Tucker, *Prophetic Sisterhood*, p. 47. This transformative effect has been a particularly prevalent theme among women rabbis. Cf. Rita J. Simon, Angela J. Scanlan, and Pamela S. Nadell, "Rabbis and Ministers: Women of the Book and the Cloth," in *Gender and Religion*, ed. William H. Swatos, Jr., (New Brunswick, N.J.: Transaction, 1993), pp. 45–52; Janet Marder, "How Women Are Changing the Rabbinate." *Reform Judaism* (Summer 1991), pp. 4–8, 41; Jennifer R. Cowan, "Survey Finds 70% of Women Rabbis Sexually Harassed." *Moment* 18 (October 1993): 37.

33. Elisabeth Schüssler Fiorenza, "Feminist Spirituality, Christian Identity, and Catholic Vision," in *Womanspirit Rising: A Feminist Reader in Religion*, eds. Carol P. Christ and Judith Plaskow (San Francisco: Harper & Row, 1979), p. 136.

34. The 1994 ordinations of women to the priesthood in the Church of England, the 1974 irregular ordinations of Episcopal women to the priesthood, and the early ordinations of women in other religious organizations have had similar effects for those who attended. For example, Episcopal Presiding Bishop Edmond Browning recalls Harris's consecration as "one of the high points of my ministry. . . ." Jay Cormier, "Diocesan Convention '94: A Conversation with the Presiding Bishop." *The Episcopal Times* (Diocese of Massachusetts) November–December 1994, pp. 6–7. Cf. Harvey Cox, "From Harris to Hutchinson—A Big Day in Boston." *The Episcopal Times* (Diocese of Massachusetts) February–March 1988, p. 8; "New Women Bishops Share Visions for an Inclusive Church," *The Flyer* (The General Commission on the Status and Role of Women in the United Methodist Church) 13 (Fall 1992): 1.

35. Acker, "Hierarchies, Jobs, Bodies," p. 171.

36. For a discussion of the relationship between power and community as they relate to gender and other variables, see Nancy C. M. Hartsock, *Money, Sex, and Power: Toward a Feminist Historical Materialism* (Boston: Northeastern University Press, 1985). Cf. Cockburn, *In the Way of Women*; Rosemary Radford Ruether, *Sexism and God-Talk: Toward A Feminist Theology* (Boston: Beacon Press, 1983); Ruether, *Women-Church*.

37. Roberts, *Religion in Sociological Perspective*, 2nd ed., pp. 294–299.

38. Cf. Acker, "Hierarchies, Jobs, Bodies," p. 173; Adrienne A. Rich, "Compulsory Heterosexuality and Lesbian Existence." *Signs* 5 (Summer 1980): 631–660; Gayle Rubin, "The Traffic in Women: Notes on the Political Economy of Sex," in *Toward an Anthropology of Women*, ed. Rayna R. Reiter (New York: Monthly Review Press, 1975), pp. 157–210; Agassi, "Theories of Gender Equality," p. 319.

39. Millet argues that men's political power over women is the fundamental political division of society, rather than class stratification. Kate Millett, *Sexual Politics*

(London: Shere, 1971), pp. 24, 38; cf. Michele Barrett, *Women's Oppression Today: Problems in Marxist Feminist Analysis* (London: NLB, 1980), p. 11; Cynthia Cockburn, *Machinery of Dominance: Women, Men, and Technical Know-How* (Boston: Northeastern University Press, 1988), p. 251.

40. For how these components apply to clergy, see Edward C. Lehman, Jr., "Status Differences Between Types of Ministry: Measurement and Effect," in *Research in the Social Scientific Study of Religion: A Research Annual* 2, eds. Monty L. Lynn and David O. Moberg (Greenwich, Conn.: JAI Press, 1990), pp. 95–116; Carroll et al., *Women of the Cloth*, pp. 116, 157; Charles Prestwood, *The New Breed of Clergy* (Grand Rapids: William B. Eerdmans, 1972), pp. 62, 86; James L. Lowery, Jr., *Peers, Tents and Owls: Some Solutions to Problems of the Clergy Today* (New York: Morehouse-Barlow, 1973); Harold C. Warlick, Jr., *How to Be a Minister and a Human Being* (Valley Forge, Pa.: Judson Press, 1982).

41. Lorber and Farrell have described the construction of gender as a process occurring through social and historical location, and as an outcome providing both a rationale and means for legitimating gender divisions in society. Judith Lorber and Susan A. Farrell, "Principles of Gender Construction," in *The Social Construction of Gender*, eds. Judith Lorber and Susan A. Farrell (Newbury Park, Calif.: Sage, 1991), p. 11. Cf. Candace West and Don H. Zimmerman, "Doing Gender," p. 14, in the same volume.

42. Cockburn, *In the Way of Women,*" p. 223.

43. Today in the United States, only the Metropolitan Community Church, Reform Judaism, the Unitarian Universalist Association, and the United Church of Christ ordain openly gay men and women not permanently committed to celibacy. For a brief discussion of the linkages between women's ordination and sexual orientation in the Episcopal Church, see Pamela W. Darling, *New Wine: The Story of Women Transforming Leadership and Power in the Episcopal Church* (Cambridge, Mass., and Boston: Cowley, 1994), pp. 197–198, 227–228.

44. Cf. Kleinman, *Equals Before God*, p. 93. Even in clergy titles, men are far more likely to be addressed by their prefix (e.g., Father, Reverend, Pastor) while women have tended to be called simply by their first name. *Report of the Executive Council's Committee on the Status of Women*, p. 17; and personal interviews with clergy.

45. Cf. Farrell, "It's Our Church, Too!" pp. 342–347; Letty M. Russell, *Household of Freedom: Authority in Feminist Theology* (Philadelphia: Westminster Press, 1987); Darling, *New Wine*, pp. 198–200.

46. Cockburn, *In the Way of Women*, p. 73. Cf. Chafetz, *Gender Equity*.

47. Cf. David L. Featherman, "Biography, Society and History: Individual Development as a Population Process," in *Human Development and the Life Course: Multidisciplinary Perspectives*, eds. Aage B. Sørensen, Franz E. Weinert, and Lonnie R. Sherrod (Hillsdale, N.J.: Lawrence Erlbaum, 1986), p. 99–141.

48. Chafetz, *Gender Equity*, p. 220.

49. Chafetz, *Gender Equity*, pp. 215–217; cf. Roberts, *Religion in Sociological Perspective*, 2nd ed., pp. 294–299.

50. "New Women Bishops Share Visions for an Inclusive Church." *The Flyer* (The General Commission on the Status and Role of Women in the United Methodist Church) 13 (Fall 1992): 5.

51. For instance, The Rt. Rev. David Ball of the Diocese of Albany attributes his recent decision to begin ordaining women at least in part to sacramental and worship experience with women clergy ordained elsewhere but licensed in his diocese. "Bishop Changes Mind, Will Ordain Women." *Episcopal Life* May 1994, p. 3.

52. James H. Thrall and James Solheim, "House of Bishops Endorses Resolution Declaring Women's Ordination Mandatory in all Dioceses, Decries Mean-Spiritedness in the Church." Episcopal News Service, File A000002Z.MSG, 29 September 1995. The resolution concurs with a proposed church canon (III.8.1) to be deliberated at the 1997 General Convention.

53. Episcopal suffragan bishop Jane Holmes Dixon has led one such retreat for women in two dioceses with a history of strong opposition to women priests—Fort Worth and Dallas—an event promoted to "nourish women's spirituality, to express it in the liturgy, and to live it out politically with integrity." "Dallas/Fort Worth." *Episcopal Life* October 1993, p. 4. Within the previous year, both dioceses had formed chapters of the feminist Episcopal Women's Caucus. Women's Bible study also is being used in a liberationist context in Africa. Cf. Susan Erdey, "The Rev. Grace Ndybahika, One of Uganda's First Women Priests, Recipient of First Diocesan Scholarship for African Students to Study in America." *The Episcopal Times* (Diocese of Massachusetts), March 1992, p. 14.

54. Kristin E. Holmes, "A Mennonite First." *The Denver Post* 27 November 1993, p. 10B; "Mennonites Elect Clemens First Woman Moderator." *Woman's Pulpit* October–December 1993, p. 6.

55. Larry Witham, "Local Adventists Rebel, Ordain Three Women." *The Sunday Washington Times* 24 September 1995, pp. A1, A16.

56. Cf. Lehman, *Gender and Work*; Ice, *Clergy Women and Their World Views*.

57. Harris was addressing the 1991 triennial gathering of Episcopal Church Women. "General Convention: Amid the Rhetoric, Some Words." *Episcopal Life* August 1991, pp. 22–23.

58. Kleinman, *Equals Before God*, p. 90.

59. Empty Tomb Inc., a religious research organization, made this prediction based upon declining contribution patterns. David Briggs, "Church Collection Plates in U.S. Very Light." *The Denver Post* 17 December 1993, p. 25A.

60. Ann Douglas, *The Feminization of American Culture* (New York: Alfred A. Knopf, 1977), p. 35.

61. Personal conversation and correspondence, 1989–1990.

62. Lyle E. Schaller, *It's a Different World!* (Nashville: Abingdon, 1987), p. 165, cf. p. 164.

63. Marder, "How Women Are Changing the Rabbinate," p. 41.

64. Cf. Rosemary Radford Ruether, *Gaia and God: An Ecofeminist Theology of Earth Healing* (San Francisco: Harper SanFrancisco, 1992).

65. Cf. Suzanne J. Kessler and Wendy McKenna, *Gender: An Ethnomethodological Approach* (Chicago: University of Chicago Press, 1985), pp. 1–41.

Bibliography

Abbott, K. "Banished from the Altar: Decision Against Catholic Girls Leaves Local Youngsters Hurt, Puzzled." *Rocky Mountain News*, 1 April 1992, pp. 60, 62.

Acker, J. "Hierarchies, Jobs, Bodies: A Theory of Gendered Organizations." In *The Social Construction of Gender*, eds. J. Lorber and S. A. Farrell, 162–179. Newbury Park, Calif.: Sage, 1991.

Agassi, J. B. "Theories of Gender Equality: Lessons from the Israeli Kibbutz." In *The Social Construction of Gender*, eds. J. Lorber and S. A. Farrell, 313–337. Newbury Park, Calif.: Sage, 1991.

Alexander, K. L., and T. W. Reilly. "Estimating the Effects of Marriage Timing on Educational Attainment: Some Procedural Issues and Substantive Clarifications." *American Journal of Sociology* 87(1): 143–156, 1981.

Allison, P. D. *Event History Analysis*. Beverly Hills: Sage, 1984.

Almquist, E. M. "Labor-Market Gender Inequality in Minority Groups." In *The Social Construction of Gender*, eds. J. Lorber and S. A. Farrell, 180–192. Newbury Park, Calif.: Sage, 1991.

"Amid the Rhetoric, Some Words." *Episcopal Life*, August 1991, pp. 22–23.

Ammerman, N. T. *Baptist Battles: Social Change and Religious Conflict in the Southern Baptist Convention*. New Brunswick, N.J.: Rutgers University Press, 1990.

Anders, S. F., and M. Metcalf-Whittaker. "Women as Lay Leaders and Clergy: A Critical Issue." In *Southern Baptists Observed: Multiple Perspectives on a Changing Denomination*, ed. N. T. Ammerman, 201–221. Knoxville: University of Tennessee Press, 1993.

Baber, K. M., and K. R. Allen. *Women and Families: Feminist Reconstructions*. New York: Guilford Press, 1992.

Baer, H. A. "The Limited Empowerment of Women in Black Spiritual Churches: An Alternative Vehicle to Religious Leadership." In *Gender and Religion*, ed. W. H. Swatos Jr., 75–92. New Brunswick, N.J.: Transaction, 1993.

Bailey, S., and B. Burrell. A *Report on the Careers of the Graduates of the Harvard*

Divinity School. Cambridge: Office of Institutional Policy Research on Women's Education, 1980.

Barfoot, C. H., and G. T. Sheppard. "Prophetic vs. Priestly Religion: The Changing Role of Women Clergy in Classical Pentecostal Churches." *Review of Religious Research* 22(1): 2–16, 1980.

Barnett, J. M. *The Diaconate: a Full and Equal Order*. New York: Seabury Press, 1981.

Barrett, M. *Women's Oppression Today: Problems in Marxist Feminist Analysis*. London: NLB, 1980.

Barwell, M. "Money Serves as Metaphor for How Church Ministers." *Episcopal Life*, July 1994, p. 10.

Beecher, C. A *Treatise on Domestic Economy*, ed. K. K. Sklar. New York: Schocken, 1977.

Bell, I. P. "The Double Standard: Age." In *Women: A Feminist Perspective*, ed. J. Freeman, 233–244. Palo Alto: Mayfield, 1979.

Bellah, R. N. *The Broken Covenant: American Civil Religion in the Time of Trial*. New York: Seabury Press, 1975.

Bellah, R. N., R. Madsen, W. M. Sullivan, A. Swidler, and S. M. Tipton. *Habits of the Heart: Individualism and Commitment in American Life*. New York: Harper & Row, 1986.

Benda, B. B., and F. A. DiBlasio. "Clergy Marriages: A Multivariate Model of Marital Adjustment." *Journal of Psychology and Theology* 20(4): 367–375, 1992.

Bendroth, M. L. "Fundamentalism and Femininity: Points of Encounter Between Religious Conservatives and Women, 1919–1935." *Church History* 61: 221–233, 1992.

Bercovitch, S. *The American Jeremiad*. Madison: University of Wisconsin Press, 1980.

Betz, N. E., and L. F. Fitzgerald. *The Career Psychology of Women*. Orlando: Academic Press, 1987.

"Bishop Changes Mind, Will Ordain Women." *Episcopal Life*. May 1994, p. 3.

Blau, F. D. "Occupational Segregation and Labor Market Discrimination." In *Sex Segregation in the Workplace: Trends, Explanations, Remedies*, ed. B. F. Reskin, 117–143. Washington, D.C.: National Academy Press, 1984.

Blau, P. M., and O. D. Duncan. *The American Occupational Structure*. New York: Free Press, 1978.

Blonston, G. "New Twist on Recession: White-Collar Blues." *The Denver Post*. 19 September 1991, pp. 2A, 15A.

Blumhofer, E. L. "The Role of Women in Pentecostal Ministry." *A/G Heritage*, Spring 1985–86, pp. 11, 14.

———. "The Role of Women in the Assemblies of God." *A/G Heritage*, Winter 1987–88, pp. 13–17.

Board for Clergy Deployment. *Their Call Answered: Women in Priesthood*. New York: The Episcopal Church, 1979.

Bock, E. W. "The Female Clergy: A Case of Professional Marginality." *American Journal of Sociology* 72(5): 531–539, 1967.

Booty, J. E. *The Servant Church: Diaconal Ministry in the Episcopal Church*. Wilton: Morehouse-Barlow, 1982.

Børresen, K. E. "Women's Ordination: Tradition and Inculturation." *Theology Digest* 40(1): 15–19, 1993.

Boyd, S. H. "A Woman's Journey Toward Priesthood: An Autobiographical Study from the 1950s Through the 1980s." In *Episcopal Women: Gender, Spirituality and Commitment in an American Mainline Denomination*, ed. C. M. Prelinger, 263–281. New York: Oxford University Press, 1992.

Brauer, J. C., ed. *The Westminster Dictionary of Church History*. Philadelphia: Westminster Press, 1971.

Braun, C. "Equality of Obligation for Women at JTS?" *Sh'ma*, 31 May 1985, p. 113.

Brenner, J., and M. Ramas. "Rethinking Women's Oppression." *New Left Review* 144: 33–71, 1984.

Brereton, V. L. "United and Slighted: Women as Subordinated Insiders." In *Between the Times: The Travail of the Protestant Establishment in America*, ed. W. R. Hutchison, 143–167. Cambridge and New York: Cambridge University Press, 1989.

Brereton, V. L., and C. R. Klein. "American Women in Ministry: A History of Protestant Beginning Points." In *Women of Spirit: Female Leadership in the Jewish and Christian Traditions*, eds. R. Ruether and E. McLaughlin, 302–332. New York: Simon and Schuster, 1979.

Briggs, D. "Catholic Churches Note Drop in Giving." *The Denver Post*, 17 December 1993, pp. 25A, 35A.

———. "Church Collection Plates in U.S. Very Light." *The Denver Post*, 17 December 1993, pp. 25A, 40A.

Briggs, S. "Women and Religion." In *Analyzing Gender: A Handbook of Social Science Research*, eds. B. B. Hess and M. M. Ferree, 408–441. Newbury Park, Calif.: Sage, 1987.

Buchanan, C. H. "The Anthropology of Vitality and Decline: The Episcopal Church in a Changing Society." In *Episcopal Women: Gender, Spirituality and Commitment in a Mainline Denomination*, ed. C. M. Prelinger, 310–329. New York: Oxford University Press, 1992.

Bucklee, S. "Let's Spread the Good News About the U.S. Church." *Episcopal Life*, August 1991, p. 31.

Bullough, V. L. *The Subordinate Sex: A History of Attitudes Toward Women*. Urbana: University of Illinois Press, 1973.

Bultmann, R. *Jesus Christ and Mythology*. New York: Charles Scribner's Sons, 1958.

Burleson, J. "A Female Priest Brings Blessings." Letter to editor. *Episcopal Life*, April 1994, p. 20.

Campbell, J. B. "Toward a Renewed Community of Women and Men." *Midstream* 30(2): 118–129, 1991.

Caplow, T. *The Sociology of Work*. New York: McGraw-Hill, 1964.

Carmody, D. L. *Women and World Religions*. Nashville: Abingdon Press, 1979.

Carroll, J. W., and R. L. Wilson. *The Clergy Job Market: Oversupply And/or Opportunity*. Multilithed report. Hartford: Hartford Seminary Foundation, 1978.

Carroll, J. W., B. Hargrove, and A. T. Lummis. *Women of the Cloth: A New Opportunity for the Churches*. San Francisco: Harper & Row, 1983.

Carter, M. J., and S. B. Carter. "Women's Recent Progress in the Professions, Or, Women Get a Ticket to Ride After the Gravy Train Has Left the Station." *Feminist Studies* 7(3): 477–504, 1981.

Catanzarite, L. M., and M. H. Strober. "Occupational Attractiveness and Race-Gender Segregation, 1960–1980." Paper presented at the Annual Meeting of the American Sociological Association, Atlanta, August 1988.

Celmer, V., and J. L. Winer. "Female Aspirants to the Roman Catholic Priesthood." *Journal of Counseling and Development* 69(2): 178–183, 1990.

Chafetz, J. S. *Gender Equity: An Integrated Theory of Stability and Change*. Newbury Park, Calif.: Sage, 1990.

Chafetz, J. S., and A. G. Dworkin. "In the Face of Threat: Organized Antifeminism in Comparative Perspective." In *The Sociology of Gender: A Text-Reader*, ed. L. Kramer, 471–486. New York: St. Martin's Press, 1991.

Chapman, A. R. *Faith, Power, and Politics: Political Ministry in Mainline Churches.* New York: Pilgrim Press, 1991.

Chapman, J. *The Last Bastion: Women Priests—The Case For and Against.* London: Methuen, 1989.

Chinnis, P. P. "Full Participation of Women in the Church: Our Time Has Come?" *Journal of Women's Ministries* 4(2): 8–9, 1988.

Christ, C. P., and J. Plaskow. "The Essential Challenge: Does Theology Speak to Women's Experience?" In *Womanspirit Rising: A Feminist Reader in Religion*, eds. C. P. Christ and J. Plaskow, 19–24. New York: Harper & Row, 1979.

"Church of Sweden Drops 'Conscience Clause.'" *The Christian Century*, 16 November 1994, p. 1072.

Clark, J. N., and G. Anderson. "A Study of Women in Ministry: God Calls, Man Chooses." In *Yearbook of American and Canadian Churches*, ed. C. H. Jacquet Jr., 271–278. Nashville: Abingdon Press, 1990.

Clark, N. "Servant of the Servants of God." In *Ministry in Question*, ed. Alec Gilmore, 28–52. London: Darton, Longman & Todd, 1971.

Cline, C. G., E. L. Toth, J. V. Turk, L. M. Walters, N. Johnson, and H. Smith. *The Velvet Ghetto: The Impact of the Increasing Percentage of Women in Public Relations and Business Communication.* San Francisco: International Association of Business Communicators Foundation, 1986.

Cobbey, N. "Dioceses Sound Alarm to National Staff." *Episcopal Life*, November 1993, pp. 1, 16.

———, ed. "Voices of General Convention." *Episcopal Life*, October 1994, pp. 18–19.

Cochran, D. "Are Deacons Necessary? No." *Episcopal Life*, August 1993, p. 14.

Cockburn, C. *In the Way of Women: Men's Resistance to Sex Equality in Organizations.* London: Industrial and Labor Relations Press, 1991.

———. *Machinery of Dominance: Women, Men and Technical Know-How.* Boston: Northeastern University Press, 1988.

Cohen, E. S. "Rabbis' Roles and Occupational Goals: Men and Women in the Contemporary American Rabbinate." *Conservative Judaism* 42: 20–30, 1989.

Cohen, M. "An Abuse of Power: Clericalism and Roles within the Church." *Modern Churchman* 34: 33–41, 1992.

Cohn, S. *The Process of Occupational Sex-Typing: The Feminization of Clerical Labor in Great Britain.* Philadelphia: Temple University Press, 1985.

Collins, R. "A Conflict Theory of Sexual Stratification." *Social Problems* 19(1): 3–21, 1971.

"Compensation Matters." *Prospectus.* Unitarian Universalist Office of Church Finances, Winter/April 1990.

Connell, R. W. *Gender and Power: Society, the Person and Sexual Politics.* Stanford: Stanford University Press, 1987.

Constitution and Canons for the Government of the Protestant Episcopal Church in the United States of America Otherwise Known as The Episcopal Church Adopted in General Conventions 1789–1991. New York: The Episcopal Church, 1991.

"Convention Clears the Clutter from Road to Ordination." *The Episcopalian*, September 1988, p. 8.

Cook, J. K., and L. C. Moorehead. *Six Stages of a Pastor's Life.* Nashville: Abingdon Press, 1990.

Corcoran, M., G. J. Duncan, and M. Ponza. "Work Experience, Job Segregation, and Wages." In *Sex Segregation in the Workplace: Trends, Explanations, Remedies*, ed. B. F. Reskin, 171–191. Washington, D.C.: National Academy Press, 1984.

Cormier, J. "Diocesan Convention '94: A Conversation with the Presiding Bishop." *The Episcopal Times*, Diocese of Massachusetts, November–December 1994, pp. 6–7.

———. "Parish 'Cluster' Ministries: A Means of Survival May Be Source of New Life for Local Congregations." *The Episcopal Times*, Diocese of Massachusetts, September 1994, pp. 8–9.

Costa, P. "A Conversation with Ronald Thiemann." *Harvard University Gazette*, 21 October 1988, pp. 6–7.

Council of Bishops of the United Methodist Church. "A Statement on the Quality and Education of Ministry for the United Methodist Church." Unpublished paper, 3 May 1991.

Cowan, J. R. "Survey Finds 70% of Women Rabbis Sexually Harassed." *Moment*, October 1993, pp. 34–37.

Cowell, A. "Fight Feminist Fringe, Bishops Told." [*The New York Times*] *The Denver Post*, 3 July 1993, p. 3A.

Cox, H. "From Harris to Hutchinson—A Big Day in Boston." *The Episcopal Times*, Diocese of Massachusetts, February–March 1989, p. 8.

———. "The 'New Breed' in American Churches: Sources of Social Activism in American Religion." *Daedalus* 96(1): 135–150, 1967.

Crompton, R., and G. Jones. *White-Collar Proletariat: Deskilling and Gender in Clerical Work*. Philadelphia: Temple University Press, 1984.

Crumm, D. "Bishops Reject Vatican Stance on Women." *The Denver Post*, 19 November 1992, p. 1A.

———. "Ordain Women, Catholics Say in Poll." *The Denver Post*, 19 June 1992, pp. 1A, 25A.

Culver, V. "Bishops Gripe at Vatican: Church Accused of Ignoring U. S. Issues." *The Denver Post*, 16 August 1995, pp. 1A, 18A.

———. "Pope Unlikely to Resolve Rifts with U.S. Catholic Protesters." *The Denver Post*, 11 July 1993, pp. 1A, 10A.

———. "Ordained Episcopal Women Face New Rebuke." *The Denver Post*, 4 June 1989, p. 4b.

"Czech Priests Defrocked." *The Christian Century*, 13 May 1992, p. 513.

Dahrendorf, R. *Life Chances: Approaches to Social and Political Theory*. London: Weidenfeld and Nicolson, 1979.

"Dallas/Fort Worth." *Episcopal Life*, October 1993, p. 4.

Daly, M. "After the Death of God the Father: Women's Liberation and the Transformation of Christian Consciousness." In *Womanspirit Rising: A Feminist Reader in Religion*, eds. C. P. Christ and J. Plaskow, 53–62. New York: Harper & Row, 1979.

———. *Gyn/ecology: The Metaethics of Radical Feminism*. Boston: Beacon Press, 1978.

———. *Beyond God the Father: Toward a Philosophy of Women's Liberation*. Boston: Beacon Press, 1973.

———. *The Church and the Second Sex*. New York: Harper & Row, 1968.

Darin, M. "They Smashed the Mold and Wear the Collar." *Episcopal Life*, July 1994, pp. 13–16.

Darling, P. W. *New Wine: The Story of Women Transforming Leadership and Power in the Episcopal Church*. Cambridge, Mass.: Cowley, 1994.

Davidman, L., and A. L. Greil. "Gender and the Experience of Conversion: The

Case of 'Returnees' to Modern Orthodox Judaism." In *Gender and Religion*, ed. W. H. Swatos Jr., 95–112. New Brunswick, N.J.: Transaction, 1993.

Davidson, W., and K. Kunze. "Psychological, Sociological, and Economical Meanings of Work in Modern Society: Their Effects on the Worker Facing Retirement." *Gerontologist* 5(3): 129–133, 159, 1965.

Dayton, D. W., and L. S. Dayton. "Women as Preachers: Evangelical Precedents." *Christianity Today*, 23 May 1975, pp. 4–7.

De Ecclesia: The Constitution on the Church of Vatican Council II Proclaimed by Pope Paul VI, November 21, 1964, ed. E. H. Peters. Glen Rock: Paulist Press, 1965.

Deckard, B. S. *The Women's Movement: Political, Socioeconomic and Psychological Issues*. New York: Harper & Row, 1975.

Declaration of the Sacred Congregation for the Doctrine of the Faith. "The Ordination of Women. Inter Insigniores, Vatican Doctrinal Congregation's Declaration on the Question of Admission of Women to the Ministerial Priesthood." *The Pope Speaks*, 15 October 1976, pp. 108–122.

Delloff, L. "Still Pioneers." *The Lutheran*, 28 November 1990, pp. 6–9.

Deming, L., and J. Stubbs. *Men Married to Ministers*. Washington, D.C.: Alban Institute, 1986.

"Discrimination Against Women." *Church & Society*, July–August 1992, pp. 95–96.

Donahoe, M., and E. Blue. *The Earl Blue Report on Clergy Disaffection*. San Francisco: Earl Blue Associates, 1970.

Donovan, M. S. "Women as Priests and Bishops." Unpublished paper. University of Arkansas-Little Rock History Seminar, 7 November 1989.

———. *Women Priests in the Episcopal Church: The Experience of the First Decade*. Cincinnati: Forward Movement, 1988.

———. *A Different Call: Women's Ministries in the Episcopal Church, 1850–1920*. Wilton, Conn.: Morehouse-Barlow, 1986.

Douglas, A. *The Feminization of American Culture*. New York: Alfred A. Knopf, 1977.

Dugan, M. H. "What Are 'Canon Nine' Clergy?" *The Mountain Echo*, (Episcopal) Diocese of Vermont, August 1992, p. 4.

Dunigan, F. J. "Perception by the Laity of the Restored Permanent Diaconate, Archdiocese of Boston: An Attitude Measurement and Analysis." Ph.D. dissertation, Catholic University of America, 1986.

Dunlap, E. D. "Consecration or Ordination: A Critical Look at the Proposal." *Circuit Rider*, November 1991, p. 8.

Dupee, F. W. *Henry James: His Life and Writings*, 2nd ed. Garden City: Doubleday, 1956.

Durkheim, E. *The Elementary Forms of the Religious Life*. New York: Free Press, 1965.

Edwards, I. "A New Life: Parish Minister Margot Campbell-Gross." *The World*, March–April 1991, pp. 19–21, 63.

Edwards, R. B. *The Case for Women's Ministry*. London: SPCK, 1989.

Eldred, O. J. *Women Pastors: If God Calls, Why Not the Church?* Valley Forge, Penna.: Judson Press, 1981.

Emerson, D. "Feminists and Religious Trailblazers." *The World*, March–April 1992, pp. 27–29.

England, P. "The Failure of Human Capital Theory to Explain Occupational Sex Segregation." *Journal of Human Resources* 17(3): 358–370, 1982.

Episcopal Clergy Directory. New York: The Church Hymnal Corp., 1972.

Episcopal Clerical Directory. New York: The Church Hymnal Corp., 1956–1968, 1975–1994.

Episcopal News Service. "The Entire Anglican Communion Mourns the Death of the Rev. Florence Li Tim Oi, First Woman Ordained a Priest." *The Episcopal Times,* Diocese of Massachusetts, April 1992, p. 11.

Erdey, S. "A Reporter's Notebook from General Convention." *The Episcopal Times,* Diocese of Massachusetts, October 1994, p. 5.

————. "The Rev. Grace Ndybahika, One of Uganda's First Women Priests, Recipient of First Diocesan Scholarship for African Students to Study in America." *The Episcopal Times,* Diocese of Massachusetts, October 1994, p. 5.

Erdner, R. A., and R. F. Guy. "Career Identification and Women's Attitudes Toward Retirement." *International Journal of Aging and Human Development* 30(2): 129–139, 1990.

Erickson, V. L. *Where Silence Speaks: Feminism, Social Theory, and Religion.* Minneapolis: Fortress Press, 1993.

Faludi, S. *Backlash: The Undeclared War Against American Women.* New York: Doubleday, Anchor Books, 1991.

Farrell, S. A. "'It's Our Church, Too!' Women's Position in the Catholic Church Today." In *The Social Construction of Gender,* eds. J. Lorber and S. A. Farrell, 338–354. Newbury Park, Calif.: Sage, 1991.

Featherman, D. L. "Biography, Society, and History: Individual Development as a Population Process." In *Human Development and the Life Course: Multidisciplinary Perspectives,* eds. A. B. Sørensen, F. E. Weinert, and L. R. Sherrod, 99–141. Hillsdale, N.J.: Lawrence Erlbaum, 1986.

Fellenbaum, G. "A Consideration of Some Factors Related to Work After Retirement." *Gerontologist* 11(1): 18–23, 1971.

Ferder, F. *Called to Break Bread? A Psychological Investigation of 100 Women Who Feel Called to Priesthood in the Catholic Church.* Mt. Ranier: Quixote Center, 1978.

Field-Bibb, J. *Women Towards Priesthood: Ministerial Politics and Feminist Praxis.* Cambridge, England: Cambridge University Press, 1991.

"Fifth GCSRW Survey Polls 1,000 Churches: Women's Participation in Local Churches Still Lags." *The Flyer,* The General Commission on the Status and Role of Women in the United Methodist Church, 12(3): 1–2, 1991–92.

Fishburn, J. F., and N. Q. Hamilton. "Seminary Education Tested by Praxis." *The Christian Century,* 1–8 February 1984, pp. 108–112.

Fishburn, P., J. Fishburn, and A. Hagy. "Are There Better Ways to Elect Bishops?" *Circuit Rider,* July–August 1992, pp. 11–12.

Fitzpatrick, R. M. "Is There a Valid Basis for a Male Priesthood?" *The Denver Post,* 15 August 1993, pp. 1D, 5D.

Floge, L., and D. M. Merrill. "Tokenism Reconsidered: Male Nurses and Female Physicians in a Hospital Setting." *Social Forces* 64: 925–947, 1986.

Foner, A., and K. Schwab. "Work and Retirement in a Changing Society." In *Aging in Society: Selected Reviews of Recent Research,* eds. M. W. Riley, B. B. Hess, and K. Bond, 71–94. Hillsdale, N.J.: Lawrence Erlbaum, 1983.

Fox, M. F., and S. Hesse-Biber. *Women at Work.* Palo Alto: Mayfield, 1984.

Furlong, M. "A Bishop to Break the Mold." *The Episcopal Times,* Diocese of Massachusetts, February–March 1989, p. 10.

Furnish, D. J. "Women in Religious Education: Pioneers for Women in Professional Ministry." In *Women and Religion in America 1900–1968,* eds. R. R. Ruether and R. S. Keller, 310–338. San Francisco: Harper & Row, 1986.

————. *DRE/DCE the History of a Profession.* Nashville: Christian Educators Fellowship, The United Methodist Church, 1976.

Gabbert, G. L. "Women in Ministry: Employment and Ordination Issues." D.Min. professional paper, the Lutheran School of Theology, 1989.

Gaustad, E. S. "The Pulpit and the Pews." In *Between the Times: The Travail of the Protestant Establishment in America*, ed. W. R. Hutchison, 21–47. Cambridge and New York: Cambridge University Press, 1989.

Gaylor, C. C. "The Ordination of Women in the Episcopal Church in the United States: A Case Study." Ph.D. dissertation, St. John's University, 1982.

"General Convention: Amid the Rhetoric, Some Words." *Episcopal Life*, August 1991, pp. 22–23.

Gibson, E. *When the Minister Is a Woman*. New York: Holt, Rinehart and Winston, 1970.

Gilbert, D., and J. A. Kahl. *The American Class Structure: A New Synthesis*. Homewood: Dorsey Press, 1982.

Gilbride, T. J., M. L. Griffith, and D. Lundquist. *The Survey of United Methodist Opinion*. Dayton: The United Methodist Church, General Council on Ministries, The Office of Research, 1990.

Gilkes, C. T. "Mother to the Motherless, Father to the Fatherless: Power, Gender, and Community in an Afrocentric Biblical Tradition." *Semeia* 47: 57–85, 1989.

Gillespie, J. B. *Women Speak: Of God, Congregations and Change*. Valley Forge, Penna.: Trinity Press International, 1995.

————. "Gender and Generations in Congregations." In *Episcopal Women: Gender, Spirituality and Commitment in an American Mainline Denomination*, ed. C. M. Prelinger, 167–221. New York: Oxford University Press, 1992.

Ginsburg, F. D. *Contested Lives: The Abortion Debate in an American Community*. Berkeley: University of California Press, 1990.

Godbey, J. C. "Unitarian Universalist Association." In *The Encyclopedia of Religion*, ed. M. Eliade, 15: 144–146. New York: Macmillan, 1987.

Goldman, A. "Black Women's Bumpy Path to Church Leadership." *The New York Times*, 29 July 1990, pp. 1, 28.

Grant, J. "Black Theology and the Black Woman." In *Black Theology: A Documentary History, 1966–1979*, eds. G. S. Wilmore and J. H. Cone, 418–433. Maryknoll: Orbis, 1979.

Greenbacker, L., and S. Taylor. *Private Lives of Ministers' Wives*. Far Hills: New Horizon Press, 1991.

Greene, D., ed. *Suffrage and Religious Principle: Speeches and Writings of Olympia Brown*. Metuchen: Scarecrow Press, 1983.

Gross, R. "Female God Language in a Jewish Context." In *Womanspirit Rising: A Feminist Reader in Religion*, eds. C. P. Christ and J. Plaskow, 167–173. San Francisco: Harper & Row, 1979.

Grove, W. B. "Appointment-Making in the West Virginia Area." *Circuit Rider*, November 1992, pp. 7–8.

Gunn, H. "Building Ministry for a New World: The Commission on Ministry." *The Record*, (Episcopal) Diocese of Michigan, May 1995, p. 6.

Gusfield, J. R. *Symbolic Crusade: Status Politics and the American Temperance Movement*. Urbana: University of Illinois Press, 1970.

Gustafson, J. M. "The Clergy in the United States." In *The Professions in America*, eds. K. S. Lynn and the editors of *Daedalus*, 70–90. Boston: Houghton Mifflin, 1965.

Hames, J. "Convention Validates Two Views on Women Priests." *Episcopal Life*, October 1994, p. 12.

Hammonds, K. A. "Taking Baby Steps Toward a Daddy Track." *Business Week*, 15 April 1991, 90–92.

Handy, C. B. *The Age of Unreason*. Boston: Harvard Business School Press, 1989.

Hansson, P. H. "Female Ministers in the Church of Sweden: Resistance and Progress." Paper presented at the Annual Meeting of the Association for the Sociology of Religion, Miami, 1993.

Hardy, E. R. "Deacons in History and Practice." In *The Diaconate Now*, ed. R. T. Nolan, 11–36. Washington, D.C.: Corpus Books, 1968.

Hargrove, B. "On Digging, Dialogue, and Decision-Making." *Review of Religious Research* 28(4): 395–401, 1987.

Harkavy, W. "War is Heck." *Westword*, 15–21 September 1993, pp. 22–29.

Harkness, G. "Pioneer Women in the Ministry." *Religion in Life* 39(2): 261–271, 1970.

Hartmann, H. "The Unhappy Marriage of Marxism and Feminism." In *Women and Revolution: A Discussion of the Unhappy Marriage of Marxism and Feminism*, ed. L. Sargent, 1–41. Boston: South End Press, 1981.

Hartsock, N. C. M. *Money, Sex, and Power: Toward a Feminist Historical Materialism*. Boston: Northeastern University Press, 1985.

Hauser, R. M., and D. L. Featherman. *The Process of Stratification: Trends and Analyses*. New York: Academic Press, 1977.

Hawes, G. R. *The Encyclopedia of Second Careers*. New York: Facts on File Publications, 1984.

Hearn, J., and P. W. Parkin. "Gender and Organizations: A Selective Review and a Critique of a Neglected Area." *Organizational Studies* 4: 219–242, 1983.

Heideman, E. P. *A People in Mission: Their Expanding Dream*. New York: Reformed Church Press, 1984.

Heilbrun, C. G. *Reinventing Womanhood*. New York: W. W. Norton, 1979.

Hendricks, C. F. *The Rightsizing Remedy: How Managers Can Respond to the Downsizing Dilemma*. Alexandria and Homewood: Society for Human Resource Management and Business One Irwin, 1992.

Hennig, M., and A. Jardim. *The Managerial Woman*. New York: Pocket Books, 1977.

Herin, M. "Issues and Recommendations." In *The Interface of Marriage and the Ministry*, ed. M. Herin, 3–14. Lake Junaluska, N.C.: Intentional Growth Center, 1981.

Hewitt, E. C. "Anatomy and Ministry: Shall Women Be Priests?" In *Women and Orders*, ed. R. J. Heyer, 39–55. New York: Paulist Press, 1974.

Hewitt, E. C., and S. R. Hiatt. *Women Priests: Yes or No?* New York: Seabury Press, 1973.

Heyer, R. J., ed. *Women and Orders*. New York: Paulist Press, 1974.

Heyward, I. C. *The Redemption of God: A Theology of Mutual Relation*. Washington, D.C.: University Press of America, 1982.

Hiatt, S. R. "Women in Research: A Subject's Reflections." *Review of Religious Research* 28(4): 386–389, 1987.

Hill, J. A. *Women in Gainful Occupations 1870 to 1920*. New York: Johnson Reprint Corp., 1972.

Hitchings, C. F. *Universalist and Unitarian Women Ministers*. Boston: Unitarian Universalist Historical Society, 1985.

Hoge, D. R. "Introduction: The Problem of Understanding Church Giving." *Review of Religious Research* 36(2): 101–110, 1994.

Hoge, D. R., and F. Yang. "Determinants of Religious Giving in American Denominations: Data from Two Nationwide Surveys." *Review of Religious Research* 36(2): 123–148, 1994.

Hoge, D. R., J. E. Dyble, and D. T. Poli. "Organizational and Situational Influences on Vocational Commitment of Protestant Ministers." *Review of Religious Research* 23(2): 133–149, 1981.

Holmes, K. E. "A Mennonite First." [*Knight-Ridder News Service*] *The Denver Post* 27 November 1993, p. 10B.

Hopke, W. E., ed. *The Encyclopedia of Careers and Vocational Guidance.* Chicago: J. G. Ferguson, 1981.

Horan, P. M., and T. A. Lyson. "Occupational Concentration of Work Establishments." *Sociological Forum* 1(3): 428–449, 1986.

Hough, J. C., Jr., "Future Pastors, Future Church: The Seminary Quarrels." *The Christian Century*, 24–31 May 1995, pp. 564–567.

Hout, M. *Mobility Tables.* Newbury Park, Calif.: Sage, 1983.

Howe, E. M. *Women and Church Leadership.* Grand Rapids: Zondervan, 1982.

Hudson, M. L. "'Shall Woman Preach?' Louisa Woosley and the Cumberland Presbyterian Church." *American Presbyterians* 68(4): 221–230, 1990.

Hulme, W. E. *Your Pastor's Problems: A Guide for Ministers and Laymen.* Garden City: Doubleday, 1966.

Hutch, R. A. *Religious Leadership: Personality, History and Sacred Authority.* New York: Peter Lang, 1991.

Hutchison, W. R. "Protestantism as Establishment." In *Between the Times: The Travail of the Protestant Establishment in America*, ed. W. R. Hutchison, 3–18. Cambridge and New York: Cambridge University Press, 1989.

———. "Discovering America." In *Between the Times: The Travail of the Protestant Establishment in America*, ed. W. R. Hutchison, 303–309. Cambridge and New York: Cambridge University Press, 1989.

Huyck, H. A. "To Celebrate a Whole Priesthood: The History of Women's Ordination in the Episcopal Church." Ph.D. dissertation, University of Minnesota, 1981.

Hyer, M. "Church Tackles Clergy 'Crisis' Head On." *Episcopal Life*, July 1990, 20–21.

Ice, M. L. *Clergy Women and Their World Views: Calling for a New Age.* New York: Praeger, 1987.

Jewett, P. K. *The Ordination of Women: An Essay on the Office of Christian Ministry.* Grand Rapids: William B. Eerdmans, 1980.

John Paul II. "Reserving Priestly Ordination to Men Alone: *Ordinatio Sacerdotalis.*" Apostolic letter. Washington, D.C.: Office for Publishing and Promotion Services, U. S. Catholic Conference, 26 May 1994.

Johnson, D. "Mormon Church Views New Threat." *The Denver Post*, 2 December 1993, p. 16A.

Johnson, E. "Wonder Working Providence of Sions Savior." *The Puritans: A Sourcebook of their Writings*, eds. P. Miller and T. H. Johnson, 1: 143–162 (New York: Harper & Row, 1963).

Johnson, J. "Mary Magdalene: Priest, Prostitute of a Model for the Post-Priesthood of Catholic Women?" *New Women, New Church*, November 1993–June 1994, pp. 22–23.

Jones, A. *Sacrifice and Delight: Spirituality for Ministry.* San Francisco: Harper SanFrancisco, 1992.

Jones, M. "25 Hottest Careers for Women." *Working Woman*, July 1995, p. 40.

Journal of the General Convention of the Episcopal Church in the United States of America. New York: The Episcopal Church, 1922–1991.

Jud, Gerald J., Edgar W. Mills, and Genevieve Walters Burch. *Ex-Pastors: Why Men Leave the Parish Ministry.* Philadelphia: Pilgrim Press, 1970.

Kanter, R. M. *Men and Women of the Corporation*. New York: Basic Books, 1977.
———. *Commitment and Community: Communes and Utopias in Sociological Perspective*. Cambridge: Harvard University Press, 1972.
Kaslow, A. J. "Saints and Spirits: The Belief System of Afro-American Spiritual Churches in New Orleans." In *Perspectives on Ethnicity in New Orleans*, ed. Committee on Ethnicity, 61–68. New Orleans, 1981.
Keller, R. S. "Women and the Nature of Ministry in the United Methodist Tradition." *Methodist History* 22: 99–114, 1984.
Kerckhoff, A. C. "The Status Attainment Process: Socialization or Allocation." *Social Forces* 55(2): 368–381, 1976.
Kerr, L. *Lady in the Pulpit*. New York: Woman's Press, 1951.
Kerwin, K. "Women Will Keep Fighting for Power, Feminist Warns." *Rocky Mountain News*, 15 August 1993, p. 28A.
Kessel, E. L. "A Proposed Biological Interpretation of the Virgin Birth." *Journal of the American Scientific Affiliation*, September 1983, pp. 129–136.
Kessler. S. J., and W. McKenna. *Gender: An Ethnomethodological Approach*. Chicago: University of Chicago Press, 1985.
Kilborn, P. T. "Good Pay Drawing More Men Into Nursing." [*The New York Times*] *The Denver Post*, 29 November 1992, p. 2A.
King, G. B. "Trends in Seminary Education 1987–1992." In *Yearbook of American and Canadian Churches 1993*, ed. Kenneth B. Bedell, 261–263. Nashville, Abingdon Press, 1993.
King, G. B., ed. *Fact Book on Theological Education for the Academic Year 1990–91*. Pittsburgh: The Association of Theological Schools, 1991.
Kirk, K. E. *Beauty and Bands and Other Papers*. Greenwich: Seabury Press, 1957.
Kleinman, S. *Equals Before God: Seminarians as Humanistic Professionals*. Chicago: University of Chicago Press, 1984.
Kraut, B. "A Wary Collaboration: Jews, Catholics, and the Protestant Goodwill Movement." In *Between the Times: The Travail of the Protestant Establishment in America*, ed. W. R. Hutchison, 193–230. Cambridge and New York: Cambridge University Press, 1989.
Krugler, J. D., and D. Weinberg-Kinsey. "Equality of Leadership: The Ordinations of Sara E. Dickson and Margaret E. Towner in the Presbyterian Church in the U.S.A." *American Presbyterians* 68(4): 245–257, 1990.
Kwilecki, S. "Contemporary Pentecostal Clergywomen: Female Christian Leadership, Old Style." *Journal of Feminist Studies in Religion* 3(2): 57–75, 1987.
LaCugna, C. M. "Catholic Women as Ministers and Theologians." *America*, 10 October 1992, pp. 238–248.
LaMagdeleine, D. R. "U.S. Catholic Church-Related Jobs as Dual Labor Markets: A Speculative Inquiry." *Review of Religious Research* 24(4): 315–327, 1986.
Larsen, E. L. "A Profile of Contemporary Seminarians Revisited." *Theological Education* 31(Supplement): 1–118.
Larsen, E. L., and J. M. Shopshire. "A Profile of Contemporary Seminarians." *Theological Education* 24: 10–136, 1988.
Larson, M. S. *The Rise of Professionalism: A Sociological Analysis*. Berkeley: University of California Press, 1977.
"Latvian Lutherans Halt Ordination of Women." *The Woman's Pulpit*, July–September 1995, p. 7.
Laws, J. L. "The Psychology of Tokenism: An Analysis." *Sex Roles* 1(1): 51–67, 1975.
Lawson, A. B. *John Wesley and the Christian Ministry*. London: SPCK, 1963.

Lehman, E. C., Jr. *Women in Ministry: Receptivity and Resistance.* Melbourne: The Joint Board of Christian Education, 1994.

———. "Gender and Ministry Style: Things Not What They Seem." In *Gender and Religion,* ed. W. H. Swatos Jr., 3–14. New Brunswick, N.J.: Transaction, 1993.

———. *Gender and Work: The Case of the Clergy.* Albany: State University of New York Press, 1993.

———. "Status Differences Between Types of Ministry: Measurement and Effect." In *Research in the Social Scientific Study of Religion: A Research Annual,* eds. M. L. Lynn and D. O. Moberg, 2:95–116. Greenwich: JAI Press, 1990.

———. "Research on Lay Church Members' Attitudes Toward Women in Ministry: An Assessment." *Review of Religious Research* 28(4): 319–329, 1987.

———. *Women Clergy in England: Sexisim, Modern Consciousness, and Church Viability.* Lewiston, N.Y.: Edwin Mellen Press, 1987.

———. "Sexism, Organizational Maintenance, and Localism: A Research Note." *Sociological Analysis* 48(3): 274–282, 1987.

———. *Women Clergy: Breaking Through the Gender Barriers.* New Brunswick, N.J.: Transaction, 1985.

———. "Organizational Resistance to Women in Ministry." *Sociological Analysis* 42(2): 101–118, 1981.

———. "Placement of Men and Women in the Ministry." *Review of Religious Research* 22(1): 18–40, 1980.

Lehman, E. C., Jr., and the Task Force on Women in Ministry. *Project SWIM: A Study of Women in Ministry.* Valley Forge, Penna.: The Ministry Council, American Baptist Churches, 1979.

Lehmann, J. M. *Durkheim and Women.* Lincoln: University of Nebraska Press, 1994.

Leidel, E. M., Jr. "Bishop, Priest, or Deacon?". Unpublished paper. New Brighton: (Episcopal) Diocese of Minnesota, n.d.

Lewis, J. "The Debate on Sex and Class." *New Left Review* 149: 108–120, 1985.

Leonard, J. E., ed. *Called to Minister . . . Empowered to Serve: Women in Ministry and Missions in the Church of God Reformation Movement.* Anderson, Ind.: Warner Press, 1989.

Lieberson, S. *Making It Count: The Improvement of Social Research and Theory.* Berkeley: University of California Press, 1985.

Lincoln, C. E., and L. H. Mamiya. *The Black Church in the African American Experience.* Durham: Duke University Press, 1990.

Lorber, J. "Dismantling Noah's Ark." In *The Social Construction of Gender,* eds. J. Lorber and S. A. Farrell, 355–369. Newbury Park, Calif.: Sage, 1991.

Lorber, J., and S. A. Farrell. "Gender Construction in the Workplace." In *The Social Construction of Gender,* eds. J. Lorber and S. A. Farrell, 135–139. Newbury Park, Calif.: Sage, 1991.

———. "Principles of Gender Construction." In *The Social Construction of Gender,* eds. J. Lorber and S. A. Farrell, 7–11. Newbury Park, Calif.: Sage, 1991.

Lowery, J. L., Jr. "'Tentmaker Priests' Contend They Have Apostolic Vocation." *The Lambeth Daily,* 21 July 1988, p. 3.

———. *Peers, Tents and Owls: Some Solutions to Problems of the Clergy Today.* New York: Morehouse-Barlow, 1973.

Luker, K. *Abortion and the Politics of Motherhood.* Berkeley: University of California Press, 1984.

Lummis, A. T. "Paradigms of Disaffiliation, Dissonance, Equity, and Feminism in Illuminating Occupational Dropout Among Clergy Women and Men." Paper presented at the Annual Meeting of the Association for the Sociology of Religion, Washington D.C., 1995.

———. "Clergy Divorce: Gendered Role Costs?" Paper presented at the Annual Meeting of the Association for the Sociology of Religion, Los Angeles, 1994.

Lynd, R. S., and H. M. Lynd. *Middletown in Transition: A Study in Cultural Conflicts*. New York: Harcourt Brace, 1937.

———. *Middletown: A Study in American Culture*. New York: Harcourt Brace, 1929.

Maccoby, M. "The Company Man." In *Organizational Shock*, ed. W. C. Hamner, 67–74. New York: John Wiley and Sons, 1980.

MacHaffie, B. J. *Her Story: Women in Christian Tradition*. Philadelphia: Fortress, 1986.

Malony, H. N., and R. A. Hunt. *The Psychology of Clergy*. Harrisburg: Morehouse, 1991.

Marder, J. "How Women Are Changing the Rabbinate." *Reform Judaism* 19(4): 4–8, 41, 1991.

Marty, M. E. "If It's not 'Mainline,' What is It?" *The Christian Century*, 8 November 1989, 1031.

———. *A Nation of Behavers*. Chicago: University of Chicago Press, 1976.

Mayer, O. "A Study of Directors of Religious Education and Their Profession." *International Journal of Religious Education* 15(2): 12, 40, 1938.

McConnell, J., and T. McConnell. "The Impact of Culture on Clergy Marriages." In *The Interface of Marriage and the Ministry: Findings of the Consultation on Clergy Marriages*, ed. M. Herin, 24–36. Lake Junaluska, N.C.: Intentional Growth Center, 1981.

McGee, G. B. "Three Notable Women in Pentecostal Ministry." *A/G Heritage*, Spring 1985–86, pp. 3–5, 12–16.

McKenna, D. L. "A Second 'Calling'". *Christianity Today*, 5 February 1988, p. 62.

Mead, L. B. *The Once and Future Church: Reinventing the Congregation for a New Misison Frontier*. Washington, D.C.: Alban Institute, 1991.

"Mennonites Elect Clemens First Woman Moderator." *The Woman's Pulpit*, October–December 1993, p. 6.

Miles, R. E., Jr., "Miles's Six Other Maxims of Management." In *Organizational Shock*, ed. W. C. Hamner, 299–310. New York: John Wiley and Sons, 1980.

Milkman, R. *Gender at Work: The Dynamics of Job Segregation by Sex During World War II*. Urbana: University of Illinois Press, 1987.

Miller, A. "Too Few Resources? Look Again: Northern Michigan Pioneers Mutual Ministry." *The Record*, (Episcopal) Diocese of Michigan, March 1994, pp. 1, 11.

Miller, P., and T. H. Johnson. "The Puritan Way of Life." In *The Puritans: A Sourcebook of Their Writings*, eds. P. Miller and T. H. Johnson, 1: 1– 63. New York: Harper & Row, 1963.

Millet, K. *Sexual Politics*. London: Shere, 1971.

Mincer, J., and S. Polachek. "Family Investments in Human Capital: Earnings of Women." *Journal of Political Economy* 82(2): S76–S108, 1974.

Moberg, David O. *The Church as a Social Institution: The Sociology of American Religion*. Englewood Cliffs, N.J.: Prentice-Hall, 1962.

Mollenkott, V. R. "An Evangelical Feminist Confronts the Goddess." *The Christian Century*, 20 October 1982, 1043–1046.

Moody, H. "Toward a Religionless Church for a Secular World." In *Who's Killing the Church?* ed. S. C. Rose, 82–92. Chicago: Renewal Magazine and Association Press, 1966.

Morgan, J. H. *Women Priests: An Emerging Ministry in the Episcopal Church* (1975–1985). Bristol, Ind.: Wyndham Hall Press, 1985.

Morrison, M. H. "Work and Retirement in an Older Society." In *Our Aging Society: Paradox and Promise*, eds. A. Pifer and L. Bronte, 341–365. New York: W. W. Norton, 1986.

Moseley, R. "Anglicans' D-day Near on Ordination of Women." [*Chicago Tribune*] *The Denver Post*, 6 March 1994, p. 9A.

Mulder, E. G. "Full Participation—A Long Time in Coming!" *Reformed Review*. 42(3): 224–245, 1989.

Murgatroyd, L. "Gender and Occupational Stratification." *Sociological Review* 30(4): 574–602, 1982.

Myers, S. J. "Women's Missionary Societies in the Methodist Episcopal Church, South." Paper presented at the Faculty Colloquium, Iliff School of Theology, Denver, May 1994.

Mylet, P. A. "Dogmatism and Acceptance of Women Priests in the Episcopal Church." Ph.D. dissertation, Northwestern University, 1988.

Nadell, P. S. "The Women Who Would Be Rabbis." In *Gender and Judaism: The Transformation of Tradition*, ed. T. M. Rudavsky, 123–134. New York and London: New York University Press, 1995.

Nason-Clark, N. "Are Women Changing the Image of Ministry? A Comparison of British and American Realities." *Review of Religious Research* 28(4): 330–340, 1987.

———. "Ordaining Women as Priests: Religious vs. Sexist Explanations for Clerical Attitudes." *Sociological Analysis* 48(3): 259–273, 1987.

Nasr, S. H. *Ideals and Realities of Islam*. London: George Allen & Unwin, 1985.

National Association of Student Financial Aid Administrators. "National Study of Theological Student Indebtedness." Unpublished study. New York: Auburn Theological Seminary, 1991.

National Center for the Diaconate and Associated Parishes, ed. *Proceedings of the Diaconate. A Unique Place in a Total Ministry*. Notre Dame: University of Notre Dame, 1979.

Neitz, M. J. "Inequality and Difference: Feminist Research in the Sociology of Religion." In *A Future for Religion? New Paradigms for Social Analysis*, ed. W. H. Swatos Jr., 165–181. Newbury Park, Calif.: Sage, 1993.

Nemeth, R. J., and D. A. Luidens. "Congregational Vs. Denominational Giving: An Analysis of Giving Patterns in the Presbyterian Church in the United States and the Reformed Church in America." *Review of Religious Research* 36(2) 111–122, 1994.

Nesbitt, P. D. "First and Second-Career Clergy: Influences of Age and Gender on the Career-Stage Paradigm." *Journal for the Social Scientific Study of Religion* 34(2): 142–171, 1995.

———. "Marriage, Parenthood and the Ministry: Differential Effects of Marriage and Family on Male and Female Clergy Careers." *Sociology of Religion* 56(4): 397–415, 1995.

———. "Dual Ordination Tracks: Differential Benefits and Costs for Men and Women Clergy." In *Gender and Religion*, ed. W. H. Swatos Jr., 27–44. New Brunswick, N.J.: Transaction, 1993.

———. "Feminization of American Clergy: Occupational Life Chances in the Ordained Ministry." Ph.D. dissertation, Harvard University, 1990.

Nester, T. R. "Doubts That Eat Away at Morale." *Circuit Rider*, March 1991, p. 9.

Neuhaus, R. J. *The Naked Public Square: Religion and Democracy in America.* Grand Rapids: William B. Eerdmans, 1984.
"New Women Bishops Share Visions for an Inclusive Church." *The Flyer,* The General Commission on the Status and Role of Women in the United Methodist Church. 13(2): 1–5, 1992.
Nielsen, J. M. *Sex and Gender in Society: Perspectives on Stratification,* 2nd ed. Prospect Heights: Waveland Press, 1990.
Nieva, V. F., and B. A. Gutek. *Women and Work: A Psychological Perspective.* New York: Praeger, 1981.
Nordhoff, C. *The Communistic Societies of the United States: From Personal Visit and Observation.* New York: Dover, 1966.
North American Association for the Diaconate. "1993 Year-end Statistics." *Diakoneo* 16 (Epiphany 1994): 6–7.
O'Faolain, J., and L. Martines. *Not in God's Image: Women in History from the Greeks to the Victorians.* New York: Harper & Row, 1973.
Official Catholic Directory. New York: Kenedy, 1991.
"One Year Later—Anglicans Accept Norm of Women Priests." *The Womans's Pulpit* 73(4): 2, 1995.
Oppenheimer, V. K. "Demographic Influences on Female Employment and the Status of Women." *American Journal of Sociology* 78(4): 946–961, 1973.
"Ordinations on Hold." *Advocate,* Diocese of Lexington, May 1991, p. 15.
Osipow, S. H. *Theories of Career Development.* New York: Appleton-Century-Crofts, 1968.
Otto, R. *The Idea of the Holy: An Inquiry into the Non-Rational Factor in the Idea of the Divine and its Relation to the Rational.* New York: Oxford University Press, 1982.
Our Professional Ministry: Structure, Support and Renewal. Boston: Unitarian Universalist Association, Commission on Appraisal, 1992.
Parsons, T. *Essays in Sociological Theory,* rev. ed. New York: Free Press, 1954.
Parvey, C. F. "The Theology and Leadership of Women in the New Testament." In *Religion and Sexism: Images of Woman in the Jewish and Christian Traditions,* ed. R. R. Ruether, 117–149. New York: Simon and Schuster, 1974.
Paul, L. *The Deployment and Payment of the Clergy.* London: Church Information Office, 1964.
Paul, R. S. *Ministry.* Grand Rapids: William B. Eerdmans, 1965.
Pavalko, R. M. *Sociology of Occupations and Professions.* Itasca: F. E. Peacock, 1971.
Penn, J. "Traditionalist 'Missionary Diocese' Forms New Denomination." *The Episcopal Times,* Diocese of Massachusetts, December 1992–January 1993, p. 13.
Pentecost, D. H. *The Pastor's Wife and the Church.* Chicago: Moody Press, 1964.
Permanent Diaconate Evaluation Committee and A. T. Lummis. *Raising Up Servant Ministry.* New York: The Episcopal Church, 1985.
Peterson, R. W., and R. A. Schoenherr. "Organizational Status Attainment of Religious Professionals." *Social Forces* 56(3): 794–822, 1978.
Pickering, W. S. F., ed. *Durkheim on Religion: A Selection of Readings with Bibliographies and Introductory Remarks.* London and Boston: Routledge and Kegan Paul, 1975.
Plater, O. "To Cut Clericalism, Don't Target Deacons." *Episcopal Life,* December 1993, p. 24.
Pohl, K. "Ministry Study Referred to Bishops for 1996." *Daily Christian Advocate,* The General Conference of the United Methodist Church, 16 May 1992, p. 8.

Poloma, M. *Assemblies of God at the Crossroads: Charisma and Institutional Dilemmas.* Knoxville: University of Tennessee Press, 1989.

Pomerleau, D. *Journey of Hope: A Prophetic Encounter in Czechoslovakia.* Mt. Ranier: Quixote Center, 1992.

Power, M. "The Making of a Woman's Occupation." *Hecate*, January 1975, pp. 25–34.

Presbyterian Clergywomen Survey 1993: Final Report. Ed. Research Services. Louisville: Presbyterian Church (U.S.A.), Congregational Ministries Division, 1993.

Presbyterian Clergywomen Survey 1993: Overview of Respondents' Comments. Ed. Research Services. Louisville: Presbyterian Church (U.S.A.), Congregational Ministries Division, 1993.

"Presbyterians Cut Staff, Reduce Ministry Units." *Episcopal Life*, September 1993, p. 3.

Prestwood, C. *The New Breed of Clergy.* Grand Rapids: William B. Eerdmans, 1972.

Purdum, S. "A Response..What is Success?" *Circuit Rider*, March 1991, pp. 7–8.

Purvis, Sally B. *The Stained Glass Ceiling: Churches and their Women Pastors.* Louisville: Westminster/John Knox Press, 1995.

Rallings, E. M., and D. J. Pratto. *Two-Clergy Marriages: A Special Case of Dual Careers.* Lanham: University Press of America, 1984.

Raming, I. "The Twelve Apostles Were Men." *Theology Digest* 40(1): 21–25, 1993.

Ranson, S., A. Bryman, and B. Hinings. *Clergy, Ministers and Priests.* London: Routledge & Kegan Paul, 1977.

Religious News Service. "Competition for Members Keeps More Money at Home." *Episcopal Life*, December 1993, p. 27.

Report of the Executive Council's Committee on the Status of Women. New York: The Episcopal Church, May 1991.

"Resistance to Ordaining Women." *The Woman's Pulpit*, October–December 1993, p. 7.

Reskin, B. F. "Bringing the Men Back In: Sex Differentiation and the Revaluation of Women's Work." In *The Social Construction of Gender*, eds. J. Lorber and S. A. Farrell, 141–161. Newbury Park, Calif.: Sage, 1991.

Reskin, B. F., and H. I. Hartmann, eds. *Women's Work, Men's Work: Sex Segregation on the Job.* Washington, D.C.: National Academy Press, 1986.

Reskin, B. F., and P. A. Roos. *Job Queues, Gender Queues: Explaining Women's Inroads into Male Occupations.* Philadelphia: Temple University Press, 1990.

———. "Status Hierarchies and Sex Segregation." In *Ingredients for Women's Employment Policy*, eds. C. Bose and G. Spitze, 3–21. Albany: State University of New York Press, 1987.

Resnick, D. A. "A Response to the "Final Report of the Commission for the Study of the Ordination of Women as Rabbis." *Conservative Judaism* 42(2): 49–58, 1989–90.

Resource Sharing Book: Programmes/Projects and Services. Geneva: World Council of Churches, 1988.

Rice, J. F. "So You Think Your Rector Is Paid Too Much." *The Episcopal Times*, Diocese of Massachusetts, October 1993, p. 16.

Rich, A. A. "Compulsory Heterosexuality and Lesbian Existence." *Signs* 5(4): 631–660, 1980.

Riley, J. "The Ordination of Women: A Matter of Economy or Theology?" *Encounter* 50(3): 219–232, 1989.

Riley, M. W., M. Johnson, and A. Foner. *Aging and Society.* New York: Russell Sage Foundation, 1972.

Riley, M. W., and J. W. K. Riley, Jr. "Longevity and Social Structure: The Potential of the Added Years." In *Our Aging Society: Paradox and Promise*, eds. A. Pifer and L. D. Bronte, 53–77. New York: W. W. Norton, 1986.

Risen, J. "Part-Time Jobs Rise While Security Drops." [*Los Angeles Times*] *The Denver Post*, 15 February 1994, p. 6A.

Robbins, T., and D. Bromley. "Social Experimentation and the Significance of American New Religions: A Focused Review Essay." In *Research in the Social Scientific Study of Religion*, eds. M. Lynn and D. Moberg, 1–28. Hillsdale, N.J.: JAI Press, 1992.

Roberts, K. A. *Religion in Sociological Perspective*, 2nd ed. Belmont: Wadsworth, 1990.

———. *Religion in Sociological Perspective*, 1st ed. Homewood: Dorsey Press, 1984.

Robinson, H. L., Jr. *Hazards of the Ministry for Dual-Clergy Couples*. Ph.D. dissertation, Fuller Theological Seminary, 1988.

Rodgers, D. T. *The Work Ethic in Industrial America 1850–1920*. Chicago: University of Chicago Press, 1978.

Roebuck, D. G. "Pentecostal Women in Ministry." *Perspectives in Religious Studies* 16(1): 29–44, 1989.

Roof, W. C., and W. McKinney. *American Mainline Religion: Its Changing Shape and Future*. New Brunswick and London: Rutgers University Press, 1987.

Roos, P. A. *Gender and Work: A Comparative Analysis of Industrial Societies*. Albany: State University of New York Press, 1985.

———. "Sexual Stratification in the Workplace: Male-Female Differences in Economic Returns to Occupation." *Social Science Research* 10(3): 195–224, 1981.

Roos, P. A., and B. F. Reskin. "Institutional Factors Contributing to Sex Segregation in the Workplace." In *Sex Segregation in the Workplace: Trends, Explanations, Remedies*, ed. B. F. Reskin, 235–260. Washington, D.C.: National Academy Press, 1984.

Rosenthal, J. M. "'Mother Church' Opens Priesthood to its Women." *Episcopal Life*, April 1994, pp. 1, 12.

Ross, C. *Who is the Minister's Wife: A Search for Personal Fulfillment*. Philadelphia: Westminster Press, 1980.

Ross, N. "Bishop Ordains First 'Local Priest.'" *The Arizona Episcopalian*, Diocese of Arizona 12(5): 1, 3, 1992.

Rowthorn, A. *The Liberation of the Laity*. Wilton: Morehouse-Barlow, 1986.

Royle, M. H. "Using Bifocals to Overcome Blindspots: The Impact of Women in the Military and the Ministry." *Review of Religious Research* 28(4): 341–350, 1987.

———. "Women Pastors: What Happens After Placement?". *Review of Religious Research* 24(2): 116–126, 1982.

Rubin, G. "The Traffic in Women: Notes on the Political Economy of Sex." In *Toward an Anthropology of Women*, ed. R. R. Reiter, 157–210. New York: Monthly Review Press, 1975.

Ruether, R. R. *Gaia and God: An Ecofeminist Theology of Earth Healing*. San Francisco: Harper SanFrancisco, 1992.

———. *Women-Church: Theology and Practice of Feminist Liturgical Communities*. San Francisco: Harper & Row, 1985.

———. *Sexism and God-Talk: Toward a Feminist Theology*. Boston: Beacon Press, 1983.

———. *New Woman New Earth: Sexist Ideologies and Human Liberation*. New York: Seabury, 1975.

Ruether, R., and E. McLaughlin, eds. *Women of Spirit: Female Leadership in the Jewish and Christian Traditions.* New York: Simon and Schuster, 1979.

Russell, A. *The Clerical Profession.* London, SPCK, 1980.

Russell, L. M. *Household of Freedom: Authority in Feminist Theology.* Philadelphia: Westminster Press, 1987.

———. "Clerical Ministry as a Female Profession." *The Christian Century,* 7–14 February 1979, pp. 125–126.

Saiving, V. "The Human Situation: A Feminine View." *The Journal of Religion* 40: 100–112, 1960.

Salem, R., and D. Stange. "Clergywomen of Ohio: Roles, Restraints, Recommendations." *Journal of Women and Religion* 7: 39–48, 1988.

Sarason, S. B. *Work, Aging, and Social Change: Professionals and the One Life-One Career Imperative.* New York: Free Press, 1977.

Sawtell, P. S. *Clergy Couples in the United Church of Christ: A Statistical Survey.* Sioux City: First Congregational United Church of Christ, 1988.

Schaller, L. E. "Suggestions for Change in the Itinerant System." *Circuit Rider,* November 1992, p. 12.

———. "Should We Close Those Small Churches?" *Circuit Rider,* July–August 1992, p. 13.

———. "Who is the Client? The Clergy or the Congregation?" In *Send Me? The Itineracy in Crisis,* ed. D. E. Messer, 87–99. Nashville: Abingdon Press, 1991.

———. *It's a Different World! The Challenge for Today's Pastor.* Nashville: Abingdon Press, 1987.

Schein, E. *Career Dynamics: Matching Individual and Organizational Needs.* Reading: Addison-Wesley, 1978.

Schlegel, A., ed. *Sexual Stratification: A Cross-Cultural View.* New York: Columbia University Press, 1977.

Schmidt, F. W. "Transcending Bureaucratic and Cultural Linkages: Women and the Church." Paper presented at the Annual Meeting of The Society for the Scientific Study of Religion and The Religious Research Association, Washington D.C., 1992.

Schmidt, J. M. "Denominational History When Gender is the Focus: Women in American Methodism." In *Reimagining Denominationalism: Interpretive Essays,* eds. R. B. Mullin and R. E. Richey, 203–221. New York: Oxford University Press, 1994.

Schoenherr, R. A. *Goodbye Father, Celibacy and Patriarchy in the Catholic Church.* New York: Oxford University Press, 1996.

Schoenherr, R. A., and L. A. Young. *Full Pews and Empty Altars: Demographics of the Priest Shortage in United States Dioceses.* Madison: University of Wisconsin Press, 1993.

———. *The Catholic Priest in the United States: Demographic Investigations.* Madison: University of Wisconsin-Madison Comparative Religious Organization Studies Publications, 1990.

Scholer, D. M. "Women in Ministry." *The Covenant Companion,* February 1984, pp. 12–16.

———. "Women in Ministry." *The Covenant Companion,* January 1984, pp. 12–13.

———. "Women in Ministry." *The Covenant Companion,* 15 December 1983, pp. 14–15.

———. "Women in Ministry." *The Covenant Companion,* 1 December 1983, pp. 8–9.

Schrank, H. T., and J. M. Waring. "Aging and Work Organizations." In *Aging in*

Society, eds. M. W. Riley, B. B. Hess, and K. Bond, 53–70. Hillsdale, N.J.: Lawrence Erlbaum, 1983.

Schreckengost, G. E. "The Effect of Latent Racist, Ethnic, and Sexual Biases on Placement." *Review of Religious Research* 28(4): 351–366, 1987.

Schüssler Fiorenza, E. *Discipleship of Equals: A Critical Feminist Ecclesia-logy of Liberation*. New York: Crossroad, 1993.

———. *Bread not Stone: The Challenge of Feminist Biblical Interpretation*. Boston: Beacon Press, 1984.

———. "Feminist Spirituality, Christian Identity, and Catholic Vision." In *Womanspirit Rising: A Feminist Reader in Religion*, eds. C. P. Christ and J. Plaskow, 136–148. San Francisco: Harper & Row, 1979.

Schwartz, F. "Management Women and the New Facts of Life." *Harvard Business Review* 67(1): 65, 1989.

Sewell, W. H., R. M. Hauser, and W. Wolf. "Sex, Schooling, and Occupational Status." *American Journal of Sociology* 86(3): 551–583, 1980.

Simon, R. J., A. J. Scanlan, and P. S. Nadell. "Rabbis and Ministers: Women of the Book and the Cloth." In *Gender and Religion*, ed. W. H. Swatos, Jr., 45–52. New Brunswick, N.J.: Transaction, 1993.

Simpson, J. B., and E. M. Story. *The Long Shadows of Lambeth X: A Critical, Eye-Witness Account of the Tenth Decennial Conference of 462 Bishops of the Anglican Communion*. New York: McGraw-Hill, 1969.

Skeat, W. W. *A Concise Etymological Dictionary of the English Language*. New York: G. P. Putnam's Sons, 1980.

Slocum, R. B. "The Diaconate: Barrier or Catalyst for Lay Ministry?" *St. Luke's Journal of Theology* 33(2): 129–145, 1990.

Smith, D. "The 'Tentmakers.'" *The Episcopal Times*, Diocese of Massachusetts, March 1991, p. 6.

Smith, H. L., and M. Grenier. "Sources of Organizational Power for Women: Overcoming Structural Obstacles." *Sex Roles* 8(7): 733–746, 1982.

Smith, P. *Daughters of the Promised Land: Women in American History*. Boston: Little, Brown, 1970.

Smith-Rosenberg, C. "Women and Religious Revivals: Anti-Ritualism, Liminality, and the Emergence of the American Bourgeoisie." In *The Evangelical Tradition in America*, ed. L. I. Sweet, 199–231. Macon: Mercer University Press, 1984.

Solheim, J. "Jubliant [sic] Vermonters Welcome Woman as Diocesan Bishop." *Episcopal Life*, December 1993, pp. 1, 7.

———. "Women's Ordination Controversy Simmers in Church of England, But Causes No Mass Exodus." Episcopal News Service: File A0000009.MSG, 12 December, 1995.

Solheim, J., J. Penn, and M. Barwell. "Report: General Convention 1994." *The Episcopal Times, Special News Section*, Diocese of Massachusetts, October 1994, pp. 2–3.

Sørensen, A. B. "Social Structure and Mechanisms of Life-Course Processes." In *Human Development and the Life Course: Multidisciplinary Perspectives*, eds. A. B. Sørensen, F. E. Weinert, and L. R. Sherrod. 177–197. Hillsdale, N.J. and London: Lawrence Erlbaum, 1986.

Sørensen, A. B., and H. Blossfeld. "Socioeconomic Opportunities in Germany in the Post-War Period." In *Research in Social Stratification and Mobility*, ed. A. L. Kalleberg, 85–106. Greenwich and London: JAI Press, 1989.

Sorge, E. "Dioceses to National Church: Think Locally, Act Locally." *Episcopal Life*, November 1993, p. 16.

Soule, G. H. "We're not Keeping the Clerical Pipeline Full." *The Episcopalian*, March 1987, pp. 16–17.

Sprigg, J. *By Shaker Hands*. New York: Alfred A. Knopf, 1975.

Stanton. E. C. *The Woman's Bible*. New York: Arno Press, 1972.

Stark, R., and W. S. Bainbridge. *The Future of Religion: Secularization, Revival, and Cult Formation*. Berkeley: University of California Press, 1985.

Steele, J. H. "Confessionals Call UMs to Reclaim and Reignite Doctrinal Heritage." *The Vision*, Rocky Mountain Conference of the United Methodist Church, June–July 1995, p. 6.

Steinfels, P. "Shortage of Qualified New Clergy Causing Alarm for U.S. Religions." *The Sunday New York Times*, 9 July 1989, pp. 1, 22.

Stendahl, B. *The Force of Tradition: A Case Study of Women Priests in Sweden*. Philadelphia: Fortress Press, 1985.

Stevens, L. "Different Voice/Different Voices: Anglican Women in Ministry." *Review of Religious Research* 30(3): 262–275, 1989.

Stewart, A. D. "Episcopal Clergy: Is There a Danger of a Clergy Shortage?" Unpublished report. New York: The Church Pension Fund, 1987.

Stewart, A. D., and M. S. West. "The Diaconate: A Call to Serve." Unpublished report. New York: The Church Pension Fund, 1991.

Stewart, C. W. *Person and Profession: Career Development in the Ministry*. Nashville and New York: Abingdon Press, 1974.

Stone, H. W. "The New Breed of Minister." *The Journal of Pastoral Care* 47(3): 286–297, 1993.

Stowe's Clerical Directory. New York: The Church Hymnal Corp., 1920–1953.

Strober, M. "Toward a General Theory of Occupational Sex Segregation: The Case of Public School Teaching." In *Sex Segregation in the Workplace: Trends, Explanations, Remedies*, ed. B. F. Reskin, 144–156. Washington, D.C.: National Academy Press, 1984.

Stuhlmueller, C., ed. *Women and Priesthood: Future Directions. A Call to Diologue*. Collegeville: Liturgical Press, 1978.

"Summary Affirmative Action Plan, Harvard University 1987." *Harvard University Gazette*, 3 April 1987, p. 9.

Sumner, D. E. *The Episcopal Church's History: 1945–1985*. Wilton: Morehouse, 1987.

Super, D. E. *The Psychology of Careers*. New York: Harper & Brothers, 1957.

Teachman, J. D., and K. A. Polonko. "Marriage, Parenthood and the College Enrollment of Men and Women." *Social Forces* 67(2): 512–523, 1988.

Telford, J., ed. *The Letters of the Rev. John Wesley*. London: Epworth Press, 1931.

The Clerical Directory. New York: The Church Hymnal Corp., 1956–1968.

The Committee for the Full Participation of Women in the Church. *Reaching Toward Wholeness: The Participation of Women in the Episcopal Church*. A 1987 Action Research study, ed. P. W. Darling. New York: The Episcopal Church Foundation, 1988.

The Documents of Vatican II, 1963–65. New York: Guild Press, 1966.

The Episcopal Church Annual. Wilton: Morehouse-Barlow, 1953–1994.

The Living Church Annual. New York: Morehouse-Gorham, 1922–1952.

The Living Church Annual and Churchman's Almanac. Milwaukee: Morehouse, 1920–1921.

"The Memphis Declaration." Statement adopted by 117 concerned United Methodists. Memphis, 25 January 1992.

The Presbyterian Placement System. Presbyterian Panel Report. Louisville: Presbyterian Survey Magazine, 1989.

The Proceedings of the Unitarian Universalist Historical Society, ed. R. E. Myers. Boston: Unitarian Universalist Association, 1984.

Thompsett, F. H. *Christian Feminist Perspectives on History, Theology and the Bible.* Cincinnati: Forward Movement, 1986.

Thrall, J. H., and J. Solheim. "House of Bishops Endorses Resolution Declaring Women's Ordination Mandatory in All Dioceses, Decries Mean-Spiritedness in the Church." Episcopal News Service: File A000002Z.MSG, 29 September 1995.

"Threshold '93: A Summary of the Study of the Organizational Structures of the Diocese as They Impact its Present and Future Mission and Ministry." *The Episcopal Times,* Diocese of Massachusetts, December 1993–January 1994, pp. 11–13.

Tocqueville, A. *Democracy in America,* ed. J. P. Mayer. New York: Anchor Books, Doubleday and Co., 1969.

Treiman, D. J., and H. I. Hartmann, eds. *Women, Work and Wages: Equal Pay for Jobs of Equal Value.* Washington, D.C.: National Academy Press, 1981.

Truesdell, M. P. "The Office of Deaconess." In *The Diaconate Now,* ed. R. T. Nolan, 143–168. Washington, D.C.: Corpus Books, 1968.

Tucker, C. G. *Prophetic Sisterhood: Liberal Women Ministers of the Frontier, 1880–1930.* Boston: Beacon Press, 1990.

Tucker, R. "Colorizing Church History." *Christianity Today,* 20 July 1992, pp. 20–23.

Tuell, J. M. "Appointment-Making in the Los Angeles Area." *Circuit Rider,* November 1992, pp. 10–11.

———. "Itineracy Revisited." *Circuit Rider,* November 1992, pp. 4–6.

Unitarian Universalist Association Directory. Boston: Unitarian Universalist Association, 1961–1994.

Unitarian Year Book. Boston: American Unitarian Association, 1920–1959.

Universalist Church of America. *Directory of Universalist Churches and Ministers.* Boston: Universalist Church of America, 1953–1956.

Universalist Church of America. *The Universalist Directory.* Boston: Universalist Church of America, 1948–1953, 1956–1957, 1959–1960.

———. *Universalist Directory and Handbook.* Boston: Universalist Church of America, 1959.

Universalist Register. Boston and Chicago: Universalist Publishing House, 1920.

Universalist General Convention, *Universalist Biennial Reports and Directory.* Boston: Universalist General Convention, 1938–1941.

Universalist Year Book. Boston: Universalist General Convention, 1931–1952.

U.S. Bureau of the Census. *Statistical Abstract of the United States.* Washington, D.C.: Government Printing Office, 1994, 1995.

———. *Census of Population and Housing, 1990: Equal Employment Opportunity File.* Washington, D.C.: Data User Services Division, 1990.

U.S. Bureau of Labor Statistics. *Employment and Earnings* 42(1). Washington, D.C.: Government Printing Office, 1995.

———. *Occupational Projections and Training Data.* Bulletin 2401. Washington, D.C.: Government Printing Office, 1992.

Vondracek, F. W., R. M. Lerner, and J. E. Schulenberg. *Career Development: A Life-Span Developmental Approach.* Hillsdale, N.J.: Lawrence Erlbaum, 1986.

Waldron, C. "Women and Resources Audit." Unpublished report. Boston: Episcopal Diocese of Massachusetts, 1986.

Waldrop, J. "Making a Career of It." *American Demographics* 11(4): 14, 1989.

Wallace, R. A. "The Social Construction of a New Leadership Role: Catholic Women Pastors." In *Gender and Religion*, ed. W. H. Swatos, Jr., 15–26. New Brunswick, N.J.: Transaction, 1993.

———. *They Call Her Pastor: A New Role for Catholic Women.* Albany: State University of New York Press, 1992.

———. "For the Record: Women Pastoral Administrators, Reflections from Interviews." *Church* 7(3): 43–48, 1991.

Warfield, E. D. "May Women Be Ordained in the Presbyterian Church?" *The Presbyterian*, 14 November 1929, p. 6.

Warlick, H. C., Jr. *How to Be a Minister and a Human Being.* Valley Forge, Penna.: Judson Press, 1982.

Webber, T. *Deep Like the Rivers: Education in the Slave Quarter Community, 1831–1865.* New York: W. W. Norton, 1976.

Weber, M. "Charismatic Authority and its Routinization." In *Religion and the Sociology of Knowledge: Modernization and Pluralism in Christian Thought and Structure*, ed. B. Hargrove, 155–165. New York: Edwin Mellen Press, 1984.

———. *Economy and Society: An Outline of Interpretive Sociology*, eds. G. Roth and C. Wittich. Berkeley: University of California Press, 1978.

———. *The Sociology of Religion.* Boston: Beacon Press, 1963.

———. *The Protestant Ethic and the Spirit of Capitalism.* New York: Charles Scribner's Sons, 1958.

Weinreich-Haste, H. *The Sexual Metaphor.* Cambridge: Harvard University Press, 1994.

"Welsh Anglicans Reject Women Priests." *The Woman's Pulpit*, July–September 1994, p. 4.

Welter, B. *Dimity Convictions: The American Woman in the Nineteenth Century.* Athens: Ohio University Press, 1976.

"Wesleyan-Holiness Women Clergy Confer in New Mexico." *The Woman's Pulpit*, October–December 1994, p. 5.

West, C. *Prophesy Deliverance! An Afro-American Revolutionary Christianity.* Philadelphia: Westminster, 1982.

West, C., and D. H. Zimmerman. "Doing Gender." In *The Social Construction of Gender*, eds. J. Lorber and S. A. Farrell, 13–37. Newbury Park, Calif.: Sage, 1991.

White, H. C. *Chains of Opportunity: System Models of Mobility in Organizations.* Cambridge: Harvard University Press, 1970.

Whitman, F. "Women Liberal Religious Pioneers." An Earth Room Talk. Boulder: Boulder Unitarian Universalist Church, 1991.

Wilkes, P. "The Hands That Would Shape Our Souls." *The Atlantic Monthly*, December 1990, pp. 59–88.

Williams, G. H. "The Ministry in the Later Patristic Period (314–450)." In *The Ministry in Historical Perspectives*, eds. H. R. Niebuhr and D. D. Williams, 60–81. New York: Harper & Row, 1956.

Williams, M. D. *Community in a Black Pentecostal Church: An Anthropological Study.* Pittsburgh: University of Pittsburgh Press, 1974.

Wilson, B. R. *Religion in Secular Society.* Baltimore: Penguin Books, 1969.

Wilson, C. R. "Cancel the Funeral: The Church is Quite Alive." *Episcopal Life*, December 1993, p. 27.

Wilson, R. L. *Drop-Outs and Potential Drop-Outs from the Parish Ministry.* A Study of the Alabama-West Florida Annual Conference. New York: The United Methodist Church, National Division of the Board of Missions, 1970.

Winthrop, J. "Journal: The Antinomian Crisis." In *The Puritans: A Sourcebook of their Writings*, eds. P. Miller and T. H. Johnson, 1: 129–143. New York: Harper & Row, 1963.

Witham, L. "Local Adventists Rebel, Ordain Three Women." *The Washington Times*, 24 September 1995, pp. A1, A16.

Wolf, F. *Moving Into the Episcopate: Resources for New Bishops*. Unpublished report prepared for The Presiding Bishop and the House of Bishops Committee on Pastoral Development. New York: The Episcopal Church, 1978.

"Women's Participation in Local Churches Still Lags." *The Flyer*, The General Commission on the Status and Role of Women in the United Methodist Church 12(3): 1–2, 1991–92.

Wortman, J. A. "One (sort of) in Christ Jesus." *The Witness*, January-February 1993, p. 23.

———. "Triennial Still a Necessity for Church Women." *Episcopal Life*, July 1991, p. 11.

———. "Deacons' Revival Brings Servant Ministry to Fore." *Episcopal Life*, June 1991, p. 7.

———. "Dioceses Redefining Roles of Deacons, Priests." *Episcopal Life*, May 1991, pp. 1, 9.

Wright, J. R. "Ministry in New York: The Non-Stipendiary Priesthood and the Permanent Diaconate." *St. Luke's Journal of Theology* 19(1): 18–50, 1975.

Zald, M. N., and J. D. McCarthy. "Religious Groups as Crucibles of Social Movements." In *Social Movements in an Organizational Society: Collected Essays*, eds. M. N. Zald and J. D. McCarthy, 67–95. New Brunswick, N.J.: Transaction, 1987.

Zaleski, P. A., and C. E. Zech. "Economic and Attitudinal Factors in Catholic and Protestant Religious Giving." *Review of Religious Research* 36(2): 158–167, 1994.

Zikmund, B. B. "Winning Ordination for Women in Mainstream Protestant Churches." In *Women and Religion in America. 1900–1968*, eds. R. R. Ruether and R. S. Keller, 339–383. San Francisco: Harper & Row, 1986.

Zikmund, B. B., A. T. Lummis, and P. M. Y. Chang. *An Uphill Calling: Ordained Women in Contemporary Protestantism*. Louisville: Westminster/John Knox Press, forthcoming 1997.

Index

Acker, Joan, 131, 168
Affirmative action, 5, 26, 42, 119–120,
    127–128, 167
Agassi, Judith Buber, 163
Age, 49, 91–92, 94–95. *See also* clergy;
    occupation; ordination; women
    clergy
Age Discrimination in Employment Act,
    94
Almquist, Elizabeth M., 48, 145
Amana (Society of True Inspiration), 16,
    198 n. 43
Ammerman, Nancy Tatom, 113
Anderson, Mother Leafy, 16
Androgyny, 6, 15, 198–199 nn. 48–49,
    203 n. 114
Anglican Lambeth Conference, 23, 37
Antifeminism, 113, 149
Apostolic succession, 7, 33, 132, 230
    n. 133
Association of Theological Schools, 25,
    91–92
Attitude change toward women clergy, 5
Authority. *See also* charisma; congrega-
    tions
  of clergy, 8, 20, 32, 111, 147–149,
    153–154, 170
  conflict over, 11, 22, 116
  legitimation of, 11, 15, 170–171, 173

and men, 10–11, 31, 107, 171
Papal, 241 n. 21
and power, 11
religious, 9–14, 22, 29, 169–171
and subordination, 113–114
and women, 6, 11, 13, 15, 17, 22,
    87, 130, 170, 173, 196–197 n. 22

Backlash, 4, 13, 21, 23, 26, 79, 89,
    107–114, 122, 124–127, 130–131,
    133, 139, 164, 166, 168–174, 240
    n. 14. *See also* feminism; feminiza-
    tion; women clergy
*Backlash: The Undeclared War Against
    American Women*, 133
Ball, David, 243 n. 51
Barfoot, Charles H., 108
Beecher, Lyman, 174
Bendroth, Margaret Lamberts, 24, 108,
    113
Bishops, 167, 241 n. 21. *See also* Epis-
    copal clergy; women clergy
Blue, Earl, 238 n. 119
Blumhofer, Edith, 24
Bock, E. Wilbur, 232 n. 28
Booth, Catherine Mumford and
    William, 204 n. 4
Bora, Katharine von, 52
Brereton, Virginia, 199 n. 58

269

Brown Blackwell, Antoinette, 23
Brown, Olympia, 23, 37, 201 n. 83
Browning, Edmund, 114, 231–232
    n. 21
Buchanan, Constance H., 102
Bucklee, Sally, 191 n. 4
Buddhism and women, 14–15
Burch, Genevieve Walters, 158
Burke, Marjorie, 200 n. 70
Burleigh, Celia, 37
Bushnell, Horace, 174

Calvinism, 204 n. 6
Career, 67, 74, 93–99, 126, 217 nn. 11,
    16. *See also* clergy; clergy career
    patterns; job(s)
Carroll, Jackson W., 5, 15, 67, 87, 94,
    97, 112, 114, 130, 155
Catanzarite, Lisa M., 220 n. 59
Chafetz, Janet Saltzman, 6, 109, 113–
    114, 124, 126, 132–133, 143, 154,
    156, 160, 166–167, 172, 233 n. 44
Charisma, 16, 131, 167
Cheek, Alison, 4
Chinnis, Pamela, 230 n. 136
Christian Coalition, 154
Christian Science Church, 17
Christianity and gender, 10, 14, 15,
    113, 197 n. 28. *See also* women's
    ordination
Church of England, 33, 92, 123, 230
    n. 3, 232 n. 30, 239 n. 123. *See
    also* women clergy; women's ordina-
    tion
Church of Sweden, 113, 123, 146. *See
    also* women clergy; women's ordina-
    tion
Civil rights movement, 9, 18
Classism, 11, 169
Clemens, Donella, 133
Clergy. *See also* Episcopal clergy; femi-
    nization; rabbinate; Unitarian Uni-
    versalist clergy; women clergy
    and age, 93–102
    career orientation of, 6–7, 30–31, 42,
    101
    class solidarity, 99, 145, 154
    compensation, 26, 101–102, 155,
    163
    crisis, 102, 154, 230 n. 3

decline of young men in the, 23, 26,
    100–106, 142–143, 145
demand for, 108, 126, 160, 208 n. 47
and education, 8, 48–49, 94, 97,
    102–103, 151, 210 nn. 15–17
financial contribution of, 147
and laity, 20, 97, 99, 146–147, 152,
    158
who leave the ministry, 35, 105, 108,
    121, 158–159
masculinization movements, 104,
    107, 149, 152
nonstipendiary, 137, 147, 155–158,
    238 n. 111
prestige, 20, 26, 31, 90–91, 101, 104,
    110, 116, 118, 121, 146–149, 154,
    156–158, 216 n. 5, 235 n. 58
projected jobs for, 105
retirements, 57, 86, 99, 143–145, 213
    n. 22, 233 n. 44
role conflicts and change, 20–21, 32,
    115, 146, 151–152, 158
second–career, 8, 50–52, 93–99, 101,
    103, 105, 136, 142, 218 n. 30
and sexual abuse, 30, 137, 151
socialization, 98–99, 110, 144
supply, 81, 115, 135, 140–144, 160,
    232 n. 30, 233 n. 41
titles, 151, 243 n. 44
traditional norm for, 30–31, 43, 52,
    102, 153
Clergy career patterns,
    and age, 93–96, 98
    and attainment, 74, 76, 83, 88, 95.
    See also Episcopal clergy
    and concurrent jobs, 155, 163
    for men over time, 28, 36, 61, 65–66,
    80–86, 100
    gender differences in, 7, 31–32, 44,
    46, 58, 64, 67, 69–71, 74, 76, 86–
    87, 96, 130, 135, 143
    traditional norm for, 45, 58, 76, 84–
    85, 95–97, 155
    trajectory, 57, 63, 71, 75–76, 83, 88,
    96
Clergy couples, 79–80, 215 n. 14. *See
    also* Episcopal clergy
Clergy leadership, 21, 85–87, 177. *See
    also* authority; religious leadership;
    women clergy

Clericalism, 145–149, 152–154, 160, 166, 173
Cockburn, Cynthia, 109–110, 113, 120, 132, 136, 163, 167, 169, 171, 196–197 n. 22, 223 n. 31, 229 n. 126
Cohn, Samuel, 145
Collins, Randall, 204 n. 2
Communication, 167, 171–172
Community, 168, 175, 177, 241 n. 22, 242 n. 36
Congregations, 40–42. *See also* clericalism; religious organizations
  and attitudes toward women clergy, 24, 87
  authority and autonomy of, 21, 29–30, 148, 231 n. 18
  and clergy compensation, 101, 125, 129, 137, 155, 227 n. 86
  and consumerization, 138–139
  declining financial resources of, 86, 136–138
  and economic dependency, 20, 91, 130, 139, 148, 200 n. 65
  and hiring of clergy, 42–43, 87, 111–112, 119, 121, 125, 127–130, 138
  labor in, 138, 155
  and men, 175
  minister's spouse in, 52
  and prestige, 31
  rural, 121, 142
  unable to afford male clergy, 20, 71
Connell, R. W., 111, 126
Cook, J. Keith, 129, 209 n. 6
Corporate downsizing, 49, 93, 213 n. 9
Cowan, Jennifer R., 71, 110
Crompton, Rosemary, 130

Daly, Mary, 21
Deaconess, 17, 24, 35, 37, 119, 123, 153, 199 n. 51, 201 n. 90
Deacon(s). *See also* Episcopal clergy
  education of, 49, 124, 155
  female, 14, 46–47, 118–120
  as job title, 46, 119, 153–154
  lay, 122–123, 147
  male, 14, 46, 62, 120
  permanent, 37, 46–47, 55, 62, 117–120, 122–125, 147–150, 153, 155, 158, 166, 210 n. 13, 225 nn. 68–

69, 235–236 nn. 70, 73, 237 nn. 101, 103
  role of, 119–120, 123, 148, 153
  and servanthood, 119–120, 225 n. 61
  transitional, 30, 33, 37, 44, 46, 54–55, 118
Denominationalism, 173–174
Deployment, 31. *See also* congregations; Episcopal Church; Episcopal clergy; Unitarian Universalist clergy
  and age norms, 94–96
  computerized, 42, 127–129
  denominational differences in, 87–88, 123, 128, 132, 156
  networks, 32, 42–43, 112, 127–128
  officials, 32, 42, 96–98, 128–129, 155, 218 n. 30
  of retirees, 99, 144–145
  women's disadvantage in, 8, 43, 96, 112, 128–129, 136
Disenfranchisement of religion, 20–21, 91
Dixon, Jane Holmes, 244 n. 53
Dobson, James, 196 n. 11
Dominance and domination, 17, 109–111, 113, 129–133, 136, 143, 168–171, 173–175
Donahoe, Michael, 238 n. 119
Donovan, Mary S., 21, 30, 228 n. 103
Douglas, Ann, 4, 20, 91, 107, 152, 203 n. 113, 200 nn. 65–66, 221 n. 3
Dugan, Michael H., 121
Durkheim, Emile, 13, 195 nn. 2–3
Dworkin, Anthony Gary, 109, 113

Ecofeminism, 176
Ecumenism, 18, 25, 154, 167–168
Eddy, Mary Baker, 17, 198 n. 48
Education. *See also* clergy; deacon; Episcopal clergy; Unitarian Universalist clergy; women clergy
  and doctoral degrees, 151
  elite status of, 103, 220 nn. 55–56
  increase over time in, 48, 90–91, 124, 151, 172, 210 n. 17, 226 n. 77
  as occupational resource, 47–48, 104, 123–124, 150–151, 210 nn. 14, 19, 226 n. 74

Education (*continued*)
  and ordination tracking, 124
  secularizing influence of, 91
  and social morality, 116
Empty Tomb Inc., 244 n. 59
Enlightenment, 11, 14, 16, 20, 174,
    196 n. 15
Episcopal Church, 7, 33, 37–38, 92,
    111, 137, 139, 146, 163, 206
    n. 24, 231 n. 20
  Church Deployment Office, 63, 79,
    128–129, 228 nn. 103, 109
  Church Pension Fund, 125, 155
  Committee on the Status of Women,
    111, 241 n. 23
  decline in congregations and commu-
    nicants, 40, 81, 101, 141, 208
    n. 47, 233 n. 36
  General Convention, 35, 37–38, 109,
    111, 145, 222 n. 15, 225 n. 64,
    244 n. 52
  General Ordination Examination, 37,
    150
  House of Bishops, 172
  House of Deputies, 230 n. 136
  and labor, 87, 100, 140, 145, 161–
    162, 215 n. 20, 233 n. 36, 231
    n. 12
  ordination in, 37, 147, 150–151. *See
    also* women's ordination
Episcopal Church Women, 200, n. 70,
    244 n. 57
Episcopal clergy,
  and age, 49–50, 65–67, 69, 71, 93–
    97, 100, 120–122, 218 n. 22
  and attainment, 76–86, 90
  as bishops, 33, 37, 42, 87, 111, 113,
    119–120, 131–132, 148, 158, 209
    n. 7, 218 n. 22, 222 n. 15, 230
    n. 133, 232 n. 22, 244 n. 53
  career tracking of, 55, 66, 71
  and church voting, 148, 157–158
  clergy couples, 80, 215 n. 18
  compensation, 118, 129, 220 n. 49,
    227 n. 86, 228 n. 109
  and conflict, 120, 123
  and continuous employment, 65, 68–
    69, 71
  and decline in men ordained, 82–83,
    100–101

  deployment of, 42–43, 97, 120–121,
    128–129, 148, 227 n. 86
  and education, 65, 69, 94, 103, 115,
    118–121, 124, 151, 220 n. 56, 236
    n. 83
  exodus of, 159
  feminization of, 39–40, 118–119
  gender differences in mobility and at-
    tainment of, 44–55, 58–71, 75–77,
    79, 84–85, 87, 96–97, 119, 125–
    127, 214 n. 5
  and male careers over time, 61, 69,
    80–86
  marriage and children, 45–46, 53, 55,
    59, 61, 71, 211 n. 32
  nonstipendiary, 118, 121, 125, 153,
    155, 157, 237 nn. 101–103
  with ordained parent, 69
  part-time work of, 125–126, 155, 227
    nn. 86, 88, 237 nn. 102–103
  and prior work experience, 51–52, 55,
    147, 211 n. 25
  and race, 35, 86
  as rectors, 43, 70, 76, 82–83, 112,
    227 n. 86, 228 n. 109
  retirements, 99, 121, 144–145
  as second career, 55, 94–97, 103, 225
    n. 66
  and secular work, 68, 71, 117, 156
  and senior level placements, 87, 96
  shortage of, 100, 140, 142
  surplus of, 61, 82, 108, 121, 140–141
  as vicars, 83
Episcopal Divinity School, 4, 226 n. 80
Episcopal laywomen, 138
Episcopal priesthood,
  and Canon 9, 120–122, 147–148,
    155, 158, 225 n. 66
  and irregular ordination of women,
    37–38, 215 n. 21
  trading up to, 147, 149, 235–236
    n. 70
  women's conflation with deacons, 46–
    47, 62, 119–120, 122, 124
Episcopal Synod of America, 111, 113
Episcopal Women's Caucus, 244 n. 53
Episcopalians United, 139
Equals Before God, 203 n. 115
Erdey, Susan, 222 n. 15
Ethics organizations, 174–175

Evangelical Protestantism,
   clergy professionalization in, 151,
      203, n. 115
   and women, 6, 16–20, 108

Faludi, Susan, 133
Family, 49, *See also* Episcopal clergy;
   women
Farrell, Susan A., 243 n. 41
Featherman, David L., 136
Federal Council of Churches, 199 n. 58
Feminism, 11, 109, 110, 164
   attacks against, 13, 113–114, 169–
      170, 196 n. 11, 240 n. 14
   and clergy, 133, 149, 168
   male support for, 41, 164, 167
   movements, 19, 21, 154, 164, 171,
      176
Feminist theology, 12, 21, 165–168,
      170, 176, 226 n. 80
Feminization, 15, 26, 122, 221 n. 3.
   See also Episcopal clergy
   backlash against, 148, 162
   and career attainment, 79, 81–84
   in clergy, 8, 38–39, 46–47, 115–119,
      164
   and compensation, 105, 116
   and job segregation, 28, 45, 115, 133,
      239 n. 3
   male concerns over, 3–4, 8, 22, 26,
      32, 102, 142, 174–176
   occupational effects of, 88, 102, 105–
      107, 134, 154, 160, 162
   and ordination requirements, 150, 225
      n. 64
   of religious education, 116
   in secular occupations, 8, 26, 88, 90–
      91, 105, 130, 140, 162
   and social change, 142–143, 161,
      177. *See also* social control
   threshold level of, 45, 74, 239 n. 3
First Amendment to the U. S. Constitution, 5, 20, 127
Frontier, 19, 200 n. 62
Fox, Mary Frank, 128
Furnish, Dorothy Jean, 116

Gender attribution, 112, 164, 177
Gender construction, 8, 112, 176–177,
   243 n. 41

Gender discrimination, 55, 129, 130,
   160, 162
Gender equality, 10, 13, 17, 114, 120,
   132, 165, 167–170, 172, 176, 195
   n. 3, 223 n. 31
Gender identity, 169–170, 175–176
Gender inequality, 123, 129, 143, 162–
   163, 169
Gender relations, 12–13, 15, 133, 170,
   172
Gender roles, 10–12, 18, 98, 169, 172,
   174
Gender segregation. *See also* feminization
   in clergy jobs, 8, 46–47, 88, 119–120,
      127, 129–130, 160–164
   in ordination tracks, 115, 122
   of networks, 128
   occupational, 86, 96, 143, 154
   in professions, 149–150
   and religion, 10, 15–17
   and wage gap, 228 n. 107
Gibson, Elsie, 71
Gilkes, Cheryl Townsend, 166
Gillespie, Joanna, 138
Glass ceiling, 3, 88, 130, 132, 228
   n. 112
Grenier, Mary, 119
Gustafson, James M., 92
Guzman, Lucia, 132

Hargrove, Barbara, 5, 161
Harris, Barbara Clementine, 38, 131–
   132, 173, 222 n. 15, 229 n. 121
Hartmann, Heidi I., 55
Harvard Divinity School, 25
Heck, Barbara, 17
Hegemony, 9, 15, 16, 166, 174
Heideman, Eugene P., 199 n. 53
Heinemann, Barbara, 16, 198 n. 43
Hesse-Biber, Sharlene, 128
Heterosexuality, 169–171. *See also* sex-
   ual orientation
Hierarchy, 164, 166–170. *See also* occu-
   pation
Hinduism, 14
Hobart, Nan, 168
Hunt, Richard A., 93, 95–96
Hutchinson, Anne, 16
Hutchison, William R., 91

Index of dissimilarity, 44–45
Individualism, 171
Individuality, 163, 166–167
International Church of the Foursquare
    Gospel, 16, 17, 108
Islam, 29, 91
    gender segregation in, 10–11
    and women, 11, 14, 15

James, Henry, Sr., 107
Jamieson, Penelope, 132
Jepsen, Maria, 132
Job(s),
    and career tracking, 57, 67, 218
        n. 28. *See also* Episcopal clergy
    de-skilling of, 26, 107, 126, 136,
        153–154, 160
Job ladder, 31, 43, 45, 64, 85
Job mobility, 57, 156, 238 n. 112. *See
    also* Episcopal clergy; Unitarian
    Universalist clergy
    and age, 66–67, 93, 95
    and attainment, 64, 214 n. 4
    definitions of, 7, 63, 73
    denominational differences in, 57, 64
    downward, 76, 79
    and education, 47
    forced, 63–65, 67, 97
    gender differences in, 64–67, 74–76,
        79, 96
    upward, 31, 45, 64–65, 74–76, 79,
        86, 88, 122, 130, 146, 213 n. 12
Job opportunities, 32, 135
    and attainment, 7, 74, 96
    competition for, 83, 105, 126
    decline in, 82–83, 153
    definition of, 6, 32, 214 n. 1
    gender differences in, 45, 58–59, 63–
        64, 74, 76, 117
    for leadership, 85, 96, 153
    for newer ordination tracks, 119–121
    and social control, 74, 76, 153
Job partition, 26, 107, 125–126
Job placements, 31, 42–43, 47, 68–69,
        153, 162. *See also* Episcopal clergy;
        Unitarian Universalist clergy
    and age, 41, 50, 94
    as associate(s), 41, 43, 45, 209 n. 6
    competition for, 82, 88, 105, 122,
        156

in congregations, 31, 41–42
denominational crossover in, 30–31,
    156
duration of, 57, 82
and economic constraints, 138, 142
entry, 31, 41, 46–47, 51, 54, 57, 64,
    75, 94
full-time, 30, 44, 71, 88, 138, 142,
    154–156, 209 n. 8
gender differences in, 44, 46, 58, 67–
    68, 71, 87, 110, 126, 130, 135,
    143, 145, 163
as interim, 43, 63, 87, 112, 145
in leadership positions, 31, 87, 96,
    105, 134
lower level, 64, 75, 88, 135
marginal, 71, 143
noncongregational, 31, 42, 157
nonstipendiary, 42, 44, 155–157,
    163
part-time, 30, 42, 44, 124, 134, 155–
    157, 163, 227 n. 88
second, 57–58, 60, 62, 64
third, 67, 69, 71
and vacancies, 32, 57
waiting time for, 44, 50
Job segregation, 127. *See also* feminiza-
    tion; gender segregation
Johnson, Edward, 198 n. 41
Jones, Alan, 216 n. 5
Jones, Gareth, 130
Jud, Gerald J., 158
Judaism, 8, 91
    and seminary, 92
    and women, 10, 87

Kant, Immanuel, 174
Kanter, Rosabeth Moss, 130
Keller, Rosemary S., 199 n. 51
Kelly, Leontine, 132
Kerckhoff, Alan, 74
Kilborn, Peter T., 104
King, Martin Luther, Jr., 9
Kirk, Kenneth E., 22
Kleinman, Sherryl, 152–153, 170, 173,
    203 n. 115
Kwilecki, Susan, 196 n. 16, 203 n. 115

Labor. *See also* clergy; Episcopal clergy;
    Unitarian Universalist clergy

alternative supplies of, 115, 145, 153, 155–156, 158

demand and supply of, 126, 136, 140, 143, 154, 233 n. 38

female exploitation, 124, 126, 130

Labor market, 30, 122, 125–126, 169

Language,

inclusive, 27, 139, 149, 162–163, 172, 192 n. 6, 203 n. 114

and male dominance, 131, 161–163

and social change, 12, 161, 163, 166

Larsen, Ellis L., 91–92, 94, 98

Lay certification programs, 36, 116, 147–148, 150

Lay pastors, 52, 123, 156

Lee, Ann, 198–199 n. 49

Lehman, Edward C., Jr., 43, 87, 112–114, 128–130, 139, 206 n. 27, 210 n. 19, 224 n. 42

Leidel, Edwin M., Jr., 155, 209 n. 7

Liberation, 9, 165–168, 170–177, 241 n. 22, 244 n. 53

Lieberson, Stanley, 123

Litigation, 151

Liturgical Movement, 146

Liturgy, 21, 146, 161

Lorber, Judith, 243 n. 41

Lowery, James L., 157–158, 238 n. 114

Luidens, Donald A., 138, 231 n. 7

Lummis, Adair T., 5, 158

Lusitanian Church, 238 n. 111

Luther, Martin, 52, 204 n. 6

Lutheran Church of Australia, 109

Lynd, Robert S. and Helen Merrell Lynd, 18

Malony, H. Newton, 93, 95–96

Marder, Janet, 176

Marginalization, 164–165, 170, 173, 177. *See also* religious organizations; women; women clergy

Marital status. *See also* Episcopal clergy; women clergy

and men, 32, 52–53, 59

and women, 12, 52–53, 71, 79–80, 212 n. 9

Marty, Martin, 196 n. 12

Matthews, Marjorie, 132

McKenna, David L., 92

McKinney, William, 210 n. 15

McLeod, Mary Adelia, 87, 113–114

McPherson, Aimee Semple, 16, 17, 108

Men,

and attainment at women's expense, 88, 122, 130, 136

and competition with women, 18, 112, 129–131, 146, 169, 174

heterosexual politics of, 111, 169–171

identity and power of, 112, 144, 169–171, 175, 242 n. 39

increased longevity and retirement of, 144, 234 nn. 50–51

supervised by women, 112, 223 n. 31

and theological conservatism, 13

women's support of, 10, 62, 113

Mennonite Church, 133, 172–173

Methodism, 3, 102, 144. *See also* United Methodist Church; Wesley; women clergy; women's ordination

British, 4, 156, 230 n. 3, 238 n. 114

clergy deployment in, 42, 87–88, 123, 128, 132, 156, 230 n. 132

lay pastors, 156

Middletown, 18

Millet, Kate, 169, 242 n. 39

Mills, Edgar W., 158

Minister's wife, 32, 52–53, 96, 211 n. 29

Ministry, 30, 137, 156, 163. *See also* clergy; deployment; deprofessionalization; Episcopal clergy; lay pastors; Unitarian Universalist clergy; women clergy

"call" to, 30–31, 36, 63, 73–74, 92, 204 n. 6

decline in the, 91, 101–102, 105, 142

gender difference in style, 5

gender shift in the, 3–4, 23–28, 32, 39–40, 46, 81, 208 n. 46

lay, 147, 149, 153, 166, 225–226 n. 69

loss of best and brightest for, 102–103

occupational viability of, 101

reasons for leaving the, 158–159

role ambiguity and conflict, 90, 99, 158

as second career, 49, 92, 95, 97–99

and secular occupations, 31, 91, 106, 151, 153, 162

Ministry (*continued*)
  specializations in, 115, 148, 151, 153, 155
  structural change in the, 20, 27–28, 114, 161
  as tentmaker occupation, 155, 237 n. 98
  time out from, 67–68
Misogynism, 164
Missionary,
  organizations, 18
  women, 17–18, 20, 23, 107
Mithraism, 14
Moore, Sister, 16
Moorehead, Lee C., 129, 209 n. 6
Muhammad, 14, 15
Mujerista movement, 166, 171
Murray, Judith Sargent, 36–37

Nason-Clark, Nancy, 12, 131
Nasr, Seyyed Hossein, 11
National Council of Christian Churches, 199 n. 58
Natural law, 10, 14, 169–170
Nemeth, Roger J., 138, 231 n. 7
Nester, Tony R., 102
New Age, 168, 175, 240 n. 14
Newman, Elizabeth Murray, 230 n. 1
Nielsen, Joyce McCarl, 109
Nineteenth Amendment of the U.S. Constitution, 108
North American Association for the Diaconate, 210 n. 13

Occupation(s). *See also* feminization; gender; gender segregation
  and age, 95, 98, 153, 219 n. 34. *See also* clergy career patterns; deployment
  attitudes toward women in, 110, 140
  and attraction for men, 105, 136, 142, 149, 162
  crowding in, 40, 82–84, 121–122, 125, 161. *See also* women clergy
  and education, 123–124
  executive management as, 146
  hierarchy in, 104, 115–116, 126, 149, 169
  hiring practices in, 119
  and human capital investment, 220 n. 59
  librarianship, 130
  nursing, 17, 104, 130, 153, 211 n. 24
  prestige of, 90–91, 116, 122–123, 140, 144–146, 148–149, 151, 153, 156, 235 n. 58. *See also* clergy
  public relations, 130
  and race, 98, 207 n. 32
  rational-choice reasoning in, 6–7
  reskilling of, 104, 149
  social work, 20, 147, 151, 153
  success in, 6, 31, 52
  teaching, 130, 147, 153. *See also* women
  truncated, 153
Occupational attainment, 211 n. 27. *See also* clergy career patterns; Episcopal clergy; feminization; job opportunities; Unitarian Universalist clergy
  and education, 47, 210 n. 14
  and mobility, 64, 74, 79, 214 n. 4. *See also* job mobility
Occupational biography, 32–33, 35, 50, 207 nn. 29–30
Occupational change, 81–82, 89, 107, 134, 136, 153, 160, 163
Occupational decline, 81, 86, 90, 158. *See also* job opportunities; ministry
Occupational differentiation, 46, 115–116, 126, 149
Occupational discrimination, 55, 95, 127, 129, 131. *See also* gender discrimination
Occupational life chances, 32
Occupational mythology, 62, 97–99, 110, 131
Occupational opportunities, 32, 47, 68. *See also* job opportunities
  and age, 96, 100
  for attainment, 6, 74, 84
  for autonomy and influence, 104–105, 209 n. 11
  decline in, 80, 84, 86, 88, 91, 105, 159
  and economic conditions, 142, 220 n. 59
  gender differences in, 71, 79, 81, 86, 96, 127–128, 130, 163, 169

and race, 207 n. 32
for women, 88, 156
Occupational privilege, 130, 152, 154
Occupational segregation, 95, 126, 163–
  164. *See also* gender segregation;
  job(s)
Occupational socialization, 51–52, 98–
  99, 113, 119
Occupational structure,
  closed and open systems, 52, 54, 211
    n. 27
  restructuring of, 107, 115, 121, 125,
    134, 136, 140, 144–145, 153, 165,
    174
Oi, Florence Li Tim, 24
Oneida community, 17
Oppression, 19, 166
Ordinatio Sacerdotalis, 15
Ordination, 29–30. *See also* Episcopal
  clergy; Unitarian Universalist clergy;
  women's ordination
  age at, 41, 49–50, 93–94, 99, 153
  applicant screening for, 8, 194 n. 28
  back door, 104
  cohorts, 33, 36
  decline in young men seeking, 100–
    102, 136, 142. *See also* clergy
  denial of, 104, 150
  and education, 47–49, 150–151
  formalized requirements for, 147,
    150–151, 153, 225 n. 64
  and gatekeeping, 150
  increase in women seeking, 4, 25,
    27, 105, 109, 136, 202–203
    n. 106
  local study programs for, 4, 117, 119,
    121, 123–124, 149
  and men, 29, 135, 210 n. 13
  newer tracks, 46, 115, 122–124, 135,
    145, 147–149. *See also* deacon(s);
    job opportunities
  and obedience, 146
  and prior work experience, 42, 50–51,
    94, 211 n. 25
  and status, 116, 147, 166
Organizational masculinization, 18, 37,
  102, 104, 107–108, 152, 175, 220
  n. 52. *See also* clergy
Organizational restructuring and change,
  93, 167

Orthodox Christianity, 10, 30
Otto, Rudolph, 196 n. 14

Palmer, Phoebe, 16, 108
Pavalko, Ronald M., 153
Parochialism, 149
Parsons, Talcott, 31, 79, 144
Parvey, Constance, 15
Patriarchy, 11, 23, 115
Pentecost, Dorothy Harrison, 211 n. 29
Pentecostal Protestantism,
  and leadership restructuring, 108, 203
    n. 115
  and women, 16–17, 20, 108, 127
Peterson, Robert W., 105
Phi Beta Kappa, 103, 220 n. 56
Pike, James A., 37
Pillar of Fire Church, 16
Pluralism, 19, 119, 177, 225 n. 62
Pope John Paul II, 13, 15, 168
Power, 11, 109, 112. *See also* authority;
  men; women
Pratto, David J., 80
Presbyterian Book of Order, 112
Presbyterian Church (U.S.A.), 137, 231
  n. 7. *See also* women clergy;
  women's ordination
Prestige, 13, 19, 32, 99, 104, 110, 114–
  115. *See also* clergy; congregations;
  occupations
Privatization, 4, 11, 20, 91, 171–172,
  200 nn. 65–66, 203 n. 113
Privilege, 11–14, 19, 105, 109, 145,
  164, 171, 173, 177. *See also* religious organizations
Profane, 11–12, 14, 16, 22
Profession(s), 30, 104. *See also* occupations
  deprofessionalization of, 90, 152–155,
    157, 160, 203 n. 115
  growth of, 91
  ministry and the clergy as, 90, 149,
    153
  professionalism in the , 123, 149,
    154, 160
  and professionalization, 30, 136, 149–
    156, 203 n. 115
  reprofessionalization of, 104, 152
  and semiprofession(s), 51, 94, 153,
    211 n. 24

Protestant Reformation, 90
Protestantism, 8. *See also* Evangelical
    Protestantism; Pentecostal Protes-
    tantism; religious organizations
    American mainline, 17, 87, 176, 196
        n. 12
    conservative, 11, 104–105, 154
    liberal, 107, 152
Puritan, 16, 33, 198 n. 41

Quaker, 14, 16, 91, 199 n. 49
Q'uran, 11

Rabbinate,
    ordination to, 243 n. 43
    reasons for leaving, 158–159
    salary and compensation, 220 n. 49,
        227 n. 88
    and women, 8, 71, 110, 176, 227
        n. 88
Racism, 7–8, 11, 166, 169, 195 n. 5
Rallings, E. M. (Bud), 80
Ranson, Stewart, 145, 159, 230 n. 3
Redeeming Christian Spiritualist
    Church, 16
Reformed Church, 10, 199 n. 53, 231
    n. 7
Religious education, 51, 116, 148, 172,
    210 n. 20, 226 n. 78. *See also* fem-
    inization; Unitarian Universalist
    clergy
Religious leadership, 102, 104, 146,
    167. *See also* authority; clergy; Epis-
    copal clergy; Unitarian Universalist
    clergy; women; women clergy
    charismatic, 15–16, 167
    in early Christianity, 14–15
    gender-related conflicts over, 108–
        109, 128, 131, 133–134, 161, 170–
        171, 195 n. 5
    gender differences in, 5, 13, 173
    lay, 19, 30, 133, 225–226 n. 69, 230
        n. 136
    male takeover of, 17–18, 21, 108
    and men, 3, 7, 21, 88, 99, 105, 114,
        130–131, 136, 145, 161, 177
    supply and demand for, 19–20
    and tradition maintenance, 113, 145
    and women, 3, 12–22, 86–88, 108,
        130–134, 161, 173, 196 n. 15

Religious movements, 8, 16–17, 88,
    102, 146, 148–149, 154, 164, 167–
    168, 170. *See also* women's move-
    ments
Religious orders, 15, 17, 90
Religious organizations, 6, 10, 17, 162.
    See also congregations; Episcopal
    Church; Unitarian Universalist
    Association
    African–American, 7, 9, 16, 18, 91,
        127, 195 n. 5
    bureaucratization in, 14, 16, 108
    consumerization trend in, 138, 152
    control of, 136, 143
    decreased vitality of, 4, 102, 107,
        191–192 n. 4, 220 n. 52
    economic concerns, 102, 133, 136–
        138, 142, 160–161, 231 n. 7
    educational level in, 47–48, 90, 210
        n. 15
    exodus from, 5, 164, 174–175
    financial contributions to, 139, 147,
        231–232 n. 21, 244 n. 59
    gender relations in, 9–12, 15, 37,
        113, 133, 164, 169, 172–173, 175
    and gender roles, 10–11, 15, 24, 108,
        130, 163, 168
    internal conflicts in, 99, 113, 130,
        139
    mainline, 11, 18–20, 22, 29, 31, 57,
        67, 71, 105, 109, 124, 127, 137,
        142, 146, 151, 154, 164, 170, 172,
        175
    and male privilege, 114, 173
    marginalization of women in, 14–18,
        21, 108, 126
    membership in, 102, 104, 108, 130,
        139–140, 142, 146, 161, 175
    nostalgia in, 109–110, 143
    and race, 7–8, 139, 166, 169
    and schism, 38, 109, 111, 208 n. 45,
        222 n. 14
    and social class, 11, 14, 33, 203
        n. 115
    structural change in, 28, 38, 81, 86,
        105, 111–114, 121–122, 135–137,
        139–140, 145, 147–148, 156, 159–
        161, 163, 173–174
    tradition maintenance in, 28, 104,
        113, 142, 145, 148

use of technology in, 104, 151
volunteer work in, 52, 80, 126,
138–139, 146–147, 155, 160, 211
n. 29
Religious Right, 170, 174, 240 n. 14
Religious revivalism, 16, 19, 20
Reskin, Barbara F., 88, 90, 105, 129,
140, 154, 162, 164, 207 n. 32,
228 n. 107, 233 n. 38
Riesman, David, 175
Ritual, 10, 146, 161–162
Roberts, Keith A., 168
Roman Catholic Church, 30, 42, 147,
233 n. 44
diminishing clergy supply, 5, 100,
122–123, 143
permanent deacons, 122, 143, 225
n. 68, 233–234 n. 45
Vatican II, 24, 202 n. 100, 225 n. 68
women's ordination issue, 5, 10, 15,
22, 24, 123, 143, 154, 167–168,
233–234 n. 45, 241 n. 21
World Youth Day Conference, 168
Roof, Wade Clark, 210 n. 15
Roos, Patricia A., 88, 94, 105, 123,
140, 162, 207 n. 32, 228 n. 107,
233 n. 38
Ross, Nan, 225 n. 66
Rousseau, Jean Jacque, 174
Royle, Marjorie Harding, 88

Sacrament, 46, 118, 146, 149. *See also*
Roman Catholic Church
Sacred, 12, 13, 16, 22, 91, 176
Saint Joseph's Spiritual Church, 16
Saiving, Valerie, 21
Salary and compensation. *See also*
clergy; congregations; Episcopal
clergy
compression, 101–102, 228 n. 109
denominational differences for
women, 88
gender disparities in, 46, 63, 71, 125,
129, 156, 163, 228 n. 107
and job sharing, 80
as measure of success, 31, 101
and men, 102, 104–105, 125, 142,
220 n. 59
and ministry, 90, 98, 101, 116, 125,
137, 145, 220 n. 49

occupational comparisons, 104, 219–
220 n. 46
Salvation Army, 29, 204 n. 4
Sarason, Seymour B., 92, 217 n. 16
Sawtell, Peter S., 80, 215 n. 14
Schaller, Lyle E., 13, 155–156, 158,
175, 196 n. 19, 226 n. 78
Schein, Edgar, 217 n. 11
Schlegel, Alice, 162
Schmidt, Frederick W., 88
Schoenherr, Richard A., 105, 143
Schrank, Harris T., 99
Schüssler Fiorenza, Elisabeth, 168
Scripture, 10, 21, 91, 113, 165, 171,
192 n. 6, 224 n. 34
Second Great Awakening, 9, 16
Secular work, 98, 105
Seminarians,
female, 13, 23, 25, 67, 98, 104, 202
n. 105, 210 n. 19
loan debt of, 101
male, 91–92, 98, 103
reasons for attendance, 92–93, 219
n. 45, 233 n. 36
second-career, 91–92, 94, 98, 103–
104
Seminary,
enrollment, 109, 124, 140, 226 n. 80
tension with denominations, 103–104,
124, 149
Seventh-Day Adventist Church, 17, 203
n. 110. *See also* women's ordination
Sexism, 8, 11, 166, 195 n. 5. *See also*
gender; gender segregation
Sexual orientation, 8, 139, 170, 176,
243 n. 43
Shakers, 17, 198–199 n. 49
Sheppard, Gerald T., 108
Shipman, Jane, 113
Shopshire, James M., 92
Slavery, 16–17, 198 n. 46
Smith, Howard L., 119
Smith, Page, 17
Social change, 12, 131, 133, 164–167,
171–173, 177. *See also* feminization
Social class, 20, 49, 169. *See also* class-
ism; religious organizations
Social control, 9, 74, 130, 139, 148,
165–167, 170–171. *See also* job op-
portunities

Social location, 166, 173, 243 n. 41
Social morality, 9–11, 15, 17, 20, 116, 142, 168–169, 174–175
Society of Friends, 29. *See also* Quaker
Sørensen, Aage B., 211 n. 27, 214 n. 4
Soule, George Hodges, 142, 233 n. 41
Stanton, Elizabeth Cady, 21, 192 n. 6, 203 n. 114
Steinfels, Peter, 97, 142
Stendahl, Brita, 111, 113, 146
Stevens, Lesley, 132
Stewart, Alexander D., 146, 210 n. 13
Stewart, Sister Wilma, 16
Stone, Howard W., 98, 220 n. 56
Strober, Myra H., 220 n. 59
Suffrage, 18, 23, 201 n. 83
Sumner, David E., 38
Super, Donald E., 95
Swenson, Mary Ann, 168, 172

The Church and the Second Sex, 21
The Psychology of Careers, 95
The Psychology of Clergy, 95
The Woman's Bible, 21, 192 n. 6, 203 n. 114
Tocqueville, Alexis de, 9, 200 nn. 65–66
Tokenism,
    effect of, 60, 76, 79, 129–132, 166–167
    and women, 3, 86, 131–133, 162, 164, 166
Tradition maintenance, 99, 113. *See also* religious leadership; religious organizations
Traditionalism, 9, 11, 16, 33, 113–115, 124, 133–134, 166, 170
Treiman, Donald J., 55
Tucker, Cynthia Grant, 107–108, 220 n. 52
Tucker, Ruth, 86

Unemployment, 94, 97, 124
Unitarian Church, 140. *See also* Unitarian Universalist clergy
Unitarian Universalist Association,
    fellowship in, 148, 151, 163, 243 n. 43
    historical roots, 33, 206 n. 24
    membership, 81, 233 n. 4

occupational structure, 36, 52, 57, 87, 95, 127, 162
polity, 55, 64
and race, 7
Unitarian Universalist clergy, 159
    age, 49–51, 60, 66, 69, 93–97, 100
    clergy couples, 80, 215 n. 18
    community minister, 36, 46, 115–116, 141, 224 n. 48
    compensation, 101, 116, 220 n. 49
    decline in men ordained, 82, 90
    deployment of, 36, 60, 65, 127–128
    dual ordination of, 117, 148, 150
    education of, 48, 50, 60, 94, 103, 117, 151
    and fellowship, 35–36, 116–117, 147, 150, 207 n. 35, 233 n. 34
    and female careers over time, 117, 135
    feminization of, 38–39, 116, 150
    gender differences in mobility and placements, 44–46, 58–60, 63–73, 78–79, 81–82, 85, 87–88, 127–128, 135, 213 n. 20
    and male careers over time, 80–82, 84–86, 88, 90
    as minister of religious education, 46–48, 116–117, 122, 148, 150, 224 n. 48
    as parish minister, 54, 117, 209 n. 11
    and prior work experience, 51–52, 54, 94, 211 n. 23
    and race, 35, 86
    retirements, 57, 86, 144
    and senior level placements, 96
    supply and demand for, 36, 57, 84, 86, 140–141, 209 n. 11
United Methodist Church, 111, 139, 147, 193 n. 14
Universal Friends, 16
Universalist Church, 140

Vietnam-era youth, 92, 100
Vocation, 6, 92, 108, 142, 204 n. 6

Wallace, Ruth A., 143, 233 n. 45
Waring, Joan M., 99
Weber, Max, 10, 13–16, 115, 129, 131, 136, 196 n. 14, 204 n. 6
Wesley, John, 3–4, 8

West, Margaret S., 146, 210 n. 13
Wetzel, Todd, 139
White, Alma, 16
White, Ellen, 17
Wicca, 168, 240 n. 14
Wilkes, Paul, 97
Wilkinson, Jemima, 16
Willard, Frances, 19
Wilson, Bryan R., 92, 154
Wilson, Robert L., 155
Witchcraft, 169, 240 n. 14
Womanist theology, 166
Woman's place, 20, 110, 161
Women. *See also* authority; religious
    leadership; religious organizations
  African-American, 16–17, 195 n. 5,
    207 n. 32
  apostles, 14, 197 n. 28
  and Bible study, 172, 244 n. 53
  career constraints of, 96, 218 n. 28
  as caregivers, 67, 96, 169
  and dependency on men, 12, 132,
    161, 166
  devaluation of the work of, 154
  and ecumenism, 5, 18, 21, 167–168,
    199 n. 58, 200 n. 72
  and education, 123, 150–151, 171
  empowerment and power of, 3, 5, 12–
    13, 22, 109, 133, 168, 171
  exploitation of, 136, 171
  family and children of, 138, 218
    n. 28
  as founders of religious groups, 16–17,
    164
  and the labor force, 6, 145, 154, 172,
    232 n. 28, 233 n. 38
  lay, 113–114, 133, 138, 166–167
  leaders, 3, 16–18, 86, 108, 132, 164,
    167, 204 n. 4.
  marginalization of, 125, 166
  men's dependency on, 113, 156,
    169
  and missionary work, 17–18, 20, 23,
    107
  preachers, 3–4, 11, 16, 20, 23, 36–
    37, 86
  and religious purity, 14, 15, 176
  and social status, 12, 15, 20, 196
    n. 21
  and spirituality, 172, 244 n. 53

  subordination of, 7, 11–12, 15–16,
    110, 126, 169–170, 229 n. 126
  as teachers, 17, 20
  and theological liberalism, 13
  traditionalist perspectives of, 4, 113–
    114, 119–120, 133, 166
  transformative interests of, 4, 13, 131,
    166, 173
  undermining of, 110–111, 169–170
  Universalist, 135
  and volunteer work, 27, 52, 80, 126,
    138, 155–156, 211 n. 29
Women clergy, 5, 168. *See also* clergy
    couples; Episcopal clergy; rabbinate;
    Unitarian Universalist clergy
  African-American, 23, 86, 127
  and age, 49–50, 60, 92, 95–96
  in the American Baptist Conference,
    5, 128–129, 210 n. 19
  in the Anglican Church of Canada,
    123
  in the Assemblies of God, 23, 24
  attitudes toward, 5, 97, 112–114, 146,
    243 n. 51
  backlash against, 107–114, 125, 133,
    136, 149, 152, 160, 162
  as bishops, 38, 87, 111, 113, 131–
    132, 222 n. 15, 229 n. 121
  building up congregations, 31, 108,
    164, 240 n. 16
  in the Church of England, 156
  in the Church of God, 5
  compensation of, 129
  and conflicts with women, 113–114,
    119–120
  in the Congregational Church
    (U.C.C.), 23, 25
  in Conservative Judaism, 5
  and dependency on men, 128, 131
  and difficulty finding jobs, 23–24, 43,
    71, 128–129
  in the Disciples of Christ, 88
  education of, 48, 50, 60, 65–66, 103,
    124, 134, 151
  Episcopal (U.S.A.), 4, 37–38, 54–55,
    70, 76–77, 79, 86–87, 103, 119,
    122, 125, 131, 145, 159–160, 172,
    191 n. 4, 202 n. 106, 233 n. 41
  erosion of support for, 23, 37, 108–
    112, 134

Women clergy (*continued*)
  exclusion and exodus of, 107–108,
    159–160
  influx of, 25, 39, 105, 136, 143, 145,
    162
  job mobility of, 65, 74–76, 130
  and job opportunities, 27, 45, 73–74,
    79, 126, 128, 145, 154, 156
  and job segregation, 126, 130
  and leadership positions, 27, 67, 86–
    87, 128, 131–133, 164
  and liberal perspectives, 12–13
  Lutheran (E.L.C.A. and pre-merger)
    88, 123, 202–203 n. 106
  and male resistance, 20, 22, 38, 201
    n. 76
  marginalization of, 86, 126, 130, 137,
    145, 149, 160
  and marital status, 52–53, 59, 80,
    142, 156, 163, 211 n. 32
  mentorship of, 31, 111, 129
  in newer ordination tracks, 122, 126,
    133–134, 149
  and occupational crowding, 117, 121–
    122, 125, 162, 164
  occupational prospects of, 27, 71, 88,
    96–97, 130, 145, 164
  and organizational change, 136, 160–
    161
  and part-time placements, 68, 71, 80,
    137, 156, 227 n. 88
  Pentecostal, 23, 196 n. 16
  Presbyterian (U.S.A.), 5, 80, 87–88,
    112, 130, 202 n. 106, 223 n. 29
  second-career, 99
  social reform interests of, 23, 71, 131,
    166–167
  Southern Baptist Convention, 5, 113
  supply and demand for, 24, 79
  Unitarian Universalist, 23, 34, 37,
    39, 47, 73, 78, 86, 107–108, 125,
    135, 162
  United Methodist Church (U.S.A.),
    5, 87–88, 123, 128, 132, 193
    n. 14, 202 n. 105
Women of the Cloth, 5, 67
Women's Christian Temperance Union,
    18–19
Women's movements, 17, 20–21, 176
  and coalitions, 163–164, 168, 172

  conflicts and co-optation of, 12, 163–
    164, 166, 167
  women-church as, 154, 164, 168
Women's ordination, 4, 152
  advocacy and support for, 5–6, 21–22,
    146, 219 n. 40, 243 n. 51
  in the African Methodist Episcopal
    Church, 24
  in the Anglican Church of Canada,
    25, 123, 191 n. 4
  in the Anglican communion, 24–25,
    191 n. 4, 201 n. 76
  in the Assemblies of God, 23, 108
  arguments against, 14, 22, 33, 159
  in British Methodist churches, 4
  in the Church of England, 25, 159,
    232 n. 30, 242 n. 34
  in the Church of Sweden, 111, 201
    n. 76, 206 n. 27, 208 n. 42, 223 n.
    25
  clergy supply and, 140, 232 n. 30
  conscience clause and, 38, 111, 172,
    208 n. 42, 223 nn. 24–25
  in Conservative Judaism, 25
  in early Christianity, 21
  in the Episcopal Church, 25, 33, 37–
    38, 88, 109, 118–120, 131, 150,
    159, 172, 209 n. 10, 215 n. 21,
    219 n. 40, 222 n. 14, 223 n. 24,
    242 n. 34, 243 n. 51
  in the Evangelical Covenant Church,
    25
  and the Evangelical Lutheran Church
    of Latvia, 109
  in Lutheran (A.L.C., L.C.A., and
    other) churches, 25, 222 n. 14
  in the Mennonite Church of North
    America, 25
  in Methodist (United States) churches,
    17, 23–24, 123
  in newer tracks, 116, 118, 122
  in the Old Catholic Church, 25
  and the Presbyterian Church of Aus-
    tralia, 109
  in Presbyterian (U.S. and U.S.A.)
    churches, 24, 140, 206 n. 27
  to the rabbinate, 8, 10, 203 n. 107
  in Reconstructionist Judaism, 25
  in Reform Judaism, 23, 25
  in the Reformed Church, 10, 109

resistance to, 22–24, 37–38, 107–109, 112, 146, 222 nn. 14–15
reversal of, 10, 23, 108–109
and the Seventh-Day Adventist Church, 173
and sexual orientation, 243 n. 43
and the Southern Baptist Convention, 10, 24, 109, 224 n. 34
in Unitarian (and) Universalist churches, 23, 37–39, 208 n. 46
women's interests in, 4, 23, 132
Women's Ordination Conference, 168

Women's organizations, 20–21. *See also* religious orders; women
takeover by men, 18, 21, 200 n. 70
World Conference of Women, 21
World Council of Churches and women, 5, 24
World War II, 24, 140, 216 n. 5, 232 n. 28
Wortman, Julie A., 149

Young, Lawrence A., 143

Zell, Katherine, 86
Zwingli, Huldrych, 86